*For Esther*

# The Clinical Interaction

# The
# CLINICAL
# INTERACTION

## WITH SPECIAL REFERENCE TO
## THE RORSCHACH

*by*

### SEYMOUR B. SARASON

*Associate Professor of Psychology*
*Yale University*

## GREENWOOD PRESS, PUBLISHERS
### NEW YORK

# CONTENTS

PART III. Individual Interpretation

# PREFACE

This book is based on a course which I have taught at Yale since 1946. Largely, I think, because my teaching duties involved the clinic as well as the classroom, I became increasingly aware of the necessity of discussing the use of any diagnostic instrument in the context of the clinical interaction. Without a thorough discussion of the variables operative in interpersonal interactions in general, and the clinical one in particular, the student tended to be test- rather than patient-centered in his clinical contacts and case reports. It came as no little surprise to me that my attempts to reorganize and reorient the course were beset by one major difficulty or lack: neither in the research literature, nor in texts on clinical psychology, nor in books about the Rorschach or any other clinical instrument was explicit and systematic attention given to the variables operative in any interpersonal interaction. This book represents an attempt to fill, in part at least, this serious gap.

A major stimulus to the writing of this book was my collaboration with Dr. Thomas Gladwin in the study of the people of Truk (see reference 58 in the bibliography of this book). The reader who is particularly interested in the interpretive process is urged to consult the monograph which in a very real sense is an integral part of the third section of this book. The scope and size of the Truk study—primarily conceived and executed by Dr. Gladwin—makes meaningful incorporation in this book of other than several protocols impossible. My participation in the Truk study was very fruitful: not only did I find it an instructive and fascinating experience but I also gained a most valued friend—which is, I think, at least par for such courses.

I am happy to acknowledge my appreciation for the many stimulating discussions I had with the staff psychologists in the VA facilities in Connecticut concerning various problems in this book. Doctors Philip Morse, Irving Frank, Larry Hemmendinger, and Jacob Levine provided me with much needed opportunities for critical discussion. Dr.

Levine was kind enough to read the entire manuscript and to make many suggestions which I am sure contributed to whatever merits this book may have. Dr. Jerry Kagan likewise read the manuscript, and I am also grateful to him for his suggestions.

It is a source of great pleasure to me to acknowledge my deep indebtedness to my brother, Irwin Sarason, who read each chapter as soon as it was written, provided me with written detailed criticisms and suggestions, and gave so much of his time for long discussions with me. In only two places in this book have I explicitly acknowledged his contribution—there were countless other places I could have made similar acknowledgments. He was of the greatest help to me in the writing of this book.

Mrs. Susan Henry typed the manuscript in most of its various stages and did so with her usual remarkable speed and quality—for which I am indeed thankful.

The dedication of this book to my wife reflects a professional and personal indebtedness the extent of which, in this instance at least, I am by far the best judge. The dedication would have been more accurate if I had indicated that this book was written for and because of her.

SEYMOUR B. SARASON

*New Haven, Connecticut*
*February, 1954*

# The Clinical Interaction

*Chapter 1*

# INTRODUCTION

CLINICAL psychology is no longer an area of specialization which can be described within the confines of a book. One might even say that to cover adequately some of the major problem areas within clinical psychology has become a somewhat overwhelming task in which both author and reader are likely at times to get confused, if not lost. When one remembers that clinical psychology as we know it today is largely a phenomenon of the last decade, one can only be amazed at the rate of its growth and the problems it has come to encompass. The clinician who received his clinical training before World War II—training which almost always had to be obtained outside the university—is probably much more aware of how his field has grown than is the newer entrant to the field. This growth, as one might expect, has not been an unmixed blessing. The strong social need for the services of the clinical psychologist, the lack of experience of university departments in clinical training, the almost total lack of contact between systematic psychological theory and clinical problems, the clinician's relative lack of sophistication and interest in research—these are some of the factors which have made for a somewhat stormy, spotty, frustrating, but stimulating period of growth. How frustrating this growth has been—how much of an unmixed blessing the growth of clinical psychology will be considered—depends on whether one is an optimist or a pessimist. The pessimist can with justice point to the plethora of unvalidated techniques which clutter the literature, the lack of rigor in so much of clinical research, and the failure of the clinician to view his problems from some explicitly stated, "organizing" theory or frame of reference. The optimist with equal justice can point to an ever growing literature on the critical evaluation of clinical techniques, the clinician's concern with problems of research design and statistical procedures, the awareness on the part of many clinicians of the need for systematic theory, and the stimulating challenge which clinical problems present as tests of the adequacy of

1

current theories. In light of the short history of modern clinical psychology this writer would prefer being classed as an optimist who would feel very unhappy if the pessimist were ever to become less vocal than he now is.

As we indicated earlier, clinical psychology is concerned with a number of problems to any one of which it is possible to devote one's entire professional career. It can justifiably be said that the tendency to concentrate one's interests and efforts in a particular area has produced the unfortunate, but perhaps inevitable, situation where one group of clinical psychologists does not understand (and is not interested in) the problems which engage the interest of other clinicians. The most unfortunate aspect of this situation is that it tends to obscure what these problems have in common. *This book stems from the belief that practically all clinical problems are concerned with data obtained from an interpersonal interaction and that regardless of how interactions differ certain variables are always operative and must be taken into account.* It is our contention that the failure to consider seriously the implications of the interpersonal nature of the clinical interaction has not only obscured what different problems have in common but has made evaluation of studies of a particular research problem extremely difficult. The reader will find little that is new in our discussion of the major variables operative in the clinical interaction. If there is any merit to our discussion it will probably stem from our emphasis that many clinicians have not taken seriously, in practice and research, what might well be termed banalities. We should perhaps make it clear that we do not consider clinical interactions essentially different from any other kind of interaction. One of the ways in which interactions differ is in the relative strength or importance of the different situational variables. In short, the clinical interaction is an instance of interactions in general.

THE PLAN OF THE BOOK

In the first part of the book we shall present and discuss the major variables operative in an interpersonal interaction. Although we have drawn upon examples from diagnostic testing and psychotherapy as a basis for our discussion, we have also attempted to choose examples from nonclinical areas in order to emphasize the generality of the variables. At the end of this first part of the book we would like to urge the reader to review carefully the studies concerned with a single problem in his field of interest with two questions in mind: To what extent have these studies explicitly recognized the variables inherent in an interpersonal interaction? To what extent might conflicting findings and opinions be a function of recognized or unrecognized differences in the role of the situational variables? We urge this active participation upon the reader because of our belief that our discussion may be more meaningful when it is viewed by the reader in light of the problems in which he is most interested.

The second part of the book is devoted to an attempt to evaluate the status of a particular clinical instrument, the Rorschach test, in light of our discussion of the situational variables. The rationale of the test, the relevant research literature, the nature of conflicting findings—these we have attempted to evaluate critically in terms of the recognition given to the major variables which affect behavior in the clinical interaction. In this part of the book the writer has done for himself what he urged the reader to do in his own field of interest. In presenting and discussing the Rorschach we have assumed that the reader has no or little familiarity with the instrument.

In the last part of the book we have attempted to indicate the problems involved in the interpretation of a single individual's Rorschach protocol. Here we have concentrated on what the clinician thinks and does in the process of interpretation, the major assumptions about the dynamics of behavior which seem necessary in such a process, and the deductive nature of the clinician's thinking. Put in another way, we have attempted to make explicit the relation between the clinician's conclusions and thinking when presented with the protocol of a particular individual.

# PART I

# Situational Variables

## Chapter 2

# OVERT AND COVERT BEHAVIOR

BEFORE discussing the diagnostic uses of any particular psychological test, one must first ask the following question: What variables must be identified in order to begin to understand a subject's behavior in any face-to-face situation? The question has been posed in this general fashion in order to emphasize that whatever the variables might turn out to be they operate in any interpersonal situation, be it psychotherapy, interviewing, or diagnostic testing. Because each situation has a different name, and many times a different purpose, there is the tendency to be more aware of the differences than the similarities and to think that the principles on the basis of which data are collected and interpreted are different from one situation to another. This has led some people, for example, to talk of "Rorschach theory" as if the principles, assumptions, and hypotheses necessary for understanding a person's Rorschach responses bear no or little relationship to those necessary for understanding his communications to a therapist. There are obvious differences in the stimulus conditions but it does not follow that the diagnostician and therapist use or need different theories for understanding the subject's behavior. The fact that so many clinicians make predictions from the testing to the therapeutic situation (or to many other situations) assumes not only some kind of continuity in the patient's behavior but also a similarity in the variables which influence his behavior in the compared situations. To assume that a different theory is needed for different situations not only limits the usefulness of the testing situation but denies the possibility of ever constructing a comprehensive theory of behavior.

The question posed above immediately raises a deceptively easy question: What is meant by "a subject's behavior"? One could point to the words used, tonal qualities, facial expressions, and physical movements. Having enumerated these factors one quickly becomes aware that the clinician makes conclusions which go beyond the observables:

7

those things which can be filmed or recorded. On the basis of these observables the clinician draws inferences about ongoing processes. In other words, the subject's behavior can be and is divided into its overt and covert aspects.

Kent (*87*, p. 19) has given an excellent summary of "what to observe" in a child's test performance:[1]

While the examiner is pretending to be busy, very little should actually escape his notice. By keeping his eyes open to the little things that make this subject's performance distinctive, he can learn much that is not included in the score.

Anything atypical about the child's physical development should be noted, especially any physical defect that might place him at a disadvantage. A speech defect or impediment is of great significance, because it might invalidate the child's score in an orally-presented test. Defective coordination might have serious effects in performance tests scored by speed. Are the child's movements jerky, or do his hands tremble?

What is the child's attitude toward the examiner? Is he friendly and responsive, shy and withdrawing, or definitely hostile? Is he curious and inquisitive? Does he snatch at the stop watch and meddle with everything within reach? Is his behavior that of a well-trained child, or is he so uninhibited as to be seriously troublesome? Does he try to be helpful in putting materials back into their boxes? Is he alert and interested, or does he behave as if bored?

Does the subject use his two hands coordinately, or is there some interference between them? Does he work lazily with one hand, while using the other hand as a support for his head? Does he let the paper slide around on the table when he touches it with the pencil, and does he straighten it with his elbow? Does he push the formboard out of place with each placement of a block? Does he respond to the increasing difficulty of a formboard series and show greater interest as the tasks make heavier demands upon his attention? If so, at what stage in the series does he hold up his head and work with both hands? Does he become easily discouraged by the difficulty of a task and say that he can't do it or that it can't be done? Is he irritated by the difficulty, and does he show it by becoming rough with the materials? When inserting a block which fits too tightly to slide into its place on a slant, does he try to force it by pounding with his fist, or does he take care to hold the block parallel with the board? How well does he follow specific instructions in a series which is preceded by a demonstration task? In the

[1] *Mental Tests in Clinics for Children,* G. H. Kent, Copyright 1950, D. Van Nostrand Company, Inc.

color cube series, does he frequently remove a block that is correctly placed? Does his comprehension of the essential principle underlying the task show improvement with practice? Does he learn to rotate the red-white or blue-yellow block consistently until he finds its correct position, or does he try two or three incorrect placements and then repeat these errors by reversing the direction of the rotation?

It may be instructive for the reader to determine for himself which of the above questions refer to overt and which to covert aspects of behavior.

## OVERT BEHAVIOR

Although it is usually assumed that a clinician's description of a patient's overt behavior is reliable in terms of inter-clinician agreement, convincing evidence for such an assumption cannot be found. Those who have been responsible for the training of clinical students will attest to the fact that there are discouragingly large individual differences in the ability to describe reliably the overt behavior of a patient. There is no evidence to suggest that graduate training reduces the range of these differences to the point where one need have no particular concern about the matter. One *hopes* that training has such an effect; one does not know that it does.

It perhaps should be emphasized that we are here talking only of those aspects of behavior which can be filmed or recorded: the overt aspects of behavior. When one studies the literature either on the psychology of testimony (67) or on the relation between patient's statements and therapist's recall (30, 129), it becomes apparent that the problem of description is by no means one which can be lightly dismissed.[2] *When one remembers that what a clinician concludes about a patient in large part represents inferences based on his description of overt behavior, the importance of the problem is obvious.*

If clinicians differ in how much they will note and remember of a

[2] One of the clinician's most revealing experiences is to listen to a recording of his interaction with a patient. He becomes embarrassingly aware of how much he forgot or was unconscious not only of the patient's behavior but *of his own behavior as well.* Were one to film as well as to record such interactions the clinician would probably benefit even more. Despite the increasing use of such training devices we do not as yet have objective indices of the extent to which a student "is changed" by such training in the sense that the validity and comprehensiveness of his description increase; and we do not know what the mechanics, duration, and goals of such supervision should be.

patient's overt behavior, then it becomes important to determine the sources of these individual differences. Why is it that individuals differ as to what aspects of a situation will be prepotent for them in the sense that they become aware of and respond to them? Posing the problem in this way implies that the clinician's response tendencies are not of equal strength or equally evocable by different aspects of the situation. What the clinician is set to see is a function both of his own habit hierarchy and of the nature of the particular situation. The following is an example of what is meant:

For the first time in his training a student was to be observed in the testing of an institutionalized child. Shortly after the testing began, the child turned and glanced out the window. The examiner then said to the child: "I bet you would like to be outside playing with the other boys." When this comment was discussed with the student the following emerged: (a) on the way to the institution he worried about what the child would be like; (b) he anticipated that the child would be aggressive and difficult to handle; (c) when he met the child he was upset because the child did not appear happy or spontaneous; (d) when he saw the child glance out the window, he felt he was doing a poor job in establishing rapport and felt he "ought to do or say something." Although this student had been observed with other kinds of children, anxiety about his performance was never as obvious as with the institutionalized child. In addition, his description of the overt behavior of these other children was far more valid and comprehensive and objective than in the above instance. It is very likely that some of the children previously seen by the student turned and glanced out the window. The student, however, was not "set" to note and respond to such behavior.

This illustration does not, of course, explain why the student reacted differentially to the different situations in which he was observed. It is presented merely to point out that the clinician's awareness of and responsiveness to the overt behavior of the patient is a function of the particular situation and ·the relative strengths of his own response tendencies.

The problem becomes much more complicated in those instances when the clinician's failure to note and respond objectively to the patient's overt behavior is a function of the fact that certain of the clinician's response tendencies are relatively weak in the sense that they do not easily become the focus either of self-awareness or of awareness by others. It is much easier to spot and understand those instances where the description of the overt behavior of the patient is related to overt characteristics of the clinician than those in which the failure to describe the patient validly is related to some non-overt characteristic of the clinician.

We are here touching upon a problem which will be discussed in later pages. Briefly stated, it concerns the relationship between what a person says he sees and the strength and handling of strong drives. For example, is the individual who is considered by others to be overtly hostile likely to be one who views other people as hostile? Is he likely to view other people as hostile if he is aware of his own hostility? If he is unaware of his own hostility, what are the relationships between his defensive reactions and his view of other people? In later pages we shall be concerned with how the clinician attempts to answer these questions when confronted with a patient. *It should be obvious, however, that when one substitutes the clinician for the patient as an object of inquiry, the same questions arise.*

Thus far we have not attempted an answer to the question of why clinicians differ as to what aspects of a situation will be prepotent for them in the sense that they become aware of and respond to them. One facet of the answer is the banal fact that individuals differ in the kinds of experiences they have had, with all that such differences imply. Too little is known about how psychologists operate *clinically* to attempt to answer the question in terms of background factors. The fact that predictions as to who will be a successful or unsuccessful clinical psychologist are discouragingly unreliable (86, 104, 137) strongly suggests that the first step is to determine the details of the clinician's operations. Before one can determine *to what* one wants to predict one should have a pretty good idea of *from what* one wants to predict (137).

Aside from personal history factors a major uncontrolled source of variation is the assumptions, implicit or explicit, which clinicians make about behavioral functioning. Differences in the kinds of assumptions made are a function both of the content of one's training and experience and of the particular theory to which one adheres. A good example of how theoretical considerations influence the clinician's perception of and behavior toward the patient can be seen in the history of psychoanalysis. In the early days of psychoanalysis it was assumed that therapeutic success was in large part a function of the degree to which unconscious material could be made conscious. Consequently, the analyst employed means which were geared to the end of making the unconscious conscious; hypnosis, early and "deep" interpretations, and a direct and rather pedagogical attitude toward the patient were not at all unusual. When, as a result of better understanding of such concepts as resistance and transference (as well as increased concern about therapeutic failures), psychoanalytic theory changed, the analyst's perception of and behavior toward the patient changed markedly. *What the analyst was set to see, in addition to his attitude toward himself and the patient (countertransference), changed when the theory changed.* The shift in the analyst's attention from the "id" to the "ego" meant that the overt as well as the covert aspects of the patient's behavior would be differently perceived and interpreted (*49, 122, 123*).

Gill and Brenman (57) have indicated how the therapist's theoretical orientation influences his behavior:

If the therapist's conceptions about psychodynamics—whether he holds them consciously or unconsciously, whether they are systematized or chaotic —influence his behavior in the therapeutic situation, and if his behavior influences the patient's productions, it must be clear that the raw data in psychotherapeutic research are inevitably influenced by the therapist's views. If a therapist believes dreams are important in helping a patient, he will show interest in the patient's dreams. Merely asking if the patient has any may result in including many more dreams in the raw data than are gathered by a therapist who is not especially interested in dreams. This is on the grossest level. The subtleties of showing interest in certain kinds of material, often not consciously detected either by therapist or patient, are manifold. They may include a questioning glance, a shifting of visual focus, a well-timed "um-hmm," a scarcely perceptible nod, or even a clearing of the throat. The therapist's conception of what his interpersonal relationship with a patient should be will also seriously influence the kind of material he obtains. If one therapist believes he should be "friendly" and another that he should be "distant," the raw data obtained by each will obviously differ.

What has been said so far is no more than saying that one cannot observe *all* overt behavior, that one does and must select those aspects to which one responds, and that such selection is in large part determined by assumptions about behavior and its interrelationships. For example, when an anthropologist goes to study a primitive culture, he obviously must select what he will observe and record for the purposes of his particular problem. But even if he narrows his problem considerably, he cannot observe and record all that is relevant to it. He makes his selection on the basis of assumptions or theoretical considerations which say, so to speak, "this is more important than that" (58). Two anthropologists with different predilections about theory but interested in the same problem will pay attention to different aspects of overt behavior. For purposes of illustration one could substitute "two psychologists" for "two anthropologists" in the previous sentence.

We have emphasized the relation between theory and observation of overt behavior for several reasons: (1) It is very easy to assume that what we say we see is a "fact" in the sense that all competent observers would note the same thing; (2) we tend to forget that what we say we see is an instance of selective reporting; (3) we tend not to make explicit the theoretical considerations which govern our selective noting and responding; (4) the more valid and comprehensive we can make psychological theory—in the sense that deductions from it are proved to be valid and consistent with each other—the more focused and effective will our training procedures be and the less will the clinician's conclusions be a function of personal fancies and idiosyncratic tendencies.

## COVERT BEHAVIOR

By covert behavior we refer to such nonobservables as attitudes toward self and others, needs or drives, purposes, defenses, fantasy, etc. In short, by covert behavior we refer to all those ongoing processes and contents which the clinician deduces from what the patient says and does. When a patient is labeled as anxious, or depressed, or perplexed, or passive, the label represents an inference made by the clinician on the basis of what the patient said or did. It is very likely that variation among observers is probably much greater for covert than for overt behavior.

The major problem—and one which will recur throughout this book —is: What are the bases and processes by which the clinician deduces covert from overt behavior? It is surprising how few systematic attempts have been made to describe the nature of this aspect of the clinician's behavior and how incomplete, unrevealing, and unsatisfactory these attempts have been—*regardless of one's evaluation of the validity of the conclusions*. For example, Schafer (*148*, p. 336) concludes his attempt by saying:

. . . I should like to point to the attempt that has been made in these pages to verbalize the step-by-step process of interpretation of test results and the elaboration of differential diagnostic arguments. It is important to the future of the practice of clinical testing that our methods of analysis be presented in publications with as great care as our conclusions. Only if these analytic principles are exposed to general view and thereby to general criticism can we hope to refine them, render them more communicable and reclaim them as much as possible from the realm of private insights and "art."

Unfortunately, Schafer's presentations, however stimulating, are unsatisfactory from the standpoint of demonstrating the ways in which the clinician utilizes theory in arriving at his conclusions. That Schafer was aware of this fact is suggested in the following quotation (*148*, p. 334):

. . . The chapter of diagnostic summaries could also have been written primarily in terms of diagnostic implications. Thus, there could have been sections on indications of anxiety, compulsiveness, modes of coping with aggressive impulses, and so forth. As it is, the reader will have to hop around among the discussions of the various groups in order to gather together all the references to any major personality characteristic. . . . The validational studies which would back up a chapter on personality characteristics are, however, woefully lacking, and any such presentation at this time would inevitably have been even more loaded down with *maybes, sometimes,* and *howevers* than this one is.

. . . The clinical summaries have been included mainly to give the reader a rough idea of the kind of person who could give each particular set of test results. This, however, is only the beginning of the job; ultimately it will be necessary to peg each conclusion from the test results into its appropriate hole in the clinical picture of the patient—confirming, amending, or amplifying the detailed clinical impressions and not merely the clinical diagnostic impression.

In his interpretation of Trukese Rorschachs Sarason (*58*) attempted to give a step-by-step account of his interpretations.

. . . One of the major things I wanted to accomplish was to give as complete a picture as possible of how I interpreted a protocol. I felt this was important for the following reasons: (a) I wanted to make clear in what relation my conclusions stood to the various aspects of the protocol; (b) I wanted ultimately to be able to ascertain where I was wrong or right and if possible why, and (c) by making the procedure "public" I was giving other psychologists an opportunity to criticize not only the conclusions but the steps by which these conclusions were arrived at. . . .

I must state that I am not particularly satisfied with the attempt to make "public" the interpretive process. As I read over the Rorschach interpretations I am aware that more went on inside my head than I was able to get down on paper (58, chap. 11).

The importance of making explicit the relation between theory and the clinician's conclusions cannot be overestimated. Until such relationships are made clear, the clinician's functioning will be more of an artistic than a scientific effort.

It might clarify the nature of the problems raised thus far in this chapter to list and describe briefly the major ways by which the clinician deduces covert from overt behavior.

1. The most "natural" way is what might be called a self-recognition process: the clinician not only notes what a person does but responds to this as if he were saying "if I acted in this way this is what I would have to feel." When a person cries, we "know" in an approximate way what he is covertly experiencing. The clinician recognizes and responds to something familiar in his own experience. He implicitly assumes that the reasons he would or did act "in this way" are in some way similar to the reasons the patient responds "in this way." The problem here is not in how the clinician arrives at a statement about covert behavior but in how he evaluates the statement. Does he accept his own conclusion as a fact requiring no further proof? Does he, as is most frequent, utilize the conclusion as a basis for further statements about other aspects of the person's behavior? If he does (and there is nothing inherently wrong in so doing), what kinds of assumptions does he make which allow him to relate one aspect of behavior to another? What does the clinician do with overt behavior which surprises him? For example, when a patient cries because he says he is happy, we are surprised; we find it hard to conceive because we have learned very different kinds of things in relation to crying.[3] The clinician attempts to interpret such overt behavior. On what bases are his interpretations made?

[3] A different aspect of the problem is seen in those instances where the overt behavior which the clinician observes is reliable and not surprising but where the covert significance attached to it is invalid because the clinician is misled by what he thinks is familiar. Davis (35) has indicated this in his studies of slum children: "The behavior which we regard as 'delinquent' or 'shiftless' or 'unmotivated' in slum groups is usually a perfectly

2. Another way in which covert is deduced from overt behavior is the use of assumptions, derived from some theory, for which there is either empirical or experimental evidence. When the overt behavior (an informal comment, a formal test response, a physicial movement, etc.) occurs, its covert significance is determined not by any self-recognition process but by the fact that it is an instance of the behavior for which a particular assumption is considered relevant. For example, when we hear a slip of the tongue, it is assumed that the individual said what he both wanted and did not want to say. Such an assumption, however, is embedded in a theoretical system, psychoanalysis, which contains constructs (unconscious, preconscious, defense, etc.) that serve as a basis for, or at the least are intimately related to, the assumption. It is not at all clear at times to what extent the clinician is aware of or utilizes the related constructs in the way in which the overall theory suggests. Another example may be appropriate here: to the first card of the Rorschach, and after six seconds, a nine-year-old boy said: "two elephants [side details] trying to pull a man apart [center detail]." This response presumably is in some meaningful way indicative of this boy's unverbalized, covert response tendencies. Beyond this assumption, however, is the question how one determines the possible significances of this response. Do we assume that this boy "identifies" with the destructive animals or with the attacked man? Or both? Regardless of which assumption one makes, how does one determine its implications for the individual's covert and overt behavior? Is his hostility, if this is concluded to be the stronger tendency, overtly discernible or only covertly experienced? What justification is there for attempting to determine the possible significances of a single verbal response? As we shall see in later pages the problem of what assumptions are employed by the clinician in interpreting the covert significances of overt behavior is a crucial and thorny one. In many cases the nature of the assumption either is not clear or has little or no justification. Until these types of assumptions and their rationale are explicitly stated, the necessary validational research cannot be done.

---

realistic, adaptive, and—in slum life—respectable response to reality" (p. 11); "the conception that aggression and hostility are neurotic or maladaptive symptoms of a chronically frustrated adolescent is an ethnocentric view of middle-class psychiatrists. In lower-class families, physical aggression is as much a normal, socially approved and socially inculcated type of behavior as it is in frontier communities" (p. 35).

The importance of the problems which have been raised in the previous pages has been well stated by Kubie (*94*):

The naturalist can stop and look at a flower as often as he pleases. He can pluck it, paint it, and photograph it, in order to show it to his colleagues. The internist and dermatologist can do the same with their observations. It will mean the dawn of a new day in clinical research in psychiatry when we can sit down together to study slowly the filmed recordings of the behavior and speech of our patients. This tool is now at hand, but it must be added that we still lack research organizations equipped with the people or the financial means to use the tool.

Most keenly do I regret this in psychoanalytic psychiatry. Here even more than in any other phase of psychiatry do we suffer from the inadequacy of our records. Freud himself pointed out the importance and complexity of this problem, and emphasized the many special technical difficulties involved in the making of psychoanalytic records. One consequence of this fact is that in fifty years of psychoanalytic literature there is not a single full protocol of even one day in the treatment of one patient; not one play-by-play record of the interaction between free association, interpretations, transference and counter-transference, and the sweep of libidinal forces in general. The consequences of this deficiency are many. So long as we depend upon unrecorded impressions and memories, the subtle differences with which we are concerned and the long drawn out period of observation become sources of error. Months of daily observation of a process which waxes and wanes continually by just perceptible increments and decrements gradually dulls the perceptions of even the keenest observer, paralyzes the memory through the monotony of repetition, and renders the written word literally useless as an instrument of record. After a time, the observer can no longer differentiate clearly and surely what the patient has said from what he himself has said, nor which came first.

This is one of the reasons why the more experienced the psychoanalyst, the greater is his preference for discussions of theories rather than of patients. Nor is it irrelevant, perhaps, to mention that because of this same need to escape the consequences of our lack of adequate records, we psychoanalysts mount our hobby-horses and ride off frantically in all directions— toward sociology, anthropology, economics, the immediate present only, infancy only, antiquity only, mythology only, endopsychic factors only, transference only, etc. All of these various interests are worthy objects of research and study, but they become angry and essentially empty battle cries when we substitute them for precise clinical observations and records.

Is it not arresting that in psychoanalysis, whose lever is interpretation and whose primary goal is insight, there should be no single factual study of the relationship of insight to health, not one objective record of the growth of insight during the course of treatment, no study of the relationship between the growth of insight and interpretation, nor between the growth of insight and the recovery of health? Conversely, there is no precise study of the relationship of insight to acute or gradual breakdown, nor even a study of the qualitative differences which exist between the insight leading to health and the insight of a schizophrenic. True, many analysts have "ideas" about these matters, but where are the protocols on which these ideas are based?

Still other deficiencies arise from the same methodological lack. Because there are no precise records, we have no objective evaluation of the relative efficacy of different concepts, different theories, different technical procedures, different ways of handling the transference situation. For the same reason, we lack any detailed studies of psychoanalytic failures, that necessary equivalent of the post-mortem of internal medicine. And for the same reason also, we lack reports from psychiatrists, analyst or otherwise, who have treated ten consecutive cases of hysterical aphonia, ten consecutive cases of agoraphobia, and other conditions. Instead we have theories and more theories, and ever new and redundant and overlapping terms. Whenever we of the psychoanalytic profession experience frustration, whenever we bump against a difficult problem, we comfort ourselves with a new theory or a new name. This was true of Freud; but let us not forget that it is even more true of the many modern messiahs. All that it is fair to say in criticism of Freud is that in this respect he set us an unfortunate example.

SOME CONCLUSIONS

At the beginning of this chapter the question was asked: What variables must be identified in order to begin to understand a subject's behavior in any face-to-face situation? It is clear from the content of this chapter that an important aspect of the question is *the problem of the psychologist* (109, 136, 138). The primary aim of the previous pages of this chapter was to indicate that although the clinician makes certain assumptions, explicit or implicit, and utilizes some kind of theoretical orientation, haphazardly or systematically, their relation to his conclusions is by no means clear. The implications of these conclusions and indications of how the problem might be attacked have been discussed by Gill and Brenman (57):

Our views here issue directly from the thesis originally stated regarding the nature of the raw data of psychotherapy: inasmuch as we believe that the emotional communication in psychotherapy is influenced by the therapist's conscious or unconscious assumptions regarding human motivation, we believe also that the therapist's translations of content into feeling, his silences, and any other contribution he may make to the therapeutic process are dictated by a rationale of which he may or may not be aware. Thus, in addition to the objective recording of the therapeutic session using any and all technical aids, another kind of recording is crucial in giving a meaningful account of a therapeutic process—the recording of the therapist's current rationale for what he is doing.

The therapist forms hypotheses constantly during the course of a psychotherapeutic hour. Some of these he states directly to the patient as the "feeling" translation of a particular content; sometimes he makes a statement to convey a feeling which for one reason or another he chooses not to express as such; sometimes he gives no translation because he is not sure of it, or he decides that the translation, though correct, would be inopportune. These hypotheses and their progressive modification should become a part of the record along with the directly observable or recordable events. This is not to say that a therapist should rob the interview of its spontaneity by constant and obsessional introspection, but that he should record his main "hunches" at the end of each interview. Every therapist, however intuitively or unsystematically, does evolve tentative hypotheses which at any given moment constitute what he calls his "understanding of the case." He even makes predictions, rarely communicated to the patient, and experiences the elation of discovery when these are borne out by subsequent events. Such predictions are prerequisite to the research record and, in the absence of the usual "controlled experimentation" of laboratory science, may prove the central methodological tool in clinical research. It will be insufficient in psychotherapeutic investigation to make predictions which are too general; nor will it suffice to predict the specific content of the patient's productions.

It will be necessary ultimately to set up highly specific hypotheses which will state what, in the investigator's opinion, will prove to be the actual turning points of the treatment; in other words, the satisfactory dealing with what kind of material will bring about a change in the patient. When our stated hypotheses in research in psychotherapy are of this order, we will have begun to tackle the problem of clinical research and to have some bases for answering the eternal question every therapist has asked himself: "Did that happen for the reasons I (later) thought?" When research in psychotherapy has evolved a genuinely inquiring rather than an eagerly empirical approach, such research records will be routinely discussed with colleagues and with members of other "schools of thought." Records of failure as well as success will be reported, with accent on the attempt to learn as much from the failures in advancing our knowledge as we now make of successes in advancing our prestige.

In later chapters we shall return to these problems and discuss them more concretely in terms of specific cases.

*Chapter 3*

# THE NATURE OF THE INSTRUCTIONS AND THE PURPOSES OF THE INTERACTION

In the previous chapter the nature of the processes whereby the clinician observes, records, and interprets overt behavior was briefly discussed and the importance of certain attendant problems stressed. In the present chapter we shall be concerned with factors influencing the behavior which the clinician observes.

To understand or explain the significances of an individual's behavior requires that one be able to specify the factors which influence the nature of his response *to the situation in which he is being observed.* If, as is banally true, an individual's behavior varies from situation to situation, then (the significance of) his behavior in any one situation is in part a function of *that* situation. Although variation in behavior from situation to situation is assumed to be lawful, the nature of the relationship between behaviors in any two situations can be stated only when it is known what the situations have in common. To predict behavior in situation B on the basis of observations in situation A assumes two things: (1) that one knows the relevant variables which influenced behavior in situation A and (2) that situation B is sufficiently similar to A in some way so as to evoke a predictable kind of behavior. Very frequently failures in prediction to the criterion situation (situation B) are attributed either to the unreliability or, in light of a failure, to the irrelevance of the criterion. While such conclusions are often true, it is sometimes overlooked that the behavior in the sample situation may be due to factors other than those considered by the investigator. Since the criterion situation is usually chosen on the basis of the investigator's *interpretation* of the behavior (which may be expressed as a score) in the sample situation, if the interpretation is faulty or incomplete then the predictions to the criterion situation are very likely to be wrong. Kelly and Fiske's (86) study, "The Prediction of Performance in Clinical Psychology," might serve as a basis for illustrating the above point.

The project was concerned with the selection of graduate students in a program of clinical psychology. The primary aim of the project was to evaluate selection procedures: how well they enabled one to predict performance in graduate school, research, diagnosis, therapy, etc. The subjects were students who had already been accepted for training; they were drawn from a large number of universities and were brought together in groups at a single location for evaluation. The following description of the "candidate's schedule" describes the nature of the assessment (*107*):

## THE CANDIDATE'S SCHEDULE

Upon arriving in Ann Arbor and reporting to the sorority house being used for housing and the actual assessment research, the assembled candidates were given a welcoming speech by the Project Director, who indicated the general nature of the program. They were told in a general way what was expected of them and assured that strict professional confidence would be maintained for all personal material gathered by the project.

That same morning the group was given a battery of objective tests. At lunch, as at all meals during the first five days, each team sat at a specified table, along with any two staff members who would not be evaluating that team. In the afternoon of the first day, the class continued taking group tests. Before the end of three days, the following tests had been taken: the Thematic Apperception Test (10 cards), the Project Sentence Completion Test, Miller Analogies, Thurstone's Primary Mental Abilities, the Allport-Vernon Study of Values, Strong Vocational Interest Blank, Guilford-Martin Battery (Inventory of Factors STDCR, GAMIN, and Personnel Inventory I), and the Minnesota Multiphasic Personality Inventory. During the third day or, sometimes, the next day, each subject took the Rorschach and the Bender-Gestalt Test, each at separate sessions.

The first afternoon, each student had an "Initial Interview" lasting one hour. The interviewer, unknown to the subject, had already studied the student's "credentials file," i.e., materials he had submitted with his application to the university. These included the transcript of his college grades, his Civil Service Form 57, and letters of recommendation submitted in his behalf. This interview was searching, but not deep lest anxiety be aroused in the subject.

During the evening of the first day, each subject filled out a Biographical Inventory, which contained over a hundred multiple-choice items about background, personal history, experiences, and preferences. He also received an outline for an autobiography he was to write within the next two days. On the third day, more objective tests were administered including the

Kuder Preference Record and the ACE Culture Test. The Strong was taken twice more: once, he filled it out as he thought it would be answered by "women in general" and finally as he thought it would be answered by "men in general." These results were not made available to the assessment staff.

Late that afternoon, each subject met his "intensive interviewer," the staff member whom he would get to know best and the person whose job it was to get to know the assigned student best. This interview was thorough and probing. By the nature of the interviewer's questions, it was obvious to each student that the interviewer had carefully examined his credentials, autobiography, Biographical Inventory, test scores, and the other materials on which the student had spent three days.

The fourth day was free for relaxation and sightseeing. The fifth day was spent in a variety of situational procedures which were observed by staff members. These situations were of three kinds: (1) a group, or team situation, in which from four to eight students participated jointly, (2) dual situations, and (3) individual situations, in which each student participated alone, in the presence of staff members only.

On the morning of the last day, the students gathered in the group testing room for their last written work, which was the completion of a sociometric questionnaire concerning his reactions to his classmates, and a rating of himself and his three teammates.

Following this, he had a final individual appointment with his interviewer. Usually the student went to this interview expecting to learn the staff's opinion of him, but came away with relatively little information, such as test scores, etc.

The predictions made on the basis of the assessment were disappointingly poor. The two major criticisms (104, 137) which have been made concern (1) the nature of the ratings scales used during assessment and (2) the failure to develop reliable or valid criterion measures. The main problem which will concern us here involves the ways in which the students reacted to or experienced the assessment situation. Many of the situations were calculated to arouse competitiveness, anxiety, and other motivational patterns. However, although the investigators hoped that each situation would arouse a particular kind of reaction in the subjects, there is no evidence that this was so. In fact, the evidence from the preliminary assessment programs indicated that the type of strength of student motivation and responsiveness could not be taken for granted (86, p. 40):

The other major lesson gained from the three preliminary assessment programs was a necessity for close attention to staff and student tolerance thresholds. Since the students at these assessment programs knew that the evaluation of their assessment performances would have no direct effect upon their professional careers, many were less than enthusiastic in their participation. The majority were as cooperative as could be expected under the trying conditions imposed upon them. However, it became quite clear that the physical and emotional tolerances of trainees had to be respected. Similarly, although the staff members applied themselves to their assessment tasks with a concentration of energy which was "above and beyond the call of duty," it became increasingly apparent that our earlier assessment plans underestimated the demands imposed by the continuous evaluation process and overestimated the energy capacity of the staff.

Unfortunately, there is no indication that this problem was controlled or studied in the main assessment program. In short, *the nature of the situation from the standpoint of the student is unknown and the range of individual differences in reaction undetermined.* To assume that such an unknown is not particularly important for purposes of prediction is to assume that what a person says or overtly does is more important than the nonverbalized attitudes or feelings which accompany or precede what he says or does. (Later on in this chapter we shall see that among college students performance on tests is clearly a function of attitudes toward taking tests, and unless these attitudes are known one is likely either not to understand the significances of the performance or to make faulty predictions.) If the students in the assessment program differed in the degree of indifference, resentment, and anxiety which the situation aroused in them, then such individual differences must in some way be accounted for in prediction to a relevant criterion situation.

Let us assume that in one or all of the group stress situations a student performs in whatever is considered to be an ineffectual manner. Let us also assume that his low rating was in part a function of the interfering effects of a fear of losing caste in the eyes of his peers and the leader, all relative strangers. (In the Kelly and Fiske study one would not know the nature of the interfering effects.) Why should one expect from the above to be able to predict the student's rated competence in clinical diagnosis or therapy? When a student operates clinically he is with *a* patient and is not in a situation where he is actively competing or interacting with peers. At the beginning of his training he may be observed by a supervisor who, unlike the leader above, plays a sympathetic and "personal" role. In the latter stages of his training personal observation by a supervisor is infrequent. In other words, the sample and criterion situations may be so dissimilar as to make it very unlikely that similar kinds of reactions will be evoked. It is, of course, possible for two overtly different situations to evoke similar kinds of reactions, and where this is the case there is usually an explicit rationale on the basis of which similarity in reaction is predicted. In the Kelly and Fiske study, however, there is no rationale which would justify the prediction that reactions to the sample and criterion situations will be correlated.[1] It should also be pointed out that in the assessment situation one observes a performance and not a series of learning trials—the student is given one trial. The clinical situation, however, is one to which the student is repeatedly exposed in such a way as to facilitate learning. It may be that the most relevant situations to compare are the assessment situation and the student's *first* supervised (personally observed) contact with a patient. Were one's predictions accurate it would be of dubious significance because the problem is not how the student reacts to and handles his first patient but to what extent the student can modify his behavior in the clinical situation in the course of his training.

One could point to other studies where the nature of the situation from the standpoint of the subject is unknown and, therefore, makes the evaluation of results a difficult task. The point does not appear to require further elaboration. What appears to be important at this point

[1] McNemar (*104*) has commented on this point: The reader "easily gets the impression that certain tests and procedures were included because someone had 'faith,' 'high confidence,' or 'high hopes' in their predictive value. That Kelly and Fiske, as analyzers and reporters, were not borne aloft by the faith and hope of their clinical brethren is evidenced by their discussion of certain correlations between tests and criterion measures. If a rationale existed for the use of a given test, and if Kelly and Fiske accepted that rationale, it is difficult to understand remarks such as 'these correlations are not easy to interpret,' or a correlation is 'of interest,' or 'two interesting validities,' or 'interesting is the finding,' or 'this relationship is somewhat unexpected.' Then there is the conspicuous absence of any discussion of the fact that a prediction based on the Bender-Gestalt correlated .41 with rated Research Competence. Perhaps this was just another unexpected *r*, difficult to rationalize." On the failure to develop adequate criterion measures McNemar says, ". . . It is sheer nonsense to have proceeded with an extensive testing and assessment prediction program without first having devised satisfactory measures of that which was to be predicted."

is discussion of the major variables in the test (or any other inter-personal) situation and their significance for clinical and research pur-poses. These variables will be discussed in the remainder of this chap-ter and the three which follow.

## THE NATURE OF THE INSTRUCTIONS

The relation between the subject's behavior and the psychologist's in-structions can most readily be seen by comparing two kinds of therapeu-tic procedures: analytic and nondirective. In the former the patient is instructed to lie on the couch and to observe the fundamental rule: to articulate whatever thoughts come into his mind regardless of how tri-fling, embarrassing, painful he may think them to be—in short, "to hold nothing back." In nondirective counseling no such instruction is given. In fact, the patient is free to choose what he wants to talk about and when he wants to do so. It would be expected, of course, that such differences in instructions should result in differences in the behavior of patients. Although such a statement may correctly be labeled as a banality, one must not confuse banality with unimportance. For ex-ample, if one is interested in predicting on the basis of nontherapeutic techniques either amenability to therapy, or the occurrence of certain kinds of reactions during therapy, or the degree of therapeutic suc-cess, the kind of therapy to be employed becomes obviously of cru-cial importance. *Since differences in therapeutic instructions result in differences in the behavior of patients, not all therapies are of equal relevance for a given prediction.* For example, if one were interested in using therapeutic information as a means of testing TAT predictions concerning sexual attitudes and practices, one would not be likely to choose nondirective counseling data because, among other reasons, the nature of the therapeutic instructions is such as to facilitate for the patient avoidance of a discussion of sexual problems. However, if one were interested in testing predictions concerning certain self attitudes, data derived from nondirective counseling might well be appropriate (*118, 119, 130*).

A study by Hutt (*81*) may be appropriate here although it is con-cerned less with the nature of the instructions verbalized to the subject than with the effect of differences in clinicians' attitude toward and handling of "standard instructions." According to the standard instruc-tions given by Terman and Merrill (*164*), once the basal age of the child has been ascertained the examination is carried up the scale until an age level has been found in which all the tests are failed. They state further that the tests at each level should be given in the order followed in the manual. It was Hutt's hypothesis that this standard procedure "offers the subject a succession of tasks of constantly increasing difficulty and therefore requires him to be able to tolerate the increasing frustrations inherent in such a situation. Such a procedure is likely to result in decreased motivation in proportion to the subject's degree of maladjustment." Hutt describes an "adaptive" testing procedure with the Binet in which if the subject fails an item he is given an easier one and if he passes an item he may be given a more difficult one. Hutt also recommends beginning with an item that does not require "considerable concentration, rapid response, or prolonged and involved verbal directions." The standard and adaptive procedures were alternately used with cases referred to an educational clinic. Results indicated that (1) the adaptive procedure did not affect the norms of the test; (2) in those cases which were rated as very well adjusted there was no difference in test score between those "standardly" tested and those "adaptively" tested; but (3) in cases rated as very poorly adjusted those who were adaptively tested did significantly better than those standardly tested. The significance of Hutt's study is that it indicates that the effect of a particular instruction in certain cases is a function not only of that instruction but of its timing.[2]

That the effect of instructions varies with the kind of case is confirmed in a series of studies (99, 100, 140, 141) of test anxiety. In the first study by Mandler and Sarason (99) a questionnaire was devised containing statements about experiences in three kinds of testing situations (see Fig. 1): an individual intelligence test, a group intelligence test, and a course examination. Two extreme groups were studied: those who almost always checked each item "anxiously" (above the median score on the item) and those who almost always checked each item "nonanxiously" (below the median score on the item). The former

---

[2] Hutt's study may possibly contain a methodological flaw. In the study the adjustment rating and testing were apparently done by the same examiners. If the examiners were prejudiced in favor of the adaptive testing method, it is conceivable that their behavior toward their subjects varied as a function of the method used and that the adjustments ratings were also contaminated. Against this possibility of bias is the fact that not all groups showed a difference between testing methods. The study deserves replication.

4.  If you know that you are going to take a group intelligence test, how do you feel *beforehand*?

I..................................I..............................I

Feel very confident          Midpoint          Feel very unconfident

9.  *While* taking a group intelligence test to what extent do you perspire?

I..................................I..............................I

Perspire not at all          Midpoint          Perspire a lot

17. Before taking an individual intelligence test, to what extent are you (or would you be) aware of an "uneasy feeling"?

I..................................I..............................I

Am not aware of it          Midpoint          Am very much
at all                                        aware of it

24. In comparison to other students, how often do you (would you) think of ways of avoiding an individual intelligence test?

I..................................I..............................I

More often than          As often as          Less often than
other students          other students          other students

26. When you are taking a course examination, to what extent do you feel that your emotional reactions interfere with or lower your performance?

I..................................I..............................I

Do not interfere          Midpoint          Interfere
with it at all                                a great deal

FIG. 1.  Some of the Questions Used in the Anxiety Questionnaire

was called high anxious (HA) and the latter low anxious (LA). Several months after the administration of the questionnaire these students were asked to participate in a psychological experiment concerning intelligence tests. The experimenter, who was not the same person who had administered the questionnaire, was not aware of the group to which a student belonged.

At the beginning of the testing session the subject was told that he was going to be given a number of intelligence tests as part of a study relating to the aptitude tests given to every Yale freshman. He was also told that his scores in the session would be compared with his aptitude test scores to make possible a better interpretation of the latter. He was presented with the Kohs Block Design Test and asked to do sample design #2 of the Wechsler Bellevue modification. He was then presented with design #13 from the Kohs Block Design Test and the total time (in seconds) needed for completion was recorded. The subject was then presented with the Digit Symbol subtest from the Wechsler-Bellevue Intelligence Test, doing the practice part first. A time limit of one minute was used for the main part, scoring number right minus number wrong. The subject was then again presented with Kohs Design #13 and, after that, again with the Digit Symbol test. This was continued until each S had completed six trials of each of the tests. Six trials were chosen in order to obtain both a representative performance curve and to minimize boredom that could appear with a large number of trials.

At this point the experimenter secretly opened an envelope, previously prepared for each subject, informing the experimenter as to which of the three experimental subgroups (success, failure, or neutral) the subject belonged. The procedure was then as follows:

*Success group.* The subject was informally told that he had done extremely well on the Kohs Block Design and Digit Symbol tests. The experimenter looked through several sheets of paper (apparently score and norm data), leafed through Wechsler's *The Measurement of Adult Intelligence,* and finally informed the subject that he had scored at approximately the 93rd to 96th percentile for a comparable college population. This was concluded by the experimenter's saying: "Let's see whether you can do as well in the second part."

*Failure group.* The procedure was the same as for the success group except that the subject was told that he had done much worse than would be expected from his aptitude scores, and that his performance fell below the 10th percentile. The experimenter then said: "Let's see whether you can do better in the second part."

*Neutral group.* The experimenter only said: "Let's go on to the second part."

Each subject was then presented with six trials of the Kohs Block Design #16 and a specially prepared Digit Symbol test of the same form as the Wechsler-Bellevue subtest but with different symbols.

For the purposes of the present chapter the following results (see Tables 1A, 1B, 1C) of this study are relevant:

1. In the low anxious group the failure instructions seemed to be most effective in the sense that those who were given such instructions tended subsequently to perform at a higher level than those receiving either success or neutral instructions.

2. In the high anxious group the neutral instructions were the most effective in terms of subsequent performance.

3. Whereas previous to these instructions the high anxious in comparison to the low anxious group tended to perform at a significantly lower level, the neutral high anxious group subsequently performed significantly better than the neutral low anxiety group.

TABLE 1A. Mean Time Scores and Standard Deviations for Both Anxiety Groups for Six Trials of First Kohs Design (Mandler and Sarason, 99)

| Trial | High Anxiety Group | | Low Anxiety Group | | t (df = 31) | $p^a$ | F | $p^a$ |
|---|---|---|---|---|---|---|---|---|
| | Mean | SD | Mean | SD | | | | |
| 1 | 199.4 | 114 | 158.2 | 107 | 1.07 | .14 | 1.15 | .05 |
| 2 | 111.1 | 78 | 82.6 | 25 | 1.36 | .08 | 9.84 | .001 |
| 3 | 76.1 | 36 | 65.1 | 12 | 1.13 | .13 | 8.83 | .001 |
| 4 | 76.2 | 35 | 58.9 | 12 | 1.86 | .04 | 8.06 | .001 |
| 5 | 74.4(60.5)$^b$ | 63(30)$^b$ | 55.4 | 11 | 1.17 | .12 | 32.88 | .001 |
| 6 | 58.9 | 20 | 54.3 | 12 | 0.78 | .22 | 2.44 | .05 |

$^a$ One tail of the distribution of t used.
$^b$ Figures in parentheses exclude one extreme case. The respective t and F values are:
t = 0.94  p = .17
F = 7.49  p = .001

TABLE 1B. Mean Time Scores for the Experimental Subgroups on the First Trial of Second Kohs Design$^b$ (Mandler and Sarason, 99)

| | High Anxiety Group | | Low Anxiety Group | | t | $p^a$ |
|---|---|---|---|---|---|---|
| | Mean | Adjusted Mean | Mean | Adjusted Mean | | |
| Neutral | 104.8 | 126.0 | 143.4 | 165.6 | 1.46 | .08 |
| Success | 197.6 | 163.6 | 106.0 | 138.0 | 0.94 | .17 |
| Failure | 204.8 | 162.2 | 146.2 | 108.6 | 1.98 | .03 |

$^a$ See footnote to Table 1A.
$^b$ Tables 1B and 1C are based on an analysis of covariance of the time scores on trial I of the second Kohs Design for the six experimental subgroups. The Ss' scores on trial I of the first Kohs Design were used as a statistical control for initial differences in Kohs Block Design performance. The resulting t-values have 23 degrees of freedom.

TABLE 1C. Significance of Difference Between Mean Time Scores of Experimental Subgroups Within the Two Anxiety Groups$^b$ (Mandler and Sarason, 99)

| | High Anxiety Group | | Low Anxiety Group | |
|---|---|---|---|---|
| | t | $p^a$ | t | $p^a$ |
| Neutral vs. success | 1.38 | .09 | 1.02 | .16 |
| Neutral vs. failure | 1.34 | .09 | 2.10 | .02 |
| Success vs. failure | 0.05 | ... | 1.01 | .16 |

$^a$ See footnote to Table 1A.
$^b$ See footnote to Table 1B.

In a subsequent study (*141*) the effect of differential instructions on test anxiety and learning was further studied. In Experiment 1 reported in this study the HA (N = 36) and LA (N = 36) groups were each split in two:

One-half of each group was told that they would be expected to finish in the time allotted to the test, and the other half being told that they were not expected to finish. The expected-to-finish group (ETF) was told that "the test is designed so that it should be fairly easy for the average college student to complete the test within the time limit. You should have little difficulty in finishing it, at least by the second or third time." After the first and third trials this group was again told that they were expected to finish. The not-expected-to-finish group (NETF) was told that the test was constructed so that nobody could finish the test within the time limit. After the first and third trials they were reminded that they should not worry about finishing because nobody could finish it. (Actually no one could or did finish the task in the time allowed.)

The test used was a modification of the Wechsler-Bellevue Digit Symbol subtest, a 50-second time limit being used for each of five trials. Five different forms of the test were devised, each form differing in the number of digit-symbol units on a line. This was done to make it difficult for the subject to determine if and to what extent he was improving from trial to trial. For each subject the order in which the five different forms were given was randomized.

Two predictions were made: (1) In the HA group those who were given the ETF (expected-to-finish) instructions would have *poorer* scores than those who were given the NETF (not-expected-to-finish) instructions; (2) in the LA group those who received the ETF instructions would have *better* scores than those who were given the NETF instructions. The results indicated that in the early trials both predictions hold up while at the end of the trials only the prediction concerning the LA groups is confirmed.

In Experiment 2, involving new subjects, the LA (N = 12) group was picked from between the 11–15th percentiles of the same distribution while the HA group (N = 12) was picked from between the 85–89th percentiles. One-half of each group received the identical introductory, "ego-involving" (EI) instructions given to all subjects in Experiment I. The other half of each group was given nonego-involving (NEI) instructions: they were *not* told that they were to be given an intelligence test which would be compared to their entrance test scores but instead were told that the examiner wanted to standardize some tasks and that "your own performance is only of importance insofar as it contributes to the total performance of a group of students." All subjects were given a trial on a Kohs design, followed by

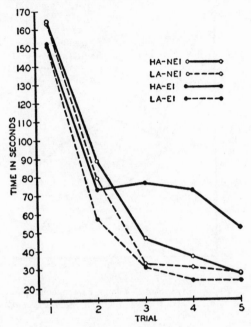

FIG. 2. Time Scores of Four Experimental Subgroups on Stylus Maze (Sarason, Mandler, and Craighill, *141*)

a trial on a stylus maze. This procedure was followed until each subject had had 5 trials on each task. Only the results of the stylus maze will be reported here. . . . Each subject received two scores on each trial: number of errors made by entering blind alleys and total time in seconds necessary for completion.

As in Experiment 1 the instruction variable was expected to have opposite effects in the HA and LA groups: (1) in the HA group those who receive ego-involving (EI) instructions will do *more poorly* than those who receive the nonego-involving (NEI) instructions; (2) in the

LA group those who receive the EI instructions will do better than those who receive the NEI instructions. Figure 2 shows the learning curves, based on time scores, for the four subgroups on the stylus maze. Figure 3 shows the curves based on error scores. In regard to the first

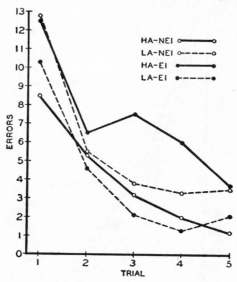

Fig. 3. Error Scores of Four Experimental Subgroups on Stylus Maze (Sarason, Mandler, and Craighill, *141*)

prediction the only trial in which it is conclusively borne out is trial 3, when time scores are used.

Although the HA-EI group *always* gets poorer mean error scores than the HA-NEI group, and is poorer on trials 3, 4, and 5 for time scores, the differences are only significant for trial 3. This is probably in part due to the large variability in each subgroup (N = 6).

In none of the trials is Prediction II borne out. However, here again, the LA-EI group *always* does better than the LA-NEI group in both mean time and error scores. These findings based on mean time and error scores tend to support the two predictions.

The most obvious finding in this study concerned the significant differences between the HA-EI and LA-EI groups. While the NEI instructions did not appear to have a differential effect on HA and LA groups, the EI instructions clearly had such an effect.

CONCLUSIONS

The most obvious conclusion that can be drawn from the above discussion is that an individual's behavior is in part a function of the nature of the instructions. More important, however, is the conclusion that instructions have a differential effect. Failure either to be aware or to take account of these differential effects may have several consequences. First, the significance of observed individual differences may be misinterpreted and unwarranted generalizations made. Second, prediction from one situation to another becomes increasingly hazardous and inaccurate where there are two situations for each of which the effect of the instructions is unknown—put in another way, one could say that the choice of the criterion situation may be made on an irrelevant or incomplete basis. Third, the clinician or researcher may overlook important ways of varying or influencing important aspects of the individual's behavior. Fourth, when, as in the case of test anxiety, differential effects amount to apparently *opposite* effects in different individuals, a "canceling out" effect may take place so that insignificant findings obscure significant ones.

It would seem important for the investigator, especially if he contemplates a series of studies on a particular problem, to ascertain the degree to which his instructions produce differential effects. Having done so he is in a position to control for them.

THE PURPOSES OF THE INTERACTION

The importance of this variable can be illustrated by again taking a problem in psychotherapy. An individual comes to a medical clinic with a variety of somatic symptoms. After he has been examined by a number of specialists and has had various laboratory tests it is concluded that there is no discernible somatic basis to his complaints and that the problem is a psychiatric one. He is then referred to a psychiatric clinic with the expectation that it will take over responsibility for the patient. The following are some of the problems the psychotherapist frequently encounters:

1. The patient was not told the purpose of the referral and frequently

expects another kind of medical examination or a new type of medication. If the therapist remains unaware that the patient has been given no idea of the purpose of the interview, he can obviously misinterpret the significance of the patient's behavior. In those instances where the therapist attempts to explain the purposes of the interview, the patient often will become resistant and uncoöperative because he does not think, nor does he want anyone else to think, that he is "a mental case." It would appear to be a mistake to interpret such resistance and unco-operativeness in the way one would if the patient were self-referred and where there had been agreement between patient and therapist about the purposes of their interaction.

2. The patient was told in very general terms that "there is nothing wrong" with him but there may be "things on his mind" which cause him to worry. Consequently, he was told, he is being referred to someone (whose professional specialty may or may not be indicated) who will be able to help him with his problems. Far more often than not the purposes of such a referral are sketchily and quickly given without any attempt to gauge the reaction of the patient to such a referral. The situation is usually handled in this way because the referring individual (a) may feel uncomfortable about the fact that he is telling the patient that he cannot help him—that someone else knows more, (b) may anticipate, rightly or wrongly, the patient's displeasure at the nature of the recommendation and want to get the referral over with as soon as possible, and, most frequently, (c) simply has had no training or supervision in the psychological aspects of the referral process. Not infrequently the patient is told nothing about the nature of psychotherapy and he comes to his first appointment with a vague, probably distorted conception of what will happen.

3. Some attempt was made to explain to the patient why he is being referred elsewhere and the nature of psychotherapy—the latter usually in terms of what a psychotherapist does. More often than not the patient is given to understand that after he has told the therapist what bothers him the therapist will then be able to state what needs to be done in order for the problems to disappear. The formula appears to be: "You talk and the doctor will then tell you what to do." Consequently, the patient sometimes becomes upset and puzzled when the therapist has no ready answers and appears to expect the patient to work things out for himself. If the therapist is not aware of the nature and source

of the patient's conception of the purposes of the interview, he may well misinterpret the significance of the patient's behavior.

Regarding the initial phase of psychotherapy Coleman (28) has pointed out that "The patient arriving for his first psychotherapeutic interview has very little idea of what is expected of him or of what to expect from the psychiatrist. The first requirements at the beginning of treatment, then, are: orientation of the patient in the process of treatment, clarification of the patient's feelings about treatment and about the therapist, and establishment of a treatment situation in which the balance between regressive and integrative trends in the patient may be maintained at a level most appropriate to the nature of his presenting problem."

In his discussion of means for improving graduate training in psychiatry Sullivan (162) has pointed out:

The first deficiency which calls for correction is orienting the candidate clearly towards the task that is to be accomplished. A remarkably varied group of preconceptions about the nature of one's personality, now presumably to be studied intensively, are brought to the work. . . .

In the phase of *formal inception of* our relationship, its ostensible goal has to be discussed explicitly, a prospective patient being led to state an adequate reason for seeking psychiatric help; a prospective training candidate, an adequate reason for seeking aid towards this sort of career. Neglect of this has been singularly costly; with unwilling or "uncooperative" patients, I have learned the wisdom of "telling them" wherein I observe their need for psychiatric help, wherein I see that their performances are obviously inadequate and inappropriate to the situation in which they are involved. This step in creating a workable relationship is simply never to be taken for granted.

The above examples have been given in order to emphasize the point that *an individual's conception of the purposes of an interaction in part determines the nature of that interaction.* A dramatic example from the area of diagnostic testing follows:

A 14-year-old boy had come to the pediatric outpatient clinic in order to get advice about overcoming his stuttering. He had been seen by a social worker who referred him to the clinical psychologist for diagnostic testing. When he showed up for the testing situation he appeared to be somewhat tense but shortly after the contact began he appeared relaxed and seemed to be cooperating in and enjoying the testing. At the outset he was told that the purposes of the testing were to determine what things he could do well, what sort of activities interested him, and what sorts of things bothered him. He was first given the Wechsler-Bellevue scale and throughout its administration the boy's behavior was in no way remarkable. The Rorschach was then given and a marked change in his behavior was noted. He became tense, had difficulty talking and began to stutter (he had not up until then). His behavior had changed to such an extent that the examiner asked him if anything was wrong. To this question the boy anxiously asked: "Do you think I'm crazy?" Questioning revealed that the week before the boy had seen the picture "The Dark Mirror" in which "crazy people" had been shown being given the Rorschach. In short, the boy's behavior changed as a function of changes in his conception of the purposes of the testing.

The following case (*139*, p. 103) is another example of how the patient's conception of the purposes of the interaction, unrelated to anything the examiner said, affected her performance and how different that performance was from other samples of her behavior. The girl had been institutionalized as a defective when fifteen years of age.

Several years after her commitment she was assigned to the hospital laboratory to do the simplest of routine tasks. After one year she was able to perform the following tasks:

1. Sterilization and chemical cleansing of glassware used in bacteriology and quantitative chemistry.
2. Preparation of bacterial media, physiological and chemical solutions used in bacteriology, hematology, and qualitative chemistry.
3. Cleansing of volumetric, graduated, and hematological pipettes and special chemical filters.
4. Complete urinalysis, except for microscopic including qualitative and quantitative sugars, albumin, acetone tests, and specific gravity.
5. Streaking and plating of bacterial cultures with aseptic technique.
6. Assistance in quantitative blood and tissue chemistry as in total proteins, lipids, sodiums, and potassiums.
7. Staining of hematology and bacterial slides.
8. Taking stool cultures and finger blood tests alone.
9. Keeping daily record of work performed.
10. All blood typing (all work is, of course, checked by the head of the laboratory).

This girl was also receiving and responding to instruction in the use of the microscope. As a result of her performance, which was a surprise to the hospital staff, she was given a psychological examination. The results of the testing were:

| Terman-Merrill (L) | M.A. | 10–6 | I.Q. | 70 |
| Arthur Point Scale | M.A. | 10–11 | I.Q. | 73 |

Rorschach

Achievement

| Reading | Grade 3.9 | Age equivalent 9–3 |
| Arithmetic | Grade 4.9 | Age equivalent 10–4 |
| Spelling | Grade 3.0 | Age equivalent 8–3 |

Before and during the examination this girl seemed very anxious and insecure. Although she had known the examiner for several years and had come to him for advice and help, she was tense, somewhat overly polite, and seemed as if she had decided to avoid at all costs doing or saying the "wrong" things. It was as if she felt that much depended on how well she did on the tests. (It is a commonly expressed attitude among institutionalized children that if they do well on their "brain" tests they might be placed back in the community at an early date.) The desire to do well, to impress and achieve, was very strong in this girl. Associated with these feelings was an equally strong anticipation of failure. Her desire to impress and achieve was so strong that even before directions for a task were completed she would nod her head knowingly, although it was evident that her anxiety about her ability to grasp directions prevented full comprehension. When she was given the memory-for-designs item on the Binet, she very quickly and inaccurately scribbled some designs which had no relationship to the originals. Questioning revealed that she thought she was to reproduce the designs as quickly as possible. When given another piece of paper and told that speed was not a factor, she did noticeably better. In light of the influence which her attitudes exerted over comprehension of directions it is not surprising that she failed almost every item involving exact recall. On items involving a sustained oral response to a verbally presented problem, she had difficulty in expressing herself, stammered a great deal, became upset, and had to be encouraged often in order to calm her and obtain a clear response. For example, it was approximately six minutes before she was able to express clearly her thoughts concerning the second verbal absurdity at eleven years. On the Rorschach, where in contrast to the Binet she could formulate her responses in her own way and where tracings eliminated much questioning by the examiner, the accuracy of form of her responses was very good, even though she tended to respond to the whole card. She was not satisfied with the irregular features of the blots but attempted to improve upon them, and her embellishments definitely enhanced the form accuracy of her responses.

Other examples can be given to illustrate the importance of being aware of the purposes of the interaction as viewed by the individual. Psychiatric screening of draftees, interviewing and testing of primitive peoples, questioning hospitalized patients in front of the professional staff—in each of these situations the evaluation of behavior must take account of the individual's conception of the purposes of the interaction.

In any interpersonal contact, be it in clinic or laboratory, the subject is given some explanation of why he is there and what will happen. It is no little surprise, therefore, to find that in the clinical and experimental literature there has been practically no discussion or investigation of the effects on the individual (and, therefore, on the particular problem being studied) of differences in the statement of the purposes of the interaction. *The stated purpose of the clinician (or experimenter) and the unstated purpose of the subject may be quite different from each other.* We are here faced with a question which, if the literature is any guide, far too few psychologists ask: "Can I assume that whatever reasons I gave to the subject for my seeing him were believed or accepted by him—or produced the motivational state I desired?" Standard texts in test administration or diagnostic testing usually contain little or no discussion of why, what, and how one communicates to a subject about the purposes of the interaction. One will not find the following questions discussed: How "honest" should one be? (One does not tell a disturbed person that one is interested in how realistic his thinking is or in what unconscious drives he is defending himself against.) How should one's statement of purpose vary with age, symptomatology, and place of testing (clinic, institution, etc.)? The absence of discussion about these and related questions is indicative not of their unimportance but of a long-standing tendency in clinical psychology to focus attention on the test materials and the subject's verbal response to them and to neglect the nature and effects of the interpersonal context. One might point out here that changes in therapeutic technique, in psychoanalysis at least, have followed changes in conception of the nature and effects of the interpersonal interaction. One might well predict that, as increasing attention is given to the nature of the interpersonal context in diagnostic testing, changes in the direction of clinical research and in the procedures of testing will come about.

In the usual diagnostic testing situation the question about the patient's conception of the interaction is answered on the basis of the clinician's impressions, the reliability of such judgments being unknown. *It does not appear to be standard practice to ask the subject, before or after testing, what his conception of the purposes of the testing were or are, even though such a direct attack might enable the clinician to evaluate his data more validly.*

The problems besetting the experimenter are no different from those of the clinician. Shaffer and Lazarus (*151*, p. 210) indicate this fact in the following:

. . . Getting the subject to perform in such a way as to provide the observer with a good sample of his characteristic reactions to most test situations is an extremely complicated task. It is often a matter of getting a subject to take the experimenter's instructions seriously or in a uniform way. This is particularly true in experiments where subjects must be subjected to psychological stress by telling them they are failing in some task. It is possible that some subjects do not become emotionally involved, in which case the experimenter has not succeeded in stressing his subjects.

Unfortunately, most experiments do not include procedures which would indicate the degree to which a subject entered seriously into the task or conceived of the situation as the experimenter hoped he would. When predictions are supported by experimental results, it is legitimate to assume that the subjects conceived of the situation as the investigator intended. However, even where significant results are obtained there are usually more than a few cases whose behavior is not in line with the predictions. When the investigator's aim is to predict to the individual case, the "exceptional" case cannot be disregarded. If discrepancies between the purposes of the investigator and the subject may result in an "exceptional" result, it would seem important for the experimenter to devise procedures for gathering data with which to evaluate this possibility.

Carlson and Lazarus (*26, 36*) report a study which is one of the few that have attempted to determine whether the reactions of the subject were those which followed from the experimenter's purposes. In this study (*36*) "three different sources of threat were used: failure, observers, and electric shock. Interviews following the experiment showed that the subjects were, in reality, responding to only one of these sources of stress, the electric shock. The proper interpretation of the subject's behavior depended on this information." The following from an article by Deese and Lazarus (*36*) is relevant:

. . . We might wish to know the effect of sophistication on the perception of threat in a failure study. In an experiment using the threat of intellectual failure on the performance of a psycho-motor task, we often tell subjects that the task measures intelligence (as in the case of the digit-symbol test). Sophisticated subjects would be more likely to question the validity of the task as a measure of intelligence, and thus remain uninvolved in the situation. We would then expect different results with the two populations. The degree of sophistication might be varied by selection of subjects on the basis of education, or by manipulating it by means of instructions.

One interesting methodological experiment that might be done is to vary sophistication by means of instructions, then interview both groups after the experiment to determine to what extent they were ego-involved in the situation. If the interview is an effective source of information about ego-involvement, then it should produce results which are in keeping with the experimental variable. . . .

In a later section on the psychologist as a variable in the testing situation we shall discuss a study by Towbin and Sarason (166) which underlines the importance of research suggested above by Deese and Lazarus. The findings of that study suggest that if the interview is limited to the experimental variable and its presumed effects, important sources of "ego-involvement" may well be overlooked. The age, status, and personal characteristics of the psychologist, for example, may well influence the effects of the experimental variable, a possibility which must be taken account of in formulating the interview.

CONCLUSIONS

Although there is general agreement about the relevance and importance of understanding both the subject's and the psychologist's conception of the purposes of the interaction, there has been in the clinical literature little discussion of why and how one communicates the purposes of the interaction and what one includes. What seems to have been even more neglected are the means of evaluating the purposes as conceived by the subject. In the experimental-clinical literature increasing attention is being given to the problem although the great bulk of research seems to operate on the presumption that what one tells a subject is believed and accepted by him in the manner intended by the experimenter.

In light of the relative absence of relevant studies it is difficult to draw conclusions about just how important the variable under discussion is. It would be simple, but unwarranted, to say that any well-trained clinician can determine how a patient is responding to the stated purposes of the interaction. The experimentalist could maintain that while not all subjects respond in the way one wants, this problem can be minimized by a variety of experimental designs. However, the *experimenter as a variable* influencing the subject's conception of the purpose of the interaction is rarely taken into account in the design. The experimenter, like the clinician, inevitably has some effect on the person with whom he is interacting—*it cannot be forgotten that the variables under discussion are present in and influence to some degree any interpersonal contact.*

## Chapter 4

## STIMULUS TASK AND TIME AND PLACE OF INTERACTION

### The Nature of the Stimulus Task

The content of the individual's responses, the accompanying expressive behavior, and the needs and attitudinal factors engendered are in part a function of the nature of the stimulus task. How an individual will react to a Rorschach card cannot be determined from knowing how he responded to a memory-for-designs test; how an individual responds to the reading of a passage does not necessarily allow us to predict the nature of his response to a sorting test. Although it is a clinical commonplace to state that an individual's behavior is in part a function of the nature of the stimulus task, the implications of such a statement are frequently either not recognized or not taken seriously. For example, despite the fact that the Binet contains a variety of stimulus tasks one frequently finds, in clinical and research studies, that the individual is described or categorized in light of his total score, be that score a mental age or intelligence quotient. In other words, it is as if the clinician assumed that the particular score reflected equally well the individual's performances on the different tasks of which the test is composed, an assumption which can rarely be made. The researcher who matches cases on the basis of total scores likewise assumes that comparable scores reflect similarity of performance on the different tasks of which the test is composed, an assumption which again can rarely be made.

The kind of thinking represented by the above practices can perhaps be clarified by an example from the field of psychopathology. In his study of a patient the clinician frequently is unable to understand the presenting symptoms in terms of their present and future significances. Too frequently as soon as the clinician attaches a label (paranoid, depressive, organic, etc.) to the patient his description of and reaction to him are largely determined by the characteristics associated

42

with the label *even though many of these characteristics were not observed in the patient.* Similarly, when in research studies patients with
a particular diagnosis are grouped together and compared to another
patient group, the assumption is made that individuals within a group
share the characteristics associated with the diagnostic label, an assumption which is usually untenable. Unfortunately, many of those
clinical psychologists who justifiably criticize the ways in which
psychiatric labels are used in research and in the clinic use their own
instruments in much the same way.

The recognition that total scores do not adequately reflect the variety
of an individual's behavior or performances has led to an approach
which has been called pattern analysis. In such an approach interest
centers not on the total scores but on the relationships which obtain
among the sub-tasks comprising the test, far more work along these
lines having been done with the Wechsler-Bellevue than with any
other psychological test. Each sub-task is assumed to elicit certain kinds
of behavior which have significances for the prediction of the individual's behavior. The following rationale for some of the sub-tasks of
the Wechsler-Bellevue is representative of the approach of many
clinicians (65, pp. 11–20):

*Comprehension.* Wechsler has postulated that this test measures "common sense" and that "Success on the test seemingly depends on the posses-
sion of a certain amount of practical information and a general ability to
evaluate past experience." This has been further extended by Rapaport to
mean that the test measures "judgment." This appears to be one of the
most cogent conclusions. . . .

*Similarities.* Wechsler has stated, "the test has certain qualitative features, the most important of which is the light which the type of responses
received throws upon the logical character of the subject's thinking
processes." Rapaport has refined this further to point out that the test is a
measure of verbal concept formation. Clinical experience shows that this
evaluation holds up well with almost all subjects. However, one primary
distinction must be made. The verbalizations presented by the patient are a
better measure of the end-product than the function; that is, the patient can
verbalize conceptual thinking when conceptualization is impaired in unfamiliar situations. Gross disturbances on this test, therefore, make one
suspect psychotic behavior. . . .

*Picture Arrangement.* Of all the subjects, this one best exemplifies the
principle that it is necessary to understand the meaning and reasoning that

lie behind test performance. The test appears to measure the ability to
function in social situations. . . . When the easiest items are failed severe
pathology is immediately suspect since it constitutes a failure to plan for
and anticipate even primary sequential processes. The difficult sequences
involve the ability to function in interpersonal situations by an automatic
analysis of the situation leading to a proper sequence of action.

*Block Design.* This subtest through the medium of visual motor coordination appears to measure the subject's ability to think abstractly and
conceptually when confronted by relatively unfamiliar performance materials. . . .

By attributing behavioral significances to each subtest and studying
the relationships among the subtests in various groups of patients it
was hoped that valuable diagnostic aids could be developed. What
seems to have been overlooked is that the objections which were raised
against the use of total test scores were equally valid for an approach
which manipulated subtest scores. For example, because an individual
gets a certain score on a subtest (Block Designs, Similarities, etc.), one
cannot assume that his performance on all items making up that
subtest has the same significances. Scheerer (*149*) has clearly indicated
the dubiousness of procedures which equate items according to either
success or failure:

Success or failure are only the *end products* of performing. As such, they
do not disclose the *how* of succeeding and the *why* of failing. Clinical and
child psychology abound in instances where results are attained by unexpected roundabout means, or where non-passing scores conceal existing
ability. To mention only a few: normal children did more poorly in a
geometric jigsaw test than did feebleminded. The former, having conceived
a clear mental picture of the final figure, were misled by first dealing with
the puzzle pieces as natural parts of the whole form. The latter, lacking
such a clear goal conception, lost no time inspecting the pieces for relations
of parts to a whole, but mechanically fitted together the matching edges of
individual pieces. In the analogies test, time:clock::warmth:_____?,
normal ten-year-olds answered with "oven"; the analogy, gift:joy::death:
_____?, was completed with "life insurance." Though both answers
were scored minus, questioning revealed that they involved analogous
thinking; namely, in the sense that "clock *makes* the time as oven *makes*
the warmth," and "what *belongs* to death as joy does to gift?" An imbecile
apparently solved correctly the Binet analogy, "brother is a boy; sister is
a_____ (*girl*)," but failed on this, "cats scratch; bees_____

(fly)." Here, however, inquiry disclosed that both responses were mechanical word associations, with neither involving any genuine understanding of the relevant relationships. The performance *result* on a test item need not provide a distinguishing measure of the processes and functions involved, a fact which often strikes us, when subnormal individuals accumulate Binet credits, despite by-passing the rationale of the task by virtue of situational or rote memory. Correspondingly, certain aphasics pass on Binet definitions, because their circumlocutions are themselves descriptive in terms of use, which suffices on the test. However, even where words of general meaning, such as "green" to denote a particular green object, are used, this does not prove ability to think in categories or concepts. A class word can be used to denote an individual object (*this* green), without implying that it is representative of a class. H. Babcock's critical comment appears in line with this observation: "Too much consideration has been given to the symbols used and too little consideration to the processes which precede the use of symbols." The problem of qualitative analysis again presents itself in the type of developmental statistics which inform us that the average child can tell time on the clock, or knows left and right on others, at the age of 6. While it remained undisputed that such training is contingent upon maturation, little interest has been shown in the mental operations necessary for either performance (except by Piaget). The four-year-old perceives as accurately as we do the *configuration*, "clock," or "other person." Why, then, can he not learn to understand the *spatial and symbol relations* on the clock's face; what the small and big hands symbolize; what their positions alone and in relation to each other signify; which respective meaning the same numbers represent, when in the hour and when in the minute context? Is a similar complexity of *relations* to be mastered when the child has to grasp the relative meaning of left and right and must learn to *shift* from one spatial frame of reference to another? Clearly, such questions are indispensable for a psychological account of what a performance is. They also demonstrate that we must investigate further whether those apparently different achievements at the same age are functionally independent, or emerge from a larger functional system, a cognitive *level* of development.

Finally, we cannot treat wrong responses as minus or zero performances, simply because they are test failures. Ignoring the factual process which leads to failure leaves a scientific gap where positive explanation is called for. . . .

Another criticism which holds either for total test or subtest scores is that *it is unjustified to assume that the ability or function in question will be manifested in the same way regardless of how one varies the nature of the stimulus task.* For example, it *may* be true that a particular test measures "ability to function in social situations" but it does not follow (1) that it measures *all* aspects of social functioning, (2) that it is the best way of measuring whatever aspect (usually not specified) of social functioning it purports to measure, and (3) that regardless of how one varies the stimulus tasks the nature or predictive usefulness of the resulting performance will be the same. To make the assumption that a single stimulus task measures "social functioning" is to assume unjustifiably that an individual functions in the same way in all social situations regardless of differences in time, composition of the group, length of social contact, and so forth. During a single day a person engages in a number of different kinds of social activities, and it is somewhat presumptuous to assume that a particular kind of stimulus task will allow one to be able to characterize the variety of responses to the variety of situations the person encounters.

In short, there has been the tendency to overlook the fact that one's conclusions are based on a particular stimulus task which tends to elicit a particular sample of behavior—a fact which seriously limits the degree to which one can generalize about the function or response pattern in question. If the objections raised against the use of total test scores were equally valid for an approach which manipulates subtest scores, one would then expect that research utilizing such an approach would not be particularly fruitful, an expectation which is largely borne out (*171,* pp. 202–207).

In the previous paragraphs emphasis has been put on the fact that differences in response are in part a function of differences in the stimulus task. It may be advisable at this point to indicate briefly a consequence of the uncritical acceptance of such an emphasis. *We are here referring to the unjustified assumption that differences in stimulus tasks (and even instructions) necessarily call for different kinds of response patterns or abilities.* For example, the fact that one test is called "verbal" and another "performance" does not necessarily mean that they do not evoke similar kinds of response patterns. It is sometimes forgotten that a "performance test" does not require the individual to articulate his verbalizations; it does not imply that no self-verbalization takes place.

That characterizing test performance on a pass-fail or adequate-inadequate basis may obscure the psychological phenomena leading up to the response can also be seen in the superficial distinction that is usually drawn between verbal and performance tests. The results of these tests are sometimes interpreted as if the psychological processes stimulated by them are mutually exclusive. Although the objective nature of the stimulus tasks in verbal and performance tests are very different, in the former the task being administered and responded to by oral speech and in the latter oral speech usually being absent, introspective analysis suggests that in both kinds of test situations self-verbalization may be present. In other words, even though oral speech may not be required for a successful solution to a performance task, in many cases the solution is mediated by a process of "talking to yourself." For example, on the nine-year level in the Binet the subject is shown a card with two designs and he is allowed to look at it for ten seconds, after which he is asked to reproduce them from memory. Although oral speech is not required of the subject, he is verbalizing to himself relationships, attaching verbal symbols to the stimulus figures, which after the card is removed may act as cues for reproducing the figures. In a Binet item like paper cutting on the nine-year level, the subject's final response also seems to be preceded by a process of self-verbalization . . . (*139*, p. 73).

Robert was a 20-year-old boy who had been institutionalized since the age of 13. His Binet mental age was 6 years and 8 months with an intelligence quotient of 44. On the Kohs block designs, using the Arthur instructions and scoring, Robert received credit for 11 of the 17 designs. He successfully finished two other designs but did not receive credit because he exceeded the time limits. For his Binet mental age his Kohs performance is extraordinary. The degree of conceptualization necessary for the solution of these designs would hardly be expected from one with his mental age. In doing the designs Robert occasionally and spontaneously verbalized aloud his procedure: "Here you need one that's all red, and here you need one that's part red. That's not right, you need this kind, etc." In effect this boy was able to verbalize a procedure, to utilize verbal symbols in attacking the problem. His motor responses were apparently mediated by self-verbalization.

John, who was an honor student in a third-year college course in testing, was asked to be the subject in a classroom demonstration of the Kohs block designs. To the surprise of everyone John had inordinate difficulty with the designs and could only complete the first eight designs. An introspective report revealed that John had been very anxious and tense because he anticipated doing poorly in front of his teacher and classmates; that the colored designs "had absolutely no meaning for him" and that he didn't know how to proceed; and that his mind was a "blank." It seemed clear from John's report that nonintellectual factors prevented him from formulating (verbalizing) a procedure (*139*, p. 74).

That different stimulus conditions may produce similar kinds of responses or results is also a major problem in psychotherapy. When one reads the writings of leading proponents (2, 44, 130, 165) of the different therapeutic approaches, one is struck forcibly by the differences in theory, therapeutic instructions and therapists' behavior—one could say that the stimulus task which the patient encounters differs markedly from one kind of therapy to another. It is because of what appears to be obvious differences that the following should be kept in mind:

1. As Watson (171, p. 546) has pointed out, there are common factors which seem to run through all major psychotherapies. Although these factors are discussed in different ways and given different emphases, they all are taken account of in the different approaches. Reference is here made to such concepts as rapport, transference, self-understanding, etc.

2. Clinical experience as well as available research (43, 77) indicates that no one therapeutic approach has a rate of success significantly above that of the other approaches. Even in regard to miracle cures it has been said that the difference in therapeutic success between "scientific" psychotherapy and the Shrine of Lourdes is probably not statistically significant.

3. Although the different forms of therapy are presumably not equally effective with all types of cases, there is no reason to believe that there are not types of cases which have benefited from therapy regardless of the approach.

From the previous paragraphs one might state that, while variations in the nature of the stimulus task are in part responsible for variations in behavior, it also appears true that variations in the nature of the stimulus task do not necessarily produce mutually exclusive or markedly different response processes or end results.

SOME CONCLUSIONS

From the standpoint of the clinician it would seem important to be acutely aware not only of the nature of the stimulus task he is presenting to a subject but also of the means whereby he can vary the nature of *that* task. The conclusion which perhaps deserves most emphasis is that psychological tests are not ordinarily constructed in a way so as to allow the clinician to vary systematically the nature of a particular stimulus task and thus be able to observe the nature of the variations in response. For example, if an individual performs poorly on a verbal similarities task (e.g., in what way are an apple and a peach alike?), it does not follow that he would necessarily perform as poorly on a similarities task in which the objects are visually presented. It seems reasonable to expect that the conclusion drawn by the clinician on the basis of both performances might be different from that based on either task alone. To concretize this point the following excerpt from a case reported elsewhere (139, p. 86) may be helpful:

*Terman-Merrill* (L). Basal year was established at 7 with final successes at 14 years. There was a marked difference in adequacy of response between items involving a verbal response to an orally presented problem and items involving a response to a visually presented stimulus. On the former items Harold's performance was hesitant and variable in efficiency. He failed vocabulary at 8 years, rhymes at 9 years, finding reasons and word-naming at 10 years, verbal absurdities at 11 and 12 years, abstract words at 12 years, and all orally presented items at 14 years. Although vocabulary was established at the 6-year level, he was able to define enough abstract words at 11 years to receive credit for the item. On many of the vocabulary items Harold seemed to comprehend the meaning of the word but did not have the facility to express it. His spontaneous conversational speech seemed well above the 6-year level. In contrast to these failures Harold passed all orally presented memory items through the 12-year level. His unpredictability with orally presented items is best seen in his performance on verbal absurdities at 9 years; he passed the first two, failed the next two, and passed the last absurdity, which is very rarely passed by defectives. That orally presented problems or face-to-face situations engender variability in efficiency can be seen when one compares his present performance on memory items with his pre-commitment performance, which led the examiner at that time to hypothecate an "organic" involvement. It would seem that in a face-to-face situation requiring an oral response to an orally presented problem efficiency of performance becomes impaired.

On items involving a response to a visually presented stimulus which may or may not involve a verbal response, Harold's performance was efficient and adequate; he passed the drawing of a diamond at 7 years, paper cutting at 9 and 13 years, memory for designs at 9 and 11 years, picture absurdities at 10 and 14 years, and bead chain and plan of search at 13 years. The only visually presented problems which Harold failed involved reading: reading and report at 10 years, Minkus completion at 12 years, and dissected sentences at 13 years. In light of Harold's general mental level it does not seem justifiable to ascribe his severe reading disability solely to an intellectual defect. When one considers his preschool and school experiences and the attitudes of self-depreciation which they probably reinforced, his reduced efficiency in face-to-face situations becomes more understandable. *Arthur Point Scale.* As might be expected from his Binet performance, Harold's score on this test, which does not require articulated verbal responses, was well within the average range. He worked quickly but reflectively with very little trial-and-error behavior. On the Porteus mazes he passed all mazes up to and including the twelfth year on the first trial, passed the 14-year maze on the second trial, failed average adult I, and passed average adult II on the second trial. On Healy P.C. I, seven of his nine placements obtained maximum scores. On his encounter with the Knox Cubes Harold's range of performance is atypical for defectives: he passed the first seven items, failed the eighth, passed the ninth, failed the tenth and eleventh, and then passed the twelfth. In the writer's experience no defective has been able to pass the twelfth Knox Cube item. Harold's performance on the Kohs Block Designs was characterized, as on the Knox and verbal absurdities (IX) on the Binet, by failure on the easier items and success on the harder ones: he passed the first design, failed the next four, passed the next two, failed the next two, passed the next one, and failed the remainder. His relatively low score and variable functioning on the Kohs do not seem to be explained by mental retardation. It is not that he lacks the intellectual power for conceptual thinking, because his performance on many Binet and Arthur items strongly suggests that he is able to formulate and sustain the correct solution to a problem. Why he is consistently adequate on the Porteus mazes, which involve formulation and criticism of a procedure, and relatively inadequate on the Kohs is not explainable at this time.

In summary it should be emphasized that in a situation which does not involve a face-to-face relationship or verbal responsiveness Harold's performance is atypical for defectives. It would seem that when he can formulate a problem in his own way (his own words?), aided by the constant presence of a visual stimulus, Harold is likely to perform efficiently. If this conclusion is correct, it suggests that previous learning situations involving face-to-face situations have engendered behavioral patterns which have interfered with efficient functioning.

It seems rather clear in this example that quality and level of memory functioning are a function of the nature of the stimulus task. Unfortunately, because of the way most tests are conceived and standardized, the clinician is unable to vary systematically the nature of the stimulus tasks. Where he now attempts to do so he is unsure of comparability in difficulty of the variations and lacks the research evidence that the variations he employs are the relevant ones.

What has been said thus far in this chapter has long been recognized and considered in experimental studies of various problems. For example, investigators (14, 34, 68, 69, 70) in the area of concept formation have long recognized that variations in the nature of the stimulus task clearly affect the rate of concept attainment and in part determine discriminability among concepts and the types of errors made. Although these experimental studies were not oriented toward the direct solution of a clinical problem, their findings and procedures are of basic importance to the clinician.

## TIME AND PLACE OF THE INTERACTION

A concrete clinical example (159) may serve as a basis for discussion of these variables. There are certain children whose pattern of behavior is sufficiently similar so as to warrant a common label: primary behavior disorder. An abnormal amount of aggressiveness, inability to form satisfactory relationships with people or objects, apparent absence of guilt feelings—these are the characteristics, present since early childhood, which apply to these children and are considered a patterned reaction to unfavorable environmental influences.

A not infrequent experience of therapists with such children is the marked discrepancy between the case history description of behavior and the child's behavior during the initial contacts (159):

It has been observed frequently that a child with a severe primary behavior disorder is friendliness and sweetness personified during the first few interviews, but thereafter, without fail, returns to the old aggressiveness. Even one of our most experienced and skilled workers felt a question arise in his mind about the correctness of the diagnosis when the boy he was interviewing for the first time was so nice that it seemed impossible to him for this to be the same little devil described in the intake worker's report. However, he soon found out. . . .

It invariably happens that when a child with conduct disorders, a child upon whom all sorts of threats and forms of punishment have been tried unsuccessfully, is finally referred to our agency, the parents have told him that we are going to show him that he cannot go on as he has done, that we are going to be very strict and severe, and so on. Naturally, the child expects unfriendliness, harshness, and threats. To his great surprise, he finds a worker who is quiet and friendly, who is interested in every little thing he mentions. She speaks to him in a civil way and does not scold him. This attitude takes him by surprise and he finds himself disarmed, having no reason or justification for a display of his usual aggressiveness. His hostility finds itself in a vacuum with nothing to fight and the surprising attitude of the worker throws him back into an attitude of friendliness. We have been using the term "surprise reaction" to indicate this behavior: finding to his surprise that there is nothing provoking his hostility, the child reverts, as it were, to the kind of behavior he may have shown before his disorder started. We would be inclined to expect that after the child has had the experience of a pleasant and warm relationship, he might be eager to continue in it, thankful to have found at last a response that he had not met with in a long time, either in his home or in school. But we find ourselves in error very soon and we want to understand what it is that brings about this change.

It seems clear in this kind of case that the child's behavior is in part a function of where the interaction is taking place. A jail, a clinic, a general hospital, a mental hospital, a school, a psychology laboratory, a private office, or some kind of assessment center—one cannot assume that all evoke in the same or different individuals samples of behavior which overtly or covertly are similar. The clinical significance of the "place variable" has been well put by Kent (87, p. 24) :[1]

Most tests are standardized by being presented to school children during school hours. Anyone who has standardized a group test in the elementary grades must have observed the immediate responsiveness of the children when they are instructed to put away their books and give their attention to a visitor who has just entered the room with a pile of papers. Anything unusual introduced into the day's work is regarded as a special treat. The children are alert, eager with curiosity, so impatient to read the test forms that it is difficult to induce them to wait for the signal to start. The test presented individually elicits a similar response. It is a special privilege to be sent to the teachers' room for an interview with a visitor, and each child enters the room with an air of expectancy. Whether for a group or an individual examination, the half-hour release from routine class work is at a premium. It is easy to obtain excellent cooperation. What is measured by the test in the collection of data for the establishment of norms is something very close to maximal achievement.

[1] *Mental Tests in Clinics for Children*, G. H. Kent, Copyright 1950, D. Van Nostrand Company, Inc.

The typical clinical interview presents a contrast that is almost painful. In most cases children are referred to the clinic because of some deficiency either in school work or in conduct. The child of school age usually feels it very keenly that he should be singled out for special examination. Consequently, he enters the room with resentment and is in no mood to do the best of which he is capable. To be sure, the tactful examiner can usually overcome his hostility and arouse some interest on his part; but it is exceptional when he brings to the examination the alert spontaneity of the normal child examined in school.

A specific example of how place influences behavior is Eron's (42) study of fantasy as elicited by the Thematic Apperception Test. His findings seemed to support his major conclusion that "fantasy productions are affected by the external objective environment of the individual, in this case a limiting, routinized, hospital environment." In this connection it might be pointed out that fantasy productions, as Coombs (29) has indicated, are a function of *when* the productions are obtained.

It should not be thought that differences in setting necessarily imply differences in the elicited behavior. The degree to which different situations may evoke similar patterns of behavior is probably in part a function, as the above case suggests, of when in a sequence of interactions a particular sample is observed. In the kind of case described above, for example, the initial interaction between therapist and child is strikingly different from the interactions between the child and other significant figures in his life. As the interaction between therapist and child goes on in time, however, similarities begin to emerge.

Bach's (11) studies of the play fantasies of young children illustrates the importance of the variables under discussion.

During the exploratory experiments with different play techniques it was noticed that the children elaborated quite extensively on doll dramatizations about resting and taking naps. Often the subjects would have all children (dolls) go to bed and have the teacher (doll) supervise them; frequently punishment would be inflicted on a "naughty" child by making him lie down in the rest room or go to sleep there. From observation of the actual behavior of the children, it was noted that all of them learned to comply in various degrees to resting or taking a nap during their day in preschool, but likewise, most of them showed avoidance responses to the rest situation. Verbal comments by the children and their overt behavior symptoms (such as their greater reluctance and slowness in going to than in leaving the rest situation) supported the initial impression gained from teacher's comments to the effect that "probably none of the children really enjoys the rest situation" (*11*, p. 32).

A theoretical analysis of the effects of the frustrating rest situation suggested certain predictions which were possible to test because of the conditions of the experiment. In reading the quotation below (*11*, p. 34) it should be borne in mind that the predictions were in part based on the assumption that *the amount of time during which differential treatment had been applied was an important variable.* Italics are those of the present writer.

For educational research reasons, two adjacent age groups (Groups III and IV) had rather different rest procedures. Each child in Group III spent only 10 to 20 minutes in the middle of the morning resting on his bed in the common bed room; in Group IV, each child was induced to take a nap for from one to two hours during the afternoon. Thus Group III can be labelled as the short rest group; and Group IV as the long nap group. This differential rest treatment had been in effect for four months prior to the play experiments. When the strength of the frustration-induced instigation to aggression is defined in terms of the degree of drive reduction which would take place if the child were not interfered with, it follows that the amount of frustration (and strength of instigation to aggression) is greater for the long nap group than for the short rest group. The reason for this is that greater delay prevents more consummatory play activity than does shorter delay. Furthermore, the long nap group was somewhat older, which factor tends not only to increase unwillingness to rest in the day time, but also to inhibit more successfully overt manifestations of aggression with respect to which no significant difference between the 2 groups was detectable on the basis of the rating material on overt destructive-aggressive behavior. *The day by day repetition of this differential interference stimulation would therefore build up more instigation toward fantasy-aggression in the long nap group than in the short rest group.* Furthermore, such fantasy-aggression should involve the teacher because she was the agent of the interference stimulation.

To test this deduction, 20 children were taken from the short rest group and were compared with 15 children taken from the long nap group in terms of mean differences between them with respect to measures of fantasy-aggression. . . .

The results are in line with the theoretically derived predictions. The long nap group (greater frustration) is significantly differentiated from the short rest group (less frustration) with respect to theoretically relevant play fantasies. In the long nap group there was: 1) a greater proportion of rest theme occurrences, 2) a greater proportion of non-stereotype dramatizations within the rest theme; 3) a greater proportion of hostile doll act aggressions within the rest theme; 4) greater elaboration of the teacher doll (agent of interference) within the rest theme, and 5) a greater relative amount of thematic aggression which involved the teacher doll.

Bach also studied fifteen children who were observed in the play situation just before their nap and twenty children who were observed after their nap.

An analysis of the rest fantasies of the group taken before rest (assumed to be anticipatory of rest) in comparison with those of the group taken after (assumed to be retrospective of rest at the time of the experiment), showed only one of five comparisons to be a statistically significant difference: the 15 pre-rest or pre-nap subjects had *less* thematic aggression within the rest theme than did the 20 post-rest or post-nap subjects. This difference was detectable for both the long nap and the short rest conditions, but when separately analysed it was no longer statistically significant. What differences there were, were more strongly shown in the long rest group than in the short.

Although the difference is not impressive, there is a trend for the subjects who, at the time of the experiment, had completed the rest or nap duties to elaborate more on the rest theme, particularly with respect to hostile aggression.

These and the previously cited findings of Bach seem to support the conclusion that the relationship between behavior and the time aspect of the interaction is probably not an unimportant one.

McHugh's (103) study of changes in I.Q. at the kindergarten level seems to be a particularly clear example of the clinical significance of the importance of the variables under discussion. The subjects in his study consisted of ninety-one children who had been registered for kindergarten. The group was homogeneous as to chronological age and about evenly divided between the sexes. Forty-five children were tested initially on Form L of the Revised Stanford-Binet and forty-six were tested initially on Form M. Each child's final test was on the form alternate to that of his initial test. Two examiners were used and every child was tested initially and finally by the same examiner. Controls were exercised for examiner bias in testing and scoring. Table 2 shows a distribution of the individual changes in M.A. from test to retest. "The children made a mean mental gain of 5.84 months in mental age from test to retest after a mean interval of 1.93 months during which time they had attended preschool a mean of 30 half day sessions." The difference between the mean mental ages was highly significant. In terms of the I.Q. the mean gain was 6.07 points, the difference between

TABLE 2.   Initial and Final Stanford-Binet Mental Age Scores
(McHugh, *103*)

| Months | Freq. 1st Test | Freq. 2nd Test |
|--------|----------------|----------------|
| 90–99 | 0 | 1 |
| 80–89 | 5 | 5 |
| 70–79 | 15 | 31 |
| 60–69 | 29 | 37 |
| 50–59 | 37 | 15 |
| 40–49 | 5 | 2 |
| N | 91 | 91 |
| Range | 44–84 mo. | 49–90 mo. |
| Mdn | 61     mo. | 67     mo. |
| Mean | 62.09 mo. | 67.93 mo. |
| S.D. | 9.04 mo. | 8.60 mo. |

$$MA1-2 = +.80 \pm .03$$
$$CR_{MA1-2} = 9.90$$

initial and final testing again being highly significant. McHugh (*103*, p. 15) interpreted his findings as follows: "It is possible that the mean gain of 6.07 I.Q. points reported in the present study, may be partially accounted for as better adjustment by the children, after some pre-school experience, to the teacher-pupil situation involved in the administration of the Stanford-Binet Test, to greater familiarity with the surroundings in which the test was administered and to what might be called a certain degree of test wisdom, having once before come through one such experience without damage." In effect McHugh's explanation is based on the following facts:

1. The initial test was presumably the first time the children had experienced such a situation.

2. The place where the children were initially seen was one to which they had never before been taken.

3. By the time of the final testing the children had already experienced many times the testlike kind of interpersonal interaction in a place which no longer was unfamiliar to them.

McHugh's analysis of the individual items rather clearly suggested that his explanation given above was a tenable one. He classified Binet items into those which required oral speech for success and those which required manual or manipulative behavior without oral speech for success. Because both forms of the Binet require a great deal more oral speech above the six-year level than they do up through that level, analysis was restricted to a comparison of individual changes from test to retest over the range of the three- through six-year levels only. Within this range children had equal opportunities to attempt manual and speech items. Table 3 shows the results of such an analysis:

. . . With approximately equal opportunity to improve in both manual and speech items from first to second test and over the same age levels of the test this group of 91 children showed 11.2% improvement in speech items as compared with 4.7% in manual items. It will also be noted that the group refused many more speech items on the first test than manual items. From these data one may infer that the mean gain of 6.07 I.Q. points obtained from 1st to 2nd tests is more closely related to an improvement in oral speech behavior during the interval between tests than to a general increase in intellectual ability. It is impossible to say whether this improvement is due to learning to use the tool of language in school or to a reduction of factors that may have operated to inhibit oral speech behavior at the time of the first test. Such factors might be: inexperience in talking to teachers, shyness in a new situation, or actual fear of the examiner who was a strange person. In view of the short period of school experience the proposed explanation in terms of reduction of factors that may have operated to inhibit oral speech behavior during the first test seems more acceptable (103, p. 21).

When an analysis identical to that above was done involving those who gained the most and those who did not gain at all in I.Q. points, the explanation in terms of improvement in the use of oral speech in the testing situation was given further support.

SOME CONCLUSIONS

A major conclusion—equally important for therapist and diagnostician—would seem to be that *awareness of the timing and place of a particular interaction makes it less likely that one will overgeneralize*

TABLE 3. Results of Analysis of Individual Binet Items 3- Through 6-year Levels for 23 Children Making Large I.Q. Gains and 38 Children Making No Gains (McHugh, *103*)

| Children | Test | Total Items Presented | Total Speech Items | % Speech Items | % Speech Passed | % Speech Failed | % Speech Refused |
|---|---|---|---|---|---|---|---|
| | | | Speech Items 3–6-Year Level Inclusive. Forms L and M | | | | |
| 23G | 1 | 407 | 213 | 52.3 | 46.9 | 42.3 | 10.2 |
| 23G | 2 | 252 | 115 | 45.8 | 71.3 | 23.5 | 5.2 |
| 38NG | 1 | 591 | 288 | 48.7 | 59.7 | 34.7 | 5.6 |
| 38NG | 2 | 487 | 242 | 49.7 | 61.6 | 36.8 | 1.6 |

| Children | Test | Total Items Presented | Total Manual Items | % Manual Items | % Manual Passed | % Manual Failed | % Manual Refused |
|---|---|---|---|---|---|---|---|
| | | | Manual Items 3–6-Year Level Inclusive. Forms L and M | | | | |
| 23G | 1 | 407 | 166 | 40.8 | 44.6 | 52.4 | 3.0 |
| 23G | 2 | 252 | 127 | 50.6 | 56.7 | 43.3 | 0.0 |
| 38NG | 1 | 591 | 276 | 46.7 | 54.3 | 44.6 | 1.1 |
| 38NG | 2 | 487 | 212 | 43.5 | 52.3 | 47.2 | .5 |

*from one's observations.* The literature on diagnostic testing abounds in instances where these variables were ignored. It is the exception rather than the rule to find in case reports or in clinical research awareness and evaluations of these variables in relation to findings or conclusions. In his survey of studies of the use of psychological tests in psychopathological prognosis Windle (*177*) points out that failure to be aware of, or to state in specific detail, the relation of the time of testing to the duration (chronicity) of illness makes comparison of studies hazardous and conflicting results likely.

It is somewhat surprising that despite the presence of evidence indicating the importance of the variables under discussion the tendency to ignore these variables is still marked. *A partial explanation of this tendency may lie in the unstated but oft made assumption that a test measures something independent of the conditions or time of measurement.* In these terms a test presumably is like an x-ray: regardless of the conditions external to the patient (the immediate environment) the "thing" being studied (e.g., a bone, intelligence, fantasy) can be observed in splendid isolation—a statement which is true neither for a test nor for an x-ray.

It would appear that the therapist more than the diagnostician has learned the importance of awareness of time factors. In most therapeutic approaches the significance of a particular patient-therapist interaction is in part determined by: (1) when in that interview the particular interaction occurred; (2) what kinds of interactions took place earlier in that interview; (3) what kinds of interactions took place in previous interviews; and (4) what took place following the interaction in question. The attempt to understand why something happened when it did is not based on a burning interest in time factors *per se* but on the practical importance of determining regularities between the patient's response, on the one hand, and external conditions, on the other hand.

*Chapter 5*

# THE PSYCHOLOGIST AS A VARIABLE

WHEN we talk in this chapter of the psychologist (clinician) as a variable influencing another person's behavior, we shall have reference to his age, status, social affiliations, and such behavioral characteristics as degree of self-confidence, responsiveness, temperament, and so forth. In Chapter 2 it was pointed out that the theory, implicit or explicit, to which a clinician subscribed in part determined how he would react to and influence a patient, a problem to which we shall return in later portions of this book. In the present chapter we shall be primarily concerned with the ways in which the social and personal characteristics of the clinician influence the behavior of the patient.

It may come as a surprise to some readers that while the clinical situation is clearly an instance of an interpersonal interaction we have little concrete evidence as to the ways in which characteristics of the clinician influence the nature of that situation. The relative absence of studies in this area is all the more surprising in light of the importance which is presumably attached to the problem. For example, very few people would disagree with the following statements, which concern practices and opinions based in part on the assumption that not all "personalities" are suited for clinical practice:

1. If all those who desired to become clinical psychologists were of similar ability and background, admission to the field would be denied to many on the basis of whatever are considered "favorable" or "unfavorable" personal characteristics.

2. Of all those who have very similar professional background and who apply for advanced training (e.g., in psychotherapy), the few who are chosen are those who are considered to have the personal qualities which make for whatever is considered "success."

3. Among practitioners in the field, variations in skill and in results achieved are obvious and in part related to variations in personal characteristics.

It should not be concluded from these statements that there is agreement about or similarity (and even clarity) in the description of those personality characteristics of the clinician which positively or adversely affect his relationships to other individuals. *What is important to bear in mind is that variations in personal characteristics exist, that they presumably make a difference in how patients' behavior is influenced, and that we have little concrete evidence of the role of such variations in the clinical situation.*

That the problems with which we are here concerned are not peculiar to the clinical situation may be seen from the following statements made by Sheatsley in connection with interviewing in public opinion polling[1] (*153*, p. 473):

Much of what we call interviewer bias can more correctly be described as interviewer *differences* which are inherent in the fact that interviewers are human beings and not machines and that they do not all work identically or infallibly. The fact that respondents, too, are human beings, with differing perceptions, judgments and personalities, simply compounds the differences which would occur even if the interviewers were engaged in evaluating physical instead of human materials. It is not to be expected, therefore, that interviewers will unfailingly bring back complete, comparable, and valid reports. Although a large number of the more obvious types of errors and biases can be overcome by appropriate methods of interviewer selection and training, some are bound to remain. Fortunately, however, it is easier for the study director to become *aware* of the biases of interviewers, and thus to discount their effects in his interpretation of the data, than it is for the clinician or experimentalist to detect his own bias when he himself collects the data. . . .

Assuming an unbiased selection of respondents, bias in the interview situation appears to come about through (1) the respondent's perception of the interviewer, and (2) the interviewer's perception of the respondent. We use the term "perception" here not in the limited physical sense but in the broader psychological sense which emphasizes the manner in which the perceptions of interviewer and respondent are influenced and modified by their wishes, expectations, and personality structure.

The interviewer's manner and appearance can, of course, alter the respondent's perception of him, but there is an abundance of experimental evidence to prove that bias may result, under certain conditions, regardless

---

[1] In reading the quotation the reader should recognize how in a nonclinical field there has been awareness (in writing and practice) of the variables discussed in this and previous chapters.

of anything the interviewer may do to eliminate it. In one study, 50 percent of a sample of non-Jewish respondents told non-Jewish interviewers that they thought Jews had too much influence in the business world, whereas only 22 percent of an equivalent sample voiced that opinion to Jewish interviewers. Similar experiments have shown that Negroes will frequently answer differently when interviewed by white people, and that working-class respondents are less likely to talk freely to middle-class interviewers. Such effects can occur easily no matter how conscientiously the interviewer attempts to be "unbiased."

The magnitude of these effects naturally varies with the way in which the respondent perceives the *situation*. Thus, in one study, it was demonstrated that Negroes spoke more frankly with white interviewers in New York than they did in Memphis, Tenn. The interviewing situation was the same in both cities, but respondents perceived it differently. By altering the respondent's perception of the situation (for example, by assuring him that his name will not be taken), these biasing effects can often be reduced, but they can seldom be eliminated.

The study director should keep these matters in mind when he selects his interviewers, and the staff should be warned of the dangers. It is for reasons of this type that interviewers, for example, are usually instructed to dress inconspicuously so that their clothes and appearance will not influence lower-class respondents; to interview the respondent privately so that his opinions will not be affected by the presence of some third person; and to adopt an informal, conversational manner in an effort to achieve the best possible rapport.

Not all interviewer effects operate through the respondent's perception of the interviewer, however. Indeed, some respondents appear to be totally immune to even the most flagrant biasing characteristics of the interviewer. Fully as important a source of bias are the interviewer's perceptions of his respondent. No matter how standardized the questionnaire may be and no matter how rigidly the interviewer may be instructed, he still has much opportunity to exercise freedom of choice during the actual interview, and it is his perception of the respondent which will determine the manner in which he asks the question, the way in which he probes, his classification of equivocal responses to precoded questions, and his recording of verbatim answers.

Interviewers do not approach each new respondent in an unstructured fashion: indeed, they often have strong expectations and stereotypes, which are more and more likely to come into play as they continue interviewing. On the basis of their past judgments, or of prior answers received from other respondents, they may, for example, quite unconsciously come to associate lack of education with ethnic or religious prejudice; or they n come to anticipate a large number of "No opinion" responses from the Negroes they interview. Such expectations will almost inevitably affect their performance.

Thus, given the same "No opinion" response from a wealthy business-man, in the one case, and from a Negro housewife in another, they may probe the former's reply, in the complete belief that an opinion *must* be lurking there somewhere, whereas in the latter they will routinely accept it without probing and go on to the next question. An experimental study has shown that when the same equivocal answer regarding aid to Europe was embedded first in an "isolationist" context of previous responses and then in an "internationalist" context, only 20 percent of the interviewers classified it in internationalist terms in the first context, but 75 percent of the same interviewers classified it as internationalist in the second context. Experiments on verbatim recording have also shown that interviewers tend to select from long answers those parts which most nearly conform to their own expectations or opinions and to discard the rest.

Cantril (25, p. 107) presents and discusses data from a number of studies which clearly support Sheatsley's statements. Table 4 shows

TABLE 4. Differences in Response Obtained by White and Negro Interviewers of Negroes in a Large Southern City (Cantril, 25)

| Would Negroes be treated better or worse here if the Japanese conquered the U.S.A.? | Negro Interviewers Reported | White Interviewers Reported |
|---|---|---|
| Better | 9% | 2% |
| Same | 32% | 20% |
| Worse | 25% | 45% |
| No opinion | 34% | 33% |
| Would Negroes be treated better or worse here if the Nazis conquered the U.S.A.? | | |
| Better | 3% | 1% |
| Same | 22% | 15% |
| Worse | 45% | 60% |
| No opinion | 30% | 24% |
| Do you think it is more important to concentrate on beating the Axis, or to make democracy work better here at home? | | |
| Beat Axis | 39% | 62% |
| Make democracy work | 35% | 26% |
| No opinion | 26% | 12% |

differences in response obtained by white and Negro interviewers of Negroes in a large southern city. Table 5 compares interviews made by middle-class and working-class interviewers.

When one considers that the number of clinician-patient interactions which involve a white clinician and a Negro patient is probably not small, the relevance of "interviewer bias" is clear. Since the number of interactions which involve clinician and patient of different social classes (but same color) is probably considerable, it is dangerous to avoid or overlook the real possibility that the clinician influences and interprets the behavior of some of his patients in ways of which he is

TABLE 5.   Comparison of Interviews Made by Middle-Class and Working-Class Interviewers (Cantril, 25)

| Opinions of Union Members Reported by Interviewers on Law Forbidding Sit-Down Strikes | Middle-Class Interviewers | Working-Class Interviewers |
| --- | --- | --- |
| Favor | 59% | 44% |
| Oppose | 29% | 39% |
| No opinion | 12% | 17% |

unaware and which have a distorting effect. *The clinician, diagnostician or therapist, cannot avoid the fact that available evidence rather clearly indicates that the social class and color of the investigator influence the professional interactions in which he engages.* That we are not at all clear as to how these variables operate in the clinical situation should not dull our sensitivity to the importance of the problem (as seems to be the case from the paucity of the available literature) but should stimulate the relevant research without which the cultural bias in our thinking and practice will remain undetected and, therefore, uncontrolled (35).

The age of the clinician is still another characteristic which, while unstudied, seems to be important. To the extent that age and prestige are correlated, and since few would dispute that differences in prestige of the clinician result in differences in the behavior of the patient, the age factor deserves discussion. The following clinical example may serve as a starting point.

The patient, who was clearly older than the writer, to whom he had been referred for therapy, was a minister in a small town where he had status and recognition. He was married, had one child, and seemed to enjoy a satisfactory relationship with his wife. His stated reason for seeking therapy was that he was not sure that he wanted to remain on in the ministry, he felt unable to think the problem through by himself, and he did not think that he functioned efficiently in his work and effectively in his interpersonal relationships. He was referred by another therapist who had much greater prestige than the writer and who in terms of age was clearly older than the patient. In the first several interviews the writer adopted a relatively passive, non-directive role, during which time the patient described his current problems and what he considered to be their background. However, it was quite apparent that the patient had difficulty talking spontaneously or upon request about what one might call truly personal feelings. In thinking over why the patient might be having difficulty in verbalizing truly personal feelings *the writer suddenly realized that if the patient was as conscious as he of the age differential, then it was understandable why the patient was having difficulty in the therapeutic sessions.* "*If I was in the position of having to reveal my problems to someone clearly younger than myself, I would probably behave in a similar fashion"—this was the substance of the writer's thinking.* At the next interview, after one of a number of long silences on the part of the patient, the writer presented to the patient in a direct way the possibility that the silences and lack of personal revelation were related to the age differential. The patient seemed immediately and visibly relieved that the matter came up and he shortly gave clear expression to his concern about it and how it affected his attitude toward and behavior in the therapy. Following this outpouring, interestingly enough, the patient stated that since the writer had guessed what was on his mind perhaps he should not evaluate his ability by his age. In subsequent sessions the patient showed no hesitation in revealing truly personal feeling.

Because of the absence of the relevant research it is impossible to state the ways in which the age of the therapist affects the patient's behavior and the course and outcome of the therapy. It may be, for example, that age is more of a factor at the beginning than at any other point in the therapy. But this is a guess, and in light of what is not known about the problem it is not even an educated guess. *What needs emphasis is the likelihood that the age of the psychotherapist is as much of a factor in his relationship to his patient as the age of any therapist or therapist-like person (dental, surgical, medical, legal, etc.) to those who come to him for help.*

That the sex of the psychologist can significantly affect a subject's behavior is shown in a study by Postman, Bronson, and Gropper (*116*).

They were primarily interested in studying the effects of two variables on recognition thresholds for tachistoscopically exposed neutral and taboo words: (1) the relative familiarity of the two classes of stimuli and (2) conditions affecting the subjects' set and readiness to give verbal reports of taboo words. We shall here be concerned only with the second variable. In reading the rationale for and design of this study the student should note the explicit recognition given to the situational variables we have thus far discussed:[2]

If Ss deliberately withhold their reports of taboo words, the thresholds for such words would appear to be unduly high. The possibility that Ss' reports are deliberately suppressed or falsified exists in every perceptual experiment and can never be completely discarded. In the case of recognition of taboo words, this problem may be critical since Ss have to give verbal responses which they have presumably been taught to avoid. It is futile to argue after the fact whether or not there was such deliberate suppression or falsification. We can, however, attempt to manipulate explicitly the conditions which we believe contribute to Ss' readiness to report faithfully what they perceive. The resulting changes in perceptual response can then provide us with an estimate of the amount of variance attributable to Ss' readiness to report.

In this experiment, manipulation of Ss' readiness to report taboo words was attempted in two ways: (a) by preliminary instructions and (b) by varying the S-E relationship.

Four different sets of instructions were used. The *Uninformed Group* was given the usual instructions for tachistoscopic recognition, without any indication that taboo words would be included among the stimuli:

This is an experiment on visual perception. We want to find out how well you can recognize words that are presented for short periods of time. When I say "Ready," fixate your eyes on this screen. About one second later a word will be flashed for a brief period of time and will appear on the screen. As soon as the word has been flashed on, write down everything you saw, including single letters, on the record sheet.

The *Informed Group* was given the same general instructions, with the following statement informing them of the presence of taboo words among the stimuli:

[2] The purposes of the interaction as conceived of by the subject were not a variable which was considered although it seems relevant to the problem of the study. Unfortunately it is extremely rare when this variable is incorporated into the design of studies, despite agreement as to its importance in interpersonal interactions.

Some of the words which will be shown are the kind not commonly used in polite society, especially in the presence of members of the opposite sex. Remember, some, not all, of the words that we will show are of this type.

The instructions given to the *Facilitation Group* were designed to discourage Ss from withholding reports of taboo words. These Ss were given the same instructions as the Informed Group with the following additional statement:

It has been found that some people find it difficult to recognize such words when they are presented for brief periods of time and are anxious about reporting them when they have seen them. In general, difficulties in seeing and reporting such words are a sign of good mental adjustment. Most normal people show this kind of reaction to some extent, particularly people who are socially successful.

To the extent that these different instructions were effective in manipulating Ss' set and readiness to report taboo words, we would expect the measured thresholds for taboo words to be (a) lower for the Informed Group than the Uninformed Group, and (b) lower for the Facilitation Group than the Informed Group, since the former is both informed about the presence of taboo words *and* encouraged to report them. It would be difficult to predict exactly where the Inhibition Group should fall since it has the advantage of expecting the appearance of taboo words but is discouraged from reporting them. In any event, the thresholds of the Inhibition Group for taboo words should be higher than those of the Facilitation Group.

An additional experimental treatment was introduced in a further attempt to manipulate Ss' readiness to report. Most of the taboo words are of a kind that one would be particularly reluctant to use in the presence of the opposite sex. Deliberate withholding of taboo words might be expected to occur more often in the presence of an E of the opposite sex than in the presence of an E of the same sex. Two Es—one male and one female—were, therefore, used in the experiment. Under each of the four major experimental conditions, each E tested two groups of Ss, one group of males and one group of females. There were, therefore, 16 different experimental subgroups. Each of the subgroups consisted of 6 Ss, giving a total of 96 Ss.

The following findings are relevant to our present discussion:

Women have higher relative thresholds for taboo words than do men. It is possible that women are less familiar with these words than are men and/or that women are more prone to selective verbal report.

Relative thresholds for taboo words are not significantly different in the presence of an E of the opposite sex than they are in the presence of an E of the same sex. There is, however, a significant tendency for all Ss to conform to instructions more fully in the presence of the female E. The E-S relationship has demonstrable effects on the observed threshold differences.

We included the first finding in order to indicate that had the purposes of the interaction as conceived of by the subject been studied data bearing on the possibility "that women are more prone to selective report" might have been obtained. The second finding, which is of major interest here, has obvious clinical relevance because it indicates that the sex of the clinician is not an unimportant variable. Whittaker, Gilchrist, and Fischer (175), concerned also with the problem of recognition thresholds of positively and negatively valued words, reported that when Negro subjects interacted with a Negro experimenter they tended to withhold responses to certain words (e.g., nigger) until the character of the stimulus was unambiguous. This suppression of response was not observed when white subjects interacted with either a white or a Negro experimenter. It is important to note that it was not until the interpersonal nature of the experimental situation was explicitly recognized that the unsatisfactory nature of previous explanations of differences in recognition thresholds became apparent (80).

AN INCIDENTAL FINDING

An unpublished study by Towbin and Sarason (166) is relevant at this point not only because of the light it sheds on the age variable but because the findings on the age variable were unexpected and incidental to the main purpose of the experiment. In an earlier study by Mandler and Sarason (see p. 26) the effect of anxiety on learning and performance in a testing-like situation was studied. They showed that a high and low anxiety group (those with extreme scores on a questionnaire designed to tap anxiety responses as elicited by the testing situation) differed in the acquisition of a response, in assembling a Kohs Block Design, and in the effects of "success," "failure," and "neutral" conditions on subsequent performance on another Kohs Design.

The design of the present (unpublished) study, while essentially the same as that of the earlier one, was modified somewhat in an attempt to study the effects of these conditions under circumstances more comparable to those of the testing situation. *The modification consisted of giving the subject only one trial before and one trial after the experimental treatment was administered, instead of the six trials before and after as in the previous study.* In addition, by interviewing subjects an attempt was made to gather data on their covert responses to various aspects of the testing situation, and to estimate the effect of this interview on subsequent performance.

The manner of choosing subjects was precisely the same as in the earlier study (see p. 26). The twenty subjects with the lowest test-anxiety and the eighteen with the highest test-anxiety scores were selected, i.e., one high anxiety (HA) and one low anxiety (LA) group. Each of these two groups was divided by random procedure into three subgroups (success, failure, and neutral). The instructions given to the subjects, the Kohs Block Designs used, and the procedure for administering the experimental treatments were identical to those described in the earlier study (99). Only the above described substitution of one trial for six, in this study, differentiated the two designs.

Although the HA group performed more slowly than the LA group on the initial trial, this difference was not significant. A comparison of the mean time scores of these groups (HA and LA) with those obtained by comparable groups on the first trial in the earlier study revealed that, while the *direction* of difference remained the same, the absolute difference between the two groups in the present study was only one-fourth as large as in the previous one. The mean time score of the HA group in this study showed that they performed faster (better) on this trial than did the LA group studied by Mandler and Sarason. While the difference between the LA groups of the two studies was not significant (p = .30), that between the two HA groups was significant at the .05 level. The success, failure, and neutral conditions did not have significantly different effects on the HA and LA groups. With the exception of the failure groups the HA-LA differences obtained in the two studies were in the same direction. It will be remembered that in the previous study, under failure conditions, the LA group performed significantly better than the HA group.

There are two major differences between the results reported here and those of Mandler and Sarason. *First,* the initial level of performance was significantly higher for the HA group in this, the second, study. *Second*, the reliable difference reported by Mandler and Sarason between their HA and LA groups under failure conditions was not found in the present study.

If, as has been assumed, the performance level of the HA group is an inverse function of the anxiety drive learned in response to the testing situation, the initial anxiety level of the HA group studied here would be considered to have been lower than that of the group reported in the earlier study. While sampling differences from year to year in Yale University classes cannot be excluded as an explanation of the differences in initial level, there is no independent evidence that this is the case. A second possibility is that some factor was present in the previous study that was absent here, and that tended to raise anxiety. While the difference in procedure, the use of one trial where six were used in the previous study, cannot be excluded as an explanation of the second difference between the results of the two studies, the presence of an anxiety-raising factor in the earlier and its absence in the present study might also account for this difference, since it was predicted by Mandler and Sarason that the increase in anxiety produced by failure would have an interfering effect on the performance of the HA group and a facilitating effect on that of the LA group. *In this connection it is interesting that the interviews, conducted after the second test-design, reveal that the subjects expected a person of high status to be conducting the experiment, and that they regarded the experimenter as a peer.* Of the sixteen subjects interviewed (chosen randomly), twelve revealed this expectancy and attitude explicitly in their answers to the interview question, "What was your impression of me?" These answers are listed below.

  1. "Well, I did spot you. Well, I asked you if you were an undergrad. I didn't think you were a teacher. I thought you'd be older."
  2. ". . . I expected somebody older."
  3. "First I thought maybe you were waiting too (for the experimenter)."
  4. "I thought you were pretty young. . . ."
  5. "I expected a heavier man, I guess. Maybe that's because my psych teacher (R) is like that."
  6. "So much younger than I thought you would be."
  7. "I have to say this? I expected to see some terrible giant. I saw you! Aha! harmless . . . that is, human. That's what I wanted to see."
  8. "I thought you were very young. I expected an older person."

9. "The impression I had before (I saw you) was that you would be some kind of big wheel like K."

10. "I wondered if you were a grad student of some sort, trying to get your master's or a Ph.D. of some sort on this project. I thought you were a nice guy . . . that there wouldn't be a very great formality involved."

11. "A little surprised. I thought you'd be a little older."

12. "I don't know . . . just another Yaley. Didn't impress me as a doctor or a psychologist, primarily because you're approximately my own age."

These answers indicate that the apparent age and status of the examiner, in relation to the subject who has concrete expectancies about them, act as potent stimuli in this situation. In support of an explanation of the differences between the two studies in terms of differences in the stimulus value of the examiners, the following is presented:

1. In comparison to the experimenter (B) in the present study the one (A) in the previous study is clearly taller, broader, and older. The age differential is four years. In addition, the experimenter (B) in the second study *looks* younger than he is.

2. Introspective reports by the two experimenters leave little doubt that while B felt insecure in his approach to and handling of the subjects, A did not experience such reactions. More specifically, while B experienced "guilt" in administering the "failure" instructions, A had no such reaction.

3. In bearing and appearance A, more than B, resembles the two faculty members mentioned in the students' answers to the interview question.

4. The near-significant difference between HA and LA subjects on the first trial in the earlier study was even more clearly demonstrated by A, who was the experimenter in a later study (*100*).

SOME CONCLUSIONS

The reader will have discerned that in this chapter we have discussed the possible influences of only the more obvious or "objective" characteristics of the psychologist in his clinical interactions. The relative lack of relevant literature has made it almost impossible to discuss how distinguishable behavioral characteristics of the psychologist influence others and determine outcomes. By "distinguishable behavioral characteristics" reference is made to those patterns of covert attitudes and overt responsiveness which presumably vary from clinician to clinician

and which in some vague way presumably are used as a basis for selection, training, and evaluation of clinical psychologists. One is forced
to conclude that if the "personality" of the clinician is as important
as it is for "success" in the clinical interaction, then the absence of
systematic research on this variable can no longer be justified.

It might be argued that the crucial aspect of the problem is not the
characteristics of the clinician but the way in which he is perceived and
responded to by his patients. The phenomenon of transference clearly
underlines the importance attached to how the patient conceives of
and reacts to the analyst—how the patient's conception of the analyst
is dependent less on what the analyst "is" than on the nature and
strength of the patient's attitude toward significant figures in his early
life. The importance of the patient's conceptions also has been emphasized by Rogers (130, p. 65):

> As our experience has moved us forward, it has become increasingly
> evident that the probability of therapeutic movement in a particular case
> depends primarily not upon the counselor's personality, nor upon his tech-
> niques, nor even upon his attitudes, but upon the way all these are experi-
> enced by the client in the relationship. The centrality of the client's percep-
> tion of the interviews has forced itself upon our recognition. It is the way
> it seems to the client which determines whether resolution of conflict, re-
> organization, growth, integration—all the elements which comprise therapy
> —will occur. Our knowledge of therapy would be far advanced if we knew
> the answers to these two questions: What does it mean that the client experi-
> ences a relationship as therapeutic? and, How may we facilitate the ex-
> periencing of a relationship as therapeutic? We do not have the answers to
> these questions, but we have at least learned to ask them.
>
> The way in which the client perceives or experiences the interviews is a
> field of inquiry which is new and in which the data are very limited. There
> has been no research as yet completed in this area, and relatively little con-
> sideration has been given to it. It is an area which appears to have great
> future significance. . . .

It does not seem fruitful to attempt to decide the relative importance of
the psychologist's characteristics and the patient's perception. We are,
as Rogers indicated, dealing with variables which interact. *The major
problem remains that of determining how variations in the clinician's
characteristic attitudes and behavior are related either to the patient's
conception of the interaction or to the outcome of the interaction.*

# Chapter 6

## ATTITUDINAL FACTORS RELATED TO PREVIOUS LEARNING

By "attitudinal factors" we refer to response tendencies (self-verbalized, or articulated, or deduced from overt behavior) whose object or referent is the self, the examiner, or other features of the external situation, present or future. *These attitudinal factors begin to operate when the individual first learns that a particular kind of situation (e.g., testing or therapeutic) is to take place. It is frequently overlooked that the clinical situation begins to affect the individual when he first learns about it.* He then begins to fantasy about it, has anticipations about it, and verbalizes to himself or to others about "the situation to be." The fact that the testing situation (in terms of the variables effecting the responses of the subject to the test materials) begins before one sees the patient has at least two important implications:

1. It is immediately apparent that it is important to know what was explained to the individual, how it was explained, and who did the communicating. Did the child first learn about the situation from his teacher, who told him that someone was going to find out why he was having trouble in school? Was he first told by his mother, who at the same time warned him how important it was for him to do well? Was the child told that he was "going to see a doctor" who was going to help him in school, help him to get over his stuttering, find out why he had stomach aches in the morning, why he urinated in his bed at night, why he could not get along with others, etc.? Was the child first told the morning of the appointed day or some days before? It seems perfectly clear that the attitudinal factors engendered in the individual toward the clinical situation are in part a function of how he first learns of the future interaction. What he says to himself about the interaction, what he fantasies, the questions he asks, his anticipations, behavioral changes or sequences—all of these are in part a function of what the individual is initially told.

73

2. Whatever has been said of the patient is equally true of the clinician. *The clinician's attitudes toward the patient take shape when he first learns that he is to see the individual.* What he reads in a case history, what is contained on a referral slip, what he has been told by others (colleague, parent, teacher, etc.)—information obtained through these media in part determine the clinician's attitudes even before he sees the patient. Very frequently the clinician is surprised when he meets the patient for the first time because the patient "in person" is simply different from what the clinician's anticipations indicated. (See case on p. 75.)

The above implications are of practical import to the clinician in that they suggest that he look beyond the attitudes which characterize the individual in the actual clinical situation. The second implication is clearly a warning to the clinician that he not overlook the fact that his own "pre-situation" anticipations and attitudes may influence in some way his own behavior in the situation.

If the attitudes discernible in the actual interaction were no different from those initially engendered, the significance which has here been attached to the initial "pre-interaction" attitudes would not be great at all. It is precisely because these initial attitudes very frequently change—in strength and manner of manifestation, if not in content— that we attach so much significance to them. *If for any kind of inter- action we could determine the conditions which gave rise to the initial attitudes, if we could determine the nature of these attitudes and the behavioral changes to which they give rise both before and during the interaction—if we could make these determinations, we would then be in a position not only to say to what other kinds of interactions we can make predictions but also to state the kinds of learning conditions which might have given rise to these kinds of attitudes to this kind of interaction.* It is axiomatic that an individual's behavior in a particular kind of situation (1) is not representative of his behavior to all or even necessarily to most kinds of situations and (2) is a function of previous experience in similar kinds of situations.

SOME EXAMPLES

It might be helpful if we illustrated through clinical material the significance of the relationships between discernible attitudes during the interaction, on the one hand, and previous attitudes toward the interaction, on the other hand. The first example, in particular, illustrates how one goes from such relationships to the problem of the conditions of previous learning.

The wife of the patient had been in an analysis with a colleague for about a year when it was decided that it was essential for her husband also to enter analysis. At the time the writer first saw the patient for analysis he knew the following about him: (a) he was against entering analysis, (b) he was jealous of his wife, (c) he frequently threatened her with bodily harm, and (d) he was also opposed to his wife's treatment although he realized that she had been helped. Before the first interview the writer more or less had developed a picture of the patient as a physically powerful, overtly aggressive, and somewhat crude individual who would be extremely difficult to handle in the analytic situation. The fact that the writer was being supervised in this, his first, analytic patient undoubtedly contributed to the above picture.

It is difficult to convey the writer's surprise when the patient first walked into his office. The patient, who had a clubbed foot and walked with a noticeable limp, was a short, slight individual—the antithesis of what the writer had expected. In the notes written after the first interview the words "puny" and "ineffectual" were used to describe the patient.

Throughout this first interview the patient was blatantly fearful, insecure, and in his own words: "I feel nervous . . . I'm shaking inside . . . I'm always thinking about my wife . . . I think a lot about my foot . . . I'm afraid of doctors, not your kind, the medical and surgical kind . . . I can't talk . . . It happens a lot of times . . . I choke up . . . When I'm talking to my wife it happens and then I cry." From his overt manner he seemed not only to fear the therapist but also to adopt a deferent, submissive manner. Neither from what the patient said or did nor from the manner in which he talked or behaved would one have deduced that during this clinical interaction the patient harbored attitudes towards himself or the therapist other than those suggested above.

It was previously stated that before the above interview the therapist knew that the patient did not want to start treatment and strongly resented his wife's treatment. *It would not be a wild leap to assume that when the possibility of treatment had first been broached to him by his wife the patient reacted hostilely not only to his wife but, in his fantasies, to his wife's therapist, who had made the recommendation.* In short, the patient's initial attitudes to the possibility of the clinical interaction probably were, among other things, of a hostile, destructive kind. If, as later evidence indicated, his initial pre-interaction attitudes were of a hostile and destructive nature, then they represent a striking contrast to those attitudes discernible in the actual interaction. In other words, the initial attitudes toward the interaction changed over a period of time from predominantly externally directed, hostile attitudes to self-derogatory, dependent, passive ones. *Since in the first and subsequent sessions it was quite clear that the patient viewed the therapist as an awesome, infallible, punitive figure of authority, it may be hypothesized that the change in attitudes is a characteristic change which takes place in connection with interactions with "authority figures"*—a hypothesis which was confirmed by data from subsequent sessions. Once the hypothesis concerning the relation between attitude change and type of interaction is considered tenable on the basis of information available at the time, the following question arises: *What were the conditions of learning previously experienced by the patient which might have given rise to this kind and sequence of attitudes toward "authority figures"?* Since in our culture parents are frequently experienced by the maturing child as authority figures, it is reasonable, having asked this question, to suspect that the patient's interactions with his parents were of a kind that would give rise to the attitudes displayed before and during the clinical interaction—a suspicion which was also borne out by subsequently obtained data.

In the above case as well as in many others the individual is apparently unaware *during the interaction* that his attitudes toward the interaction had ever been different. He is unaware that his attitudes may have changed radically and that his current behavior may, however, serve as a clue to his previous attitudes. Erickson (*40*) has demonstrated the effect of conflicting attitudes in instances where the individual is aware of only one of the conflicting attitudes. Hypnosis was the technique used in the demonstrations:

> During hypnosis the subject was told that he admired and respected Dr. D. very much but that unconsciously he was jealous of him and that because of this jealousy there would be a cutting edge to complimentary remarks which he would make. He was further told that after awakening a conversation would be started with Dr. D. in which he would take part. The subject was then awakened and the conversation begun.
>
> The topic of traveling and its contribution to personal education was

mentioned. The subject immediately brought up the fact that Dr. D. had studied both in the Middle West and in the East and that, having traveled abroad as well, he might be called cosmopolitan. He himself, he added, would like to travel and get a cosmopolitan education but in the last analysis that was what was being done by any old tramp who traveled from one part of the country to another by stealing rides on freight cars. There followed a discussion of human behavior as it reflected local environments during which the subject remarked that the man who had traveled showed a broader knowledge and better understanding of people and of cultural things; he added, however, that the same thing might possibly be said of any resident of east-side New York. . . .

The subject was told during hypnosis that he felt antagonistic, resentful and jealous of Dr. D., and that this emotional state would persist after he was awakened. He was also told that after awakening he would try to be courteous and acquiescent toward Dr. D. in every way and would appear to be willing to do anything requested of him.

After being awakened the subject seemed to be entirely at ease; he responded courteously to some casual remarks addressed to him by Dr. D. Presently Dr. D. asked him if he would mind changing his seat. The subject replied certainly not, that he would be delighted, but that *he* was quite comfortable where he was; if, however, it would make *Dr. D.* more comfortable, he would be delighted to change his seat. The request was repeated, whereupon the subject arose and asked Dr. D. to designate the precise chair in which he was to seat himself. He walked over towards the designated chair but asked Dr. D. if perhaps a certain other chair might not serve even better since the reason Dr. D. had given for his request was that he was not quite in full view of the audience. When Dr. D. insisted that the designated chair was the better one the subject, with great courtesy, still questioned, seeming nevertheless most willing to do precisely what was desired and to be hesitant only about seating himself before he was absolutely certain of Dr. D's wishes. After much insistence by Dr. D. that he seat himself the subject agreed that the chair indicated was precisely the one that he ought to sit in and proceeded to do so; but as he did so he moved the chair about six inches to one side and shifted its position so that it faced in a slightly different direction. Immediately upon seating himself he turned and politely asked, "Is this the way you would like to have me?" After a few moments of casual conversation Dr. D. found fault with his position and asked him if he would mind taking his original chair. He rose promptly, said that he would be delighted to sit anywhere that Dr. D. wished but that perhaps it would be better if he sat on the table, and offered to move the designated chair to any desired spot, suggesting some clearly unsuitable positions; finally, when urged insistently to sit in the chair he again had to move it.

The following instance of hypnotherapy cited by Wolberg (*187*) is a clinical example of the danger of the therapist's overestimating the attitudes discernible in the clinical interaction and underestimating those which were initially aroused by the prospects of the interactions:

One of my most spectacular failures with hypnosis was with a physician who asked me to hypnotize him so that he could pass his State Board examinations. He had recently completed an internship in a Midwest hospital, and had returned to New York to establish a practice which was being set up with the financial aid of his parents. By scrimping and scraping they had put their son through medical school, had supported him during his internship, and now they were about to realize their ambition of having him at home as a successful medical practitioner.

Although he realized that he would have to take his State Boards, he could find no time to study for them while interning, and, after leaving the hospital, discovered that whenever he opened a book, his mind went blank. As time passed by, he became more and more panicky, and now that the examinations were only several days away, he had become so agitated that he could scarcely contain himself. He begged me to hypnotize him and remove by suggestion his mental block; and he was quite certain that powerful pressures put upon him while he was in a trance would enable him to recall his medical studies and complete his examinations successfully.

Under ordinary circumstances, I would have refused to take this assignment; but because he was so disturbed, and because there was so little time, I consented to try to put him in a suitable frame of mind for the examination. He cooperated eagerly and entered a deep trance during which I regressed him to the period of his life while he was at medical school. He recalled many details of his studies, of which he had, in the waking state, only a faint recollection. For instance, he was brought back to his anatomic dissection laboratory, and he painstakingly went through the motions of dissecting out the radial nerve, explaining its course and distribution. In a similar way, he recalled many details of his other studies. I suggested that when he presented himself for examination he would recall as much as was necessary for him to remember. On the evening before, he would retire early and sleep soundly during the night. He would awaken refreshed with a clear mind, with sufficient vigor and self confidence to apply himself adroitly to the task of completing his examination.

On the evening before the examination, he telephoned me and asked if it might not be advisable for him to spend the night at a hotel instead of at his parents' house, because he would be able to sleep better there and thus be in a better frame of mind. I agreed that this was probably advisable.

In the late afternoon the next day, I received another telephone call from the man, and he informed me in a calm and even droll manner that never in his life before had he slept so soundly. As a matter of fact he had just gotten up, having slept through the examinations. There was no point now, he insisted, in taking the remainder of the tests. He volunteered to come to my office to talk things over.

When he reported, he seemed to be in excellent spirits. There were no signs of tension or anxiety, and he even adopted a humorous attitude towards the incident. He considered it peculiar, however, that he had slept so long, since he rarely spent more than eight or nine hours in bed. In talking, he confided that there now was no reason why he could not go back west to visit a young lady in whom he had become interested while interning. His parents had opposed his marrying the girl, and because he felt he owed them a debt, he had given up his plan to settle in her home town.

He was obviously torn between love for the girl and loyalty to his parents, and his inability to study seemed due to this conflict. He was unable to get himself to yield to the desires of his parents, nor did he wish to incur their disapproval or rebuke. Inhibition in thinking was a symptom which had for its purpose a frustration of the plans his parents had made to have him practice in New York. Guilt feelings, however, created anxiety and caused him to seek a desperate measure in hypnosis to break down his inhibition. So strong was his guilt that hypnosis was successful. When, during the trance, he realized that he might be able to remember enough to pass the examination, his conflict again became dominant and eventually it triumphed over my suggestions. His prolonged sleep was a means of escaping the possibility of becoming licensed in New York. He had obtained implied permission from me to sleep when I agreed to his plan to spend the night at a hotel. When these facts were brought to his attention, he laughed heartily and declared that no longer was he going to deceive himself. He was going to tell his parents they no longer had a claim on him. He would, as soon as he was financially capable of so doing, repay them for what they had expended towards his education.

Several years have gone by since this incident, and the man has established himself in practice in the Midwest. He is married to the young woman in question, and the situation with his parents has resolved itself more or less successfully.

I cite this case as an example of how hypnosis indiscriminately applied can fail to achieve certain goals. *It is essential to understand what motiva-*

*tions lie behind the patient's desire for hypnotherapy. These may be so dis-
torted as to militate against any satisfactory result.* [Italics mine. S. B. S.]

It is worth stressing that the attitudes which are discernible during an
interaction should not by their strength or clarity force one to under-
emphasize the importance of those attitudes which were initially
aroused by the prospects of the interaction. Wolberg's case clearly indicates that such underemphasis adversely affects the efficacy of our
practice—we are here dealing not only with what might seem to be a
theoretical point but with one apparently also of great practical significance.

Frequently the clinician, especially in the diagnostic testing situation,
is unable to determine the nature of the pre-interaction attitudes except
by deduction from the individual's behavior during the interaction. In
the cases cited above the clinician had some idea about these initial
attitudes either from what the patient said or from some other source.
*Being forced to deduce pre-interaction attitudes solely on the basis of
what one observes is in many instances the result of the failure to discuss the problem with the patient or, in the case of children, to inter-
rogate the parent.* Such failures not only make the job of the clinician
more difficult than it should be but make it more likely that the significance of the discernible attitudes will be distorted or misinterpreted.
In some instances, however, the subject's behavior during the interaction indicates the nature of his pre-interaction attitudes. For example,
if during a testing situation an individual does not appear to be tense
or frightened but there is a noticeable hand tremor when he manipulates the test material, it is justifiable to ask (1) whether his pre-
interaction attitudes were much more clearly anxiety tinged and (2)
why *this* interaction should engender such a response. If an individual
is unusually deferent and submissive to the examiner, it may well be
that in the pre-interaction period his fantasies were concerned with
themes of assertion, achievement, triumph, and hostility which as a
result of past learning he inhibits and protects himself against failure
and punishment by passive, deferent behavior. A study by Feshbach
(46) is relevant here in that it was specifically concerned with the
relationships among arousal of aggression, fantasy, and subsequent
strength of aggressive drive.

The basic experimental design used in this study is summarized in the
following paradigm: (1) arousal of aggression, (2) interpolation of fantasy

or non-fantasy activities, (3) subsequent measurement of the strength of the aggressive drive.

In order to demonstrate the effect of fantasy on motivation intensity, it was important that, insofar as possible, the motive be consistently aroused. Preliminary study indicated that an excellent means of insuring the evocation of aggression in college students was to display unmistakable and unwarranted aggression toward them. Also, it was felt that by having the hostility of the subjects directed toward a specific object or person, the measurement of aggression would be facilitated. The method of evoking aggression used in the final experiment was to insult a class of students by making several critical and disparaging remarks about the college and its student body.

The purpose of the interpolated activities was to provide one group of insulted subjects the opportunity to express their hostility in fantasy (Insult Fantasy group) and to give a comparable group of insulted subjects tasks which permitted little or no opportunity for fantasy (Insult Control group).

These two groups were then compared on subsequent measures of hostility toward the experimenter, experiment and related objects to determine if the fantasy experience resulted in less aggression than did the non-fantasy activity. Several different measures of aggression were used in order to increase the possibility of detecting any difference in aggression between the fantasy and control (non-fantasy) groups, and to increase confidence in the validity of the phenomenon of drive reduction if the predicted difference is found on several independent measures.

A control group which was not insulted was also included in the experiment (Non-Insult Fantasy group). This group engaged in the same fantasy activity as did the Insult Fantasy group. The fantasies of these two groups could then be compared to determine if any significant differences in aggressive content resulted from the hostility created in the Insult group. The Non-Insult group was also administered the same subsequent measures of aggression as the Insult groups. Comparisons between the Non-Insult and Insult groups on these measures would indicate whether the insulting attitude of the experimenter actually did arouse aggression in the insulted groups. Equally important, significant differences between the Non-Insult and Insult groups would establish the validity and usefulness of the measures of aggression with respect to this particular experimental situation. If a measure of aggression fails to discriminate between the Non-Insult and Insult groups, it would hardly be applicable to the detection of small differences between the two insulted groups.

· · · · · ·

Two experimenters were used in carrying out the study. The individual who acted as the principal experimenter was carefully selected for his ability to arouse the hostility of the subjects in the Insult groups without their realizing that his remarks were deliberately intended to achieve that end. The writer [Feshbach] acted as his assistant in each of the eleven classes which participated in the study. . . .

After the instructor left the classroom, the Insult Fantasy and Insult Control classes were subjected to the following insulting introductory remarks by the experimenter:

"All right; let's have it quiet!"

The study in which you are participating is being conducted by a research agency working on several projects. A number of quite different tests are going to be administered. One deals with a special aspect of intellectual performance. Others contain items on which we want your opinion. Now I realize that you City College students, or should I say City College grinds, have few academic interests outside of your concern for grades. This probably means that few of you have the perspective for appreciating either the nature or the importance of the tests I am about to administer. However, if you will try to look beyond your limited horizons, your cooperation will be useful. In other words, I'd like you to act like adults rather than adolescents.

My assistant will pass the tests out to you one at a time. When you receive your test put your name and class in the appropriate place. All tests will be collected at the end of the period.

There is one additional item I would like to call to your attention. As the results of the tests will not be made available to your instructor, there is absolutely no point in any of you cheating or copying.

The Non-Insult classes received a friendly introduction designed to gain their cooperation. The following comments were made to this group:

The study in which you are participating is being conducted by a research agency working on several projects. A number of quite different tests are going to be administered. One deals with a special aspect of intellectual performance. Others contain items on which we want your opinion. Now I realize that these tests may be different from those you are used to and you therefore may not feel that they are very important. However, your cooperation is requested and will be greatly appreciated.

The tests will be passed out to you one at a time. When you receive your test put your name and class in the appropriate place. All tests will be collected at the end of the period.

I would like to call to your attention that the results of the tests will not be made available to your instructor.

The fantasy activity consisted of the group administration of Thematic Apperception Test cards. The non-fantasy activity consisted of tests, such as a clerical aptitude test, which allowed little, if any, opportunity for fantasying. Three measures of aggression were used: a "geometric form-psychological test," a sentence-completion test, and an attitude questionnaire. The following statement of results is relevant for the present discussion: "The classes which had been insulted by an experimenter and were given the opportunity to express their aggression in fantasy subsequently displayed significantly less hostility toward the experimenter than a comparable insulted group which had engaged in non-fantasy activities. This difference in hostility was indicated by two different measures of aggression. The fact that two independent measures of drive strength yield similar results increases confidence in the genuineness of the phenomenon." While there are clear differences between the clinical and the above experimental situation, the results of Feshbach's study seem to be in line with what has been emphasized in this chapter, namely, that the attitudes which are initially engendered in connection with an interaction are a function of the conditions of arousal, and that these initial pre-interaction attitudes change with time and intervening activity, in strength and manifestation, so that the attitudes discernible in the interaction may be rather different from those initially engendered.

SOME CONCLUSIONS

In this chapter we have attempted to describe some relationships between attitudes during and preceding the clinical interaction. A major conclusion that might be drawn from what has been said concerns the practical importance of determining, wherever possible, what an individual was originally told about the interaction, who told it to him, and what his reactions to the communication were. It is the writer's opinion that the clinician tends to ignore the sources from which the relevant information could be derived. The practical, technical, and theoretical significance of the above conclusion has probably been given most recognition by the psychoanalyst, whose main if not sole source of information is the patient. The analyst is constantly evaluating the behavior of the patient in terms of what is revealed about attitudes toward the therapy and the therapist. In addition, the analyst evaluates the attitudes discernible in any one session in light of the attitudes revealed in previous sessions. By focusing on such attitudinal relationships the analyst aims to discover *characteristic* patterns of response to certain themes, people, and situations.

A second major conclusion concerns the significance of determining the relationships between attitudes engendered before and those manifest during the clinical interaction. Having determined the relationship between attitude change and the particular kind of interaction one is then able to focus more sharply on the kinds of previous interactions (previous conditions of learning) which may have given rise to the particular attitudes toward self and others.

## Chapter 7

# PREDICTION AND SITUATIONAL SIMILARITY

In the previous chapters we have described what appear to be some of the major variables in the clinical situation. We have used the term "major variables" because variations in each of them produce differences in the nature of the interaction. How much of a variation is necessary to produce a change in response? What is the order of importance among the variables? Are these variables independent of one another? Are these the only variables? These are questions which were not even raised in previous pages and cannot be answered at this point because of the lack of relevant studies. What was presented in previous chapters was determined by several opinions and considerations:

1. The variables presented were those which most psychologists would agree were relevant and important.

2. The importance attached to these variables was independent of the theory (analytic, learning, gestalt, etc.) to which one subscribed. In other words, *these variables were considered by psychologists to operate in interpersonal interactions even though these same psychologists might differ markedly in their theoretical conceptions of the origins, influences upon, and principles of human behavior.*

3. Despite agreement about these variables the clinician, diagnostician or therapist, seems *in his practice* to have largely overlooked or ignored them. It would not be too much of an exaggeration to say that many clinicians operate as if these variables were unimportant or simply did not exist. The ways in which tests are constructed and interpreted, descriptions of therapeutic interactions and outcomes, the manner in which pre-interaction behavior is studied and handled—these and other practices often reveal a lack of attention to the interpersonal nature of the situation.

4. The researcher, clinical or otherwise, frequently sets up his experiment as if the problems posed by his interaction with the subject required no special controls or procedures. (Obviously we refer here

only to studies involving an interaction between an experimenter and a subject, although there does not appear to be any reason why these same variables should not operate when more people are involved.) *It is difficult to refrain from speculating about the number of experimental studies which produced no results not because the theory or hypothesis was wrong but because of a failure to be aware of or control for some of the variables which have been discussed here.*

5. *The clinical interaction is just another instance of interpersonal interactions in general and there is no a priori reason for maintaining that whatever is "true" for the nonclinical interaction is not also true for the clinical one. The variables here discussed operate in any interaction.* In different kinds of interactions the different variables manifest themselves differently.

6. *The more one is aware of these situational variables and develops procedures for their detection and control, the more will one be able to understand the actual interaction and the kinds of situations to which one can appropriately predict.* Nothing that has been said so far should in any way be construed as indicating that failures in prediction will disappear if only more systematic study of and attention to these variables takes place. Improved prediction requires a detailed knowledge not only of the situational variables but also of those psychological principles (and their interrelationships) by means of which one can determine (a) how response patterns are acquired, (b) the ways in which they change in their overt and covert manifestations, and (c) the conditions (external and internal) which accompany a and b. In short, one needs in addition to a knowledge of the situational variables a valid and systematic theory of behavior. By describing and discussing the role of the situational variables only one source of improvement in prediction was presented.

AN EXAMPLE

In the course of his work the clinician makes a number of predictions concerning school progress, amenability to therapy, success of students in clinical diagnosis, effects of the various somatic therapies, and so forth. That the level of accuracy of the clinician's predictions is not exactly encouraging is probably in part due to the failure to determine adequately the likelihood that the criterion situation will elicit behavior similar to that found in the situation from which one is trying to predict. This point was taken up in Chapter 3, before the situational variables were discussed, and the study by Kelly and Fiske (86) was used there as an example of the thorny problems one encounters. Now that the situational variables have been presented, and because the problem of prediction and situational similarity is such an important one, it might be helpful if another example, this time a nonclinical one, were discussed at this point. We have chosen this study not only because of its intentionally narrow scope but because it may help the reader see how similar are the problems faced by the clinical and the nonclinical psychologist. The study by Bray (23) was entitled "The Prediction of Behavior from Two Attitude Scales." The following should give the reader an idea of Bray's preliminary considerations, methodology, and predictions.

The general outline of the study is as follows: Subjects whose scores on two attitude scales are known are introduced into a standardized behavior situation designed to elicit the same attitudes and their performance measured. Subjects representing the entire observed range of attitude are included in the behavior situation. The attitude-testing situation and the other behavior situation are kept separate in the subjects' minds. The behavior situation, finally, does not depend on abilities which might differ from subject to subject.

Specifically, the following criteria are set up for selecting attitudes to be investigated and the behavior situation with which attitude scores are to be correlated:

1. The attitudes measured by the attitude scales must be those for which stimuli expected to elicit the attitudes can be readily and realistically provided in a behavior situation.

2. The subjects must be unaware of the connection between the attitude tests and the behavior situation and unaware that their attitude is being evaluated in the behavior situation.

3. All subjects must be subjected to an identical behavior situation except for the experimental variation of certain stimuli.

4. The behavioral situation must vary from experimental group to experimental group only in respect to stimuli relevant to the attitude measured by the attitude scales.

5. The behavioral situation must not involve abilities which vary from individual to individual.

6. The behavioral situation should have a minimum of objective cues for behavior to allow for maximum operation of the attitudes involved.

7. The behavioral situation should yield a quantitative and gradated measure of performance.

These criteria were established in order to reduce all *bases* of behavior other than attitude to an absolute minimum. This purpose, of course, obviated the possibility of a "real life" behavior situation. It was felt, however, that a retreat to the laboratory provides a test of attitude scale validity relatively uncomplicated by motives other than the attitude in question. If anything, the validity of an attitude scale under controlled conditions should *overestimate* the validity of the same scale under the complex conditions of everyday life, since extraneous variability in environmental stimuli can be reduced to a minimum. It remains to be proved, furthermore, that there is any appreciable difference between the operation of a motive in the laboratory and its operation in normal life in cases where the subject is unaware that the motive is being evaluated.

This last consideration and the first criterion above led to the selection of scales of attitude toward Negroes and Jews as the two scales to be investigated. It is clearly possible, by presenting members of these minority groups as other experimental subjects, to bring a subject into contact with them without arousing his suspicion that his behavior toward them is to be evaluated. By employing a minority group member to act as a confederate, every subject can be brought into contact with the same member of the minority group who can behave in a more or less completely standardized fashion from subject to subject.

The remaining problem was the selection of a behavior situation into which the experimental subject and the minority group confederate could be introduced. In line with the above criteria, this situation should maximize response to the confederate and minimize response to other factors in the situation.

The situation chosen was one requiring the subject and the confederate to make oral judgments of the autokinetic phenomenon together. This phenomenon has been fully discussed elsewhere.[1] In brief, it involves the apparent movement of a stationary point of light in a dark room. It has been demonstrated that subjects, ignorant of the subjective nature of the phenomenon, readily give judgments of the amplitude of movement of the light. It has further been found that, when two people judge the extent of movement together orally, they tend strongly to agree in judgment. If one of these subjects is a confederate of the experimenter, the judgments of the real subject can be readily influenced. These facts led to the belief that oral judgments of the autokinetic phenomenon by each subject together with a minority group confederate would be a suitable way in which to test be-

---

[1] See Sherif (*154*).

havior toward such a minority group member. The confederates, of course, would give predetermined judgments identical for all experimental subjects. It was anticipated that the presence of a Jewish or Negro confederate, the announcement by the Jewish confederate of his religious affiliation, and the statement by the experimenter that the purpose of the research was to investigate a possible group difference would elicit the appropriate minority group attitude in the subjects. Assuming that the attitude was elicited, it was expected that it would influence behavior in the direction of more agreement with the minority group confederate or less agreement with him. Other things being equal, it was reasoned that prejudiced subjects would tend to disagree with the Jewish confederate "in order to show" a group difference and because they would not be personally attracted to a member of a group against whom they were prejudiced. On the other hand, they might tend to agree because of the stereotype of the Jew as above average in intelligence. Unprejudiced subjects, it was believed, would tend to agree with the Jewish confederate if they were actively anti-anti-Semitic because of some kind of an implicit desire to demonstrate no group differences. If their unprejudiced attitude score represented merely an absence of prejudice, no greater than average tendency to agree with the Jewish confederate would be expected. It was believed, therefore, that anti-Semitism on the average would possess more drive strength than lack of anti-Semitism, and so the over-all prediction for the subjects who were to judge with a Jewish confederate was that they would conform less closely to the confederate than subjects judging with a Gentile confederate. It was expected that this tendency would be modified somewhat by opinion that Jews are especially intelligent.

The prediction for subjects who were to judge with the Negro confederate were exactly the same, except that the stereotype of the Negro as unintelligent was expected to result in even less conformity to the Negro confederate than to the Jewish confederate.

## The two attitude scales

were administered by the instructor as a class project and not by the experimenter, in order not to reveal the connection between the scale administration and the laboratory session. The scales were administered anonymously and later identified by the experimenter from personal data requested on the same form. . . . Three groups of 50 subjects each were selected by means of a table of random numbers from the 256 individuals who had taken the attitude scales [attitudes toward Negroes and Jews]. The members of one group were to judge the autokinetic phenomenon in company with a White-

Gentile confederate. Another group was to judge with a Jewish confederate; the third was to judge with a negro confederate. All subjects were men.

Before each experimental session the subject casually found out that the other person (confederate) was "Jewish" or "Gentile." "The subjects believed their sole responsibility was to perform a psychophysical task in company, as it accidentally came about, with a partner of one or another racial or religious group."

The actual results were opposite to expectations. The group with the Jewish confederate conformed more with his judgments than did the

TABLE 6. Mean Conformity of Anti-Semitic and Not Anti-Semitic Subjects in the White-Gentile and Jewish Groups (Bray, 23)

|  | White-Gentile Group | | Jewish Group | |
|---|---|---|---|---|
|  | N | Mean | N | Mean |
| Not anti-Semitic | 26 | 1.9 | 24 | 2.0 |
| Anti-Semitic | 24 | 2.5 | 26 | 1.4 |
| Total | 50 | 2.2 | 50 | 1.7 |

|  | d.f. | Variance |
|---|---|---|
| Groups | 1 | 6.60 |
| Attitude | 1 | .00 |
| Groups × Attitude | 1 | 9.93 |
| Error | 96 | 1.38 |
| Total | 99 | |

$$F \quad \frac{\text{Groups}}{\text{Error}} = 4.78$$

$$F \quad \frac{\text{Groups} \times \text{Attitude}}{\text{Error}} = 7.20$$

other group with the Gentile confederate. When each group is divided into those who were or were not anti-Semitic "those in the Jewish group who are not anti-Semitic judge very much like those in the White-Gentile group who are not anti-Semitic. Those in the Jewish group who are anti-Semitic conform much more closely than those in the White-Gentile who are anti-Semitic. In the White-Gentile group those who are not anti-Semitic conform more closely than those who are, while in the Jewish group the opposite takes place." Table 6 shows the conformity scores of the various subgroups. Since we are not interested in Bray's results *per se*, we shall not present the Negro data except to say that the predictions tended again not to be borne out.

The following is part of Bray's explanation of the nature of his findings:

The main purpose of the study . . . was to determine the degree of relationship between attitude scores and behavior, whatever direction that behavior might take. In this respect the findings are quite clear. When subjects are divided into groups on the basis of attitude score, the mean behavior of such groups in a situation which elicits the attitude is likely to differ. The attitude scores, thus, apparently have *some* validity. It is important to note, however, that, at least in the behavior situation used in this study, it is impossible to predict the direction of this difference in behavior between the attitude groups. In the Jewish group, the prejudiced subjects conform more closely to the Jewish confederate than do the unprejudiced subjects. In the Negro group, on the other hand, it is the unprejudiced subjects who show the greater conformity.

As far as the prediction of individual behavior is concerned, the data do not show that scores on an attitude inventory reduce the errors of prediction much, if anything, over chance. Even stretching the best of the data to the one per cent fiducial limits leaves 67 per cent of the variability in individual behavior completely unaccounted for at the best and 100 per cent of it unaccounted for at the worst. If by validity is meant the prediction of an external behavioral criterion from a test score, the attitude scales used in this study are strikingly lacking in that attribute. . . .

There is one hypothesis . . . which will serve as a basis for evaluating the present results. It will be assumed that individuals have a more or less unitary acquired drive represented in some fashion by their score on an attitude scale. If this is true, there are only two conditions under which this acquired drive would not be apparent in a given behavioral situation. One is that the drive is not elicited; the other is that the drive is elicited but that other drives which are also elicited by the situation are much stronger than the attitudinal drive and modify its effect. Practically, these two alternatives are the same; other drives obscure the functioning of attitude. It is also possible that the arousal of certain acquired drives may facilitate the expression of attitude in behavior while others may hinder it.

Data derived from a personality inventory supported the explanation that the arousal of other drives may have obscured the expression of attitudes in behavior in some subjects and facilitated it in others.

Having described Bray's study, some of his results, and his major explanation, it may be instructive if the study is now viewed in terms of the variables described in the previous chapters.

1. The nature of the instructions. When the subjects took the attitude scale they were presumably instructed to be as honest and frank as possible and, in fact, they understood that their answers could not be identified by the class instructor. The attitude scales were not individually administered—*there was no face-to-face contact with or instructions from the class instructor*. In the autokinetic situation instructions were given face-to-face in the presence of a person of known religion or color. It was as if in the one situation the subject was told "Be honest—no one will know how you answer these scales" while in the other it was as if he was told "You will judge the moving light in the presence of this Jewish (or Gentile or Negro) person while I (experimenter) mark down what you say." In the autokinetic situation the subject was told, "This is an experiment in possible group differences." *It would seem that not only were the instructions literally different but they were communicated in very different kinds of interactions.*

2. The purposes of the interaction. Since the attitude scales were anonymously answered, the subject, as indicated above, probably felt that he was to be honest and frank in regard to the written items. This was certainly the purpose of the class instructor, and the anonymous condition for answering may well have created a similar purpose in the subject—there appears to be no reason for assuming otherwise. Following the autokinetic session each subject was asked the following questions:

1. "Did you find it was easy or difficult to judge the amount of movement?"

2. "Did you use any particular method to make your judgments?"

3. "Since I'm running so many subjects, I'm running two at a time. Did the other subject hinder you in making accurate judgments, did he help you, or do you think you would have judged the same if you were here alone?"

4. "Do you think we'll find a difference in the ability to make this judgment between the groups we're examining?"

After the entire research was completed approximately twenty subjects were interviewed intensively. On the basis of the answers to the above questions and the intensive interviews Bray concluded that perhaps 5 percent of the subjects were not convinced that the purpose of the laboratory session was to determine differences between Gentiles, Jews, and Negroes. Unfortunately, it is not stated how the figure of 5 percent was arrived at, but if it was solely or largely based on extrapolation from the number of subjects who in the intensive interviews admitted their doubts the figure may well be an underestimate. One may assume that some subjects could not or would not admit their doubts to the experimenter. Bray then points out:

> Three subjects, who were eventually discarded, became convinced during the course of the laboratory session that the light was not moving and stopped giving judgments. Other subjects (perhaps ten per cent of the sample) expressed doubt that the light was moving on each and every trial, but continued to give judgments because they were not sure of their suspicion.

Here it seems reasonable to assume that subjects who expressed doubts that the light was moving did not have as clear or strong a conception of the experimenter's purposes as subjects who had no doubts. For reasons stated above the figure of 10 percent probably represents a minimal figure. But more important is the possibility that those who doubted that the light moved reacted differently to the confederate from those who did not. In any event, there is little doubt that there was greater variability about the purpose of the autokinetic situation than of that involving the attitude scales. *Without the interviews the problem concerning the subject's conception of the purpose of the interaction could not even be raised and probably would have been overlooked.*

3. The nature of the stimulus task. One of the chief reasons for choosing the autokinetic situation was that it provided a minimum of objective cues for behavior and so presumably allowed for maximum operation of the attitudes involved. It was also a task markedly unfamiliar to the subject. *Varying the stimulus task either in terms of familiarity or in terms of the number of objective cues might have produced different results.* For example, if the stimulus task involved the making of judgments or discriminations in relation to familiar visual configurations, the direction of conformity between subject and confederate might have been altered. One might argue that the prejudiced subject will disagree with the appropriate confederate when the stimulus task becomes more and more familiar, primarily because the more familiar the stimulus task the greater the feelings of certainty about one's judgment and the weaker the tendency to conform to anyone else's judgments, especially when that someone else is a member

of a group one dislikes. This hypothesis is not advanced because it is a particularly compelling one but in order to emphasize that *the nature of the stimulus task limits the degree to which one can generalize, especially when the research design involves no variation of the stimulus task.*

4. The time and place of the interaction. There does not appear to be any basis for assuming that these factors played an important role in this experiment.

5. The psychologist. The attitude scales were administered by (and presumably for) an instructor with faculty status. The autokinetic situation was handled by the experimenter, who did not have faculty status and was also younger in age. These differences may or may not have been perceived by the subjects, but in the absence of relevant data one can only raise the question and leave it at that.

6. Attitudinal factors. Although Bray points out that the subjects came to the sessions without knowledge of what was actually to take place, it is reasonable to assume that each subject thought and had anticipations about what might happen. Students differ rather widely in their attitudes toward participation in psychological experiments, and differences in such pre-interaction attitudes may be related to differences in response to the confederate in the presence of the experimenter. That, as Bray maintains, personality characteristics are related to the prediction of behavior from attitude scores suggests that the response patterns engendered before and during the interaction may be important sources for the determination of the relevant personality variables. Put in another way: The ways in which an individual initially conceives of an interaction, the changes which such conceptions undergo, the attitudes experienced in the actual interaction—these may be more or as revealing of the "personality" and more relevant for the particular prediction problem than answers to a paper-and-pencil personality inventory. The problem has been put thus merely as a way of indicating that the above sequence of attitudes may be a valuable source of data and should be seriously considered when formulating one's data-gathering procedures.

It should be made abundantly clear that it is not assumed that if Bray had paid systematic attention to the situational variables his findings would have taken another direction. What we have attempted to demonstrate is that these variables might have been important and that in future studies involving prediction to a criterion situation, clinical or nonclinical, systematic attention to them might be profitable. It seems reasonable to conclude that the more aware one is of these situational variables the more appropriate will be the selection of the criterion situation, the more certainty one can have in obtained results and their interpretations, and the easier it will be to determine whether studies are comparable. It is not unusual to find that several people who independently perform a particular experiment report very conflicting findings. From their published reports one can be confident that their procedures and statistical analyses were similar, if not identical, but one usually can make no judgments either about comparability of subjects in terms of their conception of and attitudes toward the situation or about comparability of experimenters in terms of their effects on the behavior of their subjects. From the statements of the experimenter the reader might conclude that the situations were comparable. *From the standpoint of the subjects in the studies the situations might have been very different.*

## Chapter 8

## CONTINUA FOR EVALUATING RESPONSES

In previous chapters we have attempted to describe the major variables which influence an individual's behavior in an interpersonal situation. At this point we shall describe continua on the basis of which an individual's behavior can be evaluated. In the description of these continua the reader should bear several things in mind:

1. Developing meaningful continua is a necessary step toward the goal of describing lawful relationships among the important aspects of behavior.

2. The continua largely represent ways of characterizing the different aspects of the relationships between the situational variables previously described, on the one hand, and the overt response, on the other hand.

3. The continua are reflections of questions which the clinician frequently asks in determining the significances of an individual's behavior. As with the situational variables, these continua refer to aspects of behavior which are considered of great importance for the understanding of behavior.

4. As we shall see later, these continua seem to be applicable to the problem of determining the significances of responses to the Rorschach ink blots.

PHYSIOLOGICAL OR MOTOR OR AFFECTIVE CONCOMITANTS

Different aspects of a behavioral sequence vary in the degree to which physiological or motor or affective concomitants are manifest. A response, for example, may be accompanied by head shaking, frowning, puzzlement, stuttering, fidgetiness, laughter, tremors, perspiration, blushing, crying, and the like. Most responses are not accompanied by discernible affective concomitants. The "problem" response is that which one would ordinarily expect to be accompanied by some overt affective display which is surprisingly absent—an extreme example being the (usually) psychotic individual who responds to a particular situation or communication in an affectless manner whereas the normal person would have reacted with great emotion.

In the previous paragraph mention was made of some of the overt (physiological or motor or affective) concomitants of a behavioral sequence. A major problem which has concerned numerous investigators is the detection and measurement of various covert physiological responses which may accompany overt behavior. The galvanic skin response, muscle action potential, blood pressure, stomach acidity—these are some of the indices which have been studied in the attempt to understand overt behavior in various situations and types of people.

INTENSITY OR STRENGTH OF THE RESPONSE

Although physiological indices may be used to determine strength of response, it is rarely possible to obtain such measures in the clinical situation. The strength of response is frequently determined by its frequency. For example, if in therapy an individual persists in asking the therapist for ready-made solutions to his problems, we might say that adopting the dependent role is a strong tendency within him in this type of relationship. If in diagnostic testing an individual frequently responds before he considers alternative means of problem solution, impulsiveness might be said to represent a strong response tendency. There are instances, however, when a particular response is considered of undoubted strength even though it may have occurred but once during one's contact with the individual. The following is an example:

The patient was a boy of eight who had been brought to the clinic for diagnostic evaluation. He was met by the psychologist who took him via the elevator to the testing rooms. The child was fascinated by the elevator and how it worked, and he asked the psychologist if he might try to work it. To this the child was told that after they had finished their work upstairs he would be given an opportunity to do so. The boy seemed quite content but after the testing had been in progress but a short while he rather insistently asked to be allowed to run the elevator at the moment. When he was reminded that their work was not yet finished but that when it was he would be allowed to run the elevator, the boy petulantly and aggressively indicated that he wanted to do it *now* after which he would finish whatever he was supposed to do. He was allowed to run the elevator after which he returned to the room and finished the tests.

Although this boy's response to the above kind of frustration was observed but once, it would be considered a strong response. *Basic to such a consideration or judgment is the assumption that if one were in a position to observe this child's response to the frustration of his wishes, he would most frequently respond as he did in the single observed instance.* In short, the criterion of frequency is implicitly recognized.

In an earlier paragraph examples were given in which a relationship between a certain situation and response tendency was depicted, the frequency of occurrence of such a relationship being the index of strength. *Strength of response may also be reflected in the degree to which the response has generalized to a variety of types of situation.* The individual who is indiscriminately hostile might be considered as having a stronger response tendency than the one who is hostile to relatively fewer people or in fewer types of situations. The strength of the anxious response in an individual who reacts anxiously to high places might be considered as less strong than the response in one who reacts anxiously to high places, closed-in areas, thoughts of death, and the like (*61*). The anxious response has generalized more widely in the latter than in the former case.

### EXTERNAL OR INTERNAL REFERENTS OF THE RESPONSE

Behavior may be said to have its external or internal determinants in the sense that it is a function of some internal state of affairs and some aspects of the external stimulus situation. Responses vary, however, in the degree to which they reflect or refer to internal or external factors. An individual's verbalization, for example, may be directed at some external object but its contents refer almost exclusively to some past personal experience or to some present covert feelings and thoughts. Variations among individuals in the degree to which their verbalizations refer to internal and external factors are clearly seen in problem-solving situations. The verbalizations of some individuals have primarily internal referents while in other cases the verbalizations clearly refer to some aspect of the external situation. Cameron and Magaret (*24*, p. 509) have admirably described cases in which the individual's verbal behavior (as well as other aspects of behavior) consistently has little or no relation to the external situation.

As the schizophrenic patient . . . gives up his previous referents in the field of social operations, his language behavior and his thinking lose their social organization. It is not simply that he now lives in a private world; he lives in a world which provides its own asocial regulation. The usefulness of language behavior is no longer determined by its success as interpersonal communication, and the validity of thinking is no longer testable in social terms. In the following example, we see language behavior that has lost much of its conventional form; it is vague and discontinuous, like dream-talk; personal idiom has developed at the expense of social intelligibility. The end-result is something that is full of unclear, ambiguous and fragmentary approximations which convey little, but seem to imply much.

The patient, a college-trained man, is attempting to cooperate in a complicated test situation. The task confronting him is one of sorting blocks of various sizes, shapes and colors into four predetermined groups, and to formulate the principles upon which the groupings are made. Here are samples of the patient's verbalization: "That's a rectangle, substantiates angle." (*What do you mean by "substantiates"?*) " 'Substantiates' means to make a substantiation for a generality." (*And what does that mean to you?*) "In a word or two, to substantiate a generality, such must be written thoroughly." (*The names* (nonsense syllables) *on these two are different.*) "The names are different; one is 'CEV' and one is 'MUR' " —correct statement. (*What do you make of this difference?*) "The difference would be meaning that the words were different, and such are small for comparison of the generalities. . . . Same arrangement of letters substantiates such from the mixture. . . . Types are entirely different and that's a substantiation. A substantiation would mean to touch a flashlight; and if that was open and you come in contact with the battery, that would be a substantiation or a sensation generalization."

In this example, the patient manages to limit his comments to the shared problem. But the words he uses are privately endowed with vague and special meanings which he does not succeed in thoroughly communicating, in spite of his apparent intent to be understood. In the next examples which, for simplicity's sake, we shall take from attempted communication in the same problem-solving situation, other disorganized and desocialized characteristics appear. The patients are obviously talking about things which they assume their listener understands. Actually, however, they are unable any longer to communicate these matters intelligibly to anyone. The listener can infer the referents—and then only with considerable uncertainty—by learning about the patients' past from relatives, friends and physicians, whose communicative systems are not disorganized.

The first patient is a former school-teacher, who lost her position because of seriously decreased efficiency, and then became a practical nurse. Here she found herself the subject of neighborhood gossip, in which her name was linked with that of her unmarried male patient. In the block sorting test she is asked, "What is the difference between this group and that?" to which she replies, "Dividing by feeling your hand and calculating the rim. If I wrote on the blackboard my hand wouldn't give out anything at all, no chalk-mark. It's a certain light they leave careless with their work. It's light slatiness; and when I went out there to walk I found lots like that. Like these men working on the roof, keep slipping off. There's somebody copying that light all the time. How in God's name can a man keep spending money on a child and buy her clothes? And that's the way with Constance, and she going to school. They'll be going to fertilize her mind through our farm and get that light. My family took that up great. A woman in Missouri she worked on those children, boiled them and picked them and finished them. I liked to do a work there."

The second patient is a high school graduate who worked for eight years for a wholesale grocer. The patient is described as having been studious and fond of reading the classics. He looks at the experimental board which is divided into sections. "Each man has to have his way of walking on the earth. The earth is divided up like this; and these blocks —women have to be born and carry a baby up over the stars to put them out. I live up there. (*Where?*) Everything's got to live over the North Sea. The moon carries the water up. That's why nobody can eat watermelons until after I've eaten. Nobody can eat a watermelon that has green hate in it. If you eat a watermelon the next comes up with your name on it. . . . I don't have any (name) through not being born yet . . . I'm not born through food. You people have eaten food and robbed me of my birth."

In all three of these illustrations of schizophrenic talk we find obvious discontinuity and, especially in the latter two, many comments referring to matters which have nothing objectively to do with the test situation, but which the patient cannot exclude from his immediate consideration.

Although the above are examples from pathological behavior, it should be made very clear that the determination of the internal and external referents of an individual's verbalizations does *not* involve the problem of reality testing: the degree to which the relationships of the response to its internal and external referents are based on agreed-upon standards or rules of logic and reasoning. *The fact that a response falls at a particular point on one of the continua does not necessarily mean that it will fall at the same point on all or even most of the continua.*

## DEGREE OF REALITY TESTING OF THE RESPONSE

In the preceding category interest was focused on the relationship between the verbal response, on the one hand, and its internal and external referents, on the other hand. By "degree of reality testing" we refer to the *quality* of that relationship: the degree to which the response corresponds in a socially valid way to its referents. Cameron and Magaret (*24*, p. 507) have indicated the significance of this category in the general as well as in the pathological case:

Under ordinary conditions, language behavior continues to operate effectively as an instrument of interpersonal communication through almost constant use. Language behavior can also function in intrapersonal behavior, with socially valid results, provided this use conforms to the general structure of communication and is sufficiently tested against interpersonal usage. Similarly, thinking must be made to correspond with operations in the shared social field of interbehavior if it is to remain socially valid. For all but the exceptionally well-integrated social person, this means that one must continually engage in cooperative and competitive activities with other social persons, or at least return repeatedly to participative behavior, where conclusions privately arrived at can be publicly verified or contradicted. Otherwise, the individual runs the risk of developing language behavior and thinking which have private fantasy as their only validating context.

This is essentially the situation in the disorganization and desocialization characteristic of schizophrenic disorders. The progressive withdrawal from social participation, which we have witnessed in our cases, and the increasing preoccupation with fantasied achievement, frustration and escape, lead the patient deeper and deeper into behavior that, whatever its personal yield, has little or no social validity. Interpersonal communication, as we have seen, becomes intrapersonal communication; the patient converses less and less with other social persons, and more and more with fantasied persons in his pseudocommunity and autistic community. Not unlike a sleeping dreamer, the schizophrenic patient then finds the activities within his imagined context, to which his symbolic responses correspond, more lifelike and convincing than activities in the social context, to which these responses have little relevance.

In most clinical interactions, such as in diagnostic testing, it is extremely difficult to identify the internal referent of a response and, consequently, one does not have a basis for determining the extent to which a socially valid relationship exists. Since one can ordinarily describe the nature of the external stimulus situation, the quality of the relationship between the response and its external referents is in the center of the clinician's focus.

The therapeutic relationship, particularly the analytic one, provides examples of lack of congruence between the nature of the external situation and the response which is in part elicited by it. We are here referring to the patient's tendency to react (verbally or nonverbally) to the therapist as if the latter possessed qualities or characteristics which in fact he does not possess but which were characteristics of significant figures in the patient's earlier history. This *transference* of attitude and feeling might be described, when it occurs, as reflecting inadequate reality testing: the failure to see the lack of congruence between one's response and the stimulus object toward whom it is directed.

It perhaps should be emphasized that by such phrases as "reality," "socially valid," and "consensually valid" we shall have reference to what a group of trained individuals agree is either the nature of the external or "objective" situation or the degree of congruence between their manner of testing conclusions and that of the individual under study.

COMPLEXITY OF THE RESPONSE

Responses vary in the degree to which they reflect sustained mental operations as a result (or concomitant) of which events or ideas are put into a variety of relationships to each other. On the one extreme one finds a response reflecting intellectual helplessness or inertia while on the other extreme the response reflects an active, spontaneous, sustained process in which similarities and differences among ideas are examined in a way so as to change the nature of the presenting problem. *Because a response is considered to be a complex one it does not follow that it is an adequate or realistic one.* This point will become abundantly clear to the reader who studies Freud's (50) classic description of the paranoid Schreber or of the phobic Little Hans (51). In both cases—as in the case of every intellectually normal person at some time or other in his life—one will find instances where a life problem engenders complex responses which while they alter the nature of the life problem nevertheless would be considered unrealistic in the sense that they do not correspond in a socially valid way to their referents.

The complexity of human behavior as well as the current status of psychological knowledge and technique prevents the writer, as it should the reader, from assuming that the categories which have been described adequately reflect either the complexity of human behavior or the major situational variables. Every psychologist utilizes, in an explicit or implicit manner, continua by means of which aspects and sequences of behavior are ordered. Such continua reflect what the psychologist deems important for understanding and predicting behavior. That psychologists differ in the continua they use is largely due to differences in theoretical conceptions of behavior and different research interests. What we have attempted to do in the previous pages of this book is (1) to focus on a particular kind of situation, the clinical interaction, (2) to identify the major variables operating therein, and (3) to describe continua which would reflect these variables. In this attempt we have been guided not only by what clinicians and non-clinicians do in trying to understand the interpersonal interaction but also by what is considered important in such interactions regardless of one's theoretical position. In a sense, we have attacked the problem in a somewhat empirical fashion, deliberately narrowing the focus of our attention. One initially could have attacked the problem in terms of a number of theoretical systems which are all-inclusive in scope in that they are concerned with behavior from the standpoint of origins, motivation, learning, development, socialization, and the like. We chose the somewhat empirical in preference to the theoretical approach for several reasons:

1. Aside from analytic theory the major theoretical formulations have given little or no attention to the nature of the clinical interaction, and in some instances their relevance for the understanding of such an interaction is of a highly dubious sort.

2. Analytic theory, concerned primarily as it has been with the therapeutic problem and interaction, did not seem sufficiently oriented toward interactions in general to warrant using it as a starting point.

Because analytic theory has largely been shaped by therapeutically derived data it runs the risk of overemphasizing some, deëmphasizing other, and even overlooking variables.

3. By focusing on variables which apparently operate in any interpersonal interaction, and attempting to illustrate their role in a variety of settings, the likelihood is increased that one will clearly see the importance of research which seeks to study the effects of systematic variation of these variables on behavior in the particular kind of interaction in which one is interested. When one becomes aware of the significance of a particular variable in a type of interaction other than the one in which one operates, it is difficult to avoid reëxamining that variable in the context of one's work.

4. If the variables and continua are considered of importance by those with differing theoretical orientations, it indicates a certain degree of communality among the theories despite differences in language, rigor, and degree of immediate applicability.

We would like to emphasize again that the continua we have described characterize *aspects* of the relationships between the situational variables and the overt response. These continua do not reflect the complexity of behavior or even the ways in which the continua might be related to one another. The continua obviously do not relieve the psychologist of the necessity of interpreting and giving additional meaning to the data, a procedure which involves implicit or explicit assumptions about the dynamics of behavior. In short, when the psychologist goes "beyond" the continua he does so on the basis of some theory of human behavior.

In Part II we shall be discussing the ways in which responses to the Rorschach ink blots may be evaluated or "scored." Although the "language" of Rorschach scoring is different in some ways from that which we have used to describe the continua in this chapter, this should not obscure the fact that the implicit bases for most of Rorschach scoring are the continua we have here described. This could hardly be otherwise because the continua in part reflect the situational variables which operate in any interpersonal interaction, and no one has yet denied that the Rorschach situation is an interpersonal situation. The stimuli may be different and the instructions likewise may be unusual, but these are differences in degree and not kind.

The reader should bear in mind that just as the continua do not reflect the complexity of behavior in an interpersonal interaction Rorschach scores likewise reflect only aspects of a complex response process. It will not be surprising, therefore, if scoring a Rorschach is by no means the same as interpreting one. The major assumptions which appear to be utilized by the clinician in the interpretive process will be taken up after discussion of the Rorschach scoring categories.

# PART II

# The Rorschach

# Chapter 9

# THE INSTRUCTIONS

THUS far in this book we have discussed major variables in the clinical situation and some continua on the basis of which responses may be evaluated. The remainder of the book will be devoted largely to an attempt to demonstrate the relevance of the above problems in the use of a particular test, the Rorschach. Any test could have been used for purposes of illustration—there is nothing unique about the Rorschach which would require us to discuss special theories or variables.

We chose the Rorschach for several reasons: (1) It is a widely used clinical test; (2) it presents the individual with a stimulus task which is believed to elicit a clinically useful sample of an individual's response tendencies; (3) it is a test which has been regarded by some as being different in kind rather than in degree from other tests, an assumption for which there is no evidence and which runs counter, and therefore represents a challenge, to what has been said in the first half of this book; (4) it is a test in which this writer has been particularly interested. We included the last reason in order to make the point that the more one works in the clinical situation with a particular test the more one becomes convinced that it "can do" what any other test can do. *Such a conviction, of course, is no proof of the validity of the claim.* But the fact that these different tests are used in a particular kind of interpersonal interaction, the clinical situation, by clinicians who share to some degree a common training background and approach would make for some communality in the kinds of behavior observed and conclusions reached. The tendency is to attribute the "advantages" wholly to the particular test and to neglect what is contributed by the clinician's implicit use of the variables inherent in the clinical interaction. What we are here trying to emphasize is that any test can be used to illustrate the problems discussed earlier in this book and that one's choice is in part determined by one's interests and practice. It should perhaps be made clear that we are maintaining that *for pur-*

*poses of illustration* one test is as good as another. *For purposes of clinical usage,* however, the choice of test or tests should be determined by critical evaluation of available research evidence.

As soon as one attempts to evaluate the Rorschach (or any other test) in terms of our earlier discussions, it becomes quickly evident that the majority of studies which one must consider have not explicitly taken the situational variables into account. The effect of the instructions, the subject's conception of the interaction, the time and place of the inter-action—it is the rare study which takes these and other variables into account either in the design of the study or in the evaluation of the results. Consequently it is frequently difficult to place these studies in some perspective with any degree of assurance. One is often at a loss to determine how comparable these studies are even though they are presumably concerned with the same problem. In more than a few instances we shall find investigators reporting different and contra-dictory findings, the sources of which are probably differences in the role of one or several of the variables operative in any interpersonal interaction. But since the data relevant for an evaluation of these variables are usually not given, we are hard put to explain the differ-ences in the findings. To evaluate every study in terms of our earlier discussions is neither practical nor desirable. It would undoubtedly result in a degree of repetitiousness which would justifiably bore the reader. It would also, in the absence of the relevant information, force one to speculate in an unguided kind of way, a procedure which when too frequently indulged makes one uneasy about the appropriateness of one's speculations. In addition, as we have pointed out in previous pages, the fact that a study has not explicitly taken account of the situational variables does not mean that the results are invalid, nor does it necessarily mean that the investigator's conclusions are un-justified. What we have tried to indicate is that in such studies one usually does not know (1) the degree to which one can generalize from the findings, (2) what would constitute a replication of the study, and (3) how to explain differences in findings among studies.

In the pages that follow, therefore, the reader will not find every study, or perhaps the majority of studies, discussed in the detail re-quired by our earlier discussions. What we have endeavored to do is to focus in each chapter on a few studies which allow us to discuss the significance of the situational variables.

A study of various Rorschach texts (*16, 92, 121*) will quickly reveal, as Allen (*4*, p. 21) has indicated, that "The variety of verbal directions to the testee is limited only by the number of testers." Although each writer attempts to justify his instructions, and frequently presents plausible reasons for his approach, such justification is not based on any research evidence. There are studies, as we shall see later, which indicate that different instructions produce different results; but the instructions used in these studies are not those found in the major texts or utilized in clinical practice. In these studies the instructions were varied for the purposes of a particular research problem, and the results, while relevant for the particular problem, do not allow us to choose in any clear-cut fashion among the various instructions employed by clinicians. One cannot avoid the conclusion that there is a very definite need for studies comparing the most frequently used instructions. Such studies would need to focus not only on the individual's formal response to the cards but also on the differences in set or attitude engendered by the different instructions.

The following are the instructions utilized by this writer:

Perhaps when you were a child you played the game of inkblots or blotto —you would put some ink in the middle of a piece of paper, fold the paper in half, press down, and then when you would unfold it you would see all sorts of things there. I have a set of inkblots here which were once made in the same way. I am going to hand them to you one at a time and I would like you to tell me the different things you see in each of them. Some people see this, some people see that. No two people see exactly the same things. There are no right or wrong answers. Just tell me what you see. When you are through with each card give it back to me and I will give you the next one. Remember: there are no right or wrong answers. Some people see this, some people see that. Just tell me the different things you see. (The subject is then handed the first card.)

These instructions were formulated in this way because of several considerations:

1. The examiner should not give the testee any indication of what the content of a response should be. "Some people see this, some people see that. There are no right or wrong answers"—by adhering to these

words the clinician avoids giving information which would guide the testee in choosing one or another kind of content. This does not mean, of course, that these instructions have no effect on the subject, but rather that by his use of these words the examiner has not communicated to the subject that he will see "designs," or "clouds," or "people," or any other specific content.

2. The examiner should make it clear that the subject will respond on the basis of his own judgments and decisions. Whatever problems confront the subject will be resolved by him in whatever way he chooses—and whatever he does will be accepted by the clinician.

It is important to emphasize that although the instructions are intentionally of a permissive and non-leading nature, *they present the individual with a problem which he is called upon to resolve by himself in some way in the presence of another person*. In fact, one might characterize this particular clinical interaction as one in which the clinician can study a sample of how an individual makes decisions and judgments when confronted with a problem. To what other situations one can generalize from this sample of behavior depends, of course, on (1) what the individual conceives "the problem" to be and how he reacts to it, and (2) the degree of confidence, based on available research, with which such generalizations can be made. Unfortunately, the subject rarely tells us in any direct way what problems the instructions present to him, a difficulty which in no way frees the clinician from the necessity of attempting to deduce the nature of the problem as conceived of by the subject.[1] In many cases, when the test is completed, one can question the subject in a direct way about his reactions to the instructions. Although his report should not be uncritically used, and not all subjects are equally willing or able to give such a report, it is frequently possible to obtain information which would enable the clinician to be more sure of what problems were engendered by the instructions. For some reason, the post-test interview for purposes of attempting to determine such information is not standard practice in either the clinical or the experimental situation (see Chapter 3).

[1] The diagnostic importance of determining the individual's subjective definition of the test situation has been discussed at length by Schachtel (*146*). Although this article contains a number of traditional but unverified assumptions about the significance of certain Rorschach scoring categories, the student will find the discussion of the interpersonal nature of the Rorschach testing situation illuminating and helpful.

## THE NATURE OF THE STIMULUS MATERIALS

We have just indicated that the Rorschach instructions present the individual with a problem which he must solve in his own way in the presence of another person. When he is presented with the first of the ten Rorschach cards, it is clear that the nature of the stimulus materials will in some way influence the individual's conception of the problems. Ink blots, despite their too frequent appearance in popular magazines and books, are not frequently seen stimuli. If one could place stimuli on a continuum of cultural familiarity or evocation of a specifically taught and overlearned response, the Rorschach ink blots would very probably be placed at a point rather different from that of most other test stimuli. It is this kind of consideration which suggests that the Rorschach situation presents the individual with a relatively novel kind of problem for which he is unlikely to have any specifically taught and overlearned response. From the interaction of the instructions and the stimulus materials one might hypothesize that in the Rorschach situation individuals will differ in the degree to which feelings of indecision, dependence, lack of confidence, and failure will be experienced. Put in another way: *The interaction of instructions and stimulus materials will make the Rorschach situation a stressful one for many individuals.*

If our characterization of the Rorschach stimuli has some merit, one would expect that an individual's attitude toward them would change as their novel or stressful character decreased. Wallen (*170*) has presented some data in line with such an expectation. In his study the subject was seated about three feet from the experimenter. The subject was shown each card and asked whether he liked it or not. One group of normal subjects were shown the cards in the usual I-X sequence while with another group the sequence was reversed. Wallen found that in both methods of presentation there was a tendency for cards early in the sequence to be liked less than those which came later. Wallen concluded "that as adaptation to the task progresses the subject is more likely to make favorable judgments of the later cards. Many persons approach the task with timidity or apprehension, but after viewing several cards a reference frame is established, and the unusual nature of the task is less disturbing."

In evaluating an individual's behavior in relation to the Rorschach stimuli several cautions must be kept in mind:

1. By using the Rorschach one is getting a sample of behavior to a particular kind of stimulus situation. Because an individual conceives of the Rorschach situation as being stressful in a particular kind of way, it does not follow that one can generalize, or make predictions, to all stressful situations. Restricting oneself only to the use of the Rorschach immediately limits the varieties of behavior to stressful situations which one can observe. A very important research problem concerns the ways in which an individual's behavior to the Rorschach is similar to or different from behavior to other kinds of test situations. For example, does the individual who behaves in the Rorschach situation as if it were a stressful one react similarly (overtly or covertly) when given the Wechsler-Bellevue Intelligence Scale? If there are differences in behavior to these two problem-solving situations, how does one explain such a finding? What are the differences between individuals who respond similarly and those who respond differently to the two situations? To what extent are differences in behavior a function of differences in stimulus materials?

2. If the interaction between Rorschach instructions and stimulus materials makes it likely that the situation will in some degree be experienced as stressful, then a stressful reaction at the beginning of the test does not necessarily represent inadequacy or maladjustment or any other negative term one prefers. The clinician's problem is to attempt to determine the *strength and duration of the stressful experience.*

## THE PURPOSE OF THE INTERACTION

There is relatively little that can be said at this point which was not discussed in Chapter 3. The following might be added or reëmphasized.

1. Since the purpose of the interaction, as stated by the clinician and conceived of by the subject, precedes either the instructions or the presentation of the stimuli, one would expect it to be a major factor in how the individual reacts to the problem presented him.

2. In explaining the purpose of the interaction the clinician should be as frank as possible unless, as with an unusual subject or for experimental purposes, such frankness will markedly reduce the amount

of service which the clinician will be able to render. Too frequently, especially with the beginning student, the examiner unjustifiably fears that a discussion of purpose with the subject will make the relationship a difficult one—the subject will respond in a hostile fashion because "his personality is being evaluated." Such a fear is often a reflection of the clinician's own value judgment: having to take a test or go to a psychologist is an admission of failure and a sign of weakness—something few clinicians apparently enjoy thinking about. This projection of attitude on the part of the clinician can obscure the fact that the subject feels in need of help and expects to be evaluated, and such a subject can be puzzled by the clinician's evasiveness.

3. *Whatever the purpose given to the subject, the clinician should not assume that it was accepted by, or is congruent with, the purpose as conceived of by the subject.* It is the job of the clinician to deduce from the subject's overt behavior what his conception of the purpose was. Here again the post-test interview can be helpful.

THE SPONTANEOUS PERFORMANCE

1. Following the instructions the individual is handed the first card so that to the clinician, who is seated across the table, the card number on the back is in the upper left-hand corner.

2. The clinician then writes down whatever the subject says, be it a formal response or an incidental or casual remark. Should the subject ask if he can turn the card he is told, "You may hold it in any way that you please." If the subject is uncertain or puzzled and verbalizes this in the form of a request for help or clarification, the instructions are repeated to him as before. The clinician must avoid saying or doing anything which would indicate to the subject a mode of attack. For example, if after much difficulty a subject gives a response, the clinician should avoid indicating by word or action that the response is acceptable or unacceptable, "good or bad."

3. Each response is timed. In the past it has been standard practice to record the reaction time for the first response to each card. This was based on research studies with free association tests in which it was found that the longer the reaction time the more likely that the stimulus word had elicited or was in some way related to unpleasantly toned associations. Since there is no evidence that the first response to a Rorschach card is of greater significance than subsequent ones, there

seems no reason why all responses to a card should not be timed. The student will not infrequently find, for example, that the time interval between the end of the third and the beginning of the fourth response will be greater than the reaction time for the first response. Whether or not differences in reaction time among responses, regardless of their place in the sequence, reflect differences in the degree to which they are related to an individual's problem areas should be subjected to test. In addition to getting the reaction time for each response the total amount of time the card was held should be recorded.

4. If the subject gives but one response to a card, or returns the card with the statement that he does not see anything, he should not be prodded to give more responses. This practice is determined by the aim of allowing the individual to react to the cards—to handle the problem posed for him—in whatever way he chooses. If he chooses not to respond, this is accepted by the clinician and the next card is then presented. As we shall see later when "the inquiry" part of the test is discussed, the individual who initially did not give any responses to a card is given another opportunity to do so.

5. If the subject turns the card, the position to which he turns it is recorded as follows:

$\wedge$—card held right side up as presented

$\vee$—card held upside down

$<$—card held with the left side now at the top

$>$—card held with the right side now at the top

6. When the subject returns the first card, he is given the second one, and then the third, until all ten cards have been given. Care should be exercised to keep the cards in such a way that the subject does not get any preliminary view of them. It should be emphasized again that throughout the spontaneous performance portion of the test the clinician adopts a passive, non-leading attitude toward the subject's behavior. He does not judge or in any way selectively reward or punish a particular form of behavior or type of response. It is unfortunately true that many students experience great difficulty in learning to keep quiet.

THE INQUIRY

1. After the subject has handed back the last card to the clinician, the latter says: "That finishes the first part. Now I would like to go

back over each card so that I can get an idea of what it was in the card that reminded you of what you saw. If while we are going back over the cards you see something which you didn't see before or which you saw before but forgot to mention, please feel free to tell me."

2. The clinician then gives card I to the subject and says, "When you looked at the first card before you said you saw . . . (the clinician repeats verbatim the first response). What was it in the card that reminded you of that?" It is extremely important that the clinician repeat verbatim the subject's response because the aim of the inquiry is to get the subject to elaborate on the response as he initially saw it. Repeating the response verbatim increases the likelihood that the unverbalized associations which initially accompanied the response will be recalled and verbalized. The important word in the last sentence is "likelihood" because it is clear that too much time has elapsed since the response was initially given to warrant the assumption that in the inquiry the subject is only verbalizing what he originally saw in connection with the response. It would probably be closer to the true state of affairs to assume that in answer to the clinician's question the subject's response includes both what was originally unverbalized and what may be termed new associations. By repeating the response verbatim the clinician hopes to get the subject to verbalize what was previously unverbalized.

3. Since the purpose of the inquiry is to determine, for example, if the color or the texture of the card are incorporated in the response— or if the content of the response is seen as if in movement—there are times when further questions are asked about a response. When further questioning is justified and how the questions are phrased will be taken up in subsequent chapters, when measures of response characteristics will be discussed. But the student should begin to bear in mind the principle that the clinician, aside from the standard initial question given above, asks no question about a response unless there is something *in the subject's verbalization* which is ambiguous or apparently irrational. The beginning student tends to conduct the inquiry as if it were an inquisition in which the subject's verbalization is less important than the student's conception of how the response should be or was seen.

4. When the clinician is finished questioning about a response, he hands the subject a piece of tracing paper and says, "Would you please

trace what you saw so that I see it just the way you did." The value of the tracing will be taken up later. Suffice it to say at this point that the tracing represents a permanent record and, in research especially, makes the judging of the quality of the response amenable to objective study.

5. If in the performance a response was given to the card in other than the upright ( ∧ ) position, the clinician (in the inquiry) reminds the subject of this, indicates the position, and then asks the standard initial question, "What was it in the card that reminded you of . . . (verbatim repetition of the response)?"

6. If in the performance part of the test the subject "rejected" a card —he was unable to give any response to the card—he is once again given the card in the inquiry and told, "When you first saw this card you said that it did not remind you of anything. Please look at it again. Perhaps now it will remind you of something."

As was indicated before, the questioning in the inquiry is for the purpose of determining certain response characteristics. We shall now take up these response characteristics.

*Chapter 10*

# THE EXTERNAL REFERENT: LOCATION
# OF RESPONSE

ONE of the obvious ways in which Rorschach responses differ among themselves is in the amount of the external referent, the card, utilized. Some responses utilize the entire blot area, some utilize very tiny portions, while the majority utilize areas somewhere in between in size. One could, therefore, evaluate responses on a continuum of size. Traditionally, however, the area of the blot utilized for the response has been evaluated both in terms of the frequency with which it has been utilized by some normative group and in terms of size. The inclusion of the criterion of frequency stems from the fact that certain portions of each blot "stand out" more clearly than others and are therefore more frequently utilized by the subject. Judging the response in terms of the portion of the blot used is, in Rorschach terms, focusing on *the location* of the response. The following are the location symbols:

1. The whole (W) response is the easiest to judge because the individual indicates that he is using the entire blot for the response.

2. The cut-off whole (W̶) response is one in which all but a small or minor portion of the blot is used. By "small" is meant an area which is usually a projection off the main blot area. Examples follow:

CARD I
A bat—excluding one of the top or side projections

CARD II
Two bears fighting—excluding the top red area (or a response in which all but the bottom red area is used)

CARD III
Two people—excluding either or both of the red areas

CARD IV
A giant—excluding the bottom center portion

CARD V
A bat—excluding the projections at the end of "the wing"

CARD VI
A rug—excluding the top "snake-like" projection

CARD VII
Two dancing dogs—excluding the top "feather-like" projection

Although it is assumed that in terms of how an individual "perceptually grasps" the card the W̶ does not essentially differ from the W response, there is no research evidence for such an assumption. The fact that in terms of a continuum of amount of blot used the W̶ is clearly close to the W response is the only justification for grouping them together for tabulation purposes.

3. Usual details (D) are those blot areas which are the most frequently utilized. Usual areas vary greatly in size and they are obviously evaluated not on a size continuum, as in the case of W and W̶, but on the basis of frequency. At this point we must bring up a problem which will be relevant for many aspects of the Rorschach: the fact that different writers in the field use different symbols, disagree as to what is or is not a usual detail, base their list of usual details on data from different populations, and utilize different or no statistics for evaluating frequency. When one bears in mind that these same writers vary in the nature of the instructions given to the subject and in the degree of prodding or questioning in the inquiry, the task of the beginning student will clearly not be an easy one. Beck (16), Klopfer (92), and Hertz (72) have published lists of D responses. In Figure 4 we have indicated those D responses found in at least two of these lists. That, despite the limitations stated above, there is agreement about a fair number of D responses represents a crude basis for their use.

4. Space (S) responses are those in which only white space is utilized. There are several usual (DS) white space responses: The two upper white areas ("eyes" of the mask) on card I, the center white in card II, the center white in card VII, and center white ("violin" or "vase") in card IX. The discerning reader will have noted that the S response introduces a third basis for evaluating the response in terms of the external referent, namely, whether the response is to the white or black portions of the card.

5. Unusual detail (Dd, DdS) responses are determined by exclusion:

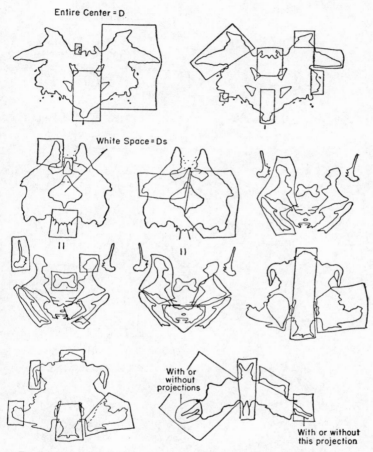

FIG 4. Usual Details Found in at Least Two of Three Published Lists

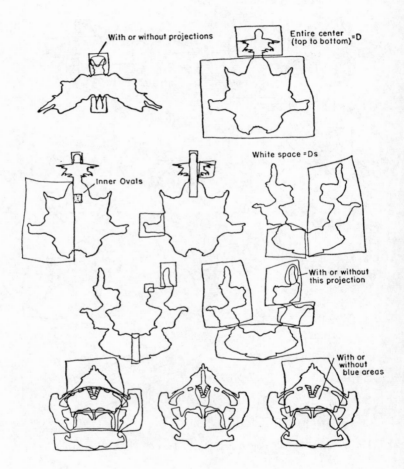

With or without projections

Entire center (top to bottom) =D

Inner Ovals

White space =Ds

With or without this projection

With or without blue areas

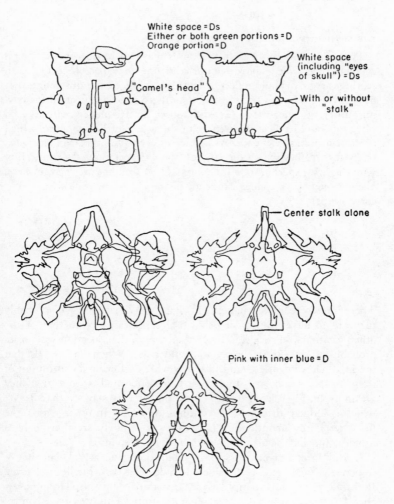

White space = Ds
Either or both green portions = D
Orange portion = D

"Camel's head"

White space
(including "eyes
of skull") = Ds

With or without
"stalk"

Center stalk alone

Pink with inner blue = D

if the response is neither W nor W̶ nor D nor DS it is scored Dd or DdS.

## THE SIGNIFICANCE OF THE W RESPONSE

That the location aspect of responses may fall in one of the several categories described above should lead one to expect that (1) each scoring category should reflect or have significance for a different aspect of behavior—if this is not the case then there is no justification for having different categories; (2) differences in frequency within each category should reflect differences in the aspect of behavior for which the category has relevance. Available research literature contains relatively few studies which directly test these expectations. In connection with the first expectation Wittenborn's (179) findings are relevant here. Using ninety-two college students he obtained the following inter-correlations:

|     | W     | D    | d    | Dd   |
|-----|-------|------|------|------|
| W   |       |      |      |      |
| D   | −.194 |      |      |      |
| d[1] | −.228 | .669 |      |      |
| Dd  | −.138 | .608 | .749 |      |
| S   | −.143 | .464 | .512 | .660 |

These intercorrelations suggest (1) that the W response will probably turn out to have a different behavioral significance from that of the other location categories and (2) that these other location categories probably reflect similar behavioral tendencies. When one recalls that the D, d, Dd categories stand for areas which differ on a continuum of frequency, it is important to note that Wittenborn also found that they are more highly related to the total number of responses than is W, which is judged in terms of a continuum of size. In other words, the more responses an individual gives the more likely are they to be a usual or unusual detail rather than a whole response.

A reading of various Rorschach publications will reveal that the W response is in some way considered to be related to intellectual level. Beck (17, p. 11), for example, says: "For a quantitative sphere of reference I rest on the results of a separate study. This was in a control

---

[1] Wittenborn utilized Klopfer's (92) scoring symbols, in which usual details are divided according to area size into large usual details (D) and small usual details (d). Also, in Klopfer's scoring W and W̶ are combined for tabulation purposes.

group ranging from the most superior to individuals maintaining themselves in the community at a sub-average level. In so far as these findings are representative, W scores for the middle two-thirds of the population are seen ranging just about from 1 to 10 (5.86 ± 4.91). It means too that many individuals at the upper end of the curve produce notably more than 10W and that many at the lower end produce none." Unfortunately, Beck's figures and conclusions are based on a control group in which intellectual level was determined not by psychological procedures but by a rather crude evaluation of social-vocational information; 73.4 percent of his cases were considered above average or higher; there were no data to indicate that it was in fact the more intelligent subjects who gave the most W; the standard deviations rather clearly indicate much overlapping between whatever groups are compared. In a later study (18), utilizing a "normal group" chosen on the basis of occupational level, there are no data presented on the relation between W and occupational level.

Wittenborn (178) presented some findings on sixty-eight college students who had taken the Rorschach and for whom scores on nine different tests of mental ability were available. "Probably no member of the present group has a verbal IQ as low as 115. The range of ability is less restricted than at first might be supposed, however; the high levels are very well represented. Moreover, some of the tests which are not relevant to general academic achievement, e.g., the measures of spatial ability, may include a very wide range of scores. In general it may be claimed that using a variety of tests which sample relatively homogeneous, specifiable abilities results in less range restriction than would result in using one general ability score, e.g., an IQ. . . . If no significant relationships are found in the present sample, it is unlikely that important linear relationships would be found in a more heterogeneous sample. . . ." The number of W was expressed as a percent of the total number of responses. For each test the "high" group was the ten students with the highest scores and the "low" group those ten with the lowest scores. None of the differences in W between the two groups was significant.

Working with the other extreme of the intelligence continuum, institutionalized mental defectives, E. K. Sarason (135) found that (1) there was a significant and *negative* relationship between W and M.A. and (2) the size of the relationship varied with etiology. In other words, those with a higher M.A. tended to have a lower number of W. It is interesting to note that the mean W percent of Wittenborn's (college students) and Sarason's subjects (mental defectives) is very similar.

In discussing the negative correlation between W and M.A., as well as the finding that her subjects gave a relatively small response total, Sarason has suggested that a crucial factor may be the subject's interpretation of the instructions. She pointed out that her subjects often verbalized that the whole blot represented "a thing" which it was up to them to discover. Having found the "thing" they were unable to change their perceptual set and look for other possibilities. This concrete attitude toward the cards was also seen in the overemphasis of the W response in both groups. "When the whole was not seen, it was because the Gestalt qualities of the figure made other areas, the usual details, more pronounced." Since this concrete interpretation of the task—the inability to shift one's approach—would be expected to vary with intellectual level, the negative correlation is not surprising. This explanation emphasizes the importance of determining the subject's conception of his task, be the subject a college student or an institutionalized defective. Such very different kinds of individuals may not differ markedly in the relative number of W which they give to the cards but they may differ markedly in why they give such responses. The student should not conclude that the above description of the defective's interpretation of the task is unique to that kind of subject. In clinical practice it is not at all unusual to find non-defective individuals who interpret the task in a similar manner. The clinician cannot avoid the necessity of determining the subject's conception of the problem.

The way in which W may be a function of the subject's conception of the problem is indicated in a study by Coffin (27).

Our general procedure was to obtain the subject's evaluation of a series of common occupations, then to suggest to him that the members of the occupations most preferred by him tend to respond in one manner, and that members of non-preferred occupations respond in a different manner. Then by administering the Rorschach test to the subject himself and examining his own responses, we were able to determine which of the available suggestions the subject had accepted, and their correspondence to his expressed attitudes.

"Suggestion" was done by having the subject read an offprint "printed in such a form as to resemble a standard reprint of a paper in a scientific journal."

To Group I was given the reprint containing suggestions that business and professional men tended to view the blot as a *whole* and that they saw chiefly *animals* in the blots, whereas laborers and WPA workers analyzed the blot into details, and tended to see inanimate objects. Group II was given a reprint with the opposite suggestion, that business and professional men analyzed the blots into *details* and saw mainly *inanimate objects,* while laborers and WPA workers saw the blot as a whole and perceived animal forms.

The results of this study clearly revealed that the subject's conception of the task, determined by the particular suggestion, influenced his responses to the Rorschach. Table 7 summarizes the findings and supports Coffin's conclusions:

TABLE 7.   Significance of Differences in Percentage of Responses
(Coffin, 27)

| Categories and Groups | M% | σm | Diff. | C.R. |
|---|---|---|---|---|
| "Wholes" | | | | |
| Group I | 38.6 | 3.77 | | |
| Group II | 7.0 | 1.18 | 31.6 | 7.98 |
| "Details" | | | | |
| Group I | 61.4 | 3.77 | | |
| Group II | 93.0 | 1.18 | 31.6 | 7.98 |
| "Animals" | | | | |
| Group I | 51.4 | 3.95 | | |
| Group II | 25.7 | 2.68 | 25.7 | 5.38 |
| "Inanimate" | | | | |
| Group I | 48.6 | 3.95 | | |
| Group II | 74.3 | 2.68 | 25.7 | 5.38 |

This experiment with ambiguous stimuli has yielded results indicating that subjects may be influenced by suggestion not only passively to accept or assent to a suggested statement, but actively to construct the imaginative situation in accordance with the suggestions given. It has further shown that the subjects do not simply interpret the situation according to any suggestion which may be given, but that the interpretation is selective and is related to attitudinal factors. Both the quantitative data and the introspective comments support the conclusion that those suggestions were accepted which were in accord with pre-existing attitudes and that these suggestions may set up Aufgaben determining the subject's own construction and interpretation of the ambiguous stimulus.

Some readers may wonder about the relevance of Coffin's study for the clinical use of the Rorschach. To such a query we would say that its significance lies in the fact that to the Rorschach, as to any other stimulus task, the subject's conception of the task is a crucial factor. Although one does not suggest to a subject what is a "good or bad" Rorschach response, the subject nevertheless comes to some conclusion about what he should do and it is this conclusion which the clinician must attempt to deduce.

Cox and Sarason (31) report a study which has relevance for the problem of the different significances of the W response. In one part of this study the behavior of the subjects was in no way influenced by any special instructions or treatment. The Rorschach was given in the manner outlined in the previous chapter. Two different groups of pre-selected subjects were used: those who had previously reported that they felt very anxious in a testing situation and those who reported either no or a minimal degree of test anxiety. The subjects were not aware of any connection between taking the Rorschach and the test-anxiety questionnaire administered several months earlier. The clinician did not know who was a high anxious (HA) or low anxious (LA) subject. These authors found, as did Eichler (38) using experimentally induced anxiety, that the more anxious subjects gave significantly fewer W responses. This finding indicates how a specific and interfering response affects how much of the stimulus an individual will become aware of. More important for our purposes here is the support which the study by Sarason and Cox, as well as that of Coffin, gives to the generalization concerning the necessity of evaluating the response in terms of covert behavior which antedates or accompanies the overt response.

The main conclusion that might be drawn from the discussion of the W response—a conclusion which holds for any Rorschach scoring category—is that one cannot attach to it anything resembling an absolute meaning. In clinical practice there is no justification for assuming that because individuals give the same number or percentage of W responses they therefore have in common certain behavioral characteristics. In research the significance attached to the W response should be determined by the kinds of subjects under study and the particular hypothesis in which one is interested. The more we learn through research the relation between a particular kind of Rorschach response, on the one hand, and variations in subjects and treatments, on the other hand, the more secure will the foundations of clinical practice be.

That W responses are not all of a piece was well pointed up by Klopfer (*92*, p. 259).[2]

A relatively high number of W, according to the tradition of the Rorschach literature, represents an emphasis on the abstract forms of thinking and the higher forms of mental activity—as, for instance, the logical or constructive activities, philosophical or religious speculation, esthetic or ethical understanding, etc.

This tradition cannot be accepted unqualifiedly; not every W can be evaluated in this manner. Certain W's are achieved by a mental inability to organize the whole card into subdivisions, an inability frequently found in certain severe forms of brain diseases. Furthermore, vague or noncommittal W interpretations, made in a high-handed manner, as butterflies, maps, islands, X-ray pictures, undefined anatomical cross sections, etc., show a minimum of effort to organize the stimulus material, to build up an all-inclusive concept; they merely utilize the crudest features of the general outline or employ a vague shading effect.

A high number of such simple or popular W's represents either a pathological condition (easily revealed by other features) or, at best, a somewhat fruitless effort to attain a higher level of mental activity without possessing the necessary qualifications. Such a trait may be called "quality ambition" (as distinct from "quantity ambition" which tries to impress with a large number of answers). To be sure, even the most brilliant subjects use some simple W's, but never in excess of half the W's produced.

The percentage of W's needs to be further qualified in the light of the form accuracy level. The fact that a record contains a high number of W's

[2] B. Klopfer and D. Mc. Kelley, *The Rorschach Technique.* Copyright 1942 and 1946 by World Book Company.

which are neither simple nor evasive does not guarantee that they represent substantial achievements in the realm of higher mental activity, as witness the various types of definitely pathological W's which are rich with the richness of nonsense.

The absence of a proportionately high number of good W's does not necessarily prove that the subject lacks capacity for higher mental activities. It may merely mean that he does not use this capacity in a way expressed by W's of high quality. For example, a very intelligent compulsion-neurotic may express an enormous drive for form accuracy and will not give a single W because he will discover in each card something which does not fit into a whole concept. However, his intellectual capacities will be revealed in other ways.

It is clear from Klopfer's statements that the W response can be evaluated in terms of at least two continua: *complexity and degree of reality testing*. In short, the W response needs to be evaluated on continua other than size. Although, as we shall see later, responses are judged on these other continua, in the case of W we know relatively little about the behavioral significances of responses which fall at different points on these continua. There is a tendency for the W responses of mental defectives and the brain-injured to be vague and unrealistic (*92, 135*). However, in these studies (1) complexity and reality testing were not stated as continua so as to allow for evaluation of *degree*, either of complexity or reality testing, and consequently (2) the behavioral significances of differences in placement on the continua cannot be stated. It is interesting to note that in the case of both mental defectives and brain-injured individuals they tend to view the Rorschach task as one in which the whole card is a "thing."

THE SIGNIFICANCE OF THE USUAL DETAILS (D)

Traditionally (*19*, p. 121; *92*, p. 260; *17*, p. 14) individuals who predominantly give D responses are described as concerned with the practical, common problems of everyday life. There is no acceptable research evidence to support such a sweeping generalization. Two considerations have probably been the basis for the generalization: (1) Since D areas are the most "obvious" ones, individuals who tend to give them are those who are concerned with the obvious aspects of everyday life; (2) individuals who are behaviorally deviant, such as psychotics and extreme neurotics, tend not to give usual details—"a deficiency in the use of normal details may point to an inability to employ such common sense or to attend to the necessary practical routine of living" (*19*, p. 121). For the first consideration to be true it would be necessary first to define "the practical, common problems of everyday life," then to obtain a reliable measure of behavior in relation to these problems so that differences among individuals can be discerned, and finally to see whether differences in the behavioral measure are related to differences in the tendency to give D. Unfortunately, this type of study has not been done, largely, it may be deduced, because of the problems involved in getting a reliable behavioral measure. In connection with the second consideration it should be pointed out that the size of the differences in D between normal and deviant groups is not of such magnitude as to have clinical significance.

It should be noted that, as in the case of W, the D responses differ among themselves in terms of complexity and degree of reality testing. In addition, they also differ in size. By taking into account these various measures of response characteristics, several problems for research might be stated:

1. If W and D were scored in terms of a complexity continuum, would individuals who give complex W responses also give complex D responses? Would individuals who give W responses indicating poor reality testing give similar D responses?

2. Would individuals whose "complexity score" for W is markedly different from that for D perform differently on simple and complex learning or problem-solving tasks?

3. Do individuals who differ in the degree to which they respond to the usual details differ in the speed with which they recognize tachistoscopically exposed stimuli which are themselves varied on some complexity continuum?

4. If *all* Rorschach responses were scored in terms of a meaningful continuum of size, would their relation to behavioral measures be higher than when they are categorized in three different ways: frequency (D, Dd), color (S), and size (W and W)?[3]

[3] The student should bear in mind that Dd (unusual) responses may be, and frequently are, greater in area size than D (usual) responses. The Dd score is by exclusion. We point this out here in order to emphasize again that the Rorschach locations do not reflect any one continuum, and we are suggesting that if any one continuum were used a more consistent and useful, if not more logical, basis for evaluation of responses would obtain.

5. How does the D response, measured in terms of the different continua, vary with differences in how the subject conceives of the task? Coffin's study (see p. 126) represents but one kind of approach to this problem.

We have presented the above research suggestions not because they are necessarily the most cogent that could have been made but in order to indicate the necessity of determining some possible significances of the D response.

What we have said about the D response should not be construed as denying the validity of the significance traditionally attributed to it. What we have attempted to point out is that its traditional significance is unproved and its testing by means of reliable behavioral measures beset with difficulties. Until the necessary research is done the clinician must interpret the significance of the D response category with extreme caution.

## THE SIGNIFICANCE OF THE UNUSUAL DETAILS (Dd)

Numerous significances have been attributed to the predominance of unusual details in a record. Escape from reality, anxiety, inferiority feelings, and a quantity ambition are some of the characteristics which have been traditionally considered to be reflected in the predominance of Dd. Here again, unfortunately, the research evidence which should serve as a foundation for such conclusions is largely lacking or methodologically defective. For example, it has been maintained that obsessive-compulsive individuals, as a result of their need for meticulousness, self-assurance, order, and avoidance of strong anxiety, tend to give an excess of unusual details, particularly those small in area size. Because the compulsive "must" perform an act it is assumed that his productivity to the Rorschach will be high. Goldfarb (60) compared the Rorschach performance of a group of obsessive-compulsive and normal adolescents and found that the obsessive-compulsive group gave significantly more responses and a higher percentage of Dd than did the normal group. However, the obsessive-compulsive group was chosen not on the basis of non-Rorschach behavior but solely on the basis of the Rorschach performance itself. If the child's Rorschach performance was similar to that which an obsessive-compulsive was *assumed* to give, the child was labeled as obsessive-compulsive. We have here a case of an assumption being treated like a fact—a degree of validity being attributed to the Rorschach which in fact it did not have. Despite this methodological flaw Goldfarb's case presentations are illuminating in that they illustrate the importance of determining the relationship between Rorschach performance and the subject's attitude toward himself and the task. The clinician of even moderate experience will probably agree that Goldfarb's cases responded in an atypical fashion. The following are samples of the Rorschach performance of some of his cases:

P. S. introduced a reservation to his response to a small detail in card I. "This looks like South America—if there was little strip here." Similarly in card VII, he stated "if you cut off this and that, it looks like Spain." Or in reference to the bottom of card VIII "if you would put a head to this, it would look like a woman's chest because the orange part stands out."

M. R. said in his response to card VI, "It may even look like a snake with its long neck, but the two wings shaped on the neck make me think otherwise."

S. K. stated in response to card I, "It looks like, if cut in half, a map of England."

S. G. pointed to the middle white space in card II and said "If this was pottery, this would be where to put things."

. . . . .

Several of the children showed more severe compulsion to meticulous description which bordered on empty verbalization. Sometimes, to keep responding, the children moved from an elaboration of response to card description or response repetition. The functional inefficacy of the results is illustrated by the following response of I. K. to card I. The painful rigidity and circuitousness in response to this card were exhibited in response to every card that followed.

4″ It might be a bat.
It looks like two ink spots—first one then another.
Part of it looks like a coast line with islands around it like a map.
In the very middle it looks like faces with hands put up. In fact it looks like a creature.
There is a hole in the middle. There is a dark line in the middle except for the hole and little dark spots. Both sides are the same except the left side is a little darker. On the right side is a few spots and the left looks like it has a belt on. The hole looks like a buckle. The outline is the same except for the left side on the bottom. It comes out. On the right side on

the hip of the creature, there is a light spot that isn't on the left side. There is a larger light spot on the left side than on the right side. There's a black spot on the right spot which isn't on the left spot. Near the top, there's on the left side a dark smudge which isn't on the right side. On the left side, just on the side near the middle, there are a lot of dark spots that aren't on the right side. In the middle of the creature's nose there is a light spot where no ink touched. On the left side there's two things coming down but there is a light spot that isn't on the right side. There's two large holes near the bottom. There's two cracks. The crack on the right is more distinct. The part in the middle that looks like a buckle has more in the left side. There's a little island on the bottom. Part of the right is taken off. Some smudges on the right side are a different shape, and darker than the left side. Directly above the right hip is a little dot that isn't on the left side. It looks like a fingerprint. On the right appears an oval shaped smudge that isn't on the left side. Approximately at a level with the creature's head, the right has some dark smudges on a line with the middle. In the hole near the bottom there are several small dots, extremely small that aren't on the right side. The white hole which looks like a buckle on the belt is a very light smudge. At the right side of the creature's head, the smudges are different.

. . . . .

H. F. showed quantity ambition in addition to a trend to meticulous elaboration of response and the aforementioned qualification trend and a seeking for reassurance. He also took 3 hours for the total performance and gave 140 responses. His associations in response to card I are offered as typical of his total performance, though in the cards that followed he showed considerably less attention to wholes and a clearer preoccupation with detail.

6″ Looks as though it might be a bat with those winglike structures on either side of a bat.
Then the body itself might be a beetle.
Then those two claw-like appendages on either side of the head are claws of a crab.
Do you want me to tell you what I see? Or what's represented?
It might be a queerly shaped island.
Then a snowflake.
Or it might be a drop of water magnified.
Upside down it might be a mask with a face, nose.
And these might be ears.
This way it might be a tree.
Then in a remote way, it might be a Gulf of Mexico.
Outline might be of an island or coast line—irregular.

Profile of a face.

Over here a hand pointing like this.

Coastline of land and islands all around.

This might be a beach—lighter gray, and tiny islands.

In a very remote way, this might look like a foot—bony part, the way it is shaped.

This dark black line might be a canal or a railroad seen from a great height.

Here it looks like a part of a nose.

This might be a cove or inlet from the sea. (Returns)

The need to be "correct," the meticulous attention to details, the frequent use of qualifying words ("looks like," "may be," "if"), the concern with order and balance of the card, the pedantic-like elaboration of a single response, the high productivity level—*it is in terms of such attitudinal factors, deduced by the clinician from the subject's overt behavior, that the significance of any particular scoring category must be evaluated.* From Goldfarb's report it would seem that he chose his "obsessive-compulsive" subjects as much on the basis of his interpretation of the covert significances of their behavior in the clinical situation as on considerations of frequency of particular scoring categories. Without the former the significance of the latter is indeed ambiguous, a point we have repeatedly made in these pages.

The writer might add at this juncture that in his own clinical experience with patients who were independently judged as having obsessive-compulsive symptoms the behavior and formal Rorschach performance was similar to that described by Goldfarb, particularly in reference to the number of responses and percentage of unusual (and frequently minute) details. *But conclusions based on clinical experiences, subject as they are to the selective influences of bias, memory, and personal pride, are far less satisfactory than those based on controlled research.*

Kates (85) compared the Rorschach performance of groups of obsessive-compulsives and "anxiety reaction patients." They were chosen on the basis of symptoms alone, independent of test results and previous diagnostic classifications. There was no significant difference between the mean I.Q. and the mean chronological age of the two groups. The obsessive-compulsives gave significantly more responses as well as a higher percentage of Dd responses.

THE INTERPRETIVE SIGNIFICANCE OF THE WHITE SPACE (s) RESPONSE

Fonda (47) has clearly summarized the status of the white space response:

When Rorschach published his inkblot test nearly thirty years ago, he assumed that space responses always indicate some sort of opposition tendency. At that time, he wrote: "It is striking to note how the study of the space response defines the neurotic aspects of the record. This is frequently the case, though I am as yet unable to say why it should be. . . . This will be known only through further experience."

Since publication of the Psychodiagnostik, the inkblots have been presented to more subjects than any other single set of stimuli in the history of psychology, and the space responses have been regularly interpreted as evidence of opposition trends. Unanimous endorsement of this practice is found in contemporary Rorschach texts and manuals, but such interpretations are still based mainly upon clinical hunches and intuition rather than clear-cut objective evidence. Indeed, Rapaport recently felt obliged to draw attention to a "dire need for verification" of the rationale underlying interpretations of the white space response.

In an attempt to test the significance traditionally attributed to the S response Fonda utilized the group Rorschach with a college population. In addition to the Rorschach the subjects were given the Guilford-Martin Personnel Inventory, and Inventory of Factors G A M I N.

Both are questionnaires comprising, altogether, 336 items which require "yes," "no," or "?" answers. The tendency to use the "?" has been shown to be a fairly consistent response set. It seems reasonable to assume that such a response set reflects a more generalized opposition tendency since it indicates that the subject is either unable or unwilling to give a definite "yes" or "no" answer. In the first case, he would be exhibiting indecisiveness; in the second, contrariness.

The following results are relevant here:

1. The number of S responses is significantly correlated with the total number of responses (R).[4]

[4] One of the most frequent findings in the Rorschach literature is that the majority of scoring symbols are correlated with total R, a fact which has been too frequently overlooked with the result that very often interpretations have been made about the frequency of a particular symbol which in fact could have been made from merely knowing the total number of responses. The student is strongly urged to become well acquainted with Cronbach's (33) excellent review of statistical methods applied to

2. The test-retest reliability was modest ($+.533$) and indicates that "only the more extreme scores should be taken as a basis for individual protocol interpretations."

3. When a subject's S score was expressed independent of total R, the correlation between S and "?" scores was .574, a statistically significant correlation but certainly not of such size as to warrant using the finding as a sole basis for conclusions about the individual case.

Bandura (13) also studied the relationship between "oppositional tendencies" and the white space response. He individually administered the Rorschach to eighty-one high-school students, who were also rated by their teachers on four traits: negativism, assertiveness, inadequacy feelings, and self-distrust. Of these four traits only negativism was significantly correlated ($+.27$) with the tendency to give white space responses. Although the correlation is too low for predicting negativistic behavior in the individual case, it does give some support to the traditional significance attributed to the white space response. Bandura also tested the hypothesis that the Rorschach white space response represents a perceptual reversal process. He correlated frequency of the white space response with rate of reversal on the Necker cube. The correlation was .35. "The Rorschach space response represents, in part at least, a perceptual reversal process. However, only a relatively small part of the variance in S is determined by a perceptual reversal tendency and other variables must be functioning as important determinants."

THE PROBLEM OF EXPECTANCY

A question which probably has been bothering the reader is: How does one know when an individual gives an excess of a particular location—what is the normal expectancy? By "normal" reference is usually made to those within the intellectually average range and presumably functioning in an efficient and independent manner. In his recent study of individuals within the average range Beck and his colleagues report that the "total productivity for the average adult is . . . 32" and that the formula for normal expectancy is 6W, 23D, and 3Dd. Klopfer (92, p. 258) expresses expectancy in terms of percentages

---

Rorschach scores. He not only gives many examples of the inappropriate use of statistics in Rorschach studies but also indicates procedures which are relevant for certain knotty Rorschach problems.

which are similar to those that would obtain if Beck's formula were so expressed.

Although Beck (*18*) gives the figure of 32 for the total productivity of the average adult, when one takes the standard deviation ($\pm 17.68$) into account the range is from approximately 15 to 50. This rather con-

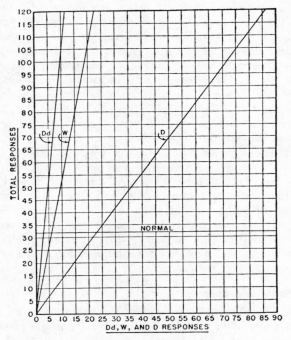

FIG. 5.  Expectancy of W, D, and Dd for Response Totals up to 120 (Beck et al., *18*)

siderable range in an average group is apparently not unusual, as the following summary from Bell (*19*, p. 118) indicates: "Rorschach found that the normal individual usually gives between 15 and 30 responses; Klopfer revised these figures upwards to 20–40 responses; Rapaport reported the normal average to be around 24. All workers are in agreement that a wide range in R may be found in normal individuals, but that less than 10 or more than 75 responses demands further examination." Since the total R within an average group can vary considerably, the question arises about the way in which the normal expectancy varies with total R. Figure 5 taken from Beck (*18*) is a graphic presentation of the expectancy of W, D, and Dd for response totals up to 120.

The data should be utilized with the following cautions in mind:

1. There are differences among Beck (*16*), Klopfer (*92*), and Rapaport (*121*) in instructions to the subject and in the manner in which the performance and inquiry are conducted, differences which may well affect total R.

2. There are no adequate normative studies in which the Rorschach performance of the subjects was evaluated in terms of such important variables as age, intellectual status, and social class (*9, 10*).

3. The number of subjects studied is usually far too small to justify using the results other than with great caution—the variability usually being too large for clinical comfort. The following, taken from Beck (*18*), indicates the unusually large variability. which is in part due to the smallness of the sample:

|     | Mean  | S.D.  |
|-----|-------|-------|
| R   | 32.65 | 17.68 |
| W   | 5.50  | 3.76  |
| D   | 22.85 | 10.49 |
| Dd  | 3.02  | 3.38  |

TRACINGS

In the chapter on administration it was recommended that after he asks the subject (in the inquiry) "What was it in the card that reminded you of (verbatim repetition of subject's verbalization in performance)?" the clinician then hand a piece of tracing paper to the subject and say, "Please trace what you saw so that I see it just the way you did." If one does not use tracings one either has to ask the subject to point out his response ("Where is the . . . ?" or "Show me the. . . .") or ask him to outline it on a sheet in which the blots are reproduced in miniature (*92*, p. 44). Tracings practically eliminate the need for questioning about location, and in the case of those subjects who react to the inquiry as a threat or an implied criticism tracings seem to give one a clearer idea of what portions of the blot are used than when this information must be verbalized.

Several experiences have impressed the writer with the importance of tracings. In working with institutionalized defectives it was very difficult to get them to delineate with anything resembling precision the portion of the blot used for a response. In addition some of the cases gave responses which according to traditional thought were well beyond the capacity of defectives (*186*), the explanation being that the writer had either misunderstood the subject or interjected his own perceptions. When responses similar in quality were traced by the subject without any help from the clinician, there was no doubt about the quality of the response or who was responsible for it.

In working with the Rorschachs of a primitive people (*58*), the fact that tracings had been obtained considerably enhanced the meaning of their verbalizations. These Rorschachs were interpreted five years after they had been given, and without tracings the anthropologist, let alone the clinician, would have been guessing about where the responses were seen.

The beginning student will find tracings a valuable aid against his tendency to assume that other people see things the way he does when they use similar words to a particular blot area.

### THE "TOTAL PATTERN"

A point which has always been stressed in the Rorschach literature is that the significance of a particular scoring category can be evaluated only in terms of the "total pattern." Bell (*19*, p. 118), for example, states that the interpretation of a record is "an artistic achievement" in which the clinician interrelates a number of variables, "a process aided but not accomplished by scoring." If by an artistic achievement is meant that the interpretive process cannot be explicitly stated or publicly communicated, or reliably repeated by others, and is not subject to the usual rules of scientific validation, then this writer must take exception—but we shall talk more about this problem in later pages. In connection with the necessity of interrelating a single scoring category with a large number of other scores the following should be said:

1. The fact that there are, for example, different categories of locations indicates that each of them presumably has a somewhat different behavioral significance. If there were no differences in their relation to a behavioral criterion, only one location symbol would be necessary. What we have indicated in this chapter is that we do not have a firm foundation for stating under what conditions the different scoring

symbols reflect behavioral differences. In addition, we have suggested that the criteria currently employed for scoring the locations are not consistent with one another and may not be the most relevant ones that could be utilized.

2. If, as we have stated, no absolute significance can be attached to a particular scoring category, then it is possible that the same score may have different significances in relation to another variable—be it another Rorschach score or an independent behavioral measure. In clinical practice, as Bell indicates, this possibility is presumably always carefully considered when Rorschach categories are compared to one another. *However, when the significance attributed to each of the scores is determined by fiat and has little or no foundation in controlled research, whatever significance is attributed to their interrelationship will probably be of very dubious validity.*

It should be made clear that the above points were made in connection with the practice of making interpretations—of a single score or combination of scores—solely on the basis of some measure of frequency. What we have tried to indicate in this chapter in relation to the location categories is the importance of basing one's interpretation on knowledge of the individual's attitudes in the clinical situation. The clinician should, of course, be acquainted with the range of normal expectancy of the group to which a particular patient is most similar, despite the criticisms to which the studies of the normal expectancy of particular groups are subject. But such studies can only serve as a point of departure in the attempt to understand the relation of the location scores to *this* patient's conception of himself in the clinical situation, regardless of whether his scores do or do not deviate from normal expectancy.

Let us consider the case of a young patient who to card I began by giving a W, then turned the card upside down and gave another W, *and then* returned the card to the examiner. The same thing happened on card II. This pattern persisted in all the cards. We might ask about this record: why does this boy give such a preponderance of W? That his W responses included an awareness and use of D indicates that the preponderance of W is not due to an inability to respond to the more "obvious" blot areas. From the speed with which he gave W responses, as well as deductions made from his comments about the cards, it was concluded that he *might* have conceived of the task as one in which the whole card must be used. If this conclusion has merit then one in effect is saying that when this boy made an initial judgment about what was expected of him, he acted persistently in accord with it even though the stimuli differ markedly in the degree to which they lend themselves to the W response. When this conclusion is taken in conjunction with the fact that he responded to each card first in its upright position and (almost always) then quickly turned the card upside down and gave another response, one might further deduce that this boy is responding in a rigid and compulsive fashion in this situation. Whatever the reasons, it is as if this boy does not or cannot easily change his method of handling the situation. It should be noted that although this boy seems to be responding in a compulsive-like way, his Dd percent is practically zero and his total R not excessive, despite an I.Q. (C.A. 9–3) of 182.

The conclusions stated above about this boy are obviously based on more than consideration of frequency of locations—a fair number of mental defectives give a preponderance of W! We might also say that the conclusions are in the form of deductions which require confirmation. That he *may be* rigid or compulsive in certain situations is not the same as saying that he *is* so. The clinician must depend on several sources of data for his attempt to confirm his conclusions: (1) the patient's observed behavior in the situation, (2) case history material, and (3) relevant research. In the case of this boy we would ask: Are there other aspects of his Rorschach performance which do not fit in with these conclusions? Does he behave similarly toward other kinds of stimulus tasks? Do the problems for which he was referred manifest the characteristics contained in the conclusions? Is there available acceptable research concerning the ways in which Rorschach performance is affected by a compulsive attitude and rigid set? What does the research literature tell us about the kinds of antecedent conditions or factors, internal and external, which give rise to rigid and compulsive behavior? Are these antecedent conditions reported in this boy's history?

Before leaving this chapter we would like to make one further observation about the contention that the significance of any Rorschach scoring category can be determined only by its relation to other scoring categories. As we have seen in this chapter, and as will become increasingly clearer in future ones, studies which have as their focus a single scoring category (e.g., W, S) do provide findings which are of clinical significance. In some instances the significance traditionally attributed to the scoring category is not supported while in others supporting evidence is found. The clinician who is not guided in his clinical work by these studies operates outside the realm of science, thereby performing a disservice to his patients as well as his profession.

That some clinicians base their conclusions on a glib, uncritical use of scoring categories (and their frequencies) is an indication not only of shoddy thinking but also of ignorance concerning the nature of the interpretive process, an ignorance which has been in part due to the emphasis usually placed on scoring in various texts. It would indeed be nice if our understanding of *an* individual required no more than a knowledge of certain scores (or points on various continua). Unfortunately, as we pointed out at the end of Chapter 8, we are not justified in depending on this at the present time. Knowledge of scores or continua does not relieve the clinician of the necessity of accounting for that which he observed but which cannot be reflected in conventional scores, of deducing the covert significance of the subject's overt responses, and of determining the significance of *this* person's behavior in *this* situation for behavior in other situations. In the individual case, scores can only be regarded as guides, the significance of which is determined by available research, the clinician's understanding of the role of the situation variables we have discussed earlier in this book, and the assumptions he makes about the dynamics of behavior. In the next few chapters, as in the present one, we shall focus our attention on the research evidence for the significances traditionally attributed to the various scoring categories. The interpretive process, which must be based as far as possible on research evidence, will be discussed in later portions of this book.

*Chapter 11*

# THE EXTERNAL REFERENT: COLOR

In the previous chapter the response was evaluated primarily in terms of how much of the blot was used as well as in terms of the particular blot area utilized (usual-unusual). In the present chapter we will discuss the color characteristics of the external referent.

SCORING (BRIGHT COLORS)

1. When bright color is used as a characteristic of a thing which has, relatively speaking, definite class characteristics the response is scored as FC. Examples follow:

CARD IX  ∨ —a colored tree, like in autumn (center strip is trunk and red portions are branches and leaves)
CARD X  ∧—blue birds
CARD II  ∧—red socks (top red)
CARD III  ∧—a red butterfly
CARD IX  ∧—a carrot, the color is just right
(top details, in tracing the projections, are omitted and the form of a carrot is apparent)

An FC scoring signifies that "the thing" seen has from a cultural standpoint readily recognizable form characteristics without which it no longer belongs to that particular class of objects. When a person in our society says "blue birds" we expect that he is seeing a particular form configuration to which we have learned to attach a particular label. An individual may give the response "blue birds" to an area which competent judges decide does not possess the configuration of form called "bird." Such a decision represents a judgment in terms of the adequacy of reality testing and does not affect the FC scoring which indicates that a definite form was intended. (Such a poor response would be scored FC—, but the problems connected with such scoring will be taken up in a separate chapter.)

2. When bright color is used as a characteristic of a thing or object

144

which has, relatively speaking, very variable form characteristics, the response is scored CF. Examples follow:

> colored clouds
> spattered blood
> colored rock
> blue water
> an explosion with all kinds of colors (an exception is "atomic explosion" to card IX in ∨ position, an example of a content which has a rather definite configuration of form which would be scored FC)

In each of these examples the object could be seen in myriad forms or shapes and still be given the same label. Clouds, for example, can have almost any number of shapes and still be called clouds—a characteristic which does not obtain for FC responses.

3. When bright color is used without any apparent attempt to describe some form characteristic, the response is scored as C. Examples follow:

> blood because it is red
> water because it is blue
> fire because it is red
> this is red, that is blue (color naming)
> the green stands for envy, the orange for hope (color symbolism)

In each of these examples the shape of the area used apparently is unimportant and is not in any way reflected in the verbalization of the response.

SCORING (WHITE AND BLACK COLORS)

*When either the black or white color is used as a characteristic of a response, the same criteria for scoring are employed as in the case of bright color responses. The scoring symbols are FC', C'F, and C'.*

It should be pointed out that the basis for scoring presented in this chapter is rather different from that utilized by other workers, Beck (16) in particular. According to Beck scoring is largely determined by what the subject says was the more important factor, color or form. For example, if to the small center detail in card X the individual says "pawnbroker's balls" and indicates in the inquiry that his response was given "because of the color," it is scored as CF. According to the criteria stated in this chapter it would be scored as FC because the content has in our culture a readily recognizable configuration of form. According to Beck a response which here would be scored as FC would be a CF if the subject indicated that "it reminded me of that because of the color." In many instances given by Beck the scoring apparently was determined by what the examiner decided was the more important, color or form.

Asking the subject about the relative importance of color and form, or deciding the scoring on the basis of the clinician's subjective estimate, is very likely to result, as Siipola (*155*) has so well shown, "in remarkably inaccurate estimates of the extent to which the presence of color actually influenced the responses." In Siipola's study

. . . The 20 colored ink blots were taken directly (literally cut out) from the standard Rorschach cards (colored cards II, III, VIII, IX, X). Parts which naturally constitute discrete subordinate units were selected and mounted separately on uniform white cards. . . . The 20 stimulus blots include practically all of the colored areas, so that color as it appears in the Rorschach Test is fully represented in our stimulus material. The 20 matched achromatic blots were carefully prepared photographic reproductions of the colored blots, identical in size and form. The achromatic rendering of the brightness values preserved the distribution of shading so that in direct comparison each matched pair looked the same except in regard to hue.

One group of subjects was exposed to the colored blots and another group to the achromatic ones. Siipola gives many instances (*155*, p. 368) in which both examiner and subject would very probably consider responses to be color influenced. *In all such instances the responses occurred with equal or greater frequency for the achromatic versions of these blots.* Clearly, then, to decide between the relative *influences* of color and form on a response on the basis either of the subject's or of the clinician's judgment is an unjustified procedure. The basis for scoring presented earlier in this chapter does not reflect an attempt to decide between the relative influences of color and form; the scoring does reflect an attempt to distinguish between two independent questions: (1) Does the individual in his verbalization *associate* the color of the blot with the object seen? (2) Does the object have a definite and readily recognizable configuration of form?[1]

---

[1] This basis for scoring, while differing markedly from that given by Beck, is very similar to that described by Klopfer (*92*, p. 142), who also points out the difficulties involved in using the subject's judgment about the relative influences of color and form.

INTERPRETIVE SIGNIFICANCE OF BRIGHT COLOR RESPONSES

In the Rorschach literature one of the most frequent assertions concerns the relation between the quality of emotional reactivity and color responses. The FC response is supposed to be characteristic of the mature and controlled adult; the CF response is supposed to reflect an impulsive and self-centered way of responding; and the C response is considered an indication of an infantile, uncontrolled mode of handling emotional or affective experiences. In the records of adults it is felt that the "most healthy" balance is one in which the number of FC responses is greater than the number of CF responses—the appearance of C responses being considered somewhat of an indication of pathology (92, p. 285). The traditional rationale underlying the assumption of relation between emotional reactivity and bright color responses has best been presented by Schachtel (145), an article with which the student should familiarize himself.

For many years studies of the validity of these broad assumptions were lacking and, too frequently, the assumptions were accepted as facts. In recent years, however, numerous studies have appeared which allow us better to evaluate the status of these assumptions. As a point of departure we would like to return to the criteria for scoring presented earlier in this chapter. Underlying these criteria were several assumptions.

*Assumption 1:* In comparison either to CF or C, the FC response requires, more often than not, a more sustained conceptual or "comparing" process whereby the concept and blot area are made to fit. Put in another way, more sustained conceptualization is required in fitting a response like "a tree with autumn colors" than a response like "splattered blood" or "water because it is blue."

If this assumption has merit, one might predict that the tendency to give FC responses would not be highly correlated with the tendency to give CF and C responses, despite the fact that all three types of responses have color as a common characteristic. This prediction seems supported by Wittenborn's (179) factor analysis of Rorschach scoring categories. Using Klopfer's scoring schema, he found that Rorschach responses (regardless of the traditional symbols attached to them) which had a relatively indefinite or "loose" configuration of form had a different factorial composition than responses which had definite class characteristics of form. "This pattern of relationships is scarcely predictable from the Rorschach literature and the scoring and interpretive practices of Rorschach workers. The present sample suggests that the superficial logical similarity between the form-color (FC) and the color-form (CF, C) responses may have little behavioral basis. If the pattern of relationships revealed in the present sample can be verified in other samples, it may be desirable to consider a revision of our current beliefs concerning the behavioral or personality significance of the form-color response." Subsequent studies by Wittenborn and Mettler (*184, 185*) and Cox and Sarason (*31*) support the assumption that responses in which form is secondary or indefinite or loose have a different behavioral significance from that of responses having a definite or precise form, regardless of whatever traditional Rorschach scoring symbol they may have.

A second assumption, adumbrated in the previous discussion, follows:

*Assumption II:* The FC response, *at the time it is given,* is a form of response in which emotional or affective factors do not intrude or are minimally present—the "intellectual" or conceptual aspect of responding predominates. The CF or C responses, at the time they are given, are forms of response in which the conceptual aspects of responding are minimally present and in which an impulsive or emotional or "uncontrolled" aspect of responding is likely to be in evidence. Put in another way, the less conceptualization a response requires the more likely that it will reflect affective or emotional factors.

From this assumption one would predict that individuals who, relative to their total number of responses, give markedly more FC than CF + C responses will be overtly less emotional than individuals in whom CF + C was greater than FC. Wittenborn and Mettler's (*185*) study of psychiatric patients is in line with this prediction. They found that the patients whose responses indicated "lack of perceptual control"—what we have here called responses with an indefinite or relatively variable form configuration—tended to be those who overtly were the most emotional. Although an individual's score for lack of perceptual control utilized CF and C responses, *the score included all other types of responses where form was vague or indefinite.* Cox and Sarason (*31*), using a very similar but not identical score, found that individuals who were highly anxious in testing situations gave more indefinite or "form secondary" responses than non-test-anxious individuals.

We have frequently pointed out in this book that predictions based on formal test results must take into account the subject's conception of or attitude toward the test and test situation. Predictions based on Rorschach categories should be no exception, *especially when such predictions are based on scoring categories which presumably reflect the subject's behavior at the time he gave his responses.* It is for this reason that we would restate the prediction based on Assumption II as follows: Individuals who, relative to their total number of responses, give markedly more FC than CF + C will be overtly less emotional than individuals in whom CF + C was greater than FC—*especially if the test situation is conceived of as a problem-solving and stressful situation.*

Although this prediction has been stated in terms of the FC, CF, C categories, the discerning reader will have already noted that in the studies cited the color categories did not possess a significance for behavior different from that of responses where bright color was *not* utilized but where the definiteness of the form was similarly evaluated. In these studies, in fact, the form-secondary black and white color (C'F, C') responses were among those grouped with bright color responses (CF, C). We tentatively stated Assumption II in terms of the bright color categories because there are studies which suggest that they *may* have under certain conditions a particular behavioral significance.

A study which is directly relevant to the prediction based on Assumption II is that of Williams (*176*). He gave the Rorschach to twenty-five college students.

After a five minute rest period following completion of the Rorschach examination, the first practice session was begun. Each subject was seated opposite the examiner and was informed, "You are about to be given a test which is an index to your general intelligence. The test which has been placed before you is known as a Digit Symbol Test. It is one frequently used in many intelligence test batteries. You will be given a number of trials on this test in which we are interested in seeing how high a score you can reach." The experimenter then carried out the standard instructions and administration of the Wechsler-Bellevue Digit Symbol Test. The test was administered five times, utilizing 60 second rest pauses between trials. The usual 90 second test period per trial was used with a Digit Symbol Test blank on which the number of test items was increased from 67 to 110 by repetition of the last 43 items. This was done to limit the possibility of any subject's completing the test before the time was up, and anticipated the possible extended range of scores which resulted from practice. The second practice session took place within 24 to 48 hours after session one. The instructions and procedure were identical with session one. Three trials were given at this time.

Following a rest period of three minutes after practice session two, control testing was instituted to obtain an average measure of maximum performance under optimum conditions. With the subject in a rested condition, three successive readministrations employing the same test and rest periods used previously were given.

Upon conclusion of the Control Period, each subject was immediately led by the experimenter to an adjoining building. He was ushered into a room in which from three to five persons including at least two females were seated before the curtains of a one-way screen. The subject was introduced to the occupants and was informed, "The tests you have recently completed will be repeated again soon. Meanwhile, I am sure you will be interested in the operation of this one-way screen. You will notice that when I part these curtains you can easily observe everything in the next room." (The experimenter opened curtains covering a one-way screen eight by four feet in size, giving a complete view of the adjoining room. A camera mounted on a tripod flush with the screen also faced directly into the adjoining room.) "Now, if you will step into the next room and seat yourself at the table facing the screen, you can see that you are unable to see through the screen while anyone on the other side may observe you." (The subject was seated at the table facing the screen. The room was in complete darkness except for two #1 Photoflood lamps focused directly upon the subject and the table before him from a distance of approximately three feet.) "Remain seated as you are. The rest of this experiment will be conducted in this room. Hold out your left hand (or right hand if subject wrote with left). I am now placing a set of electrodes on your hand, the function of which will soon be explained." (A set of brass electrodes mounted on an adjustable elastic strap was secured to the palm and back of the hand.) "I shall now leave the room. All further instructions will be given to you through a concealed loud speaker. Save any questions for the end of the experiment."

The subject was then left alone in the room and all subsequent instructions were phonographically administered. He was told that his performance was being observed and that if his test performance was not judged "up to our standards" he would be in danger of being shocked via electrodes which had been attached to his arms. The Digit Symbol Test was then administered again. Each subject received a decrement score based on his stress and pre-stress scores. The various color categories were weighted as follows: FC, 0.5; CF, 1.0; C, 1.5—the resulting sum then being divided by the number of color responses the individual gave.[2] The lower the score the greater the tendency for the FC type of responding. "In addition, each record was broken down and expressed in terms of a dichotomy between subjects showing a trend toward FC (good integration) and those showing a trend toward C (poor integration). This was done by placing all records having an average color value of .9 or less (CF tending toward FC) in the former category and those with an average color value of 1.0 or more (CF tending toward C) in the latter."

Whereas the color scores presumably reflected "emotional control," Williams employed another Rorschach measure for "intellectual control," the F+ percent (16, p. 203). A response is scored F+ when (1) the concept realistically "fits" the area of the blot used and (2) the concept does not have as a characteristic color of any kind, shading or texture, or a movement quality—the form aspects of the area are all that is incorporated in the response. When the second criterion is met but the response is a poor fit (the reality testing is poor), it is scored as F—.

The F+ percent was calculated as follows: $\dfrac{F+}{F+ \text{ and } F-} = F+\%.$

The main results of Williams' study are shown in Table 8. Although the color scores correlate significantly and in the predicted direction with decrement score under stress, the best single predictor of behavior under stress is a measure based on a group of responses evaluated in terms of reality testing. These findings raise several questions:

1. Since Williams scored the color responses according to Beck's criteria discussed earlier in this chapter, the unreliability of scoring thereby introduced may have had the effect of reducing the size of the correlations obtained whenever these color scores were utilized.

2. Williams does not present the data which would allow us to de-

[2] Weighting of color responses has long been a traditional practice and it reflects the assumption that the three bright color categories are not of equal behavioral significance in that one FC does not represent as strong a tendency as one CF or one C. Put in another way, the "healthy" way of responding should, in terms of frequency, be in much greater evidence than the "unhealthy" or uncontrolled mode of response. There is no theoretical or empirical basis for the specific weights employed.

termine whether the color results are due to the color *per se* or are a reflection of a general tendency which appears in *all* Rorschach scoring categories. Were the individuals who tended to give definite (FC) as opposed to indefinite (CF, C) form responses utilizing color also those who responded similarly when utilizing, for example, black and white color (FC', C'F, C') or shading (Fc, cF, c)?[3]

3. The results indicate that the best index of "emotional control" under stress is *not* the color scores but the F+%. The distinction be-

TABLE 8.  Comparison of Average Decrement Under Stress with Related Rorschach Factors (Williams, *176*)

| (N = 25) | r | t | p |
|---|---|---|---|
| F plus % of total record | −.606 | 3.70 | .0001 |
| F plus % of color cards | −.724 | 5.01 | .0000 |
| Integration of form with color | +.354 | 1.81 | .0359 |
| Dichotomy between poor integration and good integration | +.425 | 2.26 | .0139 |

tween "emotional control" and "intellectual control" does not appear to be a meaningful one.

4. Williams does not attempt to explain the difference in correlation between F+% of the total record and F+% of the color cards. As we shall see later, the color cards, in contrast to the achromatic ones, present a more difficult problem-solving situation, a fact which must be taken into account in evaluating the significance of color responses.

Baker and Harris (*12*) studied the speech performance of fourteen subjects under normal and stress (threat of shock) conditions. They report findings similar to those of Williams. However, it is difficult to evaluate their study critically because of the briefness of presentation of their methodology as well as the small size of their sample.

Westrope (*173*) attempted to cross-validate Williams' findings. She used four groups of subjects: twelve anxious and twelve non-anxious

---

[3] If this were true, one would have expected that the correlation between the integration of form with color score and F+ percent would have been higher than the −.082 that Williams reports. However, the means and standard deviations of each of these rather clearly indicate a bunching of scores which would in effect produce a low correlation. With a less homogeneous group and increased range of scores the correlation would probably be much higher.

college women, and twelve anxious and twelve non-anxious college men. Anxiety level was determined by Taylor's Anxiety Scale (*163*). Utilizing Williams' procedures Westrope found not one significant relationship between Rorschach scores and Digit Symbol decrement scores. However, for several reasons Westrope's study can hardly be considered a replication of the Williams study.

1. Whereas Williams used a randomly selected group of males, Westrope used selected groups of males and females.

2. Williams reported that eight practice trials prior to the three control trials were sufficient for his group to reach a stable level of performance before control testing was begun. Westrope found that the level of performance for her group "increased considerably during the three 'control' trials following only eight practice trials. Consequently it was considered necessary to increase the number of practice trials in order to reach a stable level of performance before control testing was begun." This need to depart from Williams' procedure suggests that the subjects in the two studies were in some way different.

3. *In nine of the last eleven trials (3 stress, 3 control, 5 practice) both groups of women received higher scores than the men. When the scores of the women are averaged and the same is done for the men the women receive higher scores in every one of the last eleven trials* (Fig. 1 in Westrope). Unfortunately, Westrope presents no analysis or discussion of this finding, which very strongly indicates that there was a sex difference in performance. If there was a difference in the way men and women responded to the Digit Symbol task, it is also possible that there was a similar difference in response to the Rorschach.

4. *In light of the previous point one need not labor the significance of the most incontrovertible difference between the two studies: Williams is male and Westrope is female.*

5. From the comments made by the subjects following stress it does not seem that the situation was experienced as particularly stressful. In this connection it should be noted that the average decrement score in Williams' study was 10.36 (±5.70) while in Westrope's it was 7.69 (±9.22).

Carlson and Lazarus (*26*) also attempted to replicate Williams' study and did not obtain any of his significant findings. Some of their results, however, raise certain problems:

1. Carlson and Lazarus employed two groups: (a) an experimental

group, which received the same treatment as did Williams' subjects, and (b) a control group, which was treated in the same way except that they did not experience stress on the last three trials. *Although before stress the two groups presumably were treated in the same way, the control group received higher scores on every trial—the difference in scores between the groups tending to increase from trial to trial.* These differences suggest either that the two groups were (unwittingly but) selectively treated or that the two groups were initially in some way different. The important point is that, if two groups presumably treated in the same way by the same experimenter perform differently, it is not surprising if the results obtained by that and another experimenter are different. Because two experimenters *say* they did the same thing it does not follow that they executed the procedure in a sufficiently similar manner so as to create similar effects—a problem we have previously discussed in connection with other studies (see p. 71).

2. The authors report that it was the electric shock rather than the observers or the red light which was most disturbing to the subjects. Unfortunately, Williams did not obtain data which would allow one to determine what was most disturbing to his subjects—a lack which prevents us from determining how similar were the reactions of the subjects in the two studies.

3. Carlson and Lazarus found that subjects showing greater neuroticism on Winne's Neuroticism Scale tended to show more improvement during the stress trials. Here again one cannot determine whether the subjects in the two studies were comparable in terms of neuroticism or anxiety.

We have not focused on the above points because we believe Williams is "right" and Carlson and Lazarus are "wrong." What we have tried to illustrate is that before one can compare different studies one must have a better basis than we now have for determining to what extent the experimenter-subject interactions are comparable. Unfortunately, most psychological procedures are not independent of the personality of the experimenter (or clinician), subjects differ in type of response to stress and test situations, and, as Carlson and Lazarus point out, "varying motivations and past experience of the subjects must determine the extent to which they are involved in the situation, how they interpret it, and what their response will be." In the experimental as well as in the clinical interaction the significance of the subject's response can be evaluated only in terms of the variables which are operative in such situations. Failure to take account of these variables makes statements about the comparability of studies hazardous.

Eriksen, Lazarus, and Strange (*41*) conducted a study of the relation between behavior under stress and group Rorschach scores. They did not find any significant correlations between the two. Since they used the group and not the individual Rorschach, employed a group stress situation, and induced stress in a markedly different manner, it is doubtful whether the studies are comparable. Studies by Sarason and others (*31, 99, 100, 140, 141*) with college students and Janoff (*83*) with children—in these studies the Rorschach and stress were individually administered—support Williams' findings to this extent: individuals who tend to give responses which are either of indefinite form or poor in terms of reality testing tend to perform poorly under stress. These studies do not provide the data necessary for evaluating Williams' findings in the case of color responses. Eichler's (*38*) experimental study reports findings contrary to those of Williams. Using a procedure which according to some subjects was very stressful, he found that in contrast to his non-stress group the stress group gave *lower* weighted color scores (FC = .5, CF = 1.0, C = 1.5) to a degree which was near statistical significance. Eichler does not present data on the F+% but of all other Rorschach scores he does present few were related to behavior under stress.

It is important to point out that studies of the relation between stress behavior and Rorschach performance cannot assume that "stressful instructions" articulated by the examiner are experienced by the subject in the desired fashion. As we have pointed out repeatedly in earlier pages of this book, *the experimenter as well as the clinician must attempt to determine how the subject experienced the instructions or the stated purpose of the interaction*. In this connection Cox and Sarason (*31*) concluded on the basis of their study of test anxiety and Rorschach performance:

The present writers are convinced that attempts to vary motivation in randomly chosen subjects not only yield less precise data, but also, that such results are extremely difficult to interpret. For instance, it is highly improbable that all subjects respond in the same way to situational pressures and, more significantly, it is virtually impossible, at least at the present time, to obtain any accurate estimate of the *degree* of efficacy of such experimentally induced states. If "ego-involved" instructions are given to randomly chosen subjects and if, as is quite likely, both high and low test anxious individuals are selected, then their different reactions to such instructions may easily result in a "cancelling out" of a psychologically significant difference. Finally, if induced motivations are used in attempts to test the validity of projective tests, it is only too apparent that the conditions created can be so different from those under which clinical tests are normally administered that considerable doubt is cast upon the generality of such experimental findings.

In introducing this section it was pointed out that an excess of CF + C over FC has traditionally been considered an indication of impulsive reactivity, the assumption being that since bright color is "emotion arousing," the individual whose responses do not reflect "good control" or integration of form with color is likely to express feeling in an impulsive fashion. Holtzman (79) reports a study in which he attempted to determine the relation between color responses and impulsivity.

Because any psychological test which is novel and ambiguous provides a mild stress situation for the subject, the Rorschach Test could reasonably be expected to give some measure of the degree of control ordinarily exerted by the subject when under mild stress. In view of the above findings regarding the influence of color on reactions to ink blots, the way in which the individual reacts to the colored Rorschach cards should prove particularly important in any evaluation of impulsiveness or lack of emotional control in social situations. . . .

Two independent groups of college students were carefully selected from men living in Stanford Village, a housing project of Stanford University, in such a way as to insure that each member of a particular group was intimately acquainted with all other members of the group. The two groups of subjects consisted of 24 men in Building A and 22 men in Building B, hereafter referred to as Groups A and B, respectively. The close living quarters of these two buildings were conducive to occasional friction and dissatisfaction among the students. In a sense some of the group members were in a constant "stress" situation where intragroup frustrations gave rise to aggression, avoidance of participation in the group, and similar reactions.

In a preliminary session prior to the administration of the individual Rorschach Test, each subject placed himself and all other members of his group in rank order on ten traits including impulsiveness. In this way it was possible to determine average rank values for each subject which could be used as criteria for comparison with the performance of each individual on the Rorschach Test.

The correlation between rank order in impulsivity and the ratio CF:FC was .42 and .07 for the two groups.

The above results merely confirm the feelings of many Rorschach workers that, in general, consideration of a single aspect of the Rorschach only leads to misinterpretation.

In order to overcome the difficulties encountered by isolating single test scores, an extensive analysis was made of the test data for Group B without any knowledge of the data for Group A. It was proposed that *impulsiveness would be revealed in the Rorschach in one or more of a number of ways depending upon the particular personality structure of the individual.* One subject might disclose his impulsiveness by bursting forth with a spontaneous remark pertaining to color. Another might demonstrate a lack of control by using a predominance of formless concepts or color responses having indefinite form. In order to select variables which seemed to indicate an overreactivity to the ink blots, a large number of response characteristics was studied. The Rorschach protocols in Group B were compared with the criterion data prior to any analysis of the data for Group A in order to discover patterns of scores which discriminated the most impulsive from the least impulsive individuals. On the basis of this analysis eight signs were selected which seemed logically related to impulsiveness. These were:

1. immediate remarks provoked by the color
2. the relationship of CF to FC
3. the number of C in relationship to the other color responses
4. the relationship of $(CF + cF + 2C)$ to $(Fc + FC)$
5. the ratio of mean achromatic reaction time to mean chromatic reaction time
6. the mean time per response
7. the percentage of pure form responses
8. the number of FC in relationship to the other color responses

When each of the signs was assigned a weight and a total impulsiveness score obtained, the correlation in Group B with rank order of impulsiveness was .60. This size correlation would be expected because the Rorschach signs were chosen in a way so as to maximize the correlation in this particular group. When these weighted signs were then applied to Group A, the correlation between impulsiveness scores from the Rorschach and the criterion was .49, a statistically significant find-ing. As Holtzman points out, *the impulsiveness score included more than the color scoring categories and for that reason one cannot con-clude that judgments about impulsiveness are predictable from the way in which color is used in the Rorschach situation.* His findings seem to support his conclusion that "The verification of a hypothesis predicated on the assumption that impulsiveness is revealed in a number of differ-ent ways in the Rorschach test, depending upon the individual per-sonality structure, indicates that the trait of impulsiveness, or lack of control in social situations, can be evaluated by the Rorschach test." Siipola and Taylor (*157*), in their study of response to ink blots under free and pressure conditions (see p. 217), found that the presence of color, in contrast to its absence, did tend to elicit the vague, indefinite kind of response traditionally considered characteristic of the impulsive person. They, like Holtzman, conclude that "Granting the truly re-markable potency of color to set off the primitive type of conceptualiza-tion, it is still our contention that the underlying process is one which can be induced by other stimulus dimensions and that it is unnecessary to attribute to color a unique, somewhat mysterious, connection with impulsivity."

Gardner (*55*) has also reported a study of impulsivity. He had ten subjects rated on an impulsivity-inhibition continuum by three judges who had been personally acquainted with the subjects over a period of months. "Intercorrelations between rankings of subjects by the three long-term raters were .600, .769, and .346. Inquiry revealed that the low correlation, .346 between two of the raters resulted largely from a marked difference of opinion about one subject." Gardner's results are congruent with those of Holtzman except that the correlations between color scores and impulsivity were higher.

A study by Sarason and Sarason (*143*) has relevance for the hypothe-sis concerning impulsiveness. They studied two etiologically homoge-neous groups of mental defectives who differed in that one group received scores on the Kohs Block Designs which were at least eighteen months above their Binet M.A. while the other group received scores eighteen months below their Binet M.A. When the groups were sepa-rated on this psychometric criterion, clear differences in the behavior of the two groups were discernible. The Kohs-above-Binet group were the "good" children, none of whom had ever been in need of other than ordinary discipline; their work records in the institution were excellent, they were well liked by other patients and employees, they overtly appeared deceptively "dull," and subsequent to the study almost all were placed back in the community. In the case of the Kohs-below-Binet group their institutional record is in marked contrast. "Not only do they have poor work records but their behavior in many cases has necessitated frequent, extraordinary, disciplinary action. Irregular sex behavior, runaway, stealing, laziness, extreme childishness, silliness, and incorrigibility are some of the characteristics noted in their records. Not only are they considered as poor parole possibilities but when three of this group were paroled they had to be returned after a short time to the institution." From these descriptions as well as from intimate knowledge of the cases there is little doubt that the groups differed in the tendency to react impulsively in a variety of situations. On the Rorschach, which was not given to test a hypothesis about impulsiveness, there were no significant differences between the groups either in the tendency to give FC or CF responses or for one of the categories to appear in excess. *The two groups differed significantly in that the Kohs-below-Binet group gave markedly more responses which were of poor form,* their responses frequently containing irrational features which showed a failure to critically evaluate their reactions. These findings seem to support Holtzman's (79) conclusion that impulsiveness is not predictable from color scores alone but may be manifested in the Rorschach in a number of ways. The findings also appear to be congruent with the following generalization, which seems justified on the basis of the studies so far discussed: Predictions about behavior under stress or about the degree to which strong feeling or emotion is uncontrolled are most validly made when Rorschach responses are evaluated in terms of definiteness of form and adequacy of reality testing. Predictions made solely on the basis of bright color responses do not appear to have as clinically useful a degree of validity.

In the Sarason and Sarason studies (*143, 144*) two of the tests contained bright color: the Kohs and the Rorschach. In a subsequent study Sarason and Potter (*142*) attempted to determine whether children whose responses to the five colored Rorschach cards were of poorer form quality than the responses to the five achromatic cards tended to do poorly, relative to their mental age, on the brightly colored Kohs Designs in contrast to those children whose quality level of form does not drop in the colored cards. They used behavior problem children who had a minimum I.Q. of 70 and in whom there was no question about any kind of central nervous system defect. The cases were arbitrarily divided according to the Kohs-Binet relationship used in the previous study, and the Rorschach performances of the Kohs-above-Binet and Kohs-below-Binet groups were compared. Their results suggested that poor performance on the colored Kohs Designs was associated with the inability to respond constructively to the colored Rorschach cards.

. . . The conclusion the writers draw from the data is that the presence of colored stimulation in a situation where abstraction in terms of form relationships is involved prevents some maladjusted children from functioning up to the level of their intellectual capacity. In this connection two possible, not mutually exclusive, explanations might be offered which deserve further study: (1) the presence of color stimulates emotional reactions which interfere with the intellectual functioning, (2) the presence of colors makes the visual grasp of figure-ground relationships difficult and results in emotional reactions which make for inefficient intellectual functioning. The latter explanation implies that color is a factor in that it makes visual comprehension of recognizable forms more difficult, a condition that may then result in anxiety and impulsiveness; the former explanation, the standard Rorschach one, implies that color as such may be emotionally upsetting.

On the basis of studies to be discussed later we might point out that available evidence strongly supports the explanation that the presence of color in a problem-solving situation increases the difficulty of the problem.

In the studies discussed thus far the relation of the bright color responses to other test data or some situational criterion has been the primary concern. Matarazzo, Watson, and Ulett (101) report a study of "whether a subject's perception tends to remain typical in other situations which would elicit behavior that could be scored in terms generally comparable to those of the Rorschach situation." They compared responses to the Rorschach and subjective reactions to a flickering light.

The Rorschach test was administered first in all cases and, several days later, the intermittent photic stimulation experiment was carried out. . . . The subject was seated and a flashed-opal glass screen 30′ in diameter placed about six inches from his face. Thus the flickering light filled the visual field almost entirely. Directions given to the subject were to report "any

sensations experienced other than the flashing off and on of a white light."
Frequency of stimulus was varied over 22 frequencies from 2 to 30 flashes
per second presented in ascending order. Each frequency was maintained
for forty seconds followed by forty seconds of rest. An attempt was made
to elicit some description of the subjective responses to each flicker frequency. All such sensations were recorded verbatim.

. . . . .

C was defined as any mention of color. It was felt necessary to differentiate between a response of one color and many—the latter warranting a
greater color score—and so a separate C was given for each color mentioned
in each response. A response of "many colors" was credited with one C.
No FC or CF categories were used since, in this methodological study, it
was deemed impossible to differentiate accurately among these three color
categories.

The results indicated that those who had a tendency to respond in
terms of color on the Rorschach responded similarly in the photic
stimulation experiment. This finding, however, held only for the clinically normal group and not for the clinically anxious groups. In their
discussion the authors point out that, since the anxious subject was
likely to react to the Rorschach as a stressful situation and not at all
likely to so react to the photic stimulation, a greater discrepancy between flicker and Rorschach scores among anxious than among normal
would be expected. They further suggest that the tendency of the anxious subjects to "inhibit" the CF and C type of response to the Rorschach would tend to obscure relationships between the two measures.
If their anxious subjects did in fact tend to give relatively few color
responses, it would be in line with Eichler's finding that his stress
group had lower color scores than the non-stress group. It would also
be congruent with Kates' study, in which anxious patients gave significantly fewer color responses than another patient group. It is important to point out how in the photic stimulation study emphasis is
placed on the subject's conception of and reaction to the different situations. One may hope that in future studies this problem will always be
carefully evaluated and controlled.

CHANGING THE NATURE OF THE STIMULUS

The presumed influences of color on Rorschach responses go well
beyond what has been discussed in the previous section. Many of these
influences have been subsumed under the concept of "color shock," a

concept which apparently means different things to different workers as this quotation from Rockwell, Welch, Kubis, and Fisichelli (*124*) indicates:

References to color shock appear several times in the original monograph of Rorschach. In order to grasp his concept as it finally evolved, it is necessary to put together his scattered references. They are therefore quoted verbatim, as follows:

(p. 35) "In connection with the color answers, some subjects experience an unmistakable shock, an emotional and associative stupor of varying length when the colored plate VIII appears after the preceding black ones. These subjects suddenly become helpless although previously they had been interpreting very well."

(p. 182) "Neurotic subjects suffer color shock on encountering the colored plates. This is evidence of emotional suppression."

(p. 189) Plate VIII. "There was no response for quite a while. There is a lack of associations which appears when the color plates are presented. I designate this as color shock."

Plate IX. "There was a long pause as before; it was even longer on this plate. The subject explains 'I don't know, nothing much comes to me,' expressing the associative inhibition due to color shock."

(p. 193) "Color shock . . . invariably indicates neurotic repression of affect. Suppression of color responses as expressed in color shock is a pathognomonic sign of neurotic repression of affect, and hence a very valuable and specific diagnostic aid." The essence of the phenomenon of color shock he considered to be a lack of associations appearing when the color plates are presented. This he termed "an emotional and associative stupor," apparently using the word *stupor* according to part of its precise definition, i.e., "a state of non-responsiveness." In a similar manner, he apparently selected the word "shock," using it to delimit a psychological condition which he considered analogous to the neurophysiological condition called "shock," which is defined as "a sudden depression of the nervous system" or "a condition of lowered excitability." One might summarize the views of *Rorschach* as follows: color shock is a phenomenon which appears in certain subjects when the color plates are presented; the phenomenon consists in a state of associative and emotional non-responsiveness, more or less analogous to the condition of lowered excitability seen in neurophysiological shock; the presence of color shock is a pathognomonic indication that the subject is utilizing an unconscious psychoneurotic defense mechanism, viz. neurotic repression of affect.

Since the original concept of color shock was formulated by *Rorschach,* other workers have dealt with it variously. *Harrower-Erickson* includes in

her criteria for color shock, comment preceding response, unjustified anatomical and geographical answers, and senseless repetition. *Klopfer* and
*Kelley* define color shock as *any* disturbance in responses to the color plates,
and state that to the neurotic, the color seems to constitute a new and
catastrophic situation. (The only accepted scientific definition of "catas-
trophe" is a geological one, meaning a sudden violent physical change, such
as an upheaval of the earth's surface.) These authors accept as their criteria
for color shock, those described by *Brosin* and *Fromm,* among which are
the following: exclamations indicative of newly-aroused emotions; comment by the subject indicative of anxiety, tension, stress, newly mobilized
defense mechanisms, such as undue irritation, aggressiveness, passivity, etc.;
decline in the quality of the responses; impoverished content of responses;
irregular succession of responses on the color cards when the succession on
the non-color cards is orderly; and so on.

   *Bochner* and *Halpern* state that some people, in emotional situations,
(i.e., on seeing the color plates) experience a distinct shock which results in
some disorganization. Here the authors probably do not mean that type of
disorganization which occurs in the schizophrenic and organic psychoses;
exactly what they do mean is not clear. They go on to state that sometimes
color shock is manifested, not by an avoidance of color, but rather by a
flight into color, in which the individual, like a moth drawn to a flame,
gives numerous color answers, and an increased number of responses to
the color cards. This the authors consider to have a masturbatory quality.
(Oberholzer, in a personal communication, says that this last phenomenon
was also observed by *Rorschach,* who, however, never confused it with
color shock.) *Beck* says that *Rorschach* observed that the color figures presented to the subject at certain positions in the series produced a "startle,"
and that because color was the immediate stimulus, *Rorschach* called it
"color shock." This statement by *Beck* is erroneous. *Rorschach* never used
the term "startle" in connection with the phenomenon of color shock. To
startle means precisely "to cause a violent or sudden motor response, largely
reflex, and resembling a momentary fear." This bears no resemblance to
the "state of associative and emotional stupor" described by *Rorschach*. . . .

   If one compares the original formulation of *Rorschach* to those of contemporary workers, quoted above, it becomes apparent that what was once
a precise, specific, and highly valuable concept, has been expanded so far
beyond its original limits that it is now almost meaningless.

In recent years a number of studies relevant to the concept of color
shock have been reported in which achromatic and chromatic versions
of the cards have been compared. One of the first along these lines was
that of Lazarus (95). "One group was presented the standard Group

Rorschach. After a six weeks' delay, this group was tested again using the non-color version. The other group received the non-color test first, followed six weeks later by the standard Group Rorschach." In his statistical analyses Lazarus combined his data as follows:

Group 1   Color Version                    Non-Color Version

Group 2   Non-Color Version                Color Version

The reader should bear in mind this method of grouping data because of Siipola's critique to be discussed later (p. 170). The major findings were:

1. In general, the presumed indicators of color shock appeared as frequently in the achromatic as well as in the chromatic versions of the plates.

2. The appearance of "poor form answers" decreased significantly in the absence of color. "Further investigation brought out that the change occurred in the chromatic slides, and that nearly all of the F-minus answers that dropped out when the color had been deleted from the slides were actually FC and CF responses, that is, responses making direct use of color. Therefore, when color was deleted, the responses could not be given. Apparently, then, it was the attempt to integrate the color with the form into a response that produced the higher incidence of poor form quality in the color series."

3. "The slides varied very greatly in difficulty among themselves with respect to each 'shock' index. In several indices, many of the chromatic slides tend to be more difficult than the achromatic slides, irrespective of the presence of color." Card IX, for example, in both chromatic and achromatic versions was the card most frequently rejected or elicited the fewest number of responses and the greatest number of poor form responses.

A subsequent series of studies by Siipola and colleagues (155, 156, 157) has cast doubt on Lazarus' conclusions about the influence of color. The methodology of Siipola's first study (155) has already been presented on page 146. The major findings of the first study were:

1. The reaction time to the colored blots was significantly lengthened in contrast to their achromatic versions, a finding which Lazarus could not obtain because he used the group Rorschach. "In clinical practice

. . . the relative delay in reactions to colored blots is considered a symptom of aberrant reaction to color. Our results indicate that such delay is to be expected whenever color is present and can, hence, hardly be interpreted as a deviant type of reaction."

2. When the subjects were asked after their response to a blot, "How did you like this blot?" the presence of color increased the frequency of emotional accompaniments. "For the colored version of the blots both the pleasant and unpleasant reports showed a reliable increase, whereas the neutral reports decreased by half. . . . These results indicate, then, that colored blots are affect-laden in the sense that they are more likely to arouse emotional attitudes during the process of responding. Hence they lend support to the view that the longer reaction time for colored blots is attributable to associative blocking caused by emotionally charged stimuli. But there remains the question of why colored blots are affect-laden. The results obtained here indicate again that the answer is not to be found in terms of some intrinsic power by which certain hues arouse certain emotions. A study of the kind of emotional attitudes reported for each specific hue reveals a complete lack of consistency." It must again be pointed out that data on emotional attitudes are not ordinarily obtained with the group Rorschach.

3. In general the same conceptual content was given to the matched blots which differed only in color. "Study of the properties of those blots in which color produced striking differences in comparison with the properties of those in which it produced none led to the discovery of an important clue to the manner in which stimulus-color operates. Broadly stated, the underlying principle seems to be that the manner and degree to which the presence of color affects the content of the responses will depend upon whether the specific hue of the blot happens to be appropriate or inappropriate to the conceptual objects suggested by the form of the blot. For certain blots the form suggested conceptual objects with which the specific hue was incongruent, and in these cases striking changes in content appeared when color was added. For other items, the form of the blot suggested conceptual objects to which the specific hue was clearly appropriate, and in these cases few or no changes appeared."

In the case of those blots showing a high degree of hue-form incongruity, the presence of color usually affected the content in the following manner.

Color inhibited the development of certain form-favored concepts, concepts popular for the achromatic version, which in the case of these particular blots were inappropriate to the hue. And since the hue-form incongruity had to be resolved in some manner, color forced the development of other concepts more appropriate to the specific hue. These effects are shown in our data by the fact that color usually decreased reliably the frequency of categories popular in the norm while it increased reliably the frequency of other more congruent categories which show low or zero frequencies in the norm. The total result is a fundamental change in the nature of the content when color is added. Often the most popular category for the colored version of a blot is a completely different one from that which occurs most frequently in the achromatic version.

In the case of those blots showing a low degree of hue-form incongruity color had a very different effect. Here color did not interfere with, it tended instead to reinforce, the development of the same form-favored concepts popular with the norm-group. This is shown in the data by the fact that the frequency of categories popular in the norm was either reliably increased or showed no significant change. The total result here is that no fundamental change in the nature of the content occurs when color is added. The categories of content most popular for the achromatic version of a blot are as popular, or even more popular, for the chromatic version, and the other, less popular categories show no important change.

The generalizations stated above are subject to one important limiting condition, namely, they apply only to relatively unstructured blots. If a stimulus form is highly structured, color will normally have no effect upon the content of the conceptual responses, regardless of whether the hue happens to be congruent or incongruent with the form-favored responses.

Because of their clinical significance we feel it important to quote Siipola on the deviant reactions of some subjects to those blots with high hue-form incongruity. The blot numbers referred to by Siipola are to the "cut-out" and not the regular Rorschach blots.

". . . Occasionally, in about 20 per cent of the responses to the colored blots, the subjects react by producing a novel type of conceptual responses radically different from those elicited by the achromatic forms. As shown in the data . . . , a new category of content, completely absent from the achromatic norm, may appear for the colored version of a blot. These novel conceptualizations have a distinct flavor resembling that of certain symptoms commonly noted in situations which arouse difficulty, stress, conflict, or emotional involvement. They are similar to the long-recognized phenomena ("complex indicators") which occur in associative conflict and to the more recently recognized phenomena produced under conditions of perceptual stress. Such symptoms indicate behavioral disorganization and primitivation of the conceptual process, and their presence here primarily in connection with the incongruent blots suggests that severe stress and conflict may result from the difficulties in dealing with hue-form incongruity. In the case of these novel reactions, stimulus-color may be regarded as exerting a strong, disruptive influence—it creates a highly conflictful situation demanding drastic forms of resolution. Specific examples given below illustrate prominent varieties of these novel conceptual responses.

*Color associations.* This most frequent variety of novel concepts is typified by such responses as: *blood* or *fire* to a red blot; *sky* or *sea* to a blue blot; *gold, egg,* or *butter* to a yellow blot; *grass* to a green blot. Such responses seem to represent a superficial and facile resolution of the problem created by hue-form incongruity. The concepts achieved represent objects closely associated with the specific hues of the blots; these objects are so shapeless (or of so many shapes) that they are superficially appropriate to the form of almost any unstructured blot; the symbolic meanings of the concepts seem often expressive of the aggressive or regressive attitudes likely to be aroused in a stressful situation. The dynamics of this type of response seem closely similar to those of the associations to sound (rhyming and clang responses) given in word-association tests, where the subject, under stress, gives a superficial response which may appear appropriate only through its relation to an incidental feature of the total situation.

*Far-fetched concepts.* This is a relatively frequent type of response to those stimulus blots (8 and 13) which contain well-articulated subordinate details. The conceptual response is one suggested by some small part of the blot but inappropriate to the blot as a whole. For example, the orange-colored blot 8 was seen as a *lobster, crab,* or *crustacean* in 10 per cent of the cases. The achromatic version of this blot never elicited any of these responses, although the top detail by itself was often seen as the claw of a lobster. The decrease in detail responses when color is present . . . reflects the substitution of these far-fetched concepts for them. This type of conceptual reaction resembles the response to a syllable or part of the stimulus word in an association test.

*Combinative concepts.* This is a relatively rare and interesting type of response in which concepts ordinarily given separately are combined. Examples are, for blot 3 *finger with mercurochrome* and *bloody finger,* for blot 4 *rock-like frog,* and for blot 8 *bloody cloud.* This type of response suggests a conflict between tendencies set up by the form- and the color-properties of the blot, with resolution attempted through combining their separate products. When the combination yields a meaningless concept (e.g., *bloody cloud*), it resembles the "contamination response" of the Rorschach literature and the neologism of the word-association tests.

*Stereotypy.* The repetition of a previously given conceptual response, a symptom well-recognized in association tests, occurred much more commonly for the colored than for the achromatic blots. In the case of blot 13, for example, 7 per cent of the subjects gave *wishbone* as the response to the green version whereas none did so for the achromatic version. This response was a popular response to both versions of the preceding stimulus, blot 12. This manner of resolving the difficulty sometimes led to the giving of completely absurd and illogical responses, implying a real loss of control over the conceptual processes, a "surrendering of rationality."

*Rejections.* This type of reaction occurred more than twice as frequently for the colored as for the achromatic blots. . . . In these reactions the subject spontaneously announced her inability to make anything out of the blot; and in most instances she expressed feelings of helplessness, "mental blankness," and astonishment at the peculiar mental state experienced. The phenomena of rejection are obviously closely related to the familiar "failure to answer" in word-association tests, where failure is regarded as a symptom of associative blocking resulting from conflict.

It should be pointed out that Siipola's finding that color may increase the difficulty of the task, with a resultant stress reaction, is congruent with that of Lazarus (*95*) and Sarason and Potter (*142*).

In the second study Siipola, Kuhns, and Taylor (*156*) investigated the effects of color when the same subjects were successively exposed to matched versions of chromatic and achromatic blots.

An experimental group of subjects (Group *Col-Bk*) was presented with a colored series of blots (Series I) followed by an achromatic series of blots (Series II). Each series consisted of 20 items containing an equal number of critical and noncritical items. The 10 critical colored blots and the 10 critical matched achromatic blots were embedded in Series I and II respectively. The control group (Group *Bk-Bk*) was presented with two series of achromatic blots. The blots in Series I were achromatic duplicates of the colored items presented in Series I to the experimental group; blots in Series II were identical with those presented in Series II to the experimental group. In the case of the control group, then, the 10 particular items which were critical in Series I were repeated as critical items in Series II. In the case of each of the groups an interval of one month elapsed between the two series. Immediately following the second series, a simple recognition test was given to determine the extent to which the subjects recognized the items in the second series.

The general method of procedure, stimulus material, and instructions were similar to those used in our previous experiment. . . . In brief, simple isolated stimulus forms, rather than the complex forms of the Rorschach cards, were used as stimuli, and only the subject's first spontaneous conceptual response to the blots was selected for study. The subjects consisted of a random sampling of freshmen and sophomores in a women's college; there were 72 subjects in Group *Col-Bk* and 26 in Group *Bk-Bk*.

At the end of the second exposure the subjects were asked the following:

*General impression:* "While reacting to the blots today did you find any of the blots similar to or identical with the blots you saw last time?" If the answer to the question was affirmative, "How many did you actually recognize as being identical (except for color)?"

*Recognition test:* "Let us go through the blots again to check this point. I'll give you one second to look at each one. Tell me which ones you recognized as being identical (except for color) when you originally saw the blot today. I would also like to know if you recognize any blots now which you didn't notice before." Whenever a subject reported recognition of a specific blot, "Did you recognize this blot when you first saw it today or do you remember it only now?"

The answers to these questions revealed a significant difference between the two groups: The color-black group recognized fewer blots than the black-black group. "Since all conditions except the color variable were constant for the two groups, these differences in recognition results have to be attributed to the presence or absence of color in the primary series. The presence of hue in the blots in Series I for the Group Color-Black made it much more difficult for the subjects to recognize the matched achromatic mates in Series II than was the case when hue was absent in Series I."

. . . In a preliminary experiment a group of 15 subjects was exposed to the same experimental conditions as Group *Col-Bk* except for the fact that the order of the series was reversed; the achromatic series preceded the colored series. Under these conditions, no clear differences were obtained between the recognition results for this group and the control group. These data suggest the hypothesis that an achromatic blot leaves such a clear memory trace of its form that it is easily recognizable in a later colored version, whereas a colored blot leaves such an amorphous memory trace that it is much less recognizable in a later achromatic version.

In addition, these authors found that the group which first was exposed to the colored series changed their responses on the second series significantly in contrast to the group which was exposed twice to the black series. Siipola's critique of Lazarus' design (p. 164) follows:

Lazarus designed his experiment to determine whether the presence of color in the Rorschach Test influences the results in various scoring categories. Unfortunately, his study did not deal with "color responses" and reaction time, the phenomena which we have found most likely to show the effects of color. However, the fact that color had little or no effect upon the phenomena studied stands in direct contrast with our results.

To understand the discrepancy between our results and those of Lazarus, one must be familiar with the materials and method used in his research. The materials consisted of the so-called "Color Series" in which the 10 standard Rorschach cards (5 colored and 5 uncolored) were presented and the "Noncolor Series" in which these 10 cards were all presented in achromatic form. The same subjects were used for these two series, and hence the technique involved the extraneous variable of primacy or memory. The standard method of counterbalancing the order of the series was used to equalize the effect of the memory factor upon the two series; one half of the subjects started with the Color Series and the other half with the Noncolor Series. Throughout, the data were handled by combining the results obtained from these two orders. Thus the total measure for each "series" combined the results obtained from one group of subjects upon whom the memory variable had a strong influence with those from another group upon whom there could have been no influence of memory.

The main difficulty with this experimental design arises from the use of the standard method of handling an extraneous variable when the same subjects are used in two series. This method allows for the use of subjects with strong memory influence for one half of the cases in each series. Recognition by this half of the subjects of most of the items in the second series may in itself account for the similarity of the results for the Color Series and the Noncolor Series. We have inferred that for these subjects the recognition level for the blots in the second series must have been high, despite the use of a long time interval between series, because of the following experimental conditions: use of the complete unique Rorschach blots which are more distinctly recognizable than simple forms; use of identical blots (the five achromatic Rorschach cards) rather than different blots for noncritical items in the two series; use of a relatively long period of exposure for each stimulus item. Our data indicate that the standard method happens to be inappropriate here as a method of controlling the memory factor; uniform *reduction* of the strength of the memory factor for all subjects, rather than *equalization* of its average strength at a relatively high level of recognition, is more likely to yield identifiable color effects.

By counterbalancing the order of the series, another condition was introduced, which further reduced the chances of obtaining different results for the two series. Our preliminary experiments showed that subjects using the order *black-color,* in contrast to *color-black,* had high recognition of the critical items and failed to show reliable differences in content between chromatic and achromatic blots. On the basis of our data it is apparent that for those subjects who started with the Noncolor Series the memory factor could have operated so strongly that it masked completely the effects of color. Hence the use of the method of counterbalanced series turns out to be peculiarly inappropriate to this problem in which practice effects are not equal for the two orders of presentation.

In the principal statistical treatment of the data the effects of color are necessarily obscured. The results for the five Rorschach achromatic blots are included in the total figures given for both the Color Series and the Noncolor Series. This amounts to adding what might be considered control data to what should be considered the experimental data, those obtained from the five Rorschach color cards. Actually proper control data are not available since it is impossible to determine what the effects would have been for successive presentation of achromatic versions of the critical Rorschach color cards. Hence the critical evidence to prove that color does not influence performance on the Rorschach Test is lacking.

A study of Dubrovner, Von Lackum, and Jost (37), using a design similar to that of Lazarus, supports Siipola's finding that order of presentation of the regular and photographically reproduced achromatic blots is an important variable. They found that in the group receiving the regular series first productivity *increased* in nine of the ten cards. In the group receiving first the reproduced achromatic series productivity *decreased* in all ten cards. In the case of reaction time for the first response there was a decrease in reaction time on all ten cards in the group receiving the reproduced series first while in the other group no change was discernible. In light of this study and those of Siipola, the studies of other investigators (3, 5, 113, 124, 134) in which the order of presentation was not controlled must be viewed with caution. *With this caution in mind,* in addition to the findings of other studies (106, 168), the following tentative conclusions might be drawn from our discussion:

1. Many of the so-called signs of color shock do not appear to be a function of color *per se*.

2. Color shock indices seem to appear as frequently in normal as in neurotic individuals.

3. The Rorschach cards differ markedly in difficulty when criteria such as reaction time, productivity, and rejection are utilized. Card IX tends to be most frequently rejected and elicits a long reaction time. Card X likewise elicits a long reaction time. Card VII, an achromatic card, likewise elicits a long reaction time, as does card VI.

4. In general the presence of color tends to increase reaction time.

5. In general the presence of color tends to produce both positive and negative emotional accompaniments.

6. Color can produce a hue-form incongruity which results in poor form or some other aberrant reaction.

THE INDIVIDUAL CASE

When interpreting the record of an individual it is the obligation of the clinician to avoid using assumptions which, although stated with frequency and authority in the textbooks, have little or no basis in the research literature. The fact that many clinicians are not researchers does not absolve them from critically evaluating the research literature on the instruments they employ in practice. We make these statements because of our impression that many clinicians utilize the Rorschach in a way that suggests an uncritical acceptance of traditional assumptions. The interpretive significance of color responses is a case in point. Although the research evidence strongly indicates that many generalizations made on the basis of the color categories have low validity, too frequently behavioral characteristics are attributed to an individual solely on the basis of the FC, CF, C categories. But the research findings do provide a basis which can guide the clinician in evaluating an individual's responses to the color cards whether color is associated with the content of the response or not.

1. An individual whose CF + C responses markedly outweigh his FC responses *may* be one who reacts impulsively, but the question facing the clinician is whether the impulsiveness is a general characteristic manifested in many situations or one which shows up when the individual is under stress. To decide between these alternatives the

following questions must be asked: (a) Were the CF and C responses given *in the test situation* in a manner which the clinician judges was impulsive? (b) Were the FC responses of poor form? (c) Do the non-color responses (in the colored *and* non-colored cards) also show a tendency for the form to be indefinite or poor in terms of reality testing? (d) Does the individual conceive of and react to the situation as if it were a *non*-stressful one? If these questions can be answered in the affirmative, then one might characterize the individual as one who in this situation tended to react consistently in an impulsive manner and one who in many other situations may react unreflectively. If the individual conceived of the situation as stressful, then one might limit one's prediction to a certain class of stress situations.

2. In the case of an individual who gives markedly poorer responses to the colored than to the non-colored cards, the most likely explanation may be one or a combination of the following: the elicitation of affective associations, hue-form incongruity, and a rigid set. If the content of the responses to the colored cards differs discernibly from that of the responses to the non-colored cards—especially if the content is "unpleasant"—the poor responses may reflect the inability to inhibit or "control" the emotional reaction in a way so as not to interfere with efficient functioning. In many instances there is no clear difference between the content to the colored and non-colored cards. Janis and Janis (*82*) have suggested that a free association technique employed following the standard administration may be a clinically valuable way to discriminate between the emotional significances of different contents. Their case presentations indicate that the technique deserves consideration by the clinician because it may make for more valid conclusions. It is difficult to indicate how hue-form incongruity may be recognized. One can only say that research along these lines is very necessary. It may be, for example, that some kind of post-test interview procedure might be helpful. By "rigid set" reference is made to those cases who conceive of the problem as one in which the whole card has to be used. Since it is more difficult (*15*) to give W responses to the colored cards, the persistent attempt to do so may result in responses of poor quality.

It should be pointed out, *ad nauseam* perhaps, that underlying these suggestions is the importance attached to determining the subject's conception of the situation and his behavior during it. In later pages of this book when case analyses are presented we will return again to the problems discussed above.

INTERPRETIVE SIGNIFICANCE OF THE BLACK AND WHITE COLOR RESPONSES

Traditionally this category of response has been separated from the bright colors because it presumably reflects different emotional reactions. Klopfer (92, p. 243) maintains that when the C′ categories (the black color being used far more frequently than the white) and texture categories (Fc, cF, c) outnumber the bright color responses, depressive tendencies are present. He also points out the following (92, p. 243) :[4]

C′ responses are found mainly in two situations. First, they occur in records of subjects with a very rich and variegated reaction to all sorts of stimuli from without. This combination clearly represents an artistic impressionability. Second, they may represent a "burnt child" reaction, the reaction of people who are basically responsive to emotional stimulation from outside but have experienced a series of traumatic experiences. Such subjects tend to withdraw from the "hot" bright-colored area into the safer realm of the less affective gray, black, and white hues.

The white, gray, and black surface colors used in an artistic record are often part of a bright color combination, like the white porcelain of a gayly decorated vase. In such cases it is unlikely that the use of achromatic color has any significance as an indication of depression. Such achromatic colors, forming a significant part within a concept, like snow in a colored landscape, may indicate some cold or frigid element in an otherwise warm-blooded personality.

Whenever a concept is chosen wholly because of its achromatic color, it would appear that the subject is interested in the less colorful aspects of life. Where the subject has a pronounced tendency to look for black, gray, or white objects rather than for bright ones, even when he is especially asked in testing the limits to use the color, a depressive tendency reveals itself beyond any doubt.

There is no research evidence to support most of the above contentions. While it is probably true that in our culture black is considered an unpleasant color and is associated with unpleasant situations, it does not follow that any excessive use of the black color in the Rorschach necessarily indicates depression or unpleasant affect, a point

[4] B. Klopfer and D. Mc. Kelley, *The Rorschach Technique.* Copyright 1942 and 1946 by World Book Company.

which Klopfer recognizes. It should also be noted that responses to the bright colors are frequently unpleasant ("blood," "bleeding bodies," "the red is a symbol of evil"). Whether the C' categories reflect depressive feelings can be determined only if the content of such responses is congruent with such an interpretation and if similar content is not given to the color cards. *In our opinion there is no justification for a separate C' category. Like the bright colors, black and white are properties of the external stimulus and should be scored and interpreted in the same way, a suggestion which is in keeping with Wittenborn's factor analysis of Rorschach responses (179).* The fact that some individuals give a particular kind of content to the black is as little justification for a separate scoring category as if one were to score responses to the red color separately because some people give a certain content to it.

We would like at this point to raise a question which has not been studied systematically. What is the significance of the total absence of any kind of color response? Since color (chromatic or achromatic) is an objective property of the external referent and the sequence of card presentation emphasizes that the cards are differently colored, what is the behavioral significance of the absence of any color responses? We would offer the following hypotheses:

Failure to respond with any color response does not necessarily indicate failure to be aware of the fact that the cards are colored. Failure does indicate that an *obvious* characteristic of the external stimulus was not incorporated into the formal responses. In other words, the individual's overt responsiveness was less affected by the obvious characteristic of the blots than by other factors. The individual who does not respond to *and* incorporate color in any of his responses is one whose responsiveness is determined more by internal than by external factors, and whose responsiveness changes less with changes in the external stimulus situation in comparison to those who do respond to and incorporate the obvious color characteristics of the cards in their responses. A further hypothesis would be that such individuals would also respond less spontaneously in interpersonal interactions in the sense that spontaneous expression of feeling would not be characteristic.

To test these hypotheses it would be necessary to study two groups: one which gives no color responses and one which gives many (bright and dark color responses grouped together). It would also be important that the two groups be similar in terms of total productivity to the Rorschach since differences in total number of responses might well be the crucial factor. If one assumes that these groups differ behaviorally, one would predict that their conception of and reaction to the testing situation would differ when independent measures of such attitudes are obtained. A non-test behavioral measure might be one in which the individual is observed in an interpersonal interaction by judges who are not aware of the group to which the individual belongs.

COLOR AND THE VARIABLES IN THE CLINICAL SITUATION

Few aspects of research with the Rorschach point up the significance of the variables in the clinical situation as clearly as do studies of the role of color. The nature of the instructions, variations in the nature of the stimulus materials, differences in the psychologist variable, the purposes of the interaction, attitudinal factors related to previous learning —these are the factors which we have had to consider in the attempt to evaluate the significance of the various studies. What perhaps deserves most emphasis is the fact that such an attempt quickly encounters the obstacle that the different investigators recognize and take account of these variables in differing degrees. That some investigators do not take them into account, either in design of the study or in the drawing of conclusions, can only be deplored. For example, as we pointed out earlier, the fact that in one study the experimenter was a male while in the "replication" it was a female is likely to obfuscate the issues rather than clarify them.

One cannot underestimate the impact on practice and research with the Rorschach of those studies, beginning with that of Lazarus (95), which involved *changing the nature of the stimulus materials*. In previous years a wide range of phenomena had been attributed to the fact that the cards were colored in particular ways. Not until the stimulus materials were deliberately altered did it become apparent that many of these phenomena were largely a function of stimulus characteristics other than color. It also has become apparent that the results of such studies have made more complex the clinician's task of understanding the significances of an individual's behavior to the Rorschach. The clinician's task will become even more complex when the other variables are systematically investigated, but one can predict that his conclusions will have greater validity than they now have.

PROBLEMS IN THE INQUIRY

Very frequently a subject will say, "The red (or the blue or the green, etc.) is a . . ." In most of these instances the mentioned color is not regarded as a characteristic of the content but is verbalized in order to tell the clinician the area of the blot being utilized for the response. Although the individual is obviously aware of the color, it is not scored because it is not a characteristic of the content given.

The student frequently feels perturbed when an individual's verbalization does not in any way mention or refer to color although that response is frequently given with color spontaneously mentioned as a characteristic. For example, an individual may give a response "butterfly" or "flower" or "worms" and not use any word which indicates that the color is being utilized as a characteristic of the response, even though the clinician and others have gotten the same response to the same area with the color being explicitly used. In such instances to ask further questions because the subject may be using color is to introduce a selective factor in the questioning because one can undoubtedly find other responses in the record where color may have been used but where further questioning was not attempted. The more one's questions are determined by considerations of what the subject may have utilized for his response—even though his verbalizations give no appropriate clue—the more will the inquiry resemble an inquisition and the less will the scoring reflect the subject's spontaneous behavior. The following is an example of a response for which a second question seems justified:

|  Performance  |  Inquiry  |
|---|---|
| CARD III  Two waiters | (Standard first question)  Here is the head, the arms, and the legs. |

In the inquiry the subject does not indicate why he spontaneously said *waiters* and not some other kind of person. Here it seems justified to ask: "Why *waiters*?" It was to this second question that the subject mentioned the white collar and black uniform. When a subject's verbalization in the inquiry does not explain what he spontaneously said in the performance, a second question seems justified. This second question is not determined by what the subject may have seen but by what he said he did see. Another example of where a second question seems justified follows:

CARD II  Two clowns (whole re-           (Standard first question)  They look
sponse)                                        funny the way they are posturing
                                               with their hands together, as if
                                               they are going through a comedy
                                               routine. And, of course, the cos-
                                               tumes they are wearing.

Here the subject has used a word, "costumes," which may refer to the color. If this word had not been verbalized, no further questioning would be justified. In answer to the question "What do you mean by 'the costumes'?" the subject described the black and red outfit they were wearing.

Card X often elicits responses which present scoring problems. For example, an individual may say, "The whole thing is a colorful forest scene." In the inquiry the individual points out trees, shrubs, and various kinds of animals. One question that might arise in the student's mind is whether the whole response is an FC or CF. Since "a colorful forest scene" does not belong to a class of objects or events with a definite configuration of form, the scoring would be CF. ("An under-water scene" and "a surrealist painting" would be other examples of CF scoring.) It is clear, however, that while the CF may reflect the indefinite form given to the whole card, it does not reflect either the definite forms described in the inquiry or the fact that many usual details were used for the discrete objects. The *main* scoring would be:

$$W \qquad\qquad CF$$

The discrete forms which are newly described in the inquiry are reflected in what is known as *additional* scores:

$$W \quad\Big\{ \qquad\qquad CF$$
$$D \quad\Big\{ \qquad\qquad\qquad F$$

The indented second line indicates that the response was to a usual area and was first mentioned in the inquiry. *One adds as many lines as there are discrete responses in the inquiry.* The bracket signifies that these discrete responses were integrated into one whole response. The F, which means that only the outline form of the area was used, could as well be CF or FC or any other scoring to be discussed in subsequent chapters.

The "two clowns" response given earlier presents a different scoring problem. The M in the scoring stands for the human movement aspect of the response and, for reasons to be discussed later, is scored first.

W      M, FC, FC'

Because the black and red colors are used as characteristics of a single object with a definite configuration of form (i.e., the human form), the scoring is FC and FC' rather than CF or C'F. Traditionally the M is considered as the main score while the FC and FC' are additional scores. If to all of card II an individual said, "Two people fighting with blood dripping from their bodies" the scoring would be

W      M, CF

The CF scoring reflects "the blood dripping from their bodies"—unlike the colored costumes the blood is not seen as part of the human form and because the form is clearly secondary it is scored as an additional CF. If an individual were to give a response "a man's face that is all red because it is completely covered with blood," the scoring would be FC because the blood now describes a content with a definite form. The "dripping blood" did not describe such a content even though, in one sense, it was associated with such a content (the human form).

There are times when the student will be indecisive about how to score a particular response. His uncertainty may be due to the failure to ask a justifiable question or to difficulty in deciding whether the content belongs to a class of objects with definite or indefinite form characteristics. If uncertainty is due to inadequate questioning, the student poses an impossible problem for himself if he tries to decide what the subject "really" meant. If the subject is available for recall, his answers to further questions cannot be taken as having the same significance as if they had been given at the appropriate time. If the subject is unavailable for recall, one cannot justify spending a great deal of time cogitating about one response. The student should make the best possible "guess" he can—he has no alternative. Under careful supervision the number of problems arising from inadequate questioning should markedly decrease. If the student's uncertainty is due to difficulty in deciding whether the content belongs to a class of objects with definite or indefinite form characteristics, he should consult his colleagues and decide by the consensus. In any one record the number of times this problem arises is relatively small. Since no one has ever demonstrated that a difference of one in a scoring category—for example, the difference between 3 FC and 4 FC or between 2 CF and 3 CF—is a difference which makes a difference, the student should not plague himself if he is uncertain how to score a particular response.

PRIORITY IN SCORING

Traditionally when a response contains human movement as well as other factors (color, shading, etc.) the human movement (M) is scored first (the main score) and the other factors are scored as additional. If M is absent and bright color appears with other "determinants," it is the bright color which is scored first. The priority which is given to movement and bright color is a reflection of the importance traditionally attached in interpretation to the frequency of each of these categories as well as their relationship to each other. As we have seen in this chapter, and as we shall see in subsequent ones, there is little justification for such an emphasis. When in the last part of this book we discuss the process of the interpretation of an individual protocol in its relation to the frequencies of the various scoring categories, we shall see that the problem of priority is of little importance. The usual practice in research is to adhere to some priority system and to give less weight to additional than to main scores. In the case of the white space (S) response Fonda (47) found practically no relationship between the frequency of main and additional S scores. In fact, he found that combining the main and additional scores reduced the reliability of the S score. Cox and Sarason (31) found that in connection with certain shading categories the use of additional scores had a similar effect. Until more is known about the reliability of additional scores they should be used in research with caution.

## Chapter 12

# THE EXTERNAL REFERENT: SHADING

LIKE color, shading or texture is a characteristic of the external stimulus. By shading is meant that the blot area is not seen as homogeneously colored but as having color nuances. Shading is scored when in the subject's verbalization the color nuances, which may be variations of bright or dark colors, are described as a characteristic of the content or when they are used to explain a particular configuration of form.

SCORING

1. Fc is scored when the subject's verbalization indicates that the shading is a characteristic of a content with a definite configuration of form. Examples follow.

CARD II (D). A dog. You can see his wool-like fur. (When a subject uses words like "wool" and "fur" it does not necessarily mean that he refers to the shading of the blot area. Some subjects refer to the jaggedy outline, and shading in the sense of color nuances is not a factor. When the subject uses these and similar words, he should be asked, "What do you mean *fur?*" No further questioning is justified.)

CARD IV (W). A bearskin rug (body parts pointed out). (This is a frequent response and in his answer to the first standard question in the inquiry the subject usually verbalizes spontaneously that "rug" was associated with the shading. However, some subjects will merely point out the parts and leave unexplained why he initially said bearskin or rug. In these instances one can ask: "Why a *rug?*" or "Why a *bearskin?*")

CARD IV (Dd—in addition to the top center D the subject used surrounding areas). A man's face. You can see his bushy eyebrows and eyes which look half closed. (Although the subject did not too clearly verbalize in the inquiry the use of shading, in her tracing she very carefully indicated that the nuances of color were responsible for the "bushy" and "half-closed" characteristics. Occasionally one obtains a response in which shading is not mentioned but the content is described in a manner so as to indicate that the particular blot area is not being seen as a flat surface—

181

as if the differences in shading are related to differences in depth. These may be instances of where differences in shading are used to produce a particular configuration of form although the shading is not a descriptive characteristic of the content.)

CARD VIII (bottom D). Flower petals, perhaps of an orchid. (In the inquiry the subject said, "The colors of it. The way the colors run into each other." When asked, "What do you mean 'the colors run into each other'?" the subject said, "It is not all one color because at some points they shade into each other." The scoring would be D, FC, Fc. The shading is scored in the additional column because color is traditionally scored in the main column when it appears in connection with shading. Also, the color characteristic was spontaneously verbalized whereas the shading was elicited after a second question.)

CARD IV (center bottom D). An alligator's head. You can see his eyes and the rough skin alligators have. (When asked "Why *rough?*" the subject said: "You can see the ridges in his skin from the coloring." This is an example of where a word like "coloring" does not refer to the particular color of the area as descriptive of the content but to the nuances in the color.)

2. The cF refers to those responses in which the shading is a characteristic of a content with an indefinite configuration of form. Responses such as "animal rug" or "skins" in which no specific form characteristics (e.g., legs, head part) are mentioned would be cF. "A dried up leaf which is beginning to curl up" was a response in which the subject intended no particular form but where the differences in the shading were given as the reason for the "curled up" effect—the area not being seen as a homogeneously colored, flat surface.

3. The c category refers to those responses in which the shading is a characteristic of a content in which form is presumably absent as judged by the verbalizations. Responses like "wool" or "mud" in which nothing but the shading is mentioned in the performance or inquiry would be examples of c. If in the inquiry the subject said about "mud" that "it looks streaky and mixed up like mud and the black is the right color too," the scoring would be c, C'—shading being scored before achromatic color when they appear in combination.

Klopfer (*92*, p. 125), who on the basis of Binder's work (*20*) introduced the scoring of Fc, cF, and c in this country, utilizes three other scoring categories:

1. When shading is associated with an impression of diffusion, such

as in "clouds" and "smoke," the scoring is K (where no form aspect is verbalized) or KF (where some form aspect is mentioned). The K or KF responses are by their nature vague and indefinite in form.

2. When shading is associated with an impression of depth or distance, the scoring is FK. The scoring of this category is probably unreliable because many times when the subject verbalizes the impression of distance ("people far away," "mountains in the distance") he never mentions shading, and frequently it appears that it is the contrast in size between the small area used for the response and the large unused portion that is responsible for the verbalized impression.

3. When shading is associated with "x-rays" or "topographical or relief maps" the scoring may be Fk, kF, or k.

These categories appear relatively infrequently in records and when they do their frequency is low. Although each presumably has a somewhat different diagnostic significance, as we shall see below the validity of these presumed significances has yet to be demonstrated. As in the case of the C and C' categories we see little justification for scoring the above three categories (K, FK, k) apart from the c categories.

THE INTERPRETIVE SIGNIFICANCE OF SHADING

The student who has begun to read the Rorschach literature has undoubtedly become aware that his speed of reading has suffered from the fact that different writers use different scoring symbols for the same response. This is more evident in the case of shading than in any other scoring category, a situation which is further complicated by the fact that it is not always clear whether the various writers are attributing the same significance to the same response although the scoring symbols differ. Hertz (73) made a valiant effort to compare systematically the different scorings and significances of shading responses, and the serious student is urged to read her article. The student cannot avoid the unenviable task of familiarizing himself with the "different languages" in order to translate from one scoring system to another as he goes along.

The following statements are based on Hertz's (75) discussions of the interpretive significance of the shading categories.

1. The Fc, cF, c, and FK categories each "give an index of degree of sensitivity, cautiousness, and watchful adaptability." When these responses are weighted so that those with indefinite form are given more

weight than responses with definite form, "the higher the score, the more unfree, anxious and guarded the adaptability, the more sensitive and insecure the individual and the more intense the inferiority feelings."

2. When these categories are combined and the weighted score of the indefinite form responses exceeds that of those with definite form, the more the former exceeds the latter "the more dysphoric the tones, the more the individual suffers from insecurity and inferiority consciousness, the more unfree, anxious and depressed the attitudes, and the less controlled the disturbance aroused by these feelings."

3. When the diffusion or K type of response is also evaluated, as Hertz evaluates but Klopfer does not, on the basis of definite or indefinite form, the more the indefinite forms predominate "the more negative the anxiety score, the more uncontrolled and oppressive the anxiety, and the deeper the depression to the point of resignation and apathy."

4. "Since all these shading scores reflect some anxious mood, either more peripheral feelings or deeper and more central moods, a general shading factor designated Sh has been developed as a general anxiety indication." This factor is reflected in a score in which *any* shading response in which form is primary (e.g., Fc) is given a weight of 0.5; when form is secondary, 1.0; and when form is absent, 1.5. This score is considered "an index of an adaptation which is unfree, cautious, and guarded, either conditioned by inferiority consciousness and insecurity or dictated by deep anxiety and subject to depression."

It is interesting to note that Hertz's Sh factor does not in essence depend on the traditional scoring categories of shading. *All* shading responses receive a weight depending on whether shading is a characteristic of a definite or an indefinite form—a practice which is supported by Wittenborn's (179) factor analysis of Rorschach responses.

Using the above types of Rorschach measures, as well as many others considered indicative of anxiety and depression, Hertz (75, 76) compared the Rorschachs of suicidal and non-suicidal patients as well as a group of normal subjects. She emphasizes that configurations and not isolated Rorschach factors were utilized in the study. She (75) also emphasizes "that while various patterns in each configuration have been identified and numbered, there is no intention to apply a rapid quantitative scale of interpretation. The manipulation of the patterns and the final determination of whether a configuration is present or not in a record depends upon the subjective estimate of the interpreter, which in turn is influenced by his skill, training and intuitive sense." Although Hertz concludes that many of these configurations differentiated her groups, it is very difficult to state, in light of her explicit statement about subjectivity, which configurations were crucial—especially since they were by no means mutually exclusive.

The fact that differences among examiners make for differences in their interpretation of a protocol is sufficient justification for studies which aim to determine in as objective and *communicable* a fashion as possible the differences in validity among the Rorschach signs, factors, or configurations which are employed by the clinician. Without these studies one will never be in the position to judge what is or is not valid, unless one wants to use the unsatisfactory criterion of the clinician's subjective judgments. That these studies may not be considered appropriate tests of the clinician's procedures may be due as much to the clinician's failure to state his interpretive procedure in a testable form as to the researcher's clinical naïveté. If the clinician refuses to accept the results of these studies because they are presumably inadequate tests of his procedure, one can only suggest that he clearly state the kind of scientific research which would be appropriate. The fact that the clinician maintains that a Rorschach interpretation is based not on isolated Rorschach factors but on their configuration should not obscure the fact that these configurations utilize presumably discrete scoring categories which have differing behavioral significances; otherwise there would be no need for separate categories. Researches which attempt to evaluate the differences among the separate scoring categories cannot, therefore, be summarily dismissed.

In a study of state hospital patients Wittenborn and Mettler (*185*) utilized a Rorschach score which is similar to Hertz's Sh factor. This score, which they term an index of "lack of perceptual control," is given below.

$$\frac{\Sigma\,(W + C + CF + C' + C'F + K + KF + k + kF + c + cF)}{R}$$

With the exception of W, CF, and C the scoring categories are those which are given the greatest weight in Hertz's Sh factor. The inclusion of W, CF, and C was based on a previous study (*179*) which indicated that they had a factorial composition very similar to responses in the other categories in the above formula. It is obvious that this score indicates the degree to which shading, chromatic, and achromatic color responses have contents which are of vague, indefinite, or "loose" form. The following is from Wittenborn and Mettler (185):

The present report describes two attempts to relate the lack of perceptual control score to events or variables outside the psychological testing situation. In the literature concerning frontal lobe surgery, particularly frontal lobe surgery as applied to animals as distinguished from man, observers have frequently described a change in behavior which seemingly is related to the lack of perceptual control concept applied to the Rorschach factor. It has been said that after frontal lobe surgery that animals are more distractible than they were formerly and that their behavior was less characterized by long sequences of integrated activity than formerly. Similar descriptive statements have been made concerning mental hospital patients who have been treated by psychosurgery. At any rate in an earlier study the writers predicted that after psychosurgery patients would show an increase in the lack of perceptual control score. In order to test this, both operated and control patients were examined on two occasions with the Rorschach and the respective lack of perceptual control scores computed. Among the operated patients there were increases in lack of perceptual control scores and among the non-operated patients there were decreases (presumably a result of familiarity with the Rorschach cards); the difference in knowledge and direction of changes between the operated and control groups was statistically significant. This correspondence between common beliefs concerning a change following psychosurgery and the implications of the lack of perceptual control score suggest that the lack of perceptual control score is related to the aspect of behavior in question.

It was possible to evaluate the lack of perceptual control score in a second respect. The sample comprised forty schizophrenic patients, each of whom had been hospitalized for a total period of at least three years and were considered suitable candidates for psychosurgery. All of these patients were rated by psychiatrists on a set of symptom rating scales. These rating scales have been described elsewhere and may be scored in a fashion such as to result in nine syndrome scores.[1] These syndrome scores were based on factor analyses of large samples of patients and actually refer to empirically demonstrable clusters among the 55 psychiatric symptoms which comprise the set of rating scales. Accordingly, for this sample of forty patients the

---

[1] The references for these studies (180, 181, 183) have been included in the bibliography of the present book.

lack of perceptual control score was correlated with the score for each of the symptom cluster or syndrome scores. The syndrome scores are organized so that the high scores represent numerous and severe symptoms whereas the low scores represent a relative lack of the type of pathology basic to the syndrome or symptom cluster in question.

TABLE 9.  The Correlations Between the Syndrome Scores and the Rorschach Lack of Perceptual Control Score (Wittenborn and Mettler, *185*)

| Syndrome | Correlations |
| --- | --- |
| 1. Manic | −.12 |
| 2. Schizophrenic excitement | −.30 |
| 3. Acute anxiety | −.19 |
| 4. Depressed | −.37[a] |
| 5. Paranoid schizophrenia | −.25 |
| 6. Paranoid condition | −.09 |
| 7. Conversion hysteria | .27 |
| 8. Phobic compulsive | −.24 |
| 9. Hebephrenic or "deteriorated" schizophrenia[b] | −.42[a] |

[a] Significant at 5% level.
[b] The combination of symptoms that comprises this cluster suggests "deteriorated" patient of the hebephrenic type.

Table 9 shows the correlations between scores on the various symptoms and the Rorschach score of lack of perceptual control. The correlation of −.37 supports Hertz's findings concerning the relationship between depressive feelings and the Sh factor, even though categories (CF, C) were included which traditionally have not been considered relevant for anxiety and depression. On the assumption that the lack of perceptual control score and Hertz's overall Sh factor are similar, the correlations in Table 9 do not support the conclusion that the Sh factor is *specific* for those cases with marked feelings of depression—witness the significant correlation between lack of perceptual control score and high score on the hebephrenic cluster of symptoms.[2] It should be pointed out that the lack of perceptual control score, as well as Hertz's emphasis on an overall shading score, does not permit one to decide whether the individual categories of which they are composed contribute equally to the total score. It *may* be that the individual cate-

[2] It is interesting to note, as Wittenborn indicates, that the one positive correlation in Table 9 is in the case of those patients whose intellectual efficiency and reality testing are relatively unimpaired.

gories have similar behavioral significances and that their separation from each other in scoring is unnecessary. By using separate categories one assumes they in some way have different behavioral significances, an assumption for which good evidence is lacking. In addition, since the overall scores are based on far more responses than are found in any one of the scoring categories, they are probably far more likely to correlate significantly with a criterion measure.

Eichler (*38*) has reported a study of the relation between Rorschach indices of anxiety and experimentally induced anxiety in a group of college students.

*Apparatus*

One of the important conditions defining the stress situation was the administration of electric shocks. . . . The sponge rubber electrodes were thoroughly moistened in saline solution and attached to S's left cheek and wrist with strips of adhesive tape. All of the actual apparatus for shock administration was screened from S's view.

Visible to the S was a panel, on which were mounted a number of binding posts, a fuse, an "off-on" switch, and three variable knobs labeled "motor," "lamp" and "intensity." The binding posts under the heading "high resistance" were labeled "ohms" and numbered from 50 to 1500. To the side of this panel a double-throw five-pole knife switch was prominently displayed. A group of insulated wires ran from the switch to the panel and appeared to be connected with the rest of the apparatus by wires leading behind the screen. Actually the switch and panel were not connected to any electrical source and were used solely for their suggestive effects.

The S sat in a chair directly to the side of a table on which the aforementioned pieces of electrical equipment were placed. In appearance and construction the chair suggested an "electric chair." A wide seat and high back were made of black insulating fiber board. Attached to the front of either arm was a small aluminum globe. A web belt 1 in. wide was fastened over the arms of the chair, in safety-belt fashion, after S was seated. Two shorter belts of similar width were used to fasten the S's legs to the front legs of the chair.

Also used for their suggestive effects were two dummy silver electrodes, the size of a dime and quarter respectively, a helmet, and an electric phonograph motor. The metal electrodes were attached to S's right cheek and wrist with strips of adhesive tape. The helmet consisted of a web belt to which was attached one large metal strip (extending over the subject's forehead) and two 1-in. metal squares (one on each side of S's head). Wires from the silver electrodes and the two metal squares ran toward the five-pole switch and appeared to be connected to the wires leading behind the screen. The phonograph motor, concealed behind the screen, was used to provide a continuous hum, just barely audible, suggesting to S that the complex electrical equipment was in operation.

*Procedure*

The entire experiment was divided into two sessions. During the first session all apparatus was hidden from view. The Behn-Rorschach was administered according to the procedure outlined by Beck for administering the Rorschach test, with the exception that a card was withdrawn with the remark, "All right, let us go on to the next one," after ten responses had been given to it. The test was scored using Hertz's scoring symbols. In computing the scores for each of the symbols used, each main response was counted as 1 and each additional scoring counted as 0.5.

Two groups of Ss were then formed by matching Ss individually on the following five items:

a. Number of responses.

b. Sum of weighted shading responses.

c. Presence or absence of card rejections.

d. Presence or absence of time delay on shading cards (delay defined as initial reaction time longer than the mean initial reaction time plus one average deviation).

e. Experience balance category (*constricted* type—number of M responses, one or less, and sum of weighted color responses, one or less; *dilated* type—number of M responses, four or more, and sum of weighted color responses, four or more; *average* type—that M/*sum* C ratio not falling in the constricted or dilated categories).

The two groups were also equated in respect to the following group means:

a. Number of human movement responses.

b. Number of weighted color responses.

c. Age.

d. College year.

e. Cumulative grade point average.

The groups were then randomly assigned to the stress or control conditions.

The median time interval elapsing between the first and second sessions for the experimental (stress) group was 19 days, with a range of 11 to 36 days. For the control (non-stress) group, the median time interval was 20 days, with a range of 11 to 37 days.

*Stress group.* Upon entering the room for the second session each S in the stress group was seated in the "electric chair" and the two sponge electrodes were applied to the upper left cheek and the under-surface of the left wrist, respectively. The following statement was then made:

You are participating in a physiological psychology experiment which is concerned with investigating the relationship between perception and bodily resistance to electricity. Before we deal with the perceptual aspects of the experiment, I would like you to do a simple subtraction task for me.

I want you to start from number 750 and subtract an increasing series of numbers. The series of numbers runs from 1 through 25, increasing by 1 each time. For instance, from 750 you will subtract 1, from 749 subtract 2, from 747 subtract 3, and from 744 subtract 4, and so on, until you have subtracted an amount of 25. When you have subtracted an amount of 25, the next number you will subtract *from the particular remainder you have*—do not go back to 750—will be 1 again, then 2, then 3, and so on. In other words you will never subtract an amount greater than 25, but will subtract amounts running from 1 through 25 only. You will continue subtracting, always reducing your remainder, until you reach 0 or a negative number, whichever it turns out to be.

Here is an example partly worked out, assuming we had started from 1000. [At this point an example showing the subtraction process for one series and part of another was exhibited.] From 1000 we subtract 1, from 999 we subtract 2, from 997 we subtract 3, and so on down; [pause] from 724 we subtract 24, from 700 we subtract 25, from 675 we subtract 1 again, from 674 subtract 2, thus increasing the series again. You will follow the same pattern except that you will start from 750. Remember to continue to subtract until you reach an amount of 0 or your first negative number, then stop.

This task is *not* a speed test. Please start when I tell you to. Do you have any questions? [At this point S was given a sheet of unlined paper, a pencil, and a board on which to write.]

While you are subtracting you will receive shock. The shock will come at random intervals and may occur at one or both electrode points. Each successive shock will be somewhat more intense than the preceding one; I do not have anything to do with the presentation of the shock. The shock is automatically administered by the machine.

Certain "adjustments" of the panel knobs were made and the five-pole knife switch was closed simultaneously with the activation of the phonograph motor. The subject was then told: "You can start." The E at this point was seated at the table to the back and right of the S. In this position it was possible to observe S and also operate the necessary apparatus for delivery of shock.

Shock was administered at the end of 1 minute, 2 minutes, and at the point where S had just reached a remainder in the 100's (if the subtraction was performed accurately the number was 194). The three shock volts were 25, 30, and 35, respectively. Duration of shock was a fraction of a second.

When S had finished, the paper was removed and the time required for subtraction recorded. The five-pole knife switch was opened simultaneously with the stopping of the electric motor. Two metal electrodes were then attached to S's right wrist and upper right cheek, respectively. One web belt was fastened over the arms of the chair while S's legs were fastened by two other belts to the front legs of the chair. A helmet was then adjusted on S's head. The S was then given another sheet of paper and the following statements were made:

> The next part of the experiment is rather crucial; therefore I would like you to write the following as I dictate it to you: "I do hereby pledge that I will not reveal the nature of any part of this experiment to any individual." Sign your name underneath.

The paper was removed and the following statements were made:

> We shall now go through a set of cards somewhat similar to the ones you saw last time, following the same procedure. While you are going through these cards, you will again receive shock. The shock will again come at random intervals at one or all places where the electrodes are located. Again, each succeeding shock will be somewhat more intense than the preceding one. *The longer the time interval that elapses without the receipt of shock, the more intense will the next shock be.*

The five-pole knife switch was closed simultaneously with the reactivation of the motor. The E again sat to the right and in back of S, and the Rorschach test was administered following the same procedure used with the Behn. *No shock was given during the Rorschach test.*

Upon completion of the administration of the Rorschach the switch was opened and the motor stopped. The electrodes and belts were removed and S was asked to relax in another chair near E's desk. The following statement was then made:

> This investigation is still more or less in the exploratory stage. It is felt that the experimental design used here may have produced certain feelings in the subject and that these feelings may be influencing the results

we are getting. Here is an anxiety or tension scale. Would you place a
line through this scale indicating in general how you felt while doing the
subtraction task. You may put your line at any point that you feel is the
appropriate one; it need not be directly on a number. Would you also put
another line through the scale indicating in general how you felt while
going through the ten cards for the first time, today.

The following seven-point scale was used:

| 0 | 1 | 2 | 3 | 4 | 5 | 6 |
|---|---|---|---|---|---|---|
| Completely relaxed, no anxiety or tension | | | Moderately anxious or tense | | Extremely anxious or tense | |

Before leaving the experimental room, S was reassured as to his performance on the required tasks and thanked for his cooperation. The importance of not divulging the nature of the experiment was again stressed.

*Non-stress group.* The second session for the control group was conducted
in another room, in which no apparatus was present. The following statements were made:

This session will be quite like the first one. I have here a set of cards
somewhat similar to the ones you saw last time and we shall follow the
same procedure in going through them. However, before we go through
this perception task, I want you to do a simple subtraction task for me.

(The instructions for the subtraction task utilized for the stress group
were given, beginning with "I want you to start from . . . ," and ending
with ". . . then stop.")

The following statements were added:

The task is quite simple. It is not a speed test. Do you have any questions you want to ask? O.K., you can start at any time.

Upon completion of the subtraction task, the paper was taken by E, and
the time required for the test's completion was noted. The Rorschach test
was then administered in the manner indicated previously. Upon completion of the Rorschach administration, the anxiety-tension scale was presented
with the same instructions used for the stress group.

The Behn-Rorschach, a parallel series of ink blots, "was employed to
minimize the influence of memory on the standard Rorschach administered during the second session." It was felt that previous experience

with the Rorschach might mask the influence of the stress conditions. There was a significant difference between the experimental and control groups in the number of errors made in the subtraction test and in the self-ratings on anxiety made following the standard Rorschach. There was no significant difference in time scores on the subtraction test.

The following are the major findings which tended to support the traditional predictions about Rorschach indicators of anxiety: (1) Using Hertz's Sh factor the experimental group gave significantly higher scores; (2) they gave significantly fewer W responses; (3) they gave significantly more Do responses;[3] (4) they gave significantly fewer responses. The following "did not reach an acceptable statistical level of significance but came sufficiently close to warrant considering them as suggestive findings": (1) the experimental group rejected more cards; (2) the total number of weighted color responses ($FC = .5$, $CF = 1.0$, $C = 1.5$) was less for the experimental group; (3) they gave few popular (P) responses—responses in which a *particular* content is very frequently given to a *particular* area (e.g., the people in card III, animals on card VIII). Contrary to prediction the experimental group gave significantly fewer responses in which only the outline form (F) of the area was utilized.

When Eichler's findings and procedures are viewed in light of our previous discussion, several conclusions and problems may be stated:

1. Hertz's overall shading score (Sh) does seem to reflect a *situational* anxiety. The greater the tendency for shading responses of all varieties to be of indefinite form, the more likely that the individual's behavior in the Rorschach situation is being influenced by anxiety.

2. Although the Behn ink blots are not identical with the standard series, they *are* similar, a fact which Eichler pointed out to his subjects. This raises the following question: What are the effects on a second test when the first test is similar but not identical to it? Wittenborn (*185*) has pointed out in connection with Harrower-Erickson's test-retest data with the standard cards (i.e., test-retest with *identical* cards) that "an inspection of her data revealed that the responses which

---

[3] Do, oligophrenic details, are those in which a small area of a body (animal or human) is used where normally the whole body is seen. For example, in card III the response "a person's head" would be Do because ordinarily the whole person is seen. The "oligophrenic" label was based on the belief that it was characteristic of mentally defective individuals, which is patently untrue.

comprise the lack of perceptual control factor tend to decrease and, for the most part, are less prevalent at the second administration. This is an interesting finding because it not only indicates that the lack of perceptual control determinants are affected in a similar way by familiarity with the test, but that familiarity with the test reduces the subject's susceptibility to the lack of perceptual control responses. It is plausible to suppose that perception is better controlled and less spontaneous in a familiar situation than in a grossly unfamiliar situation such as a first presentation of the Rorschach cards." Wittenborn's statement suggests that in Eichler's test-retest design the lack of perceptual control measure would lose discriminating power because form-secondary responses decrease in number. In view of this the size of the difference between the groups on the Sh factor, which weights most heavily responses of vague and indefinite form, may be unduly small. Although the difference in Sh was significant, there was great overlapping in scores.

3. Eichler tested many Rorschach signs presumed to be indicators of anxiety but aside from those given above they did not differentiate his groups.

4. In previous pages we have referred to studies which demonstrated that individuals differ markedly in degree of anxiety experienced in testing situations and that unless these differences are known significant findings may be obscured (p. 26). In Eichler's design one has no way of knowing whether his two groups contained an equal number of high and low test anxious subjects.

5. Clinicians might justifiably argue that for an individual to react anxiously to Eichler's experimental situation is realistic and in no way irrational since he was led to believe that he was in danger of being hurt. When the clinician uses the word "anxiety" he usually refers to a reaction for which there is little or no justification in reality. *The fact that the stress group was told that while taking the Rorschach they would be in danger of receiving increasing amounts of shock would in itself account for their giving fewer responses and rejecting more cards because such reactions would get the situation over with quickly—a not unrealistic way of responding.*[4]

[4] The writer is indebted to Irwin Sarason for making this point, which allows us again to emphasize the importance of determining the subject's conception of the task and his way of handling it. The importance of determining how instructions might be interpreted is obvious.

The reader may have noted that our discussion of Eichler's study has been largely in terms of the variables operating in the clinical interaction: the nature of the instructions (point 5), attitudinal factors related to previous learning (point 4), and the nature of the stimulus materials (point 2). From the standpoint of understanding the source of the anxious reaction still another variable deserves discussion, namely, the place of the interaction. Both the stress and non-stress groups were administered the Behn-Rorschach in a room in which there was apparatus which was covered. If this room looked like one in which experimentation was conducted, an anxious reaction may have been differentially engendered in some subjects. The stress group had their second session in the same room while the non-stress group had theirs in a different room. It is possible that the change in the place of interaction for the non-stress group had the effect of decreasing their initial anxiety level. In other words, the differences between the two groups on the standard Rorschach may be due not only to the interfering effects of anxiety in one group but also to the facilitating effects of changing the place of the interaction in the other group. The "place" variable may have had other effects—or it may have had no particular effects at all. The important point is that manipulating the place of the interaction *may* have effects, and unless this possibility is kept in mind its role cannot be evaluated and a source of variation in performance will remain undetected. The purposes of the interaction comprise still another variable which should be considered. One may assume that many subjects in the stress group accepted the purposes of the interactions as stated by the experimenter. But it is also likely that some subjects did not accept these stated purposes—some, for example, may have felt that this was just another "psychology experiment" which had goals other than the stated ones. Some subjects may have resented the stress procedure. If there had been some way of dividing the stress subjects according to their degree of acceptance of the stated purposes of the interaction, it is possible that those subjects who accepted the stated purposes, and reacted anxiously, differed from the non-stress group even more clearly (i.e., with less overlap) than Eichler's analysis indicates.

We should make it clear that we are not maintaining that had Eichler taken the variables of the clinical interaction more systematically into account his results would have been different. What we do maintain is that explicit recognition of the nature of the interpersonal interaction makes it more likely that one will obtain data relevant to the processes (and variables) which influence the end product, the verbalized response to the stimulus.

Cox and Sarason (31) report a study of the relation between test anxiety and Rorschach performance. They compared two groups: those with the highest and those with the lowest scores on the Test Anxiety Questionnaire (see p. 27). One half of each group took the Rorschach under standard conditions while the other half took it with ego-involving instructions. Since the ego-involving instructions did not produce any significant effects within either the low or high test anxious group, and there were no changes in the direction or statistical significances of the findings, their data are based on comparisons of all high versus all low test anxious subjects. It should be emphasized that the subjects were *preselected*: the high anxious being those who reported that they felt anxious in a test situation and the low anxious those who reported that they did not feel anxious. The following assumptions were made:

*Assumption I:* In a test situation the anxious response consists of subjective, personalized, self-centered feelings which are not task-relevant.

*Assumption II:* In a test situation the anxious response interferes with awareness and evaluation of the external stimulus.

*Assumption III:* The stronger the test anxiety the stronger is the defense against it when the need for defense is evoked.

On the basis of these assumptions the following hypotheses were stated:

1. The high anxious subjects should give significantly fewer Fc, cF, and c responses. This hypothesis involves one other assumption: This type of response is the most perceptually differentiated type of Rorschach response in that it involves awareness of and responsiveness to *differences or nuances in color*—in contrast, for example, to a C or C' response which involves awareness of and responsiveness to *one* color (e.g., red, blue, etc.) Put in another way: The c type of response involves colors and not a single color. If test anxiety interferes with awareness of the external stimulus (Assumptions I and II), one would not expect the c type of response to be in evidence. This hypothesis is the direct opposite of many traditional viewpoints.

2. The high anxious subjects should give more responses with poor form and more responses with vague or indefinite form. Using Wittenborn's lack of perceptual control score one would predict that the high anxious subjects would have higher scores (Assumption II). If the anxious response interferes with awareness and *evaluation* of the external stimulus, then one would expect that response to the stimulus to be on the uncritical, impulsive, vague side.

3. The high anxious subjects should give more movement (to be discussed in the next chapter) responses because they are assumed to reflect personal, subjective, or internal factors (Assumption I). This prediction runs counter to traditional views.

4. The high anxious subjects should display *more variability* in their records. "More specifically that, relative to low anxious subjects, high anxious individuals will yield more extreme results on the following indices: total number of responses given; number of locations used per card; reaction times for *each* response; total time for each card; and finally, in the way they respond to the stimulus material (defined operationally in terms of frequency of movement of cards). All these predictions involved the assumption that these indices are likely to be reliable indicators of 'response readiness.'" These predictions were based on Assumption III: The stronger the anxiety the stronger the defense against it and the less likely that such defensive reactions will be as consistently successful as in those cases where neither the anxiety nor the need for defense is strong.

The results of this study are contained in Table 10. Examination of the results reveals that Eichler's findings in the case of card rejections, weighted color, and total number of responses are not borne out. We have already pointed out that his findings in the case of rejections and total R may be a function of his procedure and not anxiety. The inverse relationships between anxiety and frequency of whole and popular responses confirm Eichler's findings. In general the results of this study support the predictions which were made. Cox and Sarason conclude:

From the viewpoint of the efficacy of these Rorschach anxiety signs, both the known reliability and validity of the questionnaire . . . and the internal consistency of our data afford encouraging evidence of the diagnostic efficiency of certain indices. Of particular interest are two controversial findings: the *negative* relationship between level of anxiety and frequency of

TABLE 10.   Comparison of High and Low Test Anxious Subjects
(Cox and Sarason, *31*)

| Variable | High Anxiety Group (N = 20) Mean of Transformed Percentages | Low Anxiety Group (N = 20) Mean of Transformed Percentages | P |
|---|---|---|---|
| No. of card rejections | 1.30 | 2.40 | <.50 |
| No. of W responses | 19.60 | 27.80 | .01 |
| No. of W̄ responses | 23.28 | 26.50 | .01 |
| No. of W *and* W̄ responses | 32.24 | 42.68 | .01 |
| No. of P responses | 34.20 | 39.70 | .02 |
| No. of weighted color responses | 14.40 | 15.10 | <.50 |
| No. of irrelevant verbalizations | 32.84 | 31.42 | .30 |
| No. of FM, M, and m responses | 39.42 | 31.13 | .01 |
| No. of "no form" responses | 7.90 | 2.14 | .02 |
| No. of poor form responses | 18.70 | 10.50 | .01 |
| No. of form *primary* responses | 17.12 | 22.84 | .02 |
| No. of form *secondary* responses | 18.68 | 14.40 | .05 |
| No. of sex and anat. responses | 15.52 | 14.20 | .30 |
| No. of FK and K responses | 10.32 | 8.94 | .30 |
| No. of perseverative responses | 10.52 | 6.00 | .05 |
| No. of Fc, c, and c responses | 10.32 | 15.94 | .02 |
| No. of cards given only one location | 32.42 | 31.48 | .40 |
| No. of cards given more than three locations | 12.82 | 8.24 | .05 |
| Reaction times *under* five seconds | 43.68 | 38.34 | .02 |
| Reaction times *over* fifteen seconds | 17.52 | 6.48 | .01 |
| Total times *under* twenty-five seconds | 32.58 | 31.16 | .30 |
| Total times *over* seventy-five seconds | 12.98 | 9.62 | .10 |
| No. of times moved cards | 29.52 | 28.12 | .30 |

The respective means and standard deviations were:
*HA:* Mean 25.6 responses
S.D.   11.9 responses
*LA:* Mean 20.7 responses
S.D.   13.3 responses
Neither the difference between means nor the difference between deviations
is significant (P > .05).

*surface* shading responses (Fc, cF, and c), and the form secondary results.
The former finding is congruent with our analysis and at variance with
Eichler's data. While further research is clearly indicated, it is interesting to
note that while sixteen of the twenty LA subjects obtained higher Fc scores
than the median percentage, only four of the HA subjects did, and a chi-
square test (corrected for continuity) yields P values between .01 and .02.

Exactly the same number (16 vs. 4) of subjects scored above and below the median percentage with the poor form index, although here the direction of the difference was reversed. Other measures yielding results which suggest that they may be applicable to *individual* diagnosis were number of whole and cut-off whole responses, number of movement (FM, M, and m) responses, and proportions of reaction times under five seconds: in all these cases fifteen of the HA, and only five of the LA subjects deviated from the median percentage in the direction predicted for the HA group. In all these instances a chi-square test, corrected for continuity, gave P values between .02 and .05. While the *group* results for certain other indices yielded significant differences, more overlapping in individual scores reduced the clinical significance of these findings.

The other controversial finding was obtained with the form secondary (K, C'F, C', cF, c, C, and CF) index. While the group results with this measure were significant, if Wittenborn's formula is used, precisely the opposite result is obtained (P = .002, with a two-tailed distribution). The discrepancy between these results is due to the great disparity in the number of whole responses given by our HA and LA subjects. Further work is needed before conclusive evidence can be obtained as to the relative diagnostic efficacy of these two indices.

The following picture of the effects of a specific anxious experience upon functioning seems to emerge: self-oriented or self-centered responses are evoked, awareness of the nature of the objective stimulus is impaired, and effectiveness of responsiveness to the external stimulus is reduced.

In light of our earlier discussions some other conclusions might be drawn:

1. As might have been expected, anxiety is reflected in various ways in the Rorschach and it is unjustified to assume that any particular scoring category is specific for such a reaction, a conclusion stated earlier by Hertz (75) and one that is very similar to that stated by Holtzman (78) in connection with the relationship between impulsivity and color responses.

2. Bearing the previous point in mind it seems justified to conclude that among the better indicators of anxiety and reaction to stress are measures based either on the form-quality (i.e., adequacy of reality testing) of the responses or on the degree to which responses *which incorporate some objective characteristic of the cards* (shading, bright or dark colors) are of vague or indefinite form.

3. Although the findings in the case Fc, cF, and c were predicted,

and the prediction was in a direction (less rather than more in frequency) opposite to that for other shading categories, further research
will be necessary before one can conclude that the different shading
categories have different behavioral significances.

Klatskin (90) has reported a study which is relevant in the present
discussion.

Since the Rorschach is widely used diagnostically in hospital settings, it
was decided to contrast records taken in a period of stress associated with
hospitalization with those taken on matched subjects in the absence of such
stress. In order to avoid any possible interàctions between reaction to stress
and age or intelligence, the age of subjects was limited to 18–45, and intelligence, as determined by the verbal scale of the Wechsler-Bellevue, to average
or above (i.e., IQ 90 or above). Patients on ward service only were studied,
to hold constant any hospital procedures which might influence attitude
toward the treatment received.

In selecting an experimental situation, it was desired to find an acute
temporary stress. Two situations were selected in which the patients were
assumed to be experiencing such stress: the day prior to discharge of
primiparous obstetrical patients, and the day prior to gynecological surgery.
It was demonstrated that no statistically significant differences existed between Rorschachs from these two types of patients. . . . This hospital
group was matched in age, sex, intelligence, and socio-economic status with
subjects selected as being in an everyday life situation. Clerical workers
from a large local factory were assumed to meet this requirement. . . . No
significant differences were found between the groups in age or intelligence. . . .

The surgical patients were given the Rorschach and verbal scale of the
Wechsler-Bellevue following ward rounds on the afternoon of the day
preceding surgery, as, at this time, the patient was given confirmation by
the surgeons of the intended procedure. The obstetrical patients were tested
following ward rounds of the day prior to discharge. The clerical subjects
were tested at various times throughout the working day. The examiner
introduced herself to all subjects as a doctor who was conducting a research
project on attitudes and interests of various groups of women, and asked
their cooperation in taking a test which would give data which might be
used as a normal basis for comparison. All subjects appeared cooperative.

Klatskin found that the hospital or stress group gave significantly
fewer shading (Fc, cF, c) and bright color responses, fewer responses
in general, more poor form responses, and a ratio in which CF + C

was less than FC.[5] These findings are in the main consistent with those found in other studies discussed in this and the previous chapter. The fact that the hospital group gave significantly more responses with sex and anatomy content was interpreted by Klatskin not as revealing some kind of basic personality structure but as reflecting the influence of situational factors on Rorschach performance. *Where the interaction takes place, when it takes place, and the subject's conception of the purpose of the interaction are variables which must be taken into account in evaluating the protocol.* Bleuler's comments, quoted by Klatskin (*90*), are pertinent:

If I administered the test to my patients on the hospital medical service, I got different results than when I administered the test to people who were healthy, or those who were in a psychiatric institution. The environment of a hospital creates a set to give interpretations from the field of anatomy and pathology. Not only insofar as content is concerned are the test results influenced by the environment, but also the individual Rorschach determinants . . . are affected.

## THE NEED FOR SPECIAL INK BLOTS

On the basis of our discussion in this chapter we would conclude that shading responses appear to have behavioral significances which should be studied further in future research. However, the fact that in most protocols the absolute and relative frequencies of these responses are not high—usually being below that of movement and color responses—suggests the need for a series of ink blots which would maximize the appearance of shading responses. Increasing the frequency of shading responses is likely to result in more reliable scores than we now have. Increasing the range of response among individuals makes it more likely that one would obtain significant correlations with validity criteria. One could also vary the nature of the stimulus materials in terms of degree of shading present in order to determine how the strength of the tendency to respond to shading varies with changes in the stimulus. Because we have traditionally worked with a particular set of ink blots we have no reason to assume that they are adequate for all problems.

[5] Eichler also found a lower response total (R) while Cox and Sarason did not. This apparent inconsistency may be due to the fact that Cox and Sarason were concerned with a specific anxiety, test anxiety, which a previous study (*140*) had indicated was related to a strong need for achievement. The higher response total of the high test anxious subjects would not, therefore, be unexpected.

## Chapter 13

# INTERNAL FACTORS: MOVEMENT

WHEREAS color and shading are characteristics of the external stimulus or referent, movement obviously does not reside in the cards but is a characteristic attributed to it by the subject.[1] A response is scored in the movement category when in the individual's verbalization the content is described as non-static.

SCORING

1. A response is scored as human movement (M) when people or animals are seen as if in some form of human activity. Walking, talking, resting, sleeping, standing, thinking—when words like these are used to describe human content, the scoring is M. Animals that are talking or dancing or performing some kind of uniquely human activity are likewise scored M.

2. A response is scored as animal movement (FM) when the animals are seen in an activity which, however, is not uniquely human. Birds flying, animals climbing, a dog eating, bears fighting, a snake crawling, a cow standing—when animals are described in these ways the scoring is FM.

Klopfer (92, p. 111) has also recommended the use of m in those cases where action is the result of inanimate forces: "a rock falling," "an explosion with things blown in all directions," "a woman's skirt flared out because it is being blown by the wind," "an animal falling through the air"—in these responses the action is the result of inanimate or natural forces. These responses may be either Fm, mF, or m, depending on the definiteness of the form. Since M and FM refer to contents with definite form (i.e., the human or animal form), the primacy of the form aspect is assumed whenever these responses are

[1] When we say that color and shading are objective properties of the external stimulus, we mean that people in our culture would agree that the cards are colored and also that they are not homogeneously colored. In addition, it is possible to measure their characteristics (e.g., hue, saturation).

given. As Stein (*160*) has pointed out, whereas color and shading are scored independent of the content, the M and FM scores refer to very specific contents. Whereas an FC response may be scored for a variety of contents, the M and FM scores are only scored when the content is human or animal.

INTERPRETIVE SIGNIFICANCE OF M

On the basis of her review of the literature on human movement response, Schumer (150) concluded:

There is by no means widespread agreement . . . with respect to the interpretive significance of movement responses. The Rorschach literature is replete with statements, generally in subjective and crudely defined terms, about the meaning of "M." The following are a few of the purported correlates of M which have been culled from the literature. . . .
Movement responses have been considered to be related to:
1. kinesthesis of the individual
2. delay of inner or outer impulsiveness
3. introversive functioning
4. creativeness, imagination
5. freedom and flexibility of the associative processes
6. wealth and richness of the associative processes
7. acceptance of inner impulsiveness
8. phantasies, wish-fulfillments
9. stabilization of the personality
10. ability to empathize
11. type of rapport
12. type of intelligence
13. degree of maturation
14. suggestibility
15. relationship to reality

A number of studies have appeared which test the purported relation between number of movement responses and intelligence. Tucker (*167*) correlated Wechsler-Bellevue scores with number of M as well as FM + m in a group of 100 male adult neurotic veterans. "It was found that human movement (M) scores and summed animal and minor movement (FM + m) scores correlated at the same level of significance with intelligence test scores and that the difference in the two correlations was not statistically significant. Both movement scores correlated positively and significantly with IQ's but neither correlation was high enough to indicate that movement scores could be considered predictive of intelligence. The rank order of the correlations between the two movement scores and the Wechsler subtest scores was approximately the same suggesting that the different movement scores reflect the same general areas of intelligence." Since the number of movement responses is correlated with the total number of responses (33), it is difficult to evaluate Tucker's findings because he used raw scores and not percentages. Wittenborn (178), using two groups of college students who differed significantly on tests of mental ability, found a slight tendency for those with higher M percent scores to have higher mental test scores.

There is little doubt that over the entire range of intelligence there is a significant and positive relationship between number of M and intelligence. However, the same relationship holds in the case of total number of responses (R) and it is very likely that the increase in M is a function of a productivity factor. Even were this not the case, the degree of relationship between M and intelligence is too low for clinical usage. Although mental defectives as a group tend to give no M response, E. K. Sarason (135) found a considerable minority who gave one or more such responses. In fact, Sarason and Sarason (143) found that those defectives whose intellectual efficiency was good gave far less M than those whose problem-solving behavior was poor. In her study of eminent biologists Roe (128) found that eight of her twenty subjects gave two or less M, far below what one would expect from individuals of such intellectual caliber and performance.

As Schumer (p. 203) indicated, the M response presumably is related to creativity. Rust (131) has reported a study testing this assumption. He utilized the Levy Movement Blots (132), which maximize the number of M responses one obtains from a subject.

The stimuli consist of finger paintings prepared by spreading black finger paint on the regular finger-paint paper, folding the paper so that the paint is on the inside, and then running the thumbnail over the outer surfaces in such a way that when the paper is opened, there are two symmetrical figures, one on either side of the middle crease. In this way figures of various sorts were produced. Levy, after preliminary experimentation, found seven designs that elicited a range of responses. These designs were photographed so that more than one set of cards could be used. The photographed designs are 6½″ by 9½″ and are mounted on black cardboard. Since one of these designs is used in three positions and the first design is repeated at the end, there is a total of ten cards, or ten presentations of a stimulus. The designs are in black and white and various shades of gray.

The cards are presented to each subject individually, one at a time, with the following instructions: "I am going to show you some movement blots. They show people doing something. Look at the cards and tell me what the people are doing." The subject's responses are recorded verbatim by the examiner.

The responses to the Levy Movement Blots were assessed by scales developed by Zubin (*188*). Rust used as subjects public-school children in the fourth, fifth, and sixth grades. "Since creativity is a difficult variable to measure, independent of skill, this experimenter used the ratings of creativity made by art supervisors as the best approximation of an adequate measure of creativity." Creativity was judged on a five-point scale.

In order to obtain a measure of the creativity of the subjects in this study, each subject was asked by the art supervisor in the regular art period to draw a picture of something that he would like to draw. . . . In general, each subject had as much time as he wished to complete his picture to his own satisfaction. Two different media were used in these drawings. The subjects were asked to draw one picture using only pencil and to draw one picture using whatever colors he wished. The subjects had their choice of water colors, tempera paints, or crayon and were allowed to use the medium with which they felt the most confidence, or with which they felt that they could best express their ideas.

After the productions from all of the children had been obtained, the experimenter conferred with the two art supervisors in the school system in order to obtain an adequate scale for rating the creativity of the productions. No instructions were given the raters by the experimenter, as to the basis for the ratings of creativity, except that, in so far as possible, the ratings were to be made not on the basis of skill in art, but on the basis of the type of creativity. . . . They were also asked to avoid making ratings that would reflect their personal feelings toward other aspects of the subjects' behavior. . . .

Preliminary samples of the children's drawings were obtained on which both supervisors were in agreement as to their creativity ratings. Such samples were obtained for each of the five steps in the creativity scale. These same productions were then used by the supervisors as anchoring points in making the remaining judgments of creativity. The total of these four ratings (both teachers rated each child's color and pencil production) were used to obtain the creativity rating for each subject. The reliability of independent raters is .81 on the pencil drawings and .77 on the color drawings.

The results indicated that the movement response was independent of chronological age, mental age, I.Q., and sex. Rust found a negligible relation between creativity and movement responses. "Paradoxically, there is a slight, but significant, tendency for those with lower creativity ratings to obtain somewhat higher scores on the movement scales." Rust's results are congruent with those of Roe (*125, 126, 127*), who studied twenty outstanding artists of national fame.

As we have seen earlier, a large number of different (and usually vaguely stated) significances have been attributed to the M response. That there has been practically no research evidence for many of these hypotheses does not mean that they are invalid but it certainly suggests that the clinician must proceed with caution. As a beginning step to the understanding of the M response we might begin with the fact that in such a response the individual verbalizes something (i.e., movement) which does not exist in the external stimulus. The response is obviously related to *some* aspect (e.g., contours, lines) of the external stimulus but it also contains or describes a characteristic which exists within and not outside the individual. In other words, like shading or color the M response is related to the external referent but unlike them it also reflects an internal referent. *It is because movement does not exist in the cards that one might say that the M response reflects an internal, personal, or subjective process.* Put in another way: When an individual attributes to an external stimulus a characteristic which in fact it does not possess, this characteristic reflects an internal process which itself is determined not only by current situational variables but by previous experiences as well. What we are here trying to say is that the internal process is rooted in or related to previous experiences (e.g., thoughts, interactions, perceptions, fantasies, attitudes, etc.). The relation between the external stimulus and the personal way of responding may be expressed in several ways. The internal responses may be of such strength so as to prevent the individual from becoming aware and responding in a differentiated way to the external stimulus—as in the case of the test anxious individuals who gave few shading responses (*31*). In these individuals the strength of the internal process was reflected in their tendency to give M, and their failure to respond in a more sensitive or differentiated way to the cards reflects their subjective, self-centered attitude in the situation. In the pathological case the strength of the personalized way of responding may be of such magnitude as to effectively minimize or even rule out the external stimulus as a determinant of the response. It should be clear, of course, that in characterizing the M response as a reflection of a subjective, personal process we imply nothing about the "goodness or badness" of the response in terms of such continua as complexity and reality testing. All that is meant is that at the time the response is given internal factors are in some way being reflected.

Schumer (150) has done perhaps the most extensive study of the behavioral correlates of the M response. She attempted to state some of the oft made assumptions about the significance of the M response in such a way as to make them amenable to test. Her work was based on the following assumptions and "derivations."

*Assumption I:  Movement responses reflect inner, personal and subjective factors.*

 A. Movement-oriented people are more original in the kinds of responses given to stimuli than those who are non-movement-oriented. (See Prediction 1.)
 B. Movement-oriented people respond less to objective, external cues than those who are non-movement-oriented. (See Prediction 2.)
 C. When external stimulus conditions change, movement-oriented people change their responses less than those who are non-movement-oriented. (See Prediction 5.)
 D. Movement-oriented people do not respond to stimuli in the same way that others do when the conventional mode of responding is considered. (See Predictions 3 and 4.)

*Assumption II:  Movement responses reflect a tendency to approach a problem-solving situation conceptually rather than concretely.*

 A. Movement-oriented people do better than those who are non-movement-oriented in a situation requiring conceptual activity. (See Prediction 6.)
 B. The language of movement-oriented people is more abstract than that of non-movement-oriented people. (See Predictions 7 and 8.)

*Assumption III:  Movement responses reflect a tendency to be a "thinker" rather than a "doer," that is, not to be physically active.*

A. Movement-oriented people are less impulsive than non-movement-oriented people. (See Predictions 9 and 11.)

B. Movement-oriented people are not as physically active as those who are non-movement-oriented in a problem-solving situation. (See Prediction 10.)

*Assumption IV: If the perceiving of many human movement responses represents a distinctive way of responding, then one would expect those who are movement-oriented to respond distinctively to other perceptual situations.* (See Predictions 12 and 13.)

Several measures of "movement-orientation," traditional and new, were used and the serious student is urged to consult the original study about their derivation. In presenting her results we shall give only those in which there is consistency with which the different movement measures indicated the same direction of relationship. Her subjects were ninety-five college undergraduates.

### THE WORD-ASSOCIATION TEST

The first behavioral situation investigated was the word-association technique. It was felt that this would provide an adequate test of some of the behavioral implications of Assumption I which states that "Movement responses reflect inner, personal and subjective factors." In terms of the word-association test, the relevant behavioral implications of this assumption are that movement-oriented individuals, as contrasted with non-movement-oriented ones, should tend to be more original in the kinds of responses given to stimuli, that they should tend to respond less to objective, external cues, and that they should not respond to stimuli in the same way that others do when the conventional mode of responding is considered. When phrased in terms specific to the word-association task, these behavioral implications lead to the following predictions:

*Prediction 1:* Movement-oriented subjects will give *more* unique responses than will non-movement-oriented subjects.

*Prediction 2:* Movement-oriented subjects will give *fewer* outward responses than will non-movement-oriented subjects.

*Prediction 3:* Movement-oriented subjects will give *fewer* popular responses than will non-movement-oriented subjects.

*Prediction 4:* Movement-oriented subjects will give *fewer* responses which are phrase-completions than will non-movement-oriented subjects.

.   .   .   .   .

1. *Unique responses.* Any response to a stimulus word which was not given by any other S was called a unique response. The unique responses for each S were counted and divided by the total number of responses in his protocol.

2. *Outward responses.* a. Any response which was exactly the same as either its stimulus word, a preceding stimulus word, or a preceding response word was called a repetition, provided the preceding model was not more than eight steps away. A stimulus-response unit was considered to be one step.

b. Any response which rhymed either with its stimulus word, a preceding stimulus word, or a preceding response word was called a rhyme, provided the rhymed word was not more than four steps away.

c. Any response which contained its stimulus word was called a partial repetition (e.g., lunch—lunchtime).
For each S, the number of repetitions, rhymes and partial repetitions was totalled and divided by the total number of responses in his protocol.

3. *Popular responses.* Any response to a stimulus word which was given by 32 or more S's was called a popular response. The popular responses for each S were counted and divided by the total number of responses in his protocol.

4. *Phrase-completions.* Any response which completed a conventional phrase or expression of which its stimulus word was a part was called a phrase-completion (e.g., ship—ahoy). The phrase-completions for each S were counted and divided by the total number of responses in his protocol.

The results supported Predictions 1 ("unique responses") and 2 ("outward responses"), there was a nonsignificant trend in the expected direction for Prediction 3 ("popular responses"), while for Prediction 4 ("phrase-completions") there was no supporting evidence.

THE AUTOKINETIC SITUATION

The autokinetic effect, first utilized by Sherif (*154*) and described on page 88 in connection with Bray's study, was "used in order to test one prediction relating to Assumption I, which states that movement responses reflect inner, personal and subjective factors. One relevant behavioral implication of Assumption I is that when external stimulus conditions change, movement-oriented individuals will change their responses less than will non-movement-oriented ones." The degree to which an individual would change his mode of responding (from judging alone to judging in the presence of a confederate) was called "suggestibility." The results supported the prediction that movement-oriented subjects tend to have lower suggestibility scores than those who are non-movement-oriented.

## THE VIGOTSKY TEST

The Vigotsky test was used in order to test procedures relating to Assumptions II and III. Assumption II states that "Movement responses reflect a tendency to approach a problem-solving situation conceptually rather than concretely," and Assumption III states that "Movement responses reflect a tendency to be a 'thinker' rather than a 'doer,' that is, not to be physically active." The relevant behavioral implications of Assumption II are that movement-oriented individuals, as contrasted with non-movement-oriented ones, should do better in a conceptual situation and their language should be more abstract; the relevant behavioral implications of Assumption III are that movement-oriented individuals, as contrasted with non-movement-oriented ones, should be less impulsive and not as physically active in a problem-solving situation.

The Vigotsky test was chosen to represent a problem-solving situation because (a) it presents to S a situation for which he has no *specific* learned responses as he starts to solve the problem and (b) it is a test of concept formation and reasoning ability which allows the observer to "see" the method by which S solves the problem. The problem is such that it can be approached by S on the basis of different kinds of external cues which have different degrees of "obviousness," and on the basis of different kinds of logical and reasoning processes.

When phrased in terms specific to the Vigotsky test, the behavioral implications lead to the following predictions:

*Prediction* 6:   Movement-oriented subjects will have *smaller* time-error scores in this problem than will non-movement-oriented subjects.

*Prediction* 7:   Movement-oriented subjects will be *abstract* rather than concrete in verbalizing the first "solution" of the problem.

*Prediction* 8:   Movement-oriented subjects will be *abstract* rather than concrete in verbalizing the final, correct solution of the problem.

*Prediction* 9:   Movement-oriented subjects will have a *longer* reaction time for manipulation of the blocks after demonstrations of error than will non-movement-oriented subjects.

*Prediction* 10:   Movement-oriented subjects will spend a *smaller* proportion of the total time in actual manipulation and sorting of the blocks than will non-movement-oriented subjects.

*Prediction* 11:   The first response of movement-oriented subjects in this situation will be verbal rather than manipulative.

The results supported Prediction 6 and contradicted Predictions 7 and 10. Two of the trends were in the predicted direction for Prediction 8 but were not statistically reliable. There was some supporting evidence for Prediction 11 and no supporting evidence for Prediction 9.

## THE PHI PHENOMENON SITUATION

The fourth behavioral situation involved the perception of apparent motion. This was chosen as a representative test of Assumption IV which states that "If the perceiving of many human movement responses represents a distinctive way of responding, then one would expect those who are movement-oriented to respond distinctively to other perceptual situations." The choice of this situation was based on the consideration that the perception of apparent movement is the perception of motion where there is no "real" stimulus movement; the perception of movement in the Rorschach situation similarly involves a response to static material as though it possessed dynamic characteristics.

The prediction based on Assumption IV is:

*Prediction* 12: Movement-oriented subjects will tend to differ from those who are non-movement-oriented in the *kinds* of motion seen.

Prediction 13, below, is based not so much on Assumption IV as it is on suggestions in the literature indicating that individual differences in threshold for perception of apparent motion may be related to personality organization and to the perception of Rorschach movement responses.

*Prediction* 13: Movement-oriented subjects will tend to have *lower* thresholds for perception of apparent motion than will those who are non-movement-oriented.

. . . . .

The stimuli consisted of 2 bars of reddish-orange light, each approximately 4½″ x 1½″, which were intermittently presented. The source of stimulation was 14 feet from where S sat. It is known that many variables affect the ease (threshold) with which apparent motion is seen: intensity, area and color of the stimuli, the distance between them and from S, as well as the nature and illumination of the background. It was decided, therefore, to hold these factors constant and to introduce systematic variation in one variable, time-interval between stimulations, as is traditionally done. The interval between stimulus presentations could be varied from .5 to .06 sec. With an interval between them of about .5 sec. the bars were seen as two distinct objects, flashing on and off, whereas at about .06 sec. the bars were seen as two simultaneously flashing rods. Apparent motion and its variations occurred between these points. The apparatus was so constructed that it was possible to increase or decrease the interval between exposures of each stimulus by constant, predetermined steps.

It was planned to relate the Rorschach movement measures to threshold for perception of "optimal" motion, which is a phrase used by Wertheimer to describe apparent motion which is just a perception of "sheer" motion, rather than of *something* moving. Preliminary investigation revealed large differences among Ss in their interpretations of what was meant by "optimal" motion; it was expected, therefore, that this would not be a reliable technique for obtaining Ss' threshold for perception of apparent motion. Instead, it was decided to use as the threshold the point where the stimuli changed from appearing like two rods, flashing on and off, to appearing like *one* rod in motion, or conversely, the point where the stimuli changed from appearing like one rod in motion to appearing like two separate rods flashing on and off. The appearance of *any* kind of motion, then, was used as the criterion for determining threshold.

. . . . .

In the second part of this situation, S was told:

I want you to describe the kinds of motion you see at each exposure. I am going to have you look at the stimulus for about 15 seconds and then I will switch it off. You tell me in your own words what it was that you saw, in the order that you saw it. Don't forget, tell me everything you saw.

The apparatus was then adjusted to the starting point of the series given in part 2 and the stimuli switched on for 15 seconds. After the lights were turned off, S told E what he saw, demonstrating the kinds of motion by manipulating a pencil as if it were the "swinging" rod. E was able to record, as a result, the kind, as well as the changes, in motion S perceived during the exposure period. A pictorial system of recording was used so that E could note the location of the pivot point of the moving rod, whether or not three dimensional movement was seen, etc. There were seven steps, each representing a constant decrease in interval between stimulus presentations. After each exposure period, which lasted for 15 seconds, E recorded S's report of what he saw.

The results indicated that those who received high scores on the Rorschach movement measures tended to see three-dimensional movement less frequently than those who did not receive high scores. None of the movement measures was reliably related to threshold for perception of apparent motion.

The following are Schumer's conclusions about Assumption I: Movement responses reflect inner, personal, and subjective factors.

. . . Results of the present study would indicate that the "internal response tendency" of movement-oriented individuals is manifested in other situations as well as in this simple one. The degree to which these differences in response tendencies are generalized, and their relation to previous conditions of learning can only be answered by future research.

The results in the autokinetic situation bear on the question of the generality of internal responsiveness. Because there are a minimum of external cues in this situation, the subject learns a response pattern on the basis of internal cues. With the introduction of the confederate the subject continues either to respond as before or to shift his responses in the direction of greater similarity to those of the confederate. The degree to which the subject continues to respond to a learned pattern of internal cues is probably a function of the degree of reinforcement present in previous experiences where maintaining his point of view was a factor. It would seem that the ability to withstand the outside influence of the confederate is related to how much the subject relies on his own judgment. The future problem would seem to be one of determining the nature and origins of the individual's internal or self-attitudes. In this situation, then, movement-oriented individuals shift less, are more self-consistent and apt to continue responding along lines established on the basis of internal factors than those who are non-movement-oriented.

In this study, the giving of phrase-completions and popular responses were regarded as similar types of response. These responses seem to be reflecting culturally determined ways of responding. Associating table with chair, or man with woman, or window with pane are examples of this kind of response. Movement-oriented individuals cannot be differentiated from those who are not, on the basis of this measure. It would seem, therefore, that for most individuals certain stimulus words are so frequently associated with certain kinds of verbal responses that one word, if used as a cue, immediately elicits the other word as a response. The common assumption made about movement-oriented individuals in terms of their expressing their "differentness" in all situations regardless of the context, therefore, seems unwarranted. Movement-oriented individuals seem to respond differently only within certain limits. It would seem likely that when the cultural requirements of a situation are at a minimum movement-oriented individuals will respond to a greater extent on the basis of internal cues. However, movement-oriented individuals are apparently perfectly capable of responding the way others do, i.e., in an acceptable, conventional way.

As was pointed out, the generality of these statements can only be tested by further research in which other kinds of situations are employed.

In summary then: Assumption I seems to be confirmed provided that it is interpreted to mean that in *certain* situations movement-oriented individuals do not express their personal viewpoints. The maintaining of an internally established mode of response, the lack of responsiveness to external, physical cues and the production of responses on the basis of subjective factors in the word-association test, however, seem to indicate that movement-oriented individuals have a *generalized* tendency to respond to, or to interpret stimuli in a personalized, subjective way.

The following are her conclusions about Assumption II: Movement responses reflect a tendency to approach a problem-solving situation conceptually rather than concretely.

. . . Assumption II is only partially verified in that a) movement-orientation is related to performing well in this conceptual situation; b) movement-orientation is not related to verbalizing in an abstract fashion in this particular situation.

It would seem important to consider the stimulus situation, the *context,* before attempting to predict the level of words used. Perhaps movement-orientation is actually related to cautiousness which leads to reliably more *concrete* verbalizations of incorrect solutions. It seems reasonable to relate conceptual performance (as measured by this situation) to the degree to which an individual can remain aloof from the immediate context and approach the problem in a self-critical, self-verbalizing manner. This is consistent with the results relevant to Assumption I which related movement-orientation to responsiveness to inner factors.

The following are the conclusions about Assumption III: Movement responses reflect a tendency to be a "thinker" rather than a "doer," that is, not to be physically active.

The results pertaining to this assumption indicate that movement-orientation, as defined in this study, has no relationship to "impulsiveness" as defined *temporally;* there is reason to believe, however, that movement-oriented individuals tend to verbalize rather than to sort when they are given a free choice situation which allows them to proceed in whatever way they wish.

If the tendency to verbalize, rather than to sort, is interpreted as a non-impulsive cautious approach, then this might be considered as some evidence that movement-oriented individuals are less impulsive than non-movement-oriented ones. It would seem, as a matter of fact, that temporal measures of impulsiveness are possibly not as representative as more qualitative ones.

The question of the representativeness of the measurements used is an extremely important question for studies of the present type. On the one hand, it is necessary to work with *segments,* components of total behavior which are quantifiable, since there is little way of dealing with the "total personality." On the other hand, however, the measure used to *represent* the process must always be an abstraction from it, and must always, therefore, introduce distortion. It would be desirable, of course, to construct a measure which would "get at" what is going on *inside* the individual. Until ways are found to do so, however, one can only work with mechanical and pseudo-approximations of the "real" process.

Movement-oriented people have been regarded as not being motor-oriented. That they enter actively into the present task is indicated by the fact that movement-oriented subjects actually spent *more* time than those who are non-movement-oriented in manipulation of the blocks. It would seem, therefore, that although movement-orientation might be related to an initial aloofness from the external demands of the situation, it is not necessarily a reflection of restraint. Perhaps the degree of physical activity is a function of the situation, and a function of whether or not S can reflect his internal processes in that type of situation. Certainly, the present situation easily lends itself to actual manipulative responses without reducing the requirement for conceptual activity. A more crucial test, perhaps, of whether or not movement-oriented individuals would choose a conceptual rather than a physical approach to a situation would be to construct a situation which would force the individual to choose *one* of the two approaches. In other words, in a situation where physical activity is incompatible with a conceptual approach one could determine if movement-oriented individuals engage in physical activity to the extent found in this study by observing their choice.

In summary then: Assumption III is not completely confirmed. Although movement-oriented individuals seem to be more conceptual, i.e., perform better in a conceptual situation, there is little evidence to support the notion that they are less active and more delayed in their behavior. It seems likely, however, that this may be a function of the specific situation in which they were tested. There is some evidence to support the notion that movement-oriented individuals are more cautious, less impulsive, in their first responses to this situation. This fits in well with the interpretation offered in the previous section concerning the finding that movement-oriented individuals give concrete verbalizations of first, incorrect solutions.

Schumer offered the following conclusions about Assumption IV: If the perceiving of many human movement responses in the Rorschach represents a distinctive way of responding, then one would expect those who are movement-oriented to respond distinctively to other perceptual situations.

The results indicate that the prediction pertaining to differences in kinds of motion seen between movement-oriented and non-movement-oriented subjects has been confirmed. That this is a striking result is evidenced by the fact that there has been little experimental evidence to justify Assumption IV which is implicitly made whenever a determinant is scored and interpreted. Thurstone, for example, found extremely low correlations between some Rorschach variables (including M) and several dozen perceptual tasks. . . .

. . . The nature of the obtained difference between movement-oriented and non-movement-oriented Ss in the frequency with which three dimensional motion was seen should be examined. The perception of three dimensional motion is related, perhaps, to the flexibility or to the sensitivity of S to outside cues. Most Ss do not see third dimensional motion. They visualize a rod swinging up and down or back and forth but do not perceive the extremely small interval when the stimuli are not exposed as the interval during which the stimulus seems to be moving *behind* something which blocks it from view. Perhaps the Ss who are more responsive to subtle cues from the stimulus situation (short interval between stimulus exposures) see, or "imagine" three dimensional motion; those who are movement-oriented do not. This result fits in with some of the discussion pertaining to Assumptions I and II; movement-oriented Ss are less sensitive to outside influences, less apt to respond to cues stemming from the stimulus situation.

In summary, then: Assumption IV has been confirmed. Threshold for perception of apparent movement is not related to movement orientation, but the results with respect to the perception of three dimensional motion indicate that this perceptual situation is more sensitive to learned factors than early writers in the field have admitted.

Supporting evidence for Assumption IV is found in the study by Matarazzo, Watson, and Ulett (*101*) discussed previously on page 160 in connection with color responses. They found significant relationships between Rorschach M and perception of movement with photic stimulation. Since these workers did not express the number of Rorschach M in terms of the total number of responses, it may be that as in the study of apparent motion by Klein and Schlesinger (*91*) the total number of responses is the crucial variable.

Confirmation of Schumer's Assumption I (movement responses reflect internal, subjective factors) is supported by Cox and Sarason's

(*31*) study of high and low test anxious subjects (p. 196). They predicted that since in the testing situation the high anxious subjects respond in a subjective, self-centered fashion, they should give a significantly higher M percent than the low test anxious subjects, a prediction which was confirmed by their findings (Table 10).

Siipola and Taylor (*157*) have reported a study which has relevance in our present discussion. The same ink blots employed in previous studies (*155, 156*) were now exposed under two conditions, different groups being used for each condition:

The plan of the present experiment was that of contrasting *free* and *pressure* conditions as applied to both achromatic and chromatic blots. In part *Bk,* 20 achromatic blots were presented to a group of 40 subjects under *free* conditions (Group *Bk-F*) and to another group of 60 subjects under *pressure* conditions (Group *Bk-P*). In part *Col,* 20 chromatic blots, matched with the achromatic series, were presented to a group of 40 subjects under *free* conditions (Group *Col-F*) and to another group of 72 subjects under *pressure* conditions (Group *Col-P*).

Under *free* conditions . . . the attempt was made to approximate the informal conditions used in standard Rorschach administration. The atmosphere was kept leisurely and relaxed, and the subjects were unaware of the fact that their reaction times were being recorded. The directions differed from those conventionally used only in the addition of the following statement: "Although you may think of many possible responses, I would like to have you give me only *one* response for each blot." It should be noted that the instructions still leave the subject free to define his task with respect to whether he will report his first response, a later response, or a carefully selected "best" response. In comparison to Rorschach test conditions, limitation to a single response and limitation to viewing the card in a single position were the only added restrictions of the subject's freedom. Both of these restrictions were necessary to make comparison with the data obtained under pressure conditions legitimate.

Under *pressure* conditions . . . the attempt was made to approximate the more formal conditions and atmosphere of a laboratory experiment. All of the external conditions were manipulated so as to make the subject acutely aware of his specific task, to report his very first conceptual response. As soon as the stimulus card was presented, a Springfield Timer, in full view of the subject, started and continued to run noisily until the subject began his response. The speed of the revolving pointer and the hum of the timer placed psychological pressure upon the subject to report his first reaction. . . .

The major findings were:

1. Under the free as contrasted to pressure conditions there is a significant increase in reaction time and frequency of human content.

2. Under free conditions alone the average reaction for M responses was longer than that for other types of responses. "Under our free conditions the reaction times of individuals, as measured by the median for the 20 blots, ranged from the very rapid time of 5 sec. to the very slow time of 28 sec. By splitting each of our free groups in half, we can compare the number of M responses given by the 20 slowest with that given by the 20 quickest individuals. Comparison of the results . . . shows that in the case of the achromatic blots characteristically slow subjects give reliably more M responses than do subjects who are typically fast. The addition of chroma to the blots destroys this nice, dependable relation. This suggests that the presence of hue may of itself have a specific relation to reaction time or content which masks the effect of the basic relation between M and reaction time."

The fact that under free conditions the M response is unlikely to be achieved by subjects reacting quickly proves that the mere provision of a free external situation is not in itself a sufficient condition for producing M responses. When the free situation is interpreted by the subject as a pressure situation requiring prompt reaction, M responses are as rare as they are when pressure is externally imposed. . . . One can infer, then, that the occurrence of M is specifically linked, not with mere freedom in the situation, but with a particular kind of interpretation of the free situation provided, that is, with a particular kind of attitude induced in the subject. The evidence indicates that the kind of attitude with which M is associated is an attitude directed toward full exploitation of the freedom to delay and select. The person who chooses to delay his report for a long time while he carefully develops and selects his response is the one who gives many M responses.

*In light of Schumer's hypothesis about, and findings in support of, the personal and subjective correlates of the M response, it is interesting that Siipola and Taylor offer a similar hypothesis:* "We would favor an . . . hypothesis to the effect that relatively stable self-processes are activated at the outset by the manner in which the subject relates himself to the task. If he involves himself freely and personally, self-processes of a certain kind are activated and their influence continues throughout the task to produce the type of projective process related to

M. According to this conception the self enters directly as a system of personality which once activated, persists to influence all of the sensory, perceptual, and conceptual processes, including the kinesthetic." (In connection with the kinesthetic concomitants of the M response, it should be noted that there is no evidence in the literature to support such a relationship.)

The relationship between M and the tendency to delay response is indirectly supported by the studies of Singer, Meltzoff, and Goldman (*158*) and Meltzoff, Singer, and Korchin (*105*). In these studies subjects responded to Rorschach cards following a period of hyperactivity and one in which motor responsiveness was inhibited in the sense that the subject had to delay or prolong a response over a period of time. The results indicated that subjects who had been forced to inhibit or delay responsiveness tended subsequently to give more M responses than subjects who had engaged in a non-inhibitory task.

Schumer's study raises two problems: How does one determine the nature of the subjective factors reflected in the M response? What is the relation between the nature of these responses and overt behavior? Traditionally, the first question has largely been answered in terms of the content of the responses: whether they were predominantly aggressive, passive, anxious, sexual, etc. We shall take up in later pages the problem of the interpretation of content but it is important here to point out that *subjective or internal factors may be reflected in any kind of response*. The following are examples:

A beautiful tree, the kind we used to have in our backyard when I was a child. It was my favorite tree.

That looks like a surrealist painting. It is so disorganized and ugly. I definitely don't like it.

A gnarled, withered old tree stump that looks as if it has taken quite a beating.

None of these responses would be scored as M but in each instance the verbalizations reflect something that is personal or subjective; the individual has articulated something which refers not only to some aspect of the external stimulus but to personal associations or experiences as well. These kinds of responses are utilized by the clinician in his attempt to understand the individual's attitudes and motivations, although the aspects of the response he uses are not reflected in scoring.

The point we are here trying to emphasize is that while M responses may be the best single indicator of the subject's internal and personal attitudes, there is no reason why such attitudes cannot also be reflected in non-M responses. A very fruitful and important research area would be the development of a scale or continuum whereby *all* responses could be evaluated in terms of the degree of subjective and personal factors which they reflect. Various suggestions (*160*) have been made for differentiating among M responses but there seems no logical reason why all responses could not be evaluated on a single continuum.

The second question we asked above was: What is the relation between the nature of these responses and overt behavior? Although we shall be talking more about this problem in subsequent pages, two criteria on the basis of which this question might be answered have already been suggested by the studies discussed in previous chapters:

1. The more an individual's responses which incorporate some characteristic of the external stimulus are of the vague, indefinite type the more likely that personal attitudes and motivations will be overtly expressed. Since these responses reflect, relatively speaking, an impulsive, non-conceptual way of responding, the less likely that the individual will be able to inhibit or delay the expression of personal feeling. This should be especially true in those cases where the testing situation is reacted to as if it were a stressful one. If in the testing situation, where stress is not deliberately engendered or reinforced, the individual reacts impulsively or uncritically, he is more likely to so react in "real life" situations where the level of stress and conflict can be assumed to be much stronger.

2. The more an individual's responses are of poor form, indicating irrationality or poor reality testing, the more likely that internal factors will reach overt expression. When we say that a response is of poor form, we mean that a group of peers or professionals cannot "see" the response, the individual's reasoning being in some way deviant. When we say an individual is irrational we usually mean that he is incapable of responding in an impersonal and objective manner and that personal factors intrude and affect his reactions.

Although these criteria seem justified on the basis of available research, far more research will have to be done before they can be used with other than great caution. Experienced clinicians can undoubtedly point to cases where these criteria were not met but where a central conflict or motivation was clearly discernible in overt behavior.

For example, an individual's Rorschach did not at all meet the criteria indicated above and the constellation of scores was not at all deviant. However, in this rather productive record, there were two irrational or poor form responses both of which had sexual content. The presenting problem in this case was clearly sexual and there was extensive evidence that in this particular area of functioning his overt behavior directly reflected the problem.

Very much needed are series of cases in which there is a discrepancy between the Rorschach and the overt behavioral criterion (186). Such a series would be invaluable to the clinician because it would give him a better idea than he now has of the different conditions which might give rise to similar types of overt behavior.

Up to this point we have attempted to indicate how the question of the relation between the content of M responses and overt behavior might be answered in terms of the existing research literature. The experienced clinician will rightly consider the discussion an oversimplification because *it overlooks the importance which the clinician attaches to the way in which the subject behaves in the clinical interaction.* For example, if an individual's M responses have a predominantly hostile or aggressive content and his responses in general tend to be of vague, indefinite form, the significance which the clinician attaches to this configuration will in part be a function of the subject's behavior in the clinical interaction. If in his interaction with the clinician the subject is unspontaneous, polite, compliant, and guardedly responsive, the clinician is not likely to make the same predictions as he would if the subject were ebullient, restless, petulant, argumentative, or in general spontaneous in revealing feeling. *Unfortunately, research with psychological tests rarely takes into account the interaction behavior which is a crucial part of the context giving rise to the formal test response. It is as if the researcher implicitly assumes that the fact that the data with which he works were obtained in an interpersonal interaction does not necessarily obligate him to take into account the variables that operate in such a situation.* By these statements we definitely do not mean that research which does not take the variables into

account is of little value. What we do mean is that the clinical usefulness of research will be in part a function of the degree to which the
variables which operate in an interpersonal situation are reflected in
the design of the research.

### INTERPRETIVE SIGNIFICANCE OF FM

Traditionally, FM has been assumed to reflect the influence of "the
most instinctive layers within the personality" (92, pp. 278, 114). This
assumption is based on the fact that children give many FM responses
and on clinical experience which purportedly indicates that in a subject
who "is emotionally infantile, living on a level of instinctive prompting
below his chronological and mental age, the Rorschach record of this
subject shows a predominance of FM over M" (92, p. 279). Unfortunately there is no acceptable research evidence for the assumption.
What would be necessary is to demonstrate that individuals who are
reliably judged on some independent and appropriate criterion of im-
maturity as being immature relative to their age level give a predominance of FM over M in contrast to those who are judged as mature. To
argue that because an adult gives a predominance of FM over M he is
immature because children react similarly is to give a monistic-like explanation for which there simply is no acceptable evidence. If two people have a score in common, we do not necessarily say they are behaviorally similar. For example, if a child of six obtains a mental age
of six, we do not say that he is behaviorally similar to a child of twelve
with a mental age of six.

Although we need not accept the interpretive significance traditionally attributed to FM, we should not overlook the fact that one
frequently obtains records in which no M or one or two M are given
but where many FM are present—or where the number of FM exceeds
M to a degree not explainable by the fact that it is easier to see animal
rather than human forms in the blots. One possible explanation is suggested by Pittluck's (115) study of the relation between aggressive
fantasy and overt behavior. She found that those subjects in whose
TAT stories aggression was expressed toward animals and other nonhuman objects were less overtly aggressive than subjects whose stories
described aggression toward human figures. In other words, the former
type of patient tended to displace his aggressive feelings. In regard to
the Rorschach one might offer the hypothesis that individuals who give

no or relatively few M responses, in comparison to FM, are those who either have difficulty expressing strong, personal feeling toward external figures or displace such feeling. Where no movement of any kind is present in a record the most likely hypothesis is that the individual has difficulty giving overt expression to strong, personal feelings. But it is obvious that in the case of FM much research is necessary before its interpretive significance is clear.

### INTERPRETIVE SIGNIFICANCE OF m

The justification for this scoring category is that such responses reflect tensions within the individual and appear when he "experiences his promptings from within as hostile and uncontrollable forces working upon him rather than as sources of energy at his disposal" (92, p. 279). There is no evidence to support these assumptions. Since all workers agree that these responses reflect internal and subjective factors and appear very infrequently, we see no justification for scoring them in other than the M category. Although this would require rephrasing slightly the criteria for M scoring, it would be a more defensible procedure than one in which similar responses are scored differently in the absence of supporting research.

### THE RELATION OF M TO SUM C

Traditionally a great deal of importance is attached to the relationship between M and sum C (FC = 0.5, CF = 1.0, C = 1.5) (17, p. 60). When M predominates over sum C the individual is presumably one who is introversive: responding more in terms of internal rather than external stimuli, a way of responding which characterizes his behavior in all major spheres of activities and relationships. When sum C predominates over M the individual is presumably one who is extroversive: having a ready responsiveness to the external world so that such interactions are the greatest source of satisfaction. It should be said that despite all the writing on the subject the interpretive significance of the M to sum C ratio is, as Beck (17, p. 61) states, vague. Despite this, however, it seems clear that an assumption basic to the use of this ratio is that M and C represent opposing ways of responding. Schumer's study is relevant here:

In the preceding sections, there were some references to Rorschach color variables as they related to the behavioral measures. When discussing out-

ward responses to the word-association test, variability in threshold determinations, and the perception of three dimensional movement in the phi
phenomenon situation, it was mentioned that some of the color scores were
positively related to these behavioral measures. The movement-measures
tended to be negatively related to these behavioral variables. The question
can be raised as to the "oppositeness" in interpretative meaning assigned to
movement and color scores. Many authors state that color scores, particularly CF, represent one end of a hypothetical continuum of personality control while M represents the other end. Klopfer states that "Responses using
the actual color of the blots as a determinant for the concept formation
seem to deviate from form responses in a direction which can almost be
considered as opposite to the direction of the action responses (movement
responses). . . ."

In order to throw further light on this problem, three of the Rorschach
color variables were compared to all the behavioral variables. . . . If the
assumption of exact "oppositeness" is a valid one, then 1) there would be
approximately as many significant chi-squares for the color comparisons as
there were for the movement measures, and 2) if a color measure is reliably
related to a behavioral variable, the nature of the relationship would be
opposite in direction from the way in which movement measures are related
to that variable.

[Analysis] shows that about seven per cent of the comparisons involving
color are significant at the 10 per cent level of confidence or below, whereas
27 per cent of the 70 comparisons involving the movement measures are
significant at this level or below. [The analysis] also shows that only two of
the relationships are reliable, one involving Sum C and variability of threshold determinations and the other involving %CF + C and the giving of
outward responses to the word-association test. Both of these relationships
support the "oppositeness" hypothesis. Since Sum C is highly related to the
total number of Rorschach responses and the latter is highly related to
threshold variability, these significant results involving color are not so
striking. In addition, the total number of significant relationships between
the color and behavioral variables at the various levels is not more than
could be explained by chance factors. The large number of "no relationships" between the color and behavioral variables indicates that movement
and color are not at opposite ends of a continuum.

Wittenborn's (179) factor analysis also contradicts the assumption of
oppositeness.

The factorial composition of the form-color (FC) response category is
quite different from the factorial composition of the color-form (CF) and

color response (C) categories. This result suggests that the common practice of regarding the three classes of color responses as similar in their implications for the affective features of human behavior should be viewed with reservations. In the present study, the factorial composition of the form-color response category is more similar to the factorial composition of the human movement response category than it is to the other color response categories.

Holtzman's (78) study of the relationship between the M to sum C ratio, on the one hand, and shyness and gregariousness, on the other hand, failed to give any of the expected relationships.

The student should be cautioned against a procedure and way of reasoning which is occasionally used in evaluating the M to sum C ratio (56). Let us assume that the Rorschachs of two groups are being compared and statistical tests of significance have been done for M and sum C. Let us further assume that the difference in M is significant while sum C is not. By adding the two scores one very probably will obtain another significance between the groups, but inasmuch as the difference on the combined measure is just another way of stating the differences already existing on the original measures, one is unjustified in attributing a new psychological significance to the difference on the combined score. By subtracting sum C from M one might very well be obscuring differences. Wittenborn (182) has given the statistical proof "that a difference score has no predictive value superior to the predictive values of the initial scores. It is suggested, moreover, that use of difference scores for predictive purposes possesses no unique merits . . . and in some situations may obscure the predictive merits of the variables."

At the conclusion of the chapter on shading responses the suggestion was made that since such responses did seem to have behavioral significances which were of clinical importance, it might be worth while to develop a set of blots which would maximize their appearance and give more reliable scores. In the case of the movement response this has been done, as we have seen (see p. 204), in the Levy Movement Blots, for which Zubin (188) has developed a number of scales. Unfortunately, however, there has been very little systematic work done with these blots, despite their availability and potential clinical and research value. To take but one example of how such blots may have research value: Siipola and Taylor (see p. 218) reported that "in the case of the achromatic blots characteristically slow subjects give reliably more M-responses than do subjects who are typically fast" in reaction time. This relation did not hold in the presence of color. Since Siipola and Taylor used very simplified blots, and M responses represented a relatively small percentage of all responses given, an adequate test of the stability of these findings might be one in which the individual is given achromatic and chromatic (which could be developed) versions of the Levy Movement Blots. In such a test one could also study the behavioral differences between those individuals who give M regardless of the presence or absence of bright color and those whose responses are more affected by differences in the objective nature of the stimulus. One might venture the hypothesis that these individuals would also differ in the way in which they approach and are affected by various kinds of interpersonal interactions. It may be, for example, that the differences which Schumer found between movement- and non-movement-oriented individuals would be even greater (and, consequently, of more clinical as well as of more general value) if groups were chosen in the manner suggested above, involving as it does variations in the nature of the stimulus materials.

The studies discussed in this chapter have for the most part shed only indirect light on the subjective processes which enter into the giving of the movement response. The nature of the results of these studies, however, indicating as they do the personal or subjective significance of the movement response, rather strongly suggests that this type of response may well be a sensitive indicator of the role of several of the variables affecting the nature of the clinical interaction.

1. The purposes of the interaction. If an individual conceives of the interaction as one in which areas of personal weakness and guilt may be revealed, what will be the effect on the quantity and content of his movement responses? Put more generally, since the way in which an individual conceives of the interaction involves a variety of attitudes toward self and others—truly personal reactions—what is the relation between these reactions and the quantity and quality of movement responses?

2. Attitudinal factors related to previous learning. In the study of test anxiety (see p. 198) it was found that the highly test anxious subjects gave significantly more movement responses than did low anxious subjects. But this study did not indicate how such an attitudinal factor

was reflected in the content of the movement responses. Since the clinician frequently feels unsure of his conclusions about the characteristic attitudes of an individual based on observations of overt behavior, studies of the relation between such factors and the content of human movement could be of great value to him.

3. The psychologist. Since differences in the characteristics of the psychologist are differences which appear to make a difference, it is of practical importance to study the ways in which they are reflected in the quantity and content of the movement response.

The point that we are here trying to emphasize is that there are limitations to studies which focus on the end product, the verbalized response, of a process in which many factors are operative. The studies discussed in this chapter have indicated that the movement response has or reflects personal significances. Movement responses are given in the context of a particular kind of interaction in which certain variables are operative, and future studies of the nature of these personal significances will have to deal directly with these variables. Taking these variables into account undoubtedly complicates the task of the clinician and the researcher, a consequence which would more realistically mirror the matrix of factors which antedate and influence the verbalized response. What we are here saying is that the nature of the clinical interaction requires investigation of these factors if the ultimate aim is to understand the covert significances of the overt response in the individual case.

## Chapter 14

# THE PLAIN FORM (F) RESPONSE
# AND FORM QUALITY

### THE F RESPONSE

ANY response which is not scorable in the categories previously described is scored plain F. In the F response the outline of the blot area is the only aspect of the external stimulus incorporated into the response. Since the F scoring indicates a restricted use of stimulus characteristics, and it does not reflect subjective or internal factors, it has been assumed that the individual who predominantly gives F responses is constricted in the sense that he is unable to respond in a manner which allows for the expression of internal feelings or a ready responsiveness to external stimuli. The obsessive-compulsive individual, whose defensive reactions are associated with unacceptable personal feelings and have the effect of minimizing the influence of external stimuli, is the one who is expected to give a record in which the F response predominates. Kates' (85) study, however, clearly gave contrary evidence. In the absence of relevant research, one can only say that the interpretive significance of many or few F responses is obscure.

### FORM QUALITY OF FORM LEVEL (REALITY TESTING)

When a response does not fit the chosen blot area, we say that reality testing at that particular moment is inadequate: the individual did not evaluate his response on a basis so as to take account of the external referent in a culturally accepted way. Although much importance is attached to the F+ percent as a measure of adequacy of reality testing, leading workers in the field are by no means agreed about what responses should be used as a basis for the measure or what criteria should be employed for determining "goodness or badness" of form. In her review of the history of form-level appraisal Kimball (88) has well described the differences in practice which exist among leading writers in the field, and the serious student is urged to read her article.

Form-level has been variously defined in terms of "percentage of clearly visualized forms," by Rorschach, "form accuracy," or "degree of correspondence between his [the subject's] concept and the given form qualities of the blot," by Klopfer, and "congruence with the inkblot," by Rapaport. Beck, like Rapaport, defines form-level in terms of the correspondence of the response with the "reality" that obtains in the inkblot. Inspection of these definitions of form-level would lead to the assumption that there exists a fair amount of agreement among Rorschach examiners, first with respect to the "perceptual reality of the inkblot" with which the response is to be compared, and second, concerning whether or not any given response corresponds closely to this reality.

When the form-level scores which have been published by different authors are compared, however, no such agreement is apparent. In many cases the same response has been scored F+ (good or accurate form) by one author, and F− (poor or inaccurate form) by another. These differences may be the result of lack of agreement among workers concerning the "perceptual reality" of the inkblot, differences in the standards and criteria which different workers use for comparison of the response and inkblot, or an interaction of both of these factors.

Using the published lists of Rorschach responses by Beck (*16*) and Hertz (*72*), Kimball computed the percentage of agreement in scoring (Table 11). Kimball presents several reasons for the unexpectedly large deviations in form-level scoring:

*Sample differences.* The population of Junior High School students on which Hertz's frequency tables were developed may be different from Beck's group of subjects. Beck's "normal adults" are not described, and apparently no systematic effort was made to select a sample representative of the general population. Comparisons between authors' scoring based on norms derived from the records of two very different groups of subjects violate the important principle of restriction of norms to populations similar to the one used for standardization. However, Beck's list was published with the expressed purpose of training Rorschach workers to develop standards for scoring form-level—presumably in any records they may score. In other words, Beck, without a description of the sample on which his norms are based, attributes great generality to his list of good and bad forms, as if it could be used as a general scoring standard.

Hertz explicitly states that her frequency tables should be used for scoring only the records of subjects represented by her standardization group. Undoubtedly one reason for the low percentage of agreement . . . is that

Beck's and Hertz's populations differ markedly. The unfortunate results of applying one author's scoring norms to another's varying clinical population must be apparent from a consideration of results. . . .

*Different scoring criteria for form-level.* Hertz used frequency of occurrence of each response in the records of her subjects (supplemented with her subjective judgments of similarity to frequent responses and the judgments of three to five independent judges on doubtful, infrequent responses). Beck, on the other hand, used differentiation between normal and

TABLE 11.  Percentage of Agreement Between Beck and Hertz on 165 Rorschach Responses Scored for Form Level by Both Authors (Kimball, *88*)

| Card | Number of Responses Scored by Both Authors | Percentage Agreement | Percentage Agreement Omitting P Response |
|------|---------------------------------------------|----------------------|-------------------------------------------|
| I | 40 | 75 | 72 |
| II | 7 | 70 | 50 |
| III | 3 | 66 | 66 |
| IV | 30 | 70 | 61 |
| V | 22 | 55 | 44 |
| VI | 21 | 38 | 35 |
| VII | 18 | 89 | 89 |
| VIII | 12 | 83 | 83 |
| IX | 5 | 80 | 80 |
| X | 7 | 57 | 57 |
| Total: | 165 | | |

abnormal subjects, plus his subjective comparison of "new" responses with old ones "known" to differentiate. . . .

*Different basis for selecting responses for publication.* Specific examples of form-level scoring included in the lists of the two authors were selected differently and for different purposes. Hertz apparently includes in her frequency tables all responses given by her 300 subjects, with a form-level score for each response. Beck's list, on the other hand, represents a selected sample, including (a) very common responses, considered to be the nucleus of F+, and (b) a large number of doubtful or deviating responses neither clearly F+ nor F−, on which examiners usually want help in making decisions. Obviously, inclusion of the first group of responses would tend to raise the percentage of agreement between the two authors, whereas the latter would lower it. Unfortunately, Beck does not differentiate between the very common and the borderline responses in his list.

*Responses "seen" in different ways.* In any study of extent of agreement in scoring, it is essential that both authors score, as nearly as possible, exactly the same response. It is a well-known fact that even the most frequent, "popular" Rorschach responses can be seen in many different positions and locations in the inkblots. With no inquiry material included by either author, it is impossible to be sure that both authors are scoring the same response, even though it may be labelled and scored the same for location. Since the form-level of a response varies with the position and location of the concept, no lists should be published without specification of at least three characteristics.

*Scoring of vague and variable forms.* The disposition of responses with vague or variable form by the two authors considered accounts for some of the differences in scoring noted. Hertz apparently adheres most strictly to frequency of response, disregarding whether the response as given is specific in form or vague or variable. It is impossible to determine the influence of vagueness and changeableness of form on Beck's form-level scoring. . . .

Since studies of the reliability of form-level appraisal had not been attempted, Kimball (89) had four groups of appraisers, varying with respect to experience with the Rorschach, judge 100 W responses (ten responses for each card) which had been taken from Beck's and Hertz's published lists. Ratings were made on a six-point scale.

1. Very inaccurate—blot bears no relationship at all to concept
2. Quite inaccurate
3. More inaccurate than accurate when blot is compared with concept
4. More accurate than inaccurate when blot is compared with concept
5. Quite accurate
6. Very accurate—blot corresponds to concept very closely

Kimball's major findings were as follows:

1. There was good agreement on form-level appraisal in 37 of the 100 responses.

2. "When the highest ratings for each inkblot are considered, there is marked agreement among the four groups of appraisers concerning the order of responses with respect to degree of correspondence with the inkblot. A few responses stand out for each inkblot as being selected most accurate by a large percentage of appraisers in all four groups."

3. "Inter-rater agreement is extremely variable for the 100 responses appraised. Moreover, for most of the responses the range of ratings is large, extending throughout the six-point scale. The F+ responses with the highest mean ratings were each rated as low as 1 ('no relation-

ship whatever between inkblot and concept') by at least one appraiser. Conversely, the F— responses with the lowest mean ratings were rated 4 or above ('more accurate than accurate') by some appraisers."

4. Comparison of form-level appraisal by Beck and Hertz with that by Kimball's appraisers showed marked discrepancies.

An important implication of Kimball's findings is that *because clinicians differ in criteria for scoring they also differ in how they perceive and react to the subject in the clinical interaction.* If in the process of taking the test a subject gives a response which one examiner considers "good" and another considers "bad," it is probable that the subsequent behavior (e.g., anticipation) of the clinician will be influenced by the particular judgment he makes. If he considers the response of poor form quality, his subsequent conducting of the inquiry may unwittingly become more prodding in nature as a result of his doubts about the adequacy of the subject's reality testing. The clinician may begin to reinterpret previously observed behavior in line with his altered perception of the subject. Differences in scoring criteria among examiners may result not only in differences in examiner behavior but in changes in the subject's behavior as well. The possibilities we are here discussing are identical with what frequently happens in therapeutic interactions—once the therapist makes a value judgment (i.e., he, in effect, says "This is 'healthy' and that is 'pathological' ") his perception of and behavior toward the patient are altered. *Kimball's data should serve as a reminder that just as the subject's behavior in the clinical interaction is a function of his conception of what is right and wrong, good or bad, the clinician's behavior is similarly determined.* In so far as criteria for evaluating form level are concerned, the clinician would do well to be acutely aware that his judgments and behavior are a function in some way of subjective factors. In Chapter 16 we shall return to this problem when we discuss how the social class values of the clinician influence his perception of the subject and the conclusions to which he comes.

Kimball correctly points out that the publication of lists of "empty shells of responses" for which there is no inquiry is not justified as an aid to students learning the Rorschach. Since the student is frequently unsure whether a response he obtained is like the one in a published list—and since two experienced clinicians will not infrequently disagree in appraising form level on the basis of the subject's verbalization—*the use of tracings would very probably increase the reliability of the scoring of form level,* as the studies by Cox and Sarason (*31*) and Janoff (*83*) suggest.

There are two common practices in connection with the scoring of form level and the computation of F+ percent which are questionable. The first relates to the practice of basing F+ percent only on responses which receive a plain F scoring (*16*, p. 203). If the goodness of fit between concept and blot area is considered an important indicator of an individual's adequacy of reality, it does not seem justified to use a measure which takes into account only one scoring category—especially since in clinical practice attention is paid to the adequacy of all responses. The second practice which is questionable is that of scoring as minus those responses in which no definite form is intended (e.g., rock) as well as those responses in which a definite form is indicated by the verbalization but little or no congruence with the blot is discernible. In the one case the individual is usually aware that his response is not of precise form while in the other case he is usually unaware that "something is wrong." To score both responses as minus is likely not to reflect the different processes which accompanied the response, a problem pointed out by Rapaport (*121*) and Klopfer (*92*) and reflected in their scoring systems. By grouping together responses either of vague or of definite form with responses in which congruence between blot and concept is poor, the clinician is using two different continua: one of complexity and one of adequacy of reality testing. A response like "rocks" is not complex but it does not necessarily reflect inadequate reality testing. A response in which all parts of the blot are used and specific forms are described, but which bears little semblance to the blot may be highly complex while at the same time it reflects inadequate reality testing (p. 102). If it could be demonstrated that the continua of complexity and reality testing were highly correlated, then the practice described above would be more defensible.

This writer is in accord with Kimball's (*88*) conclusions based on her review of various methods of form-level appraisal:

The criteria for scoring F+ and F— vary greatly for different authors: frequency of occurrence, differentiation between normal and abnormal subjects, empathy on the part of the examiner, and subjective evaluation of the degree of correspondence between the response and the "perceptual reality" of the inkblots have been used as a basis for form-level scoring. In many cases workers have followed Rorschach in using statistical frequency supplemented by the examiner's evaluation of infrequent or borderline responses. The logical inconsistency of adopting a criterion and arbitrarily changing to another when the first is inadequate, is apparent, and it is not likely to result in reliable scoring.

It has been shown that each criterion for form-level scoring must be supplemented to some extent by the examiner's judgment concerning correspondence between response and inkblot. Use of the scale proposed by Klopfer and Davidson requires many subjective decisions on the part of the examiner, and the end result can be no more precise or reliable than these decisions, whether expressed in quantitative terms or not. Such evaluations are undoubtedly influenced by the empathy or lack of empathy of the examiner for (a) the inkblot, (b) the concept given as a response by the subject, and (c) the concept as a response to a particular inkblot or blot area.

We cannot agree with Rapaport that a "simple test" of self-interrogation can overcome differences among examiners with respect to their readiness to empathize with a given response. Wide differences in background, training, personality characteristics and Rorschach experience make it unlikely that agreement can be reached simply or easily. Klopfer and Kelley and Brosin and Fromm have recognized the problem of examiner-involvement in form-level scoring, recommending intensive training and discipline under a recognized expert in Rorschach administration and interpretation as the only method of overcoming interference from the presence or lack of empathy for responses. However, since Rorschach interpretations are and undoubtedly will continue to be made by workers without the benefit of such intensive training and discipline, there is urgent need for formulation of a sounder basis for form-level scoring than undefined subjective evaluation.

Form-level scoring is further complicated by the use of different scoring systems by different workers, some scoring only F+ and F−, others adding plain F, and still others using four or more different classifications. It would be most helpful to students if different authors would compare their notations for form-level so that some statement of the relationship between different categories could be formulated.

At present, each author's form-level scoring must be interpreted in the light of the criteria he uses and his own definition of form-level. Furthermore, since no large representative sample of the general population has been studied with respect to Rorschach performance, the published norms for all Rorschach variables must be restricted to the records of subjects represented in the group studied by the author. Until all Rorschach workers can agree concerning the criteria for form-level scoring (or at least until they make explicit the cues in each record upon which they make their form-level estimates), such statements as ". . . the weaker the Ego, the more F— percepts appear," cannot have the same meaning for different readers, and thus cannot be validated by comparison with the experience of other clinicians.

With the increasing clinical conviction of the diagnostic importance of form-level in Rorschach records, the need for reliable methods of appraisal of form-level has become acute. No longer are clinicians content with a general statement concerning normality or abnormality based upon superior versus distorted or inaccurate form-level in Rorschach records. Now they are attempting to establish and predict levels of intelligence, in terms of I.Q. scores in some cases, on the basis of fine differentiations made between form-level of different responses in each record. Moreover, such diagnoses as "schizoid tendencies" are being made in cases of slightly distorted form-level. If such fine differences in interpretation are to be justified, it is essential that form-level scoring be made reliable and standard, so that the problem of validity can be studied. It is probable that much of the disagreement among authors concerning the interpretive significance of form-level arises from differences in definition and methods of scoring it.

The reader may have noted that the discussions of form level have been concerned primarily with evaluation of the verbalized (formal) response. An equally important problem, particularly in the case of "poor" responses, concerns the subject's own reaction or evaluation of the response. We might put the problem in the form of a question: If a subject has given a response of poor form quality, does it make any difference if upon questioning he (1) is completely satisfied with the adequacy of the response or (2) indicates some dissatisfaction with the degree of congruence between the content of the response and the blot area utilized? What we are here asking is a question which the clinician considers crucial in the therapeutic interaction—to what extent does the patient realize that his behavior (e.g., a wish, fantasy, attitude) is not justified by, or in keeping with, considerations of external reality? It is one thing if a patient unquestioningly believes that people are against him and it is another thing if he has doubts about such a belief. To focus on the belief and not on the subject's evaluation of it would obviously be neglecting an important datum—*a neglect which not only may make for an invalid prognosis but also may affect the therapist's behavior in the interaction.* The situation is no different in the case of the evaluation of the adequacy of a patient's reality testing based on considerations of the form quality of his Rorschach responses.

Another factor that must be considered in the evaluation of "poor" responses is *how the subject interpreted the instructions.* If a subject interprets the instructions to mean that one is supposed to "let his mind go"—to free-associate—then his "poor" responses do not have the same significance as those of a patient who has concluded that there is a right and wrong answer. We are here trying to indicate that, while reliability of the evaluation of form quality is necessary, it is clearly not a sufficient answer to the problem of understanding the significances of variations in form quality within and between individuals in the clinical interaction.

### JANOFF'S VALIDATION STUDY

In previous chapters we concluded on the basis of various studies that prediction of the adequacy and efficiency of behavior in stress and problem-solving situations was most validly made when all Rorschach responses were evaluated so as to reflect definiteness of form and/or adequacy of reality testing. We would like at this time to present in some detail Janoff's (*83*) attempt to validate this kind of conclusion. The subjects in the study were ninety-three fourth-grade children. The Rorschach was individually administered and tracings obtained for each response. The aim of the study is indicated in the following:

A survey of the literature was made to determine what interpretations of form quality have been advanced. Though these have been in terms of adult records, they have been applied indiscriminately in interpreting the records of children. . . .
   Form quality, or form-level, has been considered to be related to:
      Ego strength
      Ability to test reality
      Intelligence
      Clarity and accuracy of perception
      Control over intellectual processes
      Delay of impulsiveness
      Sharpness of critical appraisal
      Wealth of association process
      Repressive or constrictive control

Mental approach
Yielding to strong cultural pressure
Conceptual activity
Formal reasoning
Wealth of past experience
Ability to maintain attention
Ability to concentrate
Conscious discrimination and judgment
Stability of the personality

By selecting the most frequently agreed upon interpretations and refining the terminology, several personality variables evolved which could be measured systematically in children and related to form quality. These were then incorporated into testable "hypotheses" concerning the behavioral significance of form quality.

The general plan of the study was to test predictions stemming from these hypotheses by comparing the subjects' scores on relevant behavioral measures to Rorschach measures of form quality.

*The Hypotheses*

*Hypothesis I:* "Good form quality" reflects a cautious, unimpulsive way of responding.

*Hypothesis II:* Good form quality reflects an ability to maintain adequate control over interfering subjective and affective reactions under conditions of stress.

*Hypothesis III:* Good form quality reflects an ability to make those critical discriminations between internal and external cues necessary for realistic behavior and for adequate "reality testing."

*Hypothesis IV:* Good form quality reflects an ability to pay attention to appropriate environmental cues with a minimum of interference from irrelevant stimuli.

While these hypotheses are not mutually exclusive, it was felt that they represented somewhat different emphases and that the rejection or confirmation of each of them would contribute to a better understanding of the relation between personality and the perception of form on the Rorschach.

. . . . .

It was decided that, for the purposes of this study, none of the published lists of scores for "good" and "poor" form responses was applicable, primarily because none had been based on a sample similar to the one used here. Assigning plus and minus scores to the records of nine-year-old children on the basis of the responses of adolescents or adults appeared unjustifiable. Furthermore, the dichotomizing of all form responses into "plus" and "minus" seemed, for the purposes of this research, too unrefined. It was felt that there are differences in the accuracy of perception even within the F plus and F minus categories; some F minus responses are much "poorer" than others, and some F plus responses much more clearly perceived than others which are also traditionally scored plus. Making some provision for such differences seemed necessary in an investigation of this kind. Similarly, the published lists have presented as "F minus" many vague and variable forms. In the consideration of the accuracy of a percept in the present investigation, it was felt that the scoring of a response as "poor" would be unjustifiable if no definite form was intended by the subject.

For these reasons, then, it was apparent that a more comprehensive system of scoring form quality would be necessary. An attempt to use frequency of occurrence of each response as a quantitative basis for arriving at form quality scores for the present sample proved unfeasible because of the small number of cases and wide variation in responses. Consequently, a form-level rating scale was devised based on Klopfer and Davidson's suggestions but considerably altered. . . . A Pearson r of .90 was obtained between the writer and another psychologist who scored independently fifty responses selected at random from the protocols in the study.

All the protocols were scored blindly by the writer six months after they had been obtained. Responses of all 93 subjects to each card were scored together, and ratings for previous cards were concealed in order to avoid unconscious bias or halo effect. The tracings available for each response helped considerably in the scoring. *It should be noted that every response, regardless of whether or not it was determined primarily by form or by some other determinant (movement, color, etc.), was assigned a rating.*

"That the agreement is so high on an admittedly crude and judgmental scale can be attributed to the availability of tracings for each response, the relatively uncomplex and concrete nature of the responses of children of this age, and the similar backgrounds of the raters." Every response, regardless of the traditional scoring category into which it fell, was assigned a form-level rating. The basis for the ratings is given below.

Form quality was here thought of as a continuum, rather than as a dichotomy of "good" and "poor" form. Thus, form quality can range from those cases where a definite form is intended by the subject, and is clearly and accurately seen by him, through cases where no definite form is intended and the subject should not be penalized, to those cases where there is definite form intended, but the concept chosen does not fit the area of the ink blot indicated. Every response (regardless of whether or not an "F" would be given in usual Rorschach scoring) was given a *basal rating,* according to the directions below. Responses given a basal rating of +1.0 or above could have additional credits as explained under the section "Adding Credits" below. Minus ratings did not change, however; inaccurate responses were assigned one of four ratings depending upon the nature of the inaccuracy.

## Basal Ratings

+2.5  This is given to the unusual, complex, highly original, but obviously keen and accurate responses.

+2.0  This is given to those responses which are not unusual but which are obviously keen and accurate and refer to concepts having several definite form requirements. The Populars are not included here.

+1.5  This category is reserved for the popular responses listed by Hertz and Klopfer.

+1.0  This level is for those responses which, while accurate, represent a lower level of mental functioning requiring very little specificity, complexity, or imagination, because the concept itself is a very simple, uncomplex one. Examples are worm, ear, snake, and tree trunk.

+0.5  This level is for concepts which lack definiteness, but are not inaccurate or unjustifiable. The 0.5 concept has some suggestion of form, but does not have more than one essential form element. Examples are inlet or peninsula (because it must jut out), a leaf because the center line could represent a stem, wings, etc.

0.0  This is given to the response which is completely indefinite, in that there are *no* essential form elements present. The response is given in terms of a concept that could be most any shape. Examples are rocks, island, clouds, smoke, bushes, insides of body (when parts are not specified).

−0.5  This is given to a vague concept which is *not* applicable to the part of the blot chosen. While the concept may be considered only indefinite, its application to an unappropriate blot area is a manifestation of bad judgment on the part of the subject.

−1.0  This is given to a response which might ordinarily be given a +1.0 or higher rating, but which has one inaccurate specification or where one part of the response doesn't fit.

−2.0  This is assigned to a response where more than one specification is inaccurate, but parts of the response are still recognizable and it is evident that there has been some effort on the part of the subject to reconcile the shape of the blot area chosen and the form elements of the concept.

−3.0   This is assigned to all other responses—confabulatory responses and irrational responses where for one reason or another the subject does not bother at all to try to reconcile the shape of the blot area chosen with the form elements of the concept. There appears to be no justification whatsoever for the response given.

*Adding Credits*

Each constructive specification added one-half point credit to the basal rating (provided it was +1.0 or above) under the following conditions. (The additions to be credited were obtained from the performance proper or from the Inquiry, since it was conducted without prodding, so that all specifications were spontaneous.)

1. *The specification must exceed the essential elements of the concept.* This may take the form of: (1) mentioning a part of a concept not usually included (like seeing the claws of the bat or the protruding round eyes of the moth in Card I, along with the body and wings) or (2) pointing out a specific position (like bending over of the men in Card III or the stretching neck of a snake seen in the small upper side detail of Card IV).

2. *The specification must be independent.* For example, the pointing out of several interdependent details like the snout and ears of the usual animal heads in Card II or the eyes and eyebrows of the face in the top detail of Card IV are counted as only one specific elaboration and therefore given just one-half credit.

*Unchanged Credit*

The form-level rating of a concept remains unchanged when irrelevant specifications are mentioned by the subject, which are merely embellishments and actually do not contribute in any way to the form level of the responses.

Janoff used the following measures of form quality:

a. %F+ which consists of the ratio of the number of F+ responses to the sum of the number of F− and F+ responses. This is the traditional form-level measure which has been used most frequently by Rorschach workers. The number of F+ responses is the number of responses which have been given any one of the plus ratings. Similarly, the number of F− responses is the number of responses which have been given any one of the minus ratings.

b. %$\overline{\overline{F+}}$ which is the ratio of the number of F+ responses to the total number of responses in the protocol. This measure differs from %F+ in that it takes into account the vague responses.

c. $\overline{F+}$ which consists of the number of responses which received a rating of +2.0 or above. This gives an index of how many of the "good" responses were especially clearly defined.

d. #F− which consists of the absolute number of responses which have been given a minus rating.

e. %F− which is the ratio of the number of F− responses to the total number of responses in the protocol.

f. $\overline{F-}$ which consists of the number of responses which received a rating of −2.0 or below. This gives an index of how many responses were badly distorted.

g. $\underline{FQ}$ which is the ratio of the algebraic sum of all the form-level *ratings* to the total number of responses. This gives an index of the general perceptual quality of the entire protocol, and is, of course, a function of the relative quantities of plus, minus, and vague responses in the protocol.

The direction of the intercorrelations was in every case what would be expected if one assumed that all of the measures had something in common.

## THE HEALY PICTURE COMPLETION TEST

This test has a game-like quality for children and it was felt that certain characteristic ways of responding could be observed. The task requires the child to (a) listen to directions, (b) select from a large number of possible alternatives the ten blocks (including one sample) which will best complete a picture, and (c) view his work critically. It therefore provides an opportunity to observe impulsive and unreflective behavior.

The Healy Test was also used to test a prediction stemming from Hypothesis III, which deals with "reality testing." Hanfmann found that the incongruous placements made by schizophrenics on Form II of this test appeared to result from the disregard of the spatial relationships necessary for a realistic pictorial representation. It was expected that some of the children in this study might make inappropriate placements, and that their expressed reasons for making them might show peculiarities in their thinking resulting from failure to be self-critical and to take into account the obvious aspects of the situations depicted.

The predictions for behavior in this situation, stemming from Hypotheses I and III, are:

Table 12. Results of Chi-Square Tests Between Rorschach Form-Quality Measures and Behavioral Measures on Healy Test (Janoff, 83)

| Rorschach Form-Quality Measures | Reaching vs. Non-Reaching During Instructions | | Initial Response Time | | Number of Placements | | "Looking Over" Time | | Appropriateness of Responses | |
|---|---|---|---|---|---|---|---|---|---|---|
| | $X^2$ | P | $X^2$ | P | $X^2$ | P | $X^2$ | P | $X^2$ | P |
| %F+ | 6.72[a] | <.01 | 2.61 | .11 | 6.21 | .02 | 7.05 | <.01 | 6.76 | <.01 |
| %F+ | 6.26 | .02 | 0.17 | >.50 | 4.24 | .04 | 6.19 | .02 | 2.83 | .10 |
| F̄+ | 0.12 | >.50 | 0.00 | >.50 | 0.03 | >.50 | 0.01 | >.50 | 0.50 | >.30 |
| #F− | 7.38 | <.01 | 0.93 | >.30 | 2.07 | .16 | 4.92 | .03 | 1.26 | .26 |
| %F− | 5.42 | .02 | 0.30 | >.50 | 2.78 | .10 | 6.91 | <.01 | 8.95 | <.01 |
| F̄− | 4.60 | .04 | 0.51 | >.30 | 1.09 | .29 | 0.83 | >.30 | 3.15 | .08 |
| FQ | 5.89 | .02 | 0.93 | >.30 | 7.26 | <.01 | 10.52 | .001 | 7.00 | <.01 |

In this and in all subsequent tables, interpolated probabilities are used in all cases up to a P of .30; a P of .30 indicates a probability between .30 and .50 and a P of .50 indicates a probability of .50 or above. $X^2$ and P values will be underlined when the relationship is in the predicted direction.
[a] In this and the subsequent tables, $X^2$ and P values are given.

*Prediction* 1: "Good form" children will be able to delay a motor response until directions indicate that a response can be made.

*Prediction* 2: "Good form" children will have a *longer* reaction time for first manipulation of the blocks.

*Prediction* 3: "Good form" children will more carefully consider the possibilities before acting, as evidenced by *fewer* changes after the block has been placed.

*Prediction* 4: "Good form" children will spend a *longer* amount of time critically examining their work, when the opportunity to look over and make changes is given.

*Prediction* 5: "Good form" children will be less likely to make completely inappropriate responses.

All predictions except the second were supported by the findings (Table 12).

## THE PORTEUS MAZE SITUATION

This test consists of a series of mazes, graded in difficulty. The subject is required to trace the correct path, and, if he chooses a wrong path, is given another trial. While the Porteus mazes were designed primarily to test a form of mental ability involving planning capacity and alertness in a new situation, Porteus felt that they might be regarded as tests of temperamental capacities as well. He devised a method for scoring the test qualitatively which he found to be a valid and reliable indicator of impulsiveness. Qualitative performance in the maze test was therefore used as an additional check of the behavioral implications of Hypothesis I.

The prediction relevant to this situation was:

*Prediction* 6: "Good form" children will obtain lower qualitative scores than those with "poor form." (A *low* qualitative score indicates a *small* number of qualitative errors.)

One of the measures was significantly related to qualitative score on the Porteus. Four other measures were in the predicted direction although not significant ($p = .08, .08, .10, .19$). The consistency in the trends was interpreted as lending some support to the prediction.[1]

[1] It will be recalled (p. 156) that Holtzman (*78*) and Gardner (*55*) reported supporting evidence for the relation between impulsivity and Rorschach measures based in large part on bright color responses, those with vague or indefinite form receiving the greatest weights. It is apparent from Janoff's form-level scale that subjects who predominantly give responses of vague and indefinite form, if only in the case of bright color, will get lower scores than subjects who do not give such responses. Since the tendency to give vague response to bright color is related to the tendency to give similar responses in the

## The Kohs Blocks Stress Situation

. . . This test was used to measure intellectual control under stress and thus to test Hypothesis II. The general plan was to compare each subject's performance on this test under "normal" conditions with his performance when stress was introduced.

The Kohs Blocks were presented first as a game in which the subject was encouraged to do his best under pleasant, non-stressful conditions. Stress was then introduced by inducing a feeling of failure, relating the subject's performance on the test to school grades, to the performance of his friends, and to promotion to the fifth grade, and by threatening deprivation of the much-prized play period. It was expected that some children would show a marked decrement in performance due to stress, and that such behavior would be related to the Rorschach measures.

The following predictions were made for this situation, based on Hypothesis II:

*Prediction 7:* "Good form" children will have *less* increase in time scores under stress.
*Prediction 8:* "Good form" children will have *less* increase in ineffectual trial and error behavior, as evidenced by less increase in the number of moves under stress.

Table 13 shows the results relevant for the predictions. Prediction 8 receives greater support than Prediction 7.

## The Classroom "Stress" Situation

A measure of mental output was needed which did not require individual administration, which could be scored easily, and which could be controlled for practice effects. . . . The Wechsler-Bellevue Digit Symbol Test was used for this classroom situation. Preliminary testing on a different group of 29 children revealed that the effects of learning could be ruled out and a fairly stable level of performance obtained in seven trials. Two practice sessions were given in each classroom. At the first one, the tests were presented with the explanation that all the fourth grade children in the teacher training schools were being given them in order to try out a new method of

---

absence of bright color (*179*), it may be that the subjects in Holtzman's and Gardner's studies who received Rorschach scores indicative of impulsivity were those who also gave vague responses when bright color was not used. Color may not have been the most important variable in these studies, although, as Siipola (*155*) has demonstrated, the presence of color may make for a more difficult problem-solving situation and presumably exacerbate the tendency to respond vaguely and/or poorly.

teaching arithmetic. At this time the instructions were explained to the class and illustrated on the blackboard. The procedure was then as follows:

1. Each subject was presented with a pad containing five Digit Symbol Tests, one on a page. The teacher assisted the experimenter in making sure that all subjects understood the instructions and did a sample line of digit symbols correctly.

2. The test was administered four times, with the usual time limits of 90 seconds per trial and 60 second intervals between each trial. Precautions were taken to see that all the subjects started and stopped as directed.

TABLE 13. Results of Chi-Square Tests Between Rorschach Form-Quality Measures and Decrement Under Stress as Measured by Increases in Time Scores and Number of Moves on Kohs Test (Janoff, 83)

| | Time | | Moves | |
|---|---|---|---|---|
| | $X^2$ | P | $X^2$ | P |
| %F+ | 2.54 | .12 | 3.62 | .06 |
| %F+ | 2.13 | .15 | 4.64 | .04 |
| F+ | 0.72 | >.30 | 0.07 | >.50 |
| #F− | 1.68 | .20 | 1.22 | .27 |
| %F− | 1.22 | .27 | 2.96 | .10 |
| F− | 2.96 | .09 | 2.39 | .14 |
| FQ | 1.79 | .19 | 4.88 | .03 |

3. Four hours later the second practice session was held. Three trials were administered with rest intervals as before.

4. After a three minute rest, the control period was instituted, during which the subjects had three successive administrations to obtain an average measure of performance when working under unstressful conditions.

5. The pads were collected, and the experimenter said:

Now I'll tell you all the real reason I've been having you do these over and over again. It's been sort of practice for a game we're going to play. You've all been so nice about helping me in my work that I thought it would be fun if we played a *real* game, with prizes! How would you like that? (The children responded excitedly and enthusiastically.) Well, we'll play this game like a relay race. (This was a popular game with the children in both schools.) The rows will play against each other. Each row will be a team. The first persons in each row will race first, while the rest of the row waits. Then the second persons in each row, and so on until the whole row has done it. Keep your pads upside down and flat on your desk until your turn comes. When we're through, I'll figure out the scores. The row that has the best scores will win. That means that *every person* in the row that wins will get a prize.

The first children in each row were then instructed to begin. The other children were very excited, whispered or yelled encouragement to their row-mates. There were six rows of seats in each classroom, so that six children "raced" at a time. After 90 seconds, the first six children were stopped, and the second child in each row was instructed to get ready and given the starting signal. This procedure was continued until every child in every row had had one trial. The whole procedure was repeated two more times, to provide three trials for each child under the "game" conditions. At the conclusion, each child in the room was given a prize, on the pretext that all the children had done so well that it seemed unfair to reward any one row and exclude the others.

That this non-motor, paper-and-pencil situation approximated the competitive, exciting conditions of a game for the children was evidenced by the children's reactions during and after it. There was no indication of annoyance at having to go through the same procedure three times. The children would sit stiffly on the edges of their seats, their pencils poised expectantly, awaiting the starting signal. They tried to peer over the shoulders of their neighbors to watch their performance. Several children vehemently accused children in other rows of cheating, although the close supervision of the experimenter and the teacher insured the proper observation of the time limits. As soon as the game was over, the children demanded to know how long it would take before the results were announced. When told that all would get prizes, some were actually disappointed, for they apparently had wanted very much to have the prestige of being "winners."

The score for each test was the number of items correct. An average score for the three trials in the control non-game situation and the three trials in the game period was determined for each subject. The average score during the game period was algebraically subtracted from the average score during the pre-game control period for each subject. This difference was the measure used here. An r of .08 between this measure and the average score during the three non-game trials indicates that there was little or no relationship between the two.

*Prediction* 9: "Good form" children will show *less* decrement in performance under the excitement of competitive play.

The probability values for the seven measures of form quality were: .06, .10, .14, .15, .23, .23, and .30. The seven consistent trends found in this situation, while not statistically reliable, lend some support to Prediction 9.

TEACHERS' RATINGS

Each child was rated by his teacher on 45 scales each of which could be put in one of four categories: impulsiveness, behavior under stress, reality testing, and paying attention. Each item was stated in terms of classroom behavior and the teachers were carefully instructed in the use of the rating scales in several preliminary discussion sessions.

*Prediction* 10: "Good form" children will obtain *low* scores on ratings of impulsiveness.

*Prediction* 11: "Good form" children will obtain *low* scores on ratings of loss of control under stress.

*Prediction* 12: "Good form" children will obtain *low* scores on ratings of lack of reality testing.

*Prediction* 13: "Good form" children will obtain *low scores* on ratings of lack of attention.

Table 14 shows the results relevant to the predictions. Predictions 10, 11, and 12 are supported and there is only very slight evidence, though no contradictory evidence, to support Prediction 13.

In Janoff's study there were no significant relationships between M.A. and the form-quality measures. There was a significant relationship between total number of responses and #F−, $\overline{F+}$, and FQ (in a negative direction). "The total number of Rorschach responses is significantly related to two of the behavioral variables, and is less reliably related to one other: the giving of many responses on the Rorschach is associated with reaching and with making many placements on the Healy, and with having a poorer qualitative score on the Porteus. However, since all of these behavioral variables were found to be related to other form quality measures besides #F− and FQ it seems reasonable to assume that the obtained relationships between these variables and HF− and FQ is not entirely explained by their common relationship to number of Rorschach responses. The relationship of $\overline{F+}$ is not relevant, since this measure was not reliably related to any of the behavioral variables." Table 15 presents the number of times each measure was found to be related to the several behavioral variables at certain levels of significance.

TABLE 14. Results of Chi-Square Tests Between Rorschach Form-Quality Measures and Scores on Teachers' Ratings (Janoff, 83)

| Rorschach Form-Quality Measures | Scores on Ratings of Impulsive Behavior | | Scores on Ratings of Control Under Stress | | Scores on Ratings of Reality Testing | | Scores on Ratings of Paying Attention | |
|---|---|---|---|---|---|---|---|---|
| | $X^2$ | P | $X^2$ | P | $X^2$ | P | $X^2$ | P |
| %F+ | 3.74 | .06 | 3.14 | .08 | 3.14 | .08 | 1.89 | .18 |
| %F+ | 2.65 | .11 | 4.11 | .05 | 4.63 | .04 | 3.29 | .07 |
| F+ | 0.08 | .50 | 0.20 | .50 | 0.76 | .30 | 0.00 | .50 |
| #F- | 6.58 | .02 | 5.35 | .03 | 4.66 | .04 | 0.85 | .30 |
| %F- | 5.92 | .02 | 7.02 | .01 | 4.92 | .03 | 2.43 | .13 |
| F- | 2.38 | .14 | 1.76 | .19 | 3.10 | .08 | 1.22 | .27 |
| FQ | 1.45 | .23 | 2.54 | .12 | 4.08 | .05 | 2.13 | .15 |

. . . The most obvious finding is the complete failure of $\overline{F+}$ as a predictive measure. Not once did the relationship of this measure to any behavioral variable yield a P even approaching significance. Thus it appears that a measure such as this, which takes into consideration only the superiority and elaboration of the plus responses, has no predictive value for the kinds of behavior studied here. $\overline{F-}$ proved only slightly more valuable. The best predictive measures appear to be those involving *all* responses—good, poor, and evasive. Thus, the measure %F+, which is the ratio of the number of plus responses to the *total number* of responses in the protocol,

TABLE 15. Number of Chi-Square Tests Significant at Various Levels of Confidence for Each Rorschach Form-Quality Measure (Janoff, *83*)

|  | Number of Tests Significant at 5 Percent Level of Confidence or Below | Number of Tests Significant at the 6–15 Percent Levels of Confidence | Number of Tests Not Reaching 15 Percent Level of Confidence |
|---|---|---|---|
| %F+ | 4 | 7 | 2 |
| $\underline{\underline{\%F+}}$ | 7 | 4 | 2 |
| F+ | 0 | 0 | 13 |
| #F− | 5 | 3 | 5 |
| %F− | 6 | 4 | 3 |
| F− | 1 | 6 | 6 |
| FQ | 6 | 4 | 3 |

was reliably related to more of the behavioral variables than was %F+, which is composed of only plus and minus responses. The fact that FQ, a measure which takes into account the *ratings* of all the responses in the protocol, ranked high in the number of significant findings increases the likelihood that a measure that is composed of all the responses may be most fruitful for predicting. It will also be noted from the tables in the results sections that in some cases #F− and %F− proved to be more sensitive as predictors than the other measures. It would seem, then, that the use of more than one measure of form quality for predictive purposes might in some cases be desirable.

A study by Stein (*161*) is relevant here because he comes to a conclusion similar to that of Janoff although he used quite different procedures. He tachistoscopically exposed the Rorschach cards in both an ascending and a descending series in which exposure time varied from very brief to unlimited times. At the lower exposure times he found a tendency for responses of all kinds to be either of vague or of poor form. "When the accuracy for form responses is poor it is usually interpreted as indicating that the subject is functioning inadequately either because of emotional problems or intellectual shortcomings. The variation of F+ percent as a function of exposure time indicates that this interpretation may be valid. Low F+ percent is characteristic of those Rorschach records which are obtained at the 'stressful' shortest exposure level but it is not characteristic of those Rorschach records which are obtained at the longer exposure levels. Consequently, if a subject is permitted to work under optimal conditions without limit of time and his responses still show a poor F formation, then it seems reasonable to suppose that he is functioning under some handicap."

Of major significance in Janoff's study is the support given to the hypothesis that the tendency to give responses of poor form reflects the inability to maintain an impersonal, objective, critical attitude toward the external stimulus situation. Put in another way: the tendency to give responses of poor form reflects, especially in stress situations, the greater strength of personal, subjective factors in contrast to external factors. The support which Janoff's study lends to this hypothesis gives a firmer foundation to a hypothesis presented in the previous chapter: the degree to which the internal and subjective factors reflected in M responses reach overt expression will in part be a function of the degree of reality testing reflected in all responses. However, Janoff's cautions about the clinical use of her findings should be kept in mind.

It was not the purpose of the present study to establish relationships which would enable clinicians to predict behavior for any one child on the basis of his Rorschach performance. Instead, the study was undertaken to determine whether any relationship exists between certain kinds of behavior and the giving of good and poor form responses on the Rorschach. It was hoped that this would permit a clarification of the psychological processes underlying this aspect of the Rorschach. The results support the implicit assumption held by Rorschachers that differences in form quality reflect differences in behavior. In addition, relationships found between the Rorschach form quality measures and the samples of behavior studied here permit speculation concerning the meaning of form quality in light of general psychological theory.

It would seem relevant, however, and of clinical interest, to make some mention here of the magnitude of the relationships found. By converting the obtained chi-square values into phi coefficients and estimating the corresponding Pearson r's, estimates of the probable magnitude of the relationships between the Rorschach form quality measures and the behavioral measures were obtained. The highest $r_\phi$ was 0.54, between FQ and "looking over" time on Healy. For all other relationships which were significant at the five per cent level or below, $r_\phi$ ranged from 0.36 to 0.51. These values are somewhat low in terms of their possibilities for prediction. However, it is generally agreed among clinicians that for predicting to the individual case in the clinical situation, it is the interrelationships among the various Rorschach measures that are most useful. Thus it is probable that other Rorschach factors are related in some way to the general personality variables studied here, and that a multiple measure, composed of form quality and other appropriate variables, would prove the best predictor of all. Williams found that the combined predictive value of form quality and form-color integration in relation to intellectual control proved higher than when either Rorschach factor was used singly. It would appear, then, that a fruitful approach to the eventual validation of the Rorschach would be to investigate each of the Rorschach variables, first separately and then in combination with others. Further research is suggested in this connection from a comparison of the results obtained in Schumer's investigation of the Rorschach human movement response and the results obtained in the present study. Schumer found that individuals who gave many M's appeared to be more responsive to internal subjective factors than those who did not. While she did not attempt to separate appropriate from inappropriate responses as was done in the present study, she did suggest that perhaps internal response tendencies of movement-oriented individuals are behaviorally expressed when adherence to cultural norms is not a factor. She also found that movement-oriented individuals seemed to be more cautious and less impulsive in their first response to a situation. In view of the results obtained in the present study, it would appear, then, that the Rorschach variables of movement and form quality may not be broadly distinct from each other in terms of their relation to personality. Future research in which these two variables are studied concomitantly might contribute not only to a better understanding of the Rorschach but also to a clarification of the role of internal factors in affecting overt behavior.

Janoff's statement about the need for "clarification of the role of internal factors in affecting overt behavior" emphasizes the need for research focusing on the variables which antedate and influence the verbalized response. In other words, future research will have to deal directly with the interpersonal context in which the verbalized response appears. As Janoff indicated, the degree of accurate prediction which can be made on the basis of the formal response is not sufficient to be of great value to the clinician in the individual case. This was to be expected since the verbalized response is a reflection of the interplay of many variables. The constant problem confronting the clinician is how to determine the role of these variables in the clinical interaction. While it is of value to the clinician to know that certain types of responses reflect personal factors, it does not help him in determining how such responses differ with differences in the nature of the interpersonal interaction. It is easy to say that the way in which an individual reacts to the clinical situation is an important sample of his behavior. The thorny problem which future research must clarify is the ways in which the clinician can detect and evaluate those variables on the basis of which the nature of the sample can be described. In this book we have tried to describe some of the major variables operative in the clinical interaction; it would appear that the task of future research is to study the relation of these variables to the verbalized response.

BECK'S Z SCORE

In Janoff's rating scale for form quality two continua were used: the degree of reality testing and the degree of complexity of the response. A rather different approach to the evaluation of the continuum of complexity is represented by Beck's (15) Z or "organizational" score. Beck (16, p. 59) scores Z "when two or more portions of the figure are seen in relation to one another, and when the meaning perceived in the combination, or in any of the component portions, obtains only from the fact of this organization." The following kinds of responses receive Z scores:
1.  Whole responses
2.  Combination of distant details
3.  Combination of white with solid details
4.  Combination of adjacent details
5.  Responses in which there is an analysis-synthesis process: portions of the figure are broken up "and the elements so obtained recombined into meaningful percepts"
For each card Beck (15) calculated the frequency of each of these "organizing acts." On the assumption that the type of organizing act which appeared least frequently in a particular card was the most

difficult to perform, this type of organizational activity received the highest score while the most frequent received the lowest score. The values of each of the five types of organizing acts varied from card to card. For example, a W to card I received a lower Z score than a W to card X. An individual's organizational score consists of the summed value of all Z credits. It should be noted that not all responses receive credit for organization. For the following reasons Beck's Z score must be used with caution:

1. The numerical values of Z were derived from a study of thirty-nine "very superior" adults—a sample which is both too small and too selected to serve as a basis for determining the order of difficulty among types of response.

2. Beck presents no evidence that within his small and selected sample those who received the highest organizational score were those who in terms of other criteria functioned the most creatively or efficiently. In short, there were no validating criteria.

3. In her study of mental defectives E. K. Sarason found no relation between M.A. and Z score. "Since the Z score does not consider goodness of form, it may be obscuring . . . essential differences in the processes involved in the giving of the response. This is apparent when plus and minus concepts are assigned the same Z score for 'similar' organization. By expressing the number of minus responses that rated a Z value as a percentage of the total number of all Z responses regardless of plus or minus, a more meaningful index of the kind of organizational ability is obtained. The Z— response, in essence, is an indication that an individual's attempt at organizational activity is ineffective and reveals the unrealistic basis for his conceptualizations. Thus the higher the Z—% the more inferior the organizational ability, and good organizational ability, as reflected in a low Z—% would be expected to vary directly with degree of intelligence." Using Z— percent E. K. Sarason found that as M.A. increases Z— percent decreases, the correlations for her two groups being —.55 and —.63.

Until further validating studies are done the Z score as described and interpreted by Beck must be used with great caution. On the basis of our discussion in this chapter it would seem that evaluation of the quality of an individual's conceptual thinking or intellectual efficiency must at least be based on continua both of degree of reality testing and of complexity of response.

## Chapter 15

# THE CONTENT OF THE RESPONSE

CONTENT CATEGORIES

THUS far we have discussed Rorschach responses in terms of location (W, D, Dd) and "determinants" (movement, shading, color, plain form).[1] In the present chapter we will be concerned with a third general category: the content of the response. The following are the most frequent content categories:

| | |
|---|---|
| H | The whole human figure is described. |
| Hd | A part of the human figure is described such as an arm, or a leg, or the head, etc. |
| A | The whole animal figure is described. |
| Ad | A part of the animal figure is described. |
| At | Inner portions of the anatomy are seen. X-rays, anatomic sections, "a drawing from a medical textbook" would be put in this category. |
| A obj | This refers exclusively to animal fur, skins, animal rugs. |
| Cl | Clouds. |
| Pl | Plants: leaves, sticks, tree, petals. |
| Arch. | Architecture: houses, bridges. |
| Art | Paintings, emblems, seals, designs. |
| Geo | Mountains, valleys, peninsulas, landscapes. |
| Bl. | Blood. |
| Fi | Fire, explosions, smoke. |
| Sex | The sexual organs: penis, vagina, breasts. |
| Abs. | Abstractions: "The red is evil and the orange is hope." |
| Cl. | Articles of clothing. |
| N | Any natural object not covered by any of the previous categories. |
| obj | Any man-made object not covered by any of the previous categories. |

[1] Although movement has traditionally been labeled a determinant, it is obvious that the movement response is not "determined" by a property of the external stimulus in the same way as shading, color, and plain form.

254

As in the case of locations and determinants, not all writers use the same content categories, although these differences have aroused far less heat and discussion than have locations and determinants.

## POPULAR AND ORIGINAL RESPONSES

Blot areas differ in the range of content they elicit. Traditionally when a particular blot area frequently elicits a particular content, when such a content is given to the area it is designated P, a "popular" response. Klopfer (92) does not present any statistical criterion for determining popular responses. Beck (16, p. 191) developed his list of populars by determining the frequency of content to each W and D in each card, and when the frequency of a particular content to a given W or D was three times or more the next most frequent content it was designated as P. Hertz (72) used still another statistical criterion. Below are given the popular responses which are common to the lists of Beck and Hertz, both of whom used statistical criteria although on different age groups:

CARD I

W—a winged creature with body in center and wings at the sides

CARD II

D—(the black detail) an animal: bear, dog, etc.

S—(each entire side, including top and bottom red) a person (usually the response is a W, "two people")

CARD III

D or W—a person or two people doing something

D—(center) butterfly or moth

CARD IV

W—animal skin, pelt, rug

D—(bottom side projection) boot or shoe or foot

CARD V

W—bat, butterfly, moth

CARD VI

W—(or D when top projection is omitted) animal hide, skin, pelt

CARD VII

D—(top third of side figure usually including top projection) face or head of person

CARD VIII
D—(side detail) animal figure
D—(riblike center figure) spine, ribs, fish backbone, backbone

CARD IX
D—(bottom, side red area) person's face, head

CARD X
D—(blue side figure) crab, spider, octopus
D—(center figure between bottom inner green) rabbit's face or head
D—(bottom inner green) worm, caterpillar, snake

Although the lists of populars given by Klopfer, Beck, and Hertz are not identical, all the responses contained in each are sufficiently frequent so that the beginning student would do well to familiarize himself with all three lists.

The determination of original responses, as Hertz points out, is rather subjective. The most frequently used criterion is that a response which appears once in every hundred records is original.

INTERPRETIVE SIGNIFICANCE OF CONTENT

The following statements about the interpretive significance of the more frequent content categories are based on the writings of Beck (16, 17), Klopfer (92), and Bell (19):

1. Although it is recognized that a considerable percentage of responses will fall into the A and Ad categories, the greater the tendency for the subject to give other kinds of content "the less likely he is to be confined to the obvious, the stereotyped, or a narrow range of interests" (92, p. 215).

2. The presence of a low number (four or less) of P responses indicates a lack of conformity. "The use of five or more popular concepts seems to assure that the subject possesses capacity and interest in thinking along the same lines as other people in sufficient degree" (92, p. 216).

3. When H + A predominates over Hd + Ad it indicates an absence of criticism or an overcompensation for feelings of inferiority (19, p. 129).

4. The percentage of animal responses is an index of "adaptivity, in the sense that S recognizes intellectually the common, mundane stimuli and events of existence" (17, p. 16).

Unfortunately, there is little acceptable evidence to support these kinds of assumptions. The most solid finding in the literature is that the mentally deficient tend to give very few popular responses and a very large number of animal responses (*135*). We have already pointed out (p. 222) the fallacy of attributing similar psychological character-istics to groups or individuals who receive the same numerical score.

The possible significance of the absence of human and animal con-tent in a record may be deduced from Stein's (*160*) finding that the tendencies to give M and H are highly correlated. In four independent samples the correlations were .93, .91, .87, and .87. In the case of FM and A the correlations were not as high but statistically significant. In light of these relationships the interpretive significance of the absence of these contents will obviously be the same as of the absence of M and FM. In Chapter 13 the hypothesis was offered that the absence of M and FM indicated difficulty in expressing overtly strong personal feel-ing. Regardless of the merits of this hypothesis the important point to bear in mind is that the most frequent content categories (H, Hd, A, Ad) cannot have a very different interpretive significance from that of M and FM, since they are so highly correlated.

In contrast to the locations and determinants there has been very little research on the significance of the content of Rorschach responses. Lindner (*97*) pointed out in 1946:

On the whole, analysis of content has been among the most seriously neglected aspects of Rorschach work. Little attention has been paid to it in the literature, and among the 286 papers examined in preparation for this article, only four yielded direct content measures information, while in only 21 more were there vague indications of content significance beyond the broad categorical references. Of 38 psychiatric-psychological textbooks in which the Rorschach test was mentioned, only three evidenced an awareness that there is something to the content idea. At the same time, in informal talks with psychiatrists, psychologists and therapists of all kinds, the writers have been able to sense the conviction of most workers with the method that the possibilities of content analysis are exceptionally rich and promising. Moreover, there is hardly a clinician who, in some way or other, does not utilize content analysis in his work, however informally. Most of such work is admittedly intuitive and experiential, arising from stores of individual experiences and only checked against the findings of other observers.

In 1949 Wheeler (*174*), reviewing the literature on content indices of male homosexuality, found very few relevant studies and all of these involved subjective judgments about what constituted "homosexual content" and were in other ways methodologically unsound. Wheeler (174) attempted to evaluate twenty Rorschach content items presumably indicative of male homosexuality which had appeared in the literature and for which some relevant rationale could be stated. His subjects were 100 male patients from a mental hygiene clinic who had had a minimum of eight therapeutic interviews. Each therapist filled out a detailed questionnaire about the homosexual tendencies of the patient and, wherever possible, gave answers to specific questions about the patient's experiences, appearance, and "dynamics."

The purposes of the study and the general research plan were submitted to the entire staff of the clinic. Cooperation was solicited in designing a questionnaire which would be meaningful to the members of all three groups doing therapy: social worker, psychologist, and psychiatrist. A form was designed which representatives of each of the three groups . . . believed could be filled in by the therapists in the clinic with a minimum of misunderstanding. . . .

The therapist based [his answers to the questionnaire] upon what had occurred in therapy and in no case did he ask questions of the patient for the specific purpose of completing the questionnaire. . . .

Wheeler correctly points out that since neither the therapist's impression nor the Rorschach indices were themselves sufficiently validated, it was not justified to use either as the criterion against which the other might be validated. The main question which he posed was: "Is the therapist's impression of homosexuality similar to that which may be gained from the Rorschach and on what specific aspects of the individual's behavior is each apparently based?"

Of the twenty Rorschach content signs fourteen tended to cluster most frequently with each other and to be positively related to a small but significant degree with therapeutic judgment about homosexuality:

CARD I:   W or W̶ seen as a mask or human or animal face
CARD III:  W or W̶ seen as animals or animal-like ("dehumanized")
CARD IV:  W or W̶ seen as a human or animal; contorted, monstrous or threatening
CARD V:   W, W̶ or center D seen as a human or "humanized" animal
CARD VII:  W, W̶ or top D seen as human; female with derogatory specification
CARD VIII:  lateral D seen as an animal; several incongruous ones or one with incongruous parts

CARD IX:  upper lateral D seen as human, "dehumanized"

CARD X:  top center D seen as animals attacking or fighting over the central object

Human or animal oral detail seen anywhere in the cards

Human or animal anal detail or specification seen anywhere in the cards

Male or female genitalia seen anywhere in the cards

Feminine clothing seen anywhere in the cards

Two signs are of very questionable usefulness. They are:

CARD III:  W or W seen as humans with the sexual specification "confused"

CARD III:  W or W seen as humans with "uncertain" sexual specification

Four other signs . . . did not occur with sufficient frequency to warrant guessing about their usefulness.

It is interesting that the two signs mentioned most frequently in the literature showed the least relationship to the other signs and therapeutic judgment.

There are several aspects of Wheeler's study which make it necessary to accept his findings with much caution. It should be said that Wheeler was aware of almost all these factors:

1. In several cases the tester and therapist were the same person so that therapeutic judgment was very probably contaminated by knowledge of the Rorschach. It is not clear from the study in how many cases the therapist had read the psychologist's report which contained the Rorschach interpretation, so that contamination may have been very frequent.

2. Judgments of homosexuality by the therapist were largely based on the following questionnaire items: homosexual experience some time in the patient's life, masturbation some time in the patient's life, restriction to an exclusively male environment some time in the patient's life, effeminate appearance, and hostility toward but identification with the mother. Aside from the very subjective judgments which some of these items call for, the lack of validity data for these items in terms of the current behavior of the patient not only limits the significance of the findings but indicates the necessity of clarifying the concept of homosexuality. To correlate an instrument with judgments of dubious reliability and validity is to stack the cards unfairly against the instrument, as those who have attempted to utilize psychiatric nosologies in their research have found out.

3. The degree of relation between Rorschach content signs and

therapeutic judgments about homosexuality was highest in the case of therapists with a personal psychoanalysis, indicating what was suggested above, namely, that the concept of homosexuality does not mean the same thing to all therapists. The finding does not mean that the analytic conception of homosexuality is the most valid. It probably means that those who accept the analytic conception use it in a more consistent fashion than do those who accept other conceptions which are less systematically formulated.

Aronson (7) studied the incidence of Wheeler's twenty signs of male homosexuality in three groups: paranoid schizophrenics, non-paranoid psychotics, and normals. The two psychotic groups were equated for intellectual level, education, occupation, and length of hospitalization. Except for hospitalization, the normals were comparable to the psychotic groups. The two psychotic groups were not chosen on the basis of psychiatric diagnoses, as is usually (and unfortunately) the case, but in the following manner:

> The author read through about 75 case folders, and on the basis of the . . . data, selected the twenty cases which seemed to be most extreme with regard to the presence or absence of paranoid delusions. The remainder of the cases were discarded. The twenty extreme cases were then presented for rating to two graduate students from the University of Michigan.

The raters were instructed to read through the clinical folders of each of these twenty patients and to rate them for each of the four kinds of paranoid delusions which Freud had specifically linked with homosexual conflict: (1) delusions of persecution, (2) erotomania, (3) delusions of jealousy, and (4) megalomania. The author rated the same cases independently. Following is the rating scale on which the patients were rated for *each* of the four kinds of paranoid delusions:

    0  minimally delusional
    1  very slightly delusional
    2  slightly delusional
    3  fairly delusional
    4  markedly delusional
    5  extremely delusional
    6  maximally delusional

The raters were instructed to give high ratings to those patients whose entire symptomatology was dominated by one or more of the four kinds of paranoid delusions, and to give low ratings to those patients who exhibited primarily other types of symptoms (e.g., catatonic withdrawal). The entire psychotic population of the hospital was used as the reference group for all of these ratings. It will be noted that these ratings were not necessarily ratings of the *strength* of the delusions, but rather, of the *extent* to which the delusions pervaded the patient's symptomatology.

Since the Freudian theory of paranoia maintains that all of the four kinds of paranoid delusions are related to homosexual conflicts, it was decided to take the highest rating obtained by each patient on *any* of the four kinds of delusions as the basis for selecting him for either the paranoid or the psychotic groups. Using the *highest* rating obtained by each patient on any of the four kinds of paranoid delusions as the basis for comparison, agreement between all three raters was then computed by means of the Pearson product-moment correlation formula. The results of this analysis showed a high agreement between the three raters in their evaluations of the twenty cases. The author's ratings correlated .956 with those of one of the raters and .916 with those of the other. The ratings of the other two raters correlated .883. In 85% of the twenty cases, all three raters agreed unanimously in placing given patients into either the "high delusional group" (ratings of 4–6) or the "low delusional group" (ratings of 0–3). The agreement between the raters on these twenty cases was considered high enough to warrant the author's selection of the entire sixty cases for both of the psychotic groups, by himself.

The author read through approximately 500 case folders in selecting the thirty patients for each of the two psychotic groups. All patients who were selected for the paranoid group received ratings of "4" or more on delusions of persecution, while all patients in the non-paranoid psychotic group received ratings of "2" or less on delusions of persecution. The mean rating on delusions of persecution in the paranoid group was 4.90. The mean rating for the psychotic group was .63.

The manner of choosing the psychotic groups was crucial because Aronson's study was an attempt to test Freud's hypothesis that paranoid symptomatology represented the defense against strong homosexual tendencies. The results showed that paranoid subjects gave many more homosexual signs on the Rorschach than did either the other psychotics or the normal subjects. Aronson points out that there is no clear reason why these Rorschach content signs should reflect homosexual tendencies. Although they seem "to work," the steps or processes by which they obtain their symbolic or surplus meanings remain an unclear and unresolved theoretical problem.

Pascal, Ruesch, Devine and Suttell (*112*) gave the Rorschach in the usual manner, after which the subject was asked to point out any male or female sex organs seen in each of the ten cards. Their subjects were 28 normals, 163 neurotics, and 46 psychotics. The major findings were as follows:

1. The male population gave significantly more vagina than penis responses. Female subjects gave an equal number of both. Although the use of two male examiners may have produced this sex difference, Shaw (*152*) using a different procedure for obtaining responses obtained similar findings with a group of normal male subjects.

2. "For both male and female subjects, Card VI yields the greatest percentage of responses and is highest in the number of subjects responding to it. The data show, in addition, that Card VI elicits from a majority of subjects, both male and female, a masculine symbol. For men, Card V seems to elicit the least number of responses while for women Card VIII occupies this position."

3. In conformance with expectations from psychoanalytic theory (*45*) anal responses were given almost exclusively by the paranoid subjects.

4. "Except for the breast response to Card I, given most often by psychotics and neurotics, we did not find a difference between nosological groups with respect to these most frequent responses."

5. Table 16 shows the contents given to identical areas in the standard Rorschach and in the "testing the limits" or post-Rorschach procedure. "Our data show that when an elongated object or human or animal appendage is seen in the protocol, the area used is apt to be called a penis in testing the limits for sex. Whether or not one can make the inference that the protocol response symbolized a penis is not proved by such a finding, but, we feel, is strong presumptive evidence that such may be the case. . . ."

The findings with regard to card VI should not be taken as evidence that a long reaction time to card VI, or rejection of the card, *necessarily* means that the individual has some kind of sexual conflict or inhibition. Since many people in our culture have been taught to avoid talking about sex and not to mention genitalia, difficulty with card VI *may* reflect the influence of social learning and not some kind of internal conflict in relation to sexual practices. What we are here trying to emphasize is not that the above reactions may not be significant in the

TABLE 16. Area and Content of "Limits" Responses Related to Area and Content of Protocol Responses (Pascal et al., *112*)

| Limits Response | Content of Identical Area in Protocol | No. Resp. | Percent Total |
|---|---|---|---|
| Penis | Inanimate, elongated objects—monuments, spearheads, totem poles, swords, smoke stacks, candlesticks, etc. | 61 | 28 |
| | Animal or human appendages—animal tails, human or animal legs, arms, heads, noses, hands, teeth, fangs, etc. | 124 | 56 |
| | Penis | 8 | 4 |
| | Miscellaneous—things hanging in cave, dead women over a cliff, etc. | 26 | 12 |
| | | 219 | 100 |
| Vagina | Butterfly | 20 | 13 |
| | Invaginated objects—opened flowers, vases, spittoons, muffs, etc. | 36 | 23 |
| | Parts of human body—opened mouth, opened stomach, heart, pelvis, etc. | 18 | 11 |
| | Parts of animals—wolf's jaw, space between head of rabbit, rear of animals, etc. | 13 | 8 |
| | Vagina | 12 | 8 |
| | Blood | 8 | 5 |
| | Miscellaneous—eruption, inside looking out to light, clouds, zipper, x-rays | 51 | 32 |
| | | 158 | 100 |
| Breasts | Breasts | 16 | 43 |
| | Paired objects—2 dead ducks, 2 heads, hills, airplane wings, etc. | 6 | 16 |
| | Miscellaneous—sunrise, top of vase, face of monster, etc. | 15 | 41 |
| | | 37 | 100 |
| Anus | Animal parts—rear of animal, turtle, mouth, etc. | 4 | 27 |
| | Dirt or related—caterpillar coming from hole, train from tunnel | 2 | 13 |
| | Parts of body—pelvis, digestive tract, etc. | 4 | 27 |
| | Miscellaneous—burst pimple, x-ray, anus, etc. | 5 | 33 |
| | | 15 | 100 |

individual case but rather that any judgment based on a single test indicator, without regard to important variables which determine an individual's behavior in an interpersonal interaction, is likely not to be valid. If the judgment based on card VI is consistent with judgments made on the basis of responses to other cards, the situation is somewhat different although even here one must guard against the tendency of uncritically forcing an interpretation on the data. It has been pointed out by many that statements about sexual maladjustment are likely to be correct not because the data we use are necessarily correct but because sexual maladjustment in our culture is apparently so frequent.

In his clinical evaluation of the Rorschachs of the people of Truk, Sarason (58) found that many more men than women rejected card VI. His conclusion, which was congruent with the ethnographic data, that men had certain strong conflicts in the sexual areas was based on more than card VI. For example, long reaction times and card rejections were characteristic of the Truk records. In the case of some males card VI was rejected much quicker than other rejected cards. The question asked was: Why was card VI rejected so much quicker—why did he not hold the card longer? In other words, the significance of behavior to card VI was considered in light of behavior to other cards. The significance of rejection of card VI was also considered in light of the fact that genital responses were not infrequently given. In short, a single indicator was not the basis for any conclusion about sexual behavior. Some of the Trukese cases will be presented in full in later pages, where the present point will be elaborated.

The finding by Pascal et al. of the relation between the outline shape of the original response and the sexual response given in the post-Rorschach procedure is of much clinical importance because it appears to lend *some* support to the practice of attributing sexual meanings to responses of particular shapes and contents (e.g., candlestick = penis, opened mouth = vagina, train from tunnel = anus). But these important findings, which other workers should attempt to duplicate, do not tell us the relation between these possibly "symbolic" responses and overt behavior. It would be unjustified, for example, for the clinician to conclude that an individual who gives many (and we have little idea how much "many" is) responses with elongated shapes is sexually inhibited or preoccupied or maladjusted. We know far too little about the relation between verbal and other forms of overt behavior to make such statements. What is very much needed is research in which the Rorschach contents of groups who differ on explicit and reliable behavioral criteria are compared. By "explicit and reliable behavioral criteria" we do not mean words like neurotic, psychotic, schizophrenic, etc. Such words mean different things to different people and the subjects grouped under any of these labels are heterogeneous rather than homogeneous in terms of either overt behavior or etiology.[2] Far too frequently the clinician's perception of and behavior toward the patient is too much determined by the particular diagnosis previously made, be that diagnosis a tentative or final one. If the clinician knows that a patient is thought to be schizophrenic, his thinking about and behavior toward the patient is influenced by knowledge of such a fact. This is not in itself "bad" or to be avoided. What is to be avoided is the tendency to focus only on what supports the diagnosis and to unwittingly ignore contrary evidence. The important thing that the clinician must remember is that *his* behavior in the clinical interaction is influenced by his preconceptions and those of others about the patient. As we have indicated in earlier pages of this book, the principles which are utilized to understand a patient's behavior are necessary when the focus of our interest is the behavior of the psychologist in the clinical interaction.

Pascal and Herzberg (*111*) attempted to determine the discriminatory value of their procedure for "testing the limits for sex" (TLS) in a prison population. They studied four groups:

Controls: N = 19, the non-sexual deviates. All of these subjects were imprisoned for non-sexual crimes. . . . Insofar as could be determined from other prisoners, none of these individuals were known as sexual deviants within the prison.

Rapists: N = 19. All of these subjects were imprisoned for rape of women of child-bearing age.

Pedophiliacs: N = 20. All of these subjects were imprisoned for rape of pre-pubertal females, age 12 or younger.

Homosexuals: N = 20. All of these subjects were imprisoned for homosexual practices.

In all major comparison there was little differentiation between rapists and controls. "If we take heterosexual behavior between adults as our

[2] The difficulty of using psychiatric nomenclature is illustrated by Bradway and Heisler's (*22*) study of content and diagnostic groupings. They concluded: "Limitations of this study are that psychiatric diagnoses are fallible and are inconsistent from one institution to another. . . . Even with these limitations, the results show the need for caution in using any one response or kind of response in making diagnostic evaluations from the Rorschach. None of the factors or content was associated exclusively with any one diagnosis, so that none appears to be pathognomonic. . . ."

standard, then it is difficult to see how the rapists differ from the controls in sexual behavior *per se*. The rapist may be more aggressive; he may have less judgment, but he does not differ from the standard in sexual act and object. Other parameters of behavior need to be studied if controls are to be differentiated from rapists. The rapist commits a sex crime, legally defined, but from the point of view of actual sexual behavior, he is not a sexual deviant.

"The case is different for the pedophiliacs and homosexuals. The pedophiliacs differ from the standard in age of sexual object, from the point of view of our mores. The homosexuals differ from the standard in sexual object and sexual act. They have in common a failure to abide by the mores of our culture with respect to sexual act and object."

When rapists and controls were grouped and compared to the other two groups, two significant findings emerged:

1. When a subject's responses were compared to the most frequently given TLS responses ("sex populars"), the pedophiliac-homosexual groups gave significantly more deviant or nonpopular responses than the control-rapist group.

2. "The mean number of cards rejected per subject shows a progression from controls to homosexuals, the homosexuals showing almost twice as many rejections as the controls, with the rapists and pedophiliacs somewhere in between. In the rejection of Card VI, the 'male' card, the groups are undifferentiated, but in the rejection of Card VII, the 'female' card, the homosexuals show twice as many rejections as the controls. Card IX is also rejected twice as often by the homosexuals as it is by the controls."

The significance of these findings is somewhat limited by the fact that the sexually deviant subjects may have viewed the testing procedure differently from the way the other groups did, a possibility which could account for their greater card rejections. If it had been shown that the groups did not differ in their conception of the nature and purpose of the clinical interaction, one would feel more secure about the findings. In any event the TLS procedure does appear to be a potentially valuable clinical procedure. It would be an interesting research project to determine whether the responses in the standard protocol which appear to be related to certain sexual responses in the TLS elicit similar sexual associations with a non-Rorschach procedure, e.g., the free-association test. If such a finding would emerge when the stimulus conditions are varied, the generality of the findings of the TLS procedure would be considerably enhanced.

Elizur (39) began his study of content by assuming that anxiety and hostility are measurable variables and that A and H scores of the Rorschach Content Test (RCT) were valid means for their measurement. Below is presented a description of the scale in addition to instructions for scoring given to judges who were used for determining reliability:

*The scale.* Capital and small letters were utilized in the scoring system. A capital letter was used whenever anxiety and hostility were expressed obviously and explicitly in the responses. Small letters were used for responses which revealed anxiety and hostility to a lesser degree or in a fairly clear *symbolic* manner. A capital letter (A, H) counted twice as much as a small letter (a, h). Responses which implied both anxiety and hostility were given the combined score "ah" which was counted as 1 "a" plus 1 "h." The final scores were made up by the weighted sum of all "a"s and "h"s, and are referred hereafter simply as the "a" and "h" scores of each record, or by a common name, RCT scores.

The writer attempted to make the scoring system as objective as possible . . . though he is fully aware of arbitrary factors which entered into that "objectivity." The following rules served as practical clues:

1. Emotions expressed explicitly or implicitly were scored accordingly: fear, horror, disgust, etc.—"A"; reproach, hatred, etc.—"H."
2. Percepts like snakes, witches, bats, dragons, which have a fearful connotation in our culture, were scored "A" regardless of whether or not the subject expressed his feelings verbally. Percepts which usually arouse disgust, like spiders, were scored "a."
3. Derogatory expressions like "ugly," "stupid," etc., were scored "H"; slightly derogatory indications such as "overpolite men," "gossiping women," were scored "h."
4. Responses like "headless people," "cut-off fingers," etc., which could easily be interpreted as denoting anxiety as well as hostility (sadistic tendencies) were scored "ah."
5. Doubtful cases were sometimes decided by means of an analogy to other responses in the same record or to the general tendency revealed in the record.
6. The decision was always made on the basis of the response taken as a

whole rather than on a single word. Thus "pretty *clouds* on a soft summer day," was scored neutral, while "thunder *clouds* crashing in the sky," was scored "A," though both responses centered around the word "clouds."

. . . . .

*The scorers and the training given.* Eight graduate students in the guidance department of Teachers College, Columbia University, were willing to serve as volunteer scorers. None of them had had any previous training in the Rorschach technique, but they all had a general background in psychology. They were given copies of the instructions for scoring which are printed below and were asked to read them carefully. A discussion period of about forty minutes followed later, and then fifteen records were handed over to them for independent scoring.

*The instructions.* The following were the instructions given to the scorers.

### INSTRUCTIONS FOR SCORING

The attached fifteen records consist of sets of responses given by fifteen individuals to ten ink blots. You are to read carefully the responses of each record and to score only those which contain elements of anxiety and hostility. Any scorable response might be assigned one of the following scores: "A" or "H" to responses containing clear cut evidence of anxiety or hostility respectively; "a" or "h" to responses with a smaller degree of the same elements and "ah" to responses containing both anxiety and hostility. All other responses are considered "neutral" and are left blank.

The scores of each record are to be summed up into two general scores of "total a" and "total h." Each "A" is counted as 2 "a"s, each "H" as 2 "h"s, and an "ah" score is counted as 1 "a" + 1 "h." The following will illustrate the various ways in which anxiety and hostility may be expressed in the responses, and will serve as a guide for scoring.

### 1. Emotions and Attitudes Expressed or Implied (A, a, H, h)

Responses which reveal feelings or attitudes of fear, unpleasantness, sorrow, pity and the like are scored "A," those containing hatred, dislike, criticism, derogation and the like "H." Responses which manifest such feelings or attitudes to a smaller degree are scored accordingly "a" or "h."

Note that the feeling or attitude may be related to the observer (like an animal that he is afraid of) as well as to the figure perceived in the ink blot (a person or an animal being frightened or sad). Note also that feelings or attitudes are often *implied* rather than expressed overtly (thus "a dangerous place" implies fear and "a silly face" implies derogation).

Examples:

A: A frightening giant; a weeping child; a dangerous crevice; darkness and gloom.

a: An unpleasant animal.

H: A type of man I hate; an ugly figure; a stupid animal; an angry face; a quarrelsome person.

h: Gossiping women; two butlers making each other compliments.

## 2. Expressive Behavior (A, H)

Watch the behavior of the figure perceived as to whether it indicates anxiety or hostility. In the first case score "A," in the latter "H."

Examples:

A: A girl escaping; a retreating animal; a rabbit running away.

H: Two animals fighting with each other; they squashed the butterfly; a wolf devouring its prey; a killed animal.

## 3. Symbolic Responses (a, h)

No far fetched symbolic interpretations are asked for in the present scoring system, but whenever a response reveals a clear symbolic meaning it is scored accordingly "a" or "h."

Examples:

a: An unbalanced figure; dead leaves; a tree with broken branches; scarecrow; an impression of coldness.

h: The red represents struggle; a primitive war-mask.

## 4. Cultural Stereotypes of Fear (A, a)

Certain percepts, which are assumed to have a general connotation of fear in our culture are to be scored "A" even if they appear without any further elaboration. Percepts which are usually connected with a moderate degree of unpleasantness should be scored "a." The latter score should also be given to responses containing a religious element. In observing the present rule, adhere closely to the following examples rather than enlarging unduly upon the extent of the stereotypes.

Examples:

A: Bats; snakes; monsters; witches; a human skeleton or skull; dead man or dead animal; blood; atomic bomb; volcano; clouds; fire; smoke.

a: Spiders; mosquitoes; totem pole; church; priest.

### 5. Objects of Aggression (H, h)

Responses containing objects which are usually used for aggressive purposes are to be scored "H" or "h." (Note that "atomic bomb" is scored "A" for in it the element of fear is much more pronounced.)

Examples:

H: Arrow; gun; pistol.
h: Pliers; knife; teeth.

### 6. Double Connotation (ah)

Responses that contain clear evidence of both, anxiety and hostility, or which leave you in doubt as to whether they contain the one or the other factor, are to be scored "ah."

Examples:

ah: Headless person; an injured bear; a child with cut-off arms; a torn butterfly; a policeman; an animal going to attack you, I feel somewhat scared.

### 7. Unscorable or "Neutral" Responses

There is of course no sharp line between scorable and unscorable responses. The following examples of borderline cases which were selected as occurring most frequently, should be left unscored. However, the same "neutral" response, if elaborated further could become an "A" or "H" response. Thus, "an insect," according to the following list is "neutral," but "an unpleasant or dangerous insect" should receive an "A," a "fighting insect," an "H" score.

### Examples of Unscored Responses:

1. Animals: Frogs; mice; bugs; crabs; bears.
2. Anatomical: Spinal cord; X-ray pictures; bones; lungs, etc.
   (Exception: Human skeleton or skull "A.")
3. Miscellaneous: Coat of arms; rocks; skin of an animal.

The correlations between the average scores of the judges and Elizur were .89, .93, and .98 for a, h, and a + h respectively. In addition to the Rorschach each subject (college student who volunteered) filled out a questionnaire containing items on fears and phobias and lack of self-confidence and also rated himself on control of fear, worry, general shyness, sexual shyness, and feelings of inferiority. Each subject was interviewed and rated on four variables (submissiveness, dependency, anxiety, and hostility), about which he was asked to talk. Table 17 and Table 18 show the major relationships between the a and h scores and the criterion measures. The results in Table 17 indicate that higher scores on the "a" variable are associated with higher scores on the fear and phobia questionnaire items, higher self-ratings on "control" items, and higher ratings based on the interviews.[3] The results in Table 18

TABLE 17. Correlation Coefficients Between RCT Scores and Indications of Anxiety (Elizur, *39*)

| Variable | Correlation With | |
|---|---|---|
| | a | h |
| Questionnaire (N = 30) | | |
| Fears and phobias | .58[b] | .23 |
| Lack of self-confidence | .39[a] | .28 |
| Both items combined | .61[b] | .31 |
| Self-rating (N = 30) on control of | | |
| Fear | .39[a] | .17 |
| Worry | .42[a] | .05 |
| General shyness | .17 | .14 |
| Sexual shyness | .46[b] | .26 |
| Feelings of inferiority | .52[b] | .09 |
| All items combined | .52[b] | .19 |
| Interview (N = 20) | | |
| Anxiety | .71[b] | −.16 |

[a] Significant at the .05 level.
[b] Significant at the .01 level.

indicate that higher "h" scores are positively related to the relevant items in the questionnaire and self-ratings although the interview ratings are significantly related to both a and h measures. Other findings not reported in the tables were that both a and h score were positively, significantly, and approximately equally correlated with aloofness, ideas of reference, and depression.

Although Elizur concludes that the "RCT appears to be a valid technique for the assessment of the subject's anxiety and hostility," there are several factors which suggest that such a conclusion is too sweeping:

1. Two of the criterion measures, the questionnaire and self-ratings,

[3] It is doubtful whether any significance can be attached to the interview ratings because the interview was conducted immediately after the Rorschach administration and the interviewer's ratings were very probably biased by the Rorschach responses he had just obtained. The writer is indebted to Irwin Sarason for pointing this out.

do not involve overt behavior. The third measure, the interview, did involve observation of overt behavior, but since the subjects were asked to talk about the variables also contained in the other two measures, it is not possible to decide to what extent the interview ratings are based on verbal material contained in the other measures. In other words, a conclusion which seems justified from the data is that the RCT appears to reflect how an individual *says* he feels and acts. This point appears to

TABLE 18.   Correlation Coefficients Between RCT Scores and Indications of Hostility (Elizur, *39*)

| Variable | Correlation With | |
|---|---|---|
| | a | h |
| Questionnaire (N = 30) | | |
| (1) Self-blame | .19 | .44[a] |
| (2) Subject regarded as good natured | −.29 | .27 |
| (3) Subject was a "goodygoody" child | −.06 | .53[b] |
| (4) Subject believes that people are hostile | .22 | .55[b] |
| (5) Subject believes that people are selfish | .06 | .21 |
| All items combined | −.02 | .74[b] |
| Self-ratings (N = 30) on control of hostile and aggressive feelings against | | |
| (1) Friends | .18 | .15 |
| (2) Members of the family | .03 | .38[a] |
| (3) Minority groups | .15 | .37[a] |
| All items combined | .16 | .45[a] |
| Interview (N = 20) | | |
| Hostility | .46[a] | .60[b] |

[a] Significant at the .05 level.
[b] Significant at the .01 level.

have been recognized by Elizur: "An interesting field of investigation would probably be the comparison of an individual's RCT scores with his behavioral patterns, since such a study may possibly throw light on the question of how a person's system of tension may affect his behavior."

2. Although the results in Tables 17 and 18 indicate that a and h are correlated to different degrees with the criterion measures, Elizur did not determine whether the differences between the correlations (e.g., between .39 and .17 with fear in Table 17) were significant. Since he had a relatively small sample of cases (N = 30) the difference between two correlations has to be rather large to represent a statistically signifi-

cant difference. If, as is very likely, some of the differences between the correlations are not significant, the discriminatory value of differences in score on "a" vs. "h" is reduced.

The above points should not obscure the fact that Elizur's study represents the first serious and systematic attempt to evaluate anxiety and hostility from the content of Rorschach responses. He has presented a reliable procedure which deserves further study.

Elizur's study raises some thorny theoretical problems which have cropped up (and plagued us) in our discussions more than a few times. The problems may be put in the form of questions: If, according to self-report, individuals differ on a particular variable, how will the differences be reflected in overt behavior? If individuals do not differ on a particular variable, what factors account for the fact that they frequently differ in the way that variable is overtly manifested? If an individual is low on a particular variable (e.g., no or little anxiety is reported), how does one determine whether or not this represents a defense against experiencing the variable in question? What is the relation between type and strength of defense and overt behavior?[4] These questions are obviously not peculiar to the Rorschach but to all problems which involve determining the significance of verbal responses for overt and covert behavior. In the case of the Rorschach the tendency has been to assume that these questions are answerable from an individual's responses, an assumption which *may* be true but for which there is no acceptable evidence. As we shall see in subsequent pages there is suggestive evidence that some clinicians can answer some

[4] It is our opinion that the covert and overt behavioral significance of Rorschach content will in part be a function of the individual's dominant defense mechanisms. For example, in Aronson's study (p. 260) paranoids gave more "homosexual" signs than other groups. If, as is likely, the majority of the paranoids were not consciously aware of homosexual tendencies (of which one would *assume* they were once conscious) then in such individuals the relation between Rorschach content, on the one hand, and conscious awareness and overt behavior, on the other hand, would be an *inverse* one: little or no conscious awareness or behavioral manifestation of homosexual tendencies is related to the marked presence of certain Rorschach content. In these cases projection is the mechanism of defense. In Elizur's study, however, the relation was a *direct* one: The greater the conscious awareness of anxiety or hostility, the greater the incidence of anxious or hostile content. In these cases we know nothing of the dominant mechanisms of defense but it would be our guess that as drastic a mechanism as projection would not be the dominant one. Although our opinion of the role of defense mechanisms may be in error, there is little doubt that the relation between Rorschach content and overt and covert behavior is not as simple or direct as Elizur's data might suggest.

of these questions in what appears to be a valid fashion, but since their procedures are not explicitly stated, and there is no evidence that their results can be duplicated by others as is required in science, one can only conclude that these problems are as yet unanswerable from the Rorschach—or for that matter from any other clinical instrument. This state of affairs should not be interpreted as a reflection on our clinical instruments but should indicate our lack of an adequate psychological theory which spells out the relevant variables and their interrelationships in such a way that the means by which the theory can be tested become clear.

Aside from the unresolved theoretical problems, we would like to suggest that our use of language may be interfering with a clearer understanding of the problems we have been discussing. We are here referring to the tendency to use words—like "anxiety" and "hostility"—in such a way that their referents are obscure. For example, how helpful it is to describe a person as hostile? Obviously, he is not hostile *all* the time or to *all* people. Nor does such a statement tell us how the person views his "hostility," if at all. To conclude from an analysis of the Rorschach that an individual is hostile is not to differentiate him from a great many other people, a point which has been well made by Cronbach (32). Similar statements could be made in connection with the use of "anxiety," "sexual conflict," "aggressive," etc. To use these kinds of words as if they were akin to Platonic essences not only prevents one from discriminating at all among individuals but makes the development of a behavioral criterion measure much more difficult. In the case of the content of Rorschach responses we doubt whether in the long run it will be fruitful to continue to talk of "anxious," or "sexual," or "hostile" content. The problem of the clinician is not to determine whether an individual is hostile or not but rather to attempt to state the object or objects of the hostility, the strength of that kind of hostile response, the likelihood that the specific hostility will reach overt expression, and the ways in which this hostility is related to other problems and characteristic modes of response. To what extent an analysis of Rorschach content, and for that matter an analysis of the total protocol, will enable one to answer these kinds of questions will be determined only on the basis of research yet to be done.

In this and previous chapters we have indicated the limitations of analyses and predictions made on the basis of the verbalized or formal response. We have pointed out the importance of evaluating a particular type of response in terms of the variables operative in the clinical interaction. The interpretation of the significances of content is no exception to the rule. To indicate one facet of the problem we might ask this question: What are the significances which might be attached to the *absence of content* (e.g., sexual, hostile, etc.) which ordinarily appears to some extent in most records? If there is no anxious content, few clinicians would maintain that the individual does not experience strong anxiety in some areas of functioning. If there is no sexual content, the clinician would not jump to the conclusion that this is an area in which the individual experiences no conflict. It is our contention that the significance of the absence of content must in part, at least, be based on an understanding of the individual's conception of and attitudes toward the clinical interaction. In the therapeutic interaction the failure of the patient to talk about certain areas of functioning is usually a function of the attitudes engendered by the nature of the interaction. It frequently appears that the patient, consciously or unconsciously, avoids talking about something because it is an area of strong conflict. Since in the diagnostic testing interaction the task of the clinician frequently is to determine areas of conflict and characteristic modes of defense against recognition and/or verbal expression of conflicts, the greater the attention given to determining the nature of the patient's covert responses to the clinical interaction the better will one understand the significances of the content which he does *and* does not give. Although we ordinarily do not ask the patient to tell us about his areas of conflict, anxiety, or guilt, the fact that he is being given tests—that he is in some way being evaluated by a professional specialist—mobilizes his conflicts and the defenses learned in relation to them. While the formal response to the stimulus materials is one basis for understanding the patient's problems, one must constantly keep in mind that it is the end product of a variety of reactions engendered by the variables operative in the clinical interaction.

## Chapter 16

# THE PSYCHOLOGIST

In Chapter 5 we pointed out that one of the most important variables affecting the behavior of an individual in an interpersonal interaction is the psychologist: his age, sex, status, behavior. In the present chapter we will be concerned with the influence of the clinician when he is administering and interpreting the Rorschach.

Those who are responsible for the clinical training of students are constantly aware of the wide differences which exist in how students react to and handle the clinical interaction (p. 9). That these individual differences are cause for concern to clinical supervisors is a reflection of the assumption that the behavior of the patient is influenced to an unknown degree by the behavior of the clinician. This is reflected in the following statements by Joel (*84*), who points out that the overt and covert behavior of the clinician influences the subject:

It has been argued that the effect of the examiner should be reduced to a minimum by assuming a constant warm attitude which does not change under the impact of the subject's personality. There can be no argument about the desirability of a friendly attitude on the part of the examiner or about its beneficial effect on rapport. But we make a fundamental mistake if we believe that the assumed attitude of the examiner can really nullify the dynamics of the testing situation. Clinical psychologists are human and, the assumed attitude of warmth notwithstanding, they react to different subjects in different ways, partly because of irrational attitudes. So we must reckon with the effect of the examiner's actual, continuously changing feelings underneath the assumed attitudes. Even if it were possible for the examiner always actually to feel the way he pretends he does, we should not forget that the subject reacts not only to the examiner's real attitude, but also to what he thinks the examiner's attitude is. This phenomenon is independent of the examiner's real attitude; it varies with different examiners,

276

thereby vitiating or at least complicating the rapport-making efforts of any examiner.

Although there has been relatively little research on the problem, the few available studies indicate that a person's responses to the Rorschach are in part a function of who the clinician is. One of the first solid pieces of evidence along these lines was the finding during World War II that there were significant differences among examiners in the total number of responses they tended to elicit from their subjects (64). This finding stimulated Lord (98) to study the problem with the following design:

An experimental design was constructed which aimed toward controlling as many variables as possible. The basic unit of the study was 36 males between the ages of 19 and 27. They were selected at random from a list of approximately 200 college sophomores enrolled in an introductory course in general psychology. Each subject was given three Rorschachs at four to six weeks' intervals. Each of the three Rorschachs was administered by a different person.

The three administrators, A, B, and C, were females, not different in any grossly apparent way; i.e., no one of the three was outstandingly fat or thin, ugly or beautiful. Administrators A and C were brunettes, B was a reddish-blonde. The age range among the three was twelve years, with B the youngest and C the oldest. Each administrator holds a degree in psychology and has had several years' experience in the use of the Rorschach according to the Klopfer technique.

The Rorschach tests were given in a systematic or rotated order so that twelve subjects received control tests first, twelve second, and twelve third. Twelve received negative tests and twelve received positive tests first. The second and third testing sessions were similarly varied.

No subject was tested twice by the same person. Twelve were tested first by Administrator A, second by B, and third by C. The other administrations were distributed similarly. Each administrator used exactly the same technique for the administration of the Rorschach Test, regardless of the affective loading of the pre-test situation and regardless of whether the administration was the first, second, or third for the subject.

The negative and positive situations included two simple card-sorting tests administered prior to the Rorschach test for the purpose of setting the effective tone of the session. Identical directions, terminology, and techniques were used in both the negative and positive pre-tests; however, the tone of the administrations was differently slanted. Specific directions for the administration of the three sessions were followed explicitly and without variation by the three administrators. These directions were as follows:

## ADMINISTRATION

*Neutral.* Standard Rorschach procedure will be used. The administrator will be courteous but business-like in manner. She must attempt to avoid either negative or positive affective loading of the situation. There will be no pre-tests nor any gathering of biographical data.

*Negative administration.* The administrator will assume the role of a harsh, rejecting, authoritarian figure. She must be deliberately unconcerned about the subject, not look at him while asking questions, preparing tests, or giving directions; never smile, give directions in a voice of dictatorial harshness, make every "Hm!" sound like a sneer.

*Positive administration.* The administrator will be personally warm, charming, appreciative in manner. She must look at subject with a smile while asking questions, preparing tests, or giving directions in an encouraging tone of voice, making every "Hm!" sound like a compliment for work well done.

The following administration will be used verbatim for *both* negative and positive administrations:

Are you Mr. Blank? Come with me! This room. Sit here.

What is your full name? You have an address? Freshman, Sophomore, Junior? Your birthdate?

Are you familiar with an ordinary deck of playing cards? (Place deck face down, with one black nine on the bottom of the pack.) When I say GO turn the cards, one at a time, and pull out all the black nines here and the red tens here (indicate areas with gestures). Work as fast as you can. Ready? Go! (Answer any questions only by repeating words in the foregoing instructions. Note any cheating, i.e., number of times subject turns two or more cards at a time; also note any errors in carrying out instructions or any requests for repetition of instructions. Record time.)

Hm! Some speed! (Leave nines and tens; shuffle remaining cards; replace, face down, before subject.)

Now, when I say GO, turn the cards, one at a time, and see how many face cards—Jacks, Queens, and Kings—you can pull out before I say STOP. Put the red face cards on the black nines and the black face cards on the red tens. Ready? Go! (Allow thirty seconds.)

STOP! (Count face cards and record number.)

Hm! Not bad!

(The Rorschach Test will follow using the same instructions as for the neutral administration.)

The most important (and pervasive) finding in this study was that the number (first, second, or third) or type (neutral, positive, negative) of administration was *less* important in producing variation in the records obtained than examiner differences. The study was not designed to determine the ways in which the three examiners differed behaviorally, so that one does not know, as Lord points out, "what specific and measurable factors in an examiner's personality will bring about what specific and measurable factors in a subject's Rorschach protocol." Sanders and Cleveland (*133*) attempted to study this question. They selected nine graduate students as "examiners."

. . . None had had any extensive contact with projective tests; some had taken the Thematic Apperception Tests as part of a research study; none had interpreted or used these tests in a clinical setting. In order to insure that the examiners have an adequate theoretical and practical background for clinical testing it was required that the volunteers have completed a course in advanced personality theory.

The twelve volunteers were informed that a good introduction to projective tests entailed the experience of taking them. They were asked, therefore, to arrange two periods of two hours each when they could take a battery of tests. The Rorschach was administered individually to all twelve by one of the authors and, during this testing, the subject was seated with his back to the examiner because it was hoped that this would standardize the interpersonal situation between them. Following testing, the examiner discussed some of the administrative details as part of an introductory training session. Of the twelve volunteers, nine were finally chosen by the authors. The selection criteria were adequate motivation, dissimilar personalities, and absence of obvious physical deviations.

The examiners were given training and supervision in the Rorschach. The inquiry section of the administration of the test was conducted in a specified, standardized manner.

After this training period, the examiners were permitted to begin the testing of subjects assigned to them. The first two administrations of the Rorschach were observed by the authors through one-way screens, without the examiners being aware of this. The purpose of this check was to see that all test procedures were correctly fulfilled. All examiners then came for individual conferences. At this time, any errors in technique observed by the authors were discussed with the examiners and their specific problems in testing were resolved. Each examiner was assigned 30 subjects to be tested during the 1949 Fall semester. The only criterion for assignment was the matching of available free time of examiner and subject. Since all the subjects offered from three to seven free periods, it was assumed that there was a random assignment of subjects. Each examiner tested approximately twenty per cent of his subjects at night. Several testing rooms were used in an irregular manner so as to randomize any environmental effects. All of these rooms were in University buildings and were specially designed for individual testing. Each subject was given a code number, and standard directions for orienting the subject to the Rorschach were read by the examiner. Following the test administration, the examiner gave the subject a questionnaire in which the subject was asked to respond concerning his feelings about the examiner. The questionnaire was filled in by the subject only after the examiner had left the room and the completed questionnaire was then sealed in an envelope and placed in a box in the testing room.

The questionnaire contained items indicative of either anxiety or hostility. "Since this measure of examiner anxiety and hostility was established on the basis of the subject's description of the examiners it is inferred that this criterion provides an index of that aspect of the examiner's anxiety and hostility which is overt and apparent to the subject." The Rorschachs of the nine examiners were scored for anxiety and hostility according to Elizur's RCT test (p. 267). This measure was assumed to indicate "the anxiety and hostility present in the examiner's perceptual and fantasy living and hence is covert rather than that acted out by the examiners." The major findings were as follows:

1. There were significant differences among examiners in the number of responses they tended to obtain from their subjects. When the correlation between R and the individual scoring categories was taken into account, significant differences among examiners remained.

2. The three examiners ranked highest, in comparison to the three ranked lowest, on overt anxiety elicited more responses, more S responses, and more color responses.

3. The three examiners with the highest, in comparison to the three with the lowest, covert anxiety score (RCT) elicited more human movement responses, more H content, a smaller A percent more shading responses, and higher hostility scores (RCT).

4. The more overt the hostility of the examiners the less the hostile content elicited, more shading and animal (A percent) responses were given, and fewer H responses were found.

5. Compared to examiners who rank low on covert hostility, the high examiners elicited few shading responses, less A percent, more hostile content, more content categories, and more H responses.

6. Using a questionnaire "indicating the degree of emotional closeness and liking which they (the subject) felt towards their examiner," it was found that examiners were liked differently by their subjects.

Inspection of the subjects' feelings as expressed on these items reveals that examiners rated low on overt anxiety or hostility are described as "close friends" while examiners described as most anxious or most hostile are liked "mildly" or "somewhat." The low anxiety or hostility ranked examiners are liked "a great deal" or "pretty much" and according to their subjects these examiners would be "affectionate" or "rather warm" with children. In contrast, high anxiety or hostility examiners would be only "tolerant" or "pay some attention to it (child)."

A chi-square test was also made of the responses to questionnaire items referring to emotional distance between the three examiners ranked low on anxiety according to Elizur's measure. This chi-square value failed to attain statistical significance. That is, subjects did not indicate any significant difference in their degree of liking or desire for emotional distance between examiners who are ranked high or low on covert anxiety. However, the more covertly hostile (Elizur's RCT) the examiners the more the subjects like them and the "closer" the subjects want to be to these examiners.

The findings might more clearly be presented as follows:

Examiners high on *overt hostility*
elicit
higher A%
higher Y (Beck's symbol for shading)
less H
lower hostility score

Examiners high on *covert hostility*
elicit
lower A%
less Y
more H
greater hostility score

Examiners high on *overt anxiety*
elicit
a greater R
more C
more S

Examiners high on *covert anxiety*
elicit
greater hostility score
more M and H
more Y

Although these findings strongly indicate that Rorschach scores vary with examiner differences, there are several factors which suggest that authors' interpretation of some of their findings must be viewed with caution.

1. Although the authors conclude, as the above findings suggest, that there is an inverse relation between overt and covert hostility and certain Rorschach scores, they fail to attach importance to the significant and *negative* correlation (—.79) between the measures of overt and covert hostility: the examiners who were rated highly hostile by the subjects gave low hostile scores (RCT) on the Rorschach. Since this correlation indicates that the measures of covert and overt hostility were not independent of each other—that they were measures of much the same thing—one cannot draw any conclusions about the differential effects of either overt or covert hostility. *However, one should not overlook the importance of this negative correlation because it should caution the clinician against the oft made assumption that the amount of a particular content on the Rorschach is positively related to overt behavior, a point we have discussed in the previous chapter.*

2. In interpreting their findings the authors make assumptions about the interpretive significance of some of the scoring categories which are of dubious validity. For example, increased shading = increased passivity, increased A percent = increased stereotypy, and increased M = more fantasy. There is little or no evidence for any of these assumptions and it is unwarranted to assume that the presence of one indicates the presence of the other.

Examiners ranked high or low on covert anxiety obtain a small but significant number of differences in the Rorschach scores of their subjects. The more anxious examiners do not elicit significantly more responses from their subjects than do the ones who are less covertly anxious. However, they do elicit more hostile content, more passive trends (Y per cent) and more fantasy and self awareness (M and H). In this case, the subjects apparently are not aware of the source of the anxiety, even though certain of their perceptions on the Rorschach Tests are influenced by the anxiety. At any rate, the subjects indicate no significant differences in their degree of liking for these high and low ranked examiners. The nature of their reaction, in general, in the presence of this kind of anxiety may be interpreted as a relatively less active one than in the presence of anxiety of which they are more consciously aware. It may be that the subjects tend to avoid acting out their disturbance. They indulge in increased fantasy, probably with a hostile content and they become more passive. This is in contrast with the relatively more active and outwardly directed efforts in the presence of overt examiner anxiety.

In light of our discussions in previous chapters we would conclude that the above interpretations are to a large extent unwarranted. A more cautious interpretation would be that the overtly anxious examiner tends to elicit a greater, externally directed responsiveness in contrast to the less overtly anxious examiner, while the examiner with a high ranking on covert anxiety tends to elicit a more subjective, hostility-tinged responsiveness in contrast to examiners with a low ranking on covert anxiety. One could argue that the subject with an overtly anxious examiner is less likely to be aware of himself or to be set to give expression to his personal motives or internal reactions than the subject with an examiner who, while he may be covertly anxious, does not overtly behave in an anxious way.

Despite these criticisms the study by Sanders and Cleveland represents an important and ingenious attempt to tackle a long-neglected problem, one which has significance for interactions in general.

Alden and Benton (1) studied the relationship of sex of examiner to incidence of Rorschach responses with sexual content. Male hospitalized subjects were used. "One hundred Rorschach records were drawn from the files, fifty of them secured by the female examiner and fifty by the male examiner. The selection was a random one except for the fact that records with less than ten responses were discarded." They found no differences between the male and female examiners although, as they point out, the design of the study does not rule out the possibility that personality differences or similarities rather than the sexual factor might have been the important factors. In addition, by excluding cases whose Rorschachs contained less than ten responses, the investigators might well have been excluding cases which would have been relevant to one of the hypotheses which gave rise to the study, namely, that the male patients would be inhibited by a female examiner.

One can only hope that in years to come the influence of the clinician on the behavior of the subject will not remain a neglected area. We feel this is an important problem not only because of our special interest in the Rorschach but because of the significance of the problem for interactions in general and personality theory in particular. For example, Sanders and Cleveland found a negative correlation between measures of overt and covert hostility, whereas in the case of anxiety they found no particular relationship. These findings suggest the possibility that not all response tendencies are reacted to or defended against by the individual in the same way. It may be that response tendencies (e.g., hostility, sexuality) which in our culture are "punished" when overtly expressed are likely to be expressed overtly in a different way from the case of response tendencies where cultural restrictions are not as strong. Perhaps the important factor is not the cultural one but the characteristic way an individual has learned to cope with what he considers to be dangerous tendencies. We are here obviously dealing with problems which are of general significance and it may well be that the Rorschach, consisting as it does of definable stimuli utilized in a specific kind of situation, can be a valuable instrument in research on these problems.

DIFFERENCES IN INTERPRETATION

In the previous section we were concerned with the influence of the clinician on the behavior of the subject during the clinical interaction. Equally important problems are how clinicians differ in (1) the rationale or assumptions upon which their interpretive procedures are based and (2) the degree to which their own values, dominant response tendencies, or conflicts (e.g., hostility) influence the content of interpretations. On the second problem there has been practically no research, despite the fact that clinical supervisors recognize it as a crucial problem in training and one of the goals of training is to have the student learn to interpret the data he obtains in a manner uninfluenced by problems or characteristics peculiar to himself. Even were clinicians not aware that the interpretation of a patient's protocol is influenced by personal or subjective factors, the experimental literature (8, 96, 102) on the relationship between internal needs and perception of external stimuli would force the problem into the center of our attention. However, it is unfortunate but true that we know very little either about how interpretations of Rorschach protocols are affected by the clinician's own personality or about the degree to which training reduces the importance of the problem (138).

The question of how clinicians differ in the rationale or assumptions upon which interpretations are based is also one for which there are no clear-cut answers. Many times in our discussions we have seen that a number of the interpretive significances attributed to various scores or ratios are either unproved or simply not supported by available research. To base an interpretation, as is frequently done, on frequencies and combinations of scores and to lose sight at the same time of the fact that the significances attributed to many of these scores are unwarranted is a most dangerous procedure. As has been pointed out elsewhere (58):

One does not have to read far in the Rorschach literature in order to conclude that some workers view the scoring categories as the chief if not sole basis for interpretation. The frequency of the various types of responses is determined, ratios within and between categories are computed, and one need only know what each category and ratio stands for in order to write an interpretation. What some workers do not seem to realize is that the assumptions underlying each category are largely unproved.

The most flagrant examples of the use or abuse of the "counting" method are those studies in which a more or less homogeneous group of subjects is given the Rorschach, the frequencies computed, and the interpretation written in such a manner as to suggest that the constellation of frequencies is somehow unique for this group and that the behavioral characteristics described in the interpretation are valid. A somewhat more sophisticated, albeit unwarranted, use of the counting method is found in those studies in which contrasting groups are given the Rorschachs and differences between the responses of the two groups emerge. It is usually then assumed that whatever psychological differences are implied by the differences in Rorschach responses are in fact reflected in the behavior of the two groups— even though the Rorschach differences were not predicted and no independent evidence is presented that the behavior of the groups reflects the differences. The reverse side of the coin is found when no Rorschach differences emerge between the two groups and one concludes that behaviorally the two groups are not different. One might more justifiably conclude that the Rorschach as used may not be a discriminating instrument.

Auld (9, 10) has indicated how an uncritical acceptance of traditional assumptions can result in conclusions which not only are unwarranted but reflect clinicians' implicit "middle-class centered" values (9).

A survey of the literature on the Rorschach test did not disclose any comparative study of the way people belonging to different social classes differ in their responses. Indeed, the information about the influence of age, sex, education, and intelligence—all of which are known to be psychologically important—is also scanty. It happens, however, that the authors of two studies used groups of subjects that are similar except for social class. Hertz [74] reported on the Rorschach responses given by 41 upper-middle-class boys who were 15 years old at the time of testing. Schachtel [59] reported on 500 lower-class boys who were from 9 to 17 years old at time of testing (average age was 14 years, 6 months).[1] It seems likely, therefore, that Hertz's group and Schachtel's group differ importantly only in social class and variables related to social class.

A comparison of Hertz's report with Schachtel's shows that the middle-class boys differ strikingly from the lower-class boys in their responses to the test. As can be seen [below], the middle-class boys gave more human-movement responses, more animal-movement responses, more form-color responses, color-form responses, and more pure color responses. The differences in number of human-movement responses, form-color responses, and color-form responses are all statistically significant by the chi-square test (and hence cannot be attributed to chance sampling fluctuations). The middle-class boys also gave, on the average, a larger total number of responses (32, as compared to 26 for the lower-class boys). The larger total for the middle-class group, however, does not fully explain the larger number of movement and color responses, because if movement and color responses were figured as percentages of the total rather than as ordinary numbers, the middle-class boys would still come out higher on movement and color.

### Rorschach Responses of Cleveland Upper-Middle-Class and of Boston Lower-Class

| Variable | Cleveland Mean | Boston Mean |
|---|---|---|
| Total number of responses | 31.7 | 26.2 |
| Human-movement responses | 3.7 | 1.2 |
| Animal-movement responses | 3.2 | 1.2 |
| Form-color responses | 2.1 | 0.5 |
| Color-form responses | 1.0 | 0.4 |
| Pure color responses | 0.4 | 0.1 |

Since it is not absolutely certain that social status is the only important way in which these two groups of boys differ, and it is possible that differences in methods of administering the test have also had some effect on the results, these findings are not conclusive. They do suggest, however, that social class has a marked influence on the way people respond to the Rorschach test.

[1] The numbers in brackets refer to the Bibliography of this book.

Most Rorschach experts, in fact, would interpret the average lower-class profile of test scores . . . very differently from the average middle-class profile. . . . According to Rorschach experts, a person who gives a large number of human-movement (M) responses has a "rich inner life," is imaginative and intelligent. Thus they would say that the middle-class boys have a much richer inner life and are more imaginative and intelligent. According to Rorschach experts, the human-movement (M) response is "more mature" than the animal-movement (FM) response; the animal-movement response represents a childish expression of inner needs. Therefore, a well-adjusted person should give more M responses than FM. It can be seen that the middle-class boys give more M than FM, but the lower-class boys do not.

Similarly, Rorschach experts would give a quite different interpretation to the color responses of the two groups. According to Rorschach experts, color responses reveal the emotional life of the person and indicate how he behaves toward other people. Rorschach experts believe that form-color (FC) responses are more mature and "better controlled" than color-form (CF) responses. Color-form responses are said to be better controlled than pure color (C) responses. It is desirable, therefore, that FC responses far outweigh the CF and C responses. It is also desirable to have a moderate number of color responses, since lack of such responses is taken to indicate lack of ability to express one's emotions. Obviously, then, the lower-class boys would be said to be more immature and less well controlled (since they have as many CF responses as FC) and to be less responsive to their environment and lacking in emotional warmth (since they have fewer color responses of all kinds).

But are middle-class boys actually richer in inner life, more mature, emotionally warmer, and better controlled? Indeed, they may be; but since the validity of the Rorschach test has not yet been convincingly demonstrated, there is little reason to believe that this *is* so. It seems more probable that the Rorschach experts ascribe these less desirable traits to the lower-class group because its pattern of responses is *different* from the pattern that the experts are familiar with. Most of the normal people that the Rorschach experts have tested were middle-class people; hence the experts' notion of a normal Rorschach record is derived from the test responses of middle-class people.

Psychologists who have collected data showing how normal persons respond to the Rorschach have almost always studied middle-class groups. For example, Hertz [71] studied the responses of 300 adolescents. Almost all of them belonged to the middle class. Persons using Hertz's norms have forgotten her caution: "Attempts to apply such norms to groups materially different from that herein described must be made with caution." Ames,

Learned, Metraux, and Walker [6] offered normative data based on the test records of 650 children from 2 to 10 years old. Most of these children came from middle-class families. Thus the responses of only a limited segment of the population—people belonging to the middle class—have been used as reference points for what is "normal."

*Although many clinicians base their interpretations on a dictionary-like use of scoring categories, the published interpretations of leading writers in the field rather clearly reveal that they are based on more than scoring categories.* In fact, a careful study of these interpretations might well force one to the following conclusions: (1) The frequencies within and between the scoring categories are, at best, a starting point for interpretation, and (2) the "qualitative" rather than the quantitative aspects of the record are the major focus of and basis for the interpretation. Schachtel (147), for example, in his study of the Rorschachs of delinquent and non-delinquent concluded that "the differences in terms of isolated Rorschach scores between the delinquents and non-delinquents are very much smaller than the similarities are. The differences become more marked when the total configurations of the Rorschach records are studied with methods of qualitative rather than quantitative analysis." The fact that Schachtel (59) was able, on the basis of protocols which he himself had not obtained, to separate delinquents from non-delinquents far beyond chance expectations clearly suggests that the qualitative rather than the quantitative aspects of the protocols were of crucial importance. What, therefore, are these qualitative aspects, or what is a qualitative analysis? We shall be unable to answer these questions satisfactorily because published interpretations largely contain conclusions about the individuals and not the detailed, step-by-step analysis which led up to the conclusions. To answer these questions we need to know in as great detail as possible what the clinician does from the beginning to the end of the interpretive process. Where does he start and why does he start there? What assumptions about the dynamics of behavior does he utilize and how are these related to his interpretive procedure? When, why, and how are those aspects of a protocol which are not reflected in the formal scoring utilized? Until the data necessary for answering these kinds of questions are available the interpretive procedure cannot be evaluated and, more important, communicated (136).

Although we do not have satisfactory answers to the questions asked above, the interpretive procedure seems to be based largely on the following considerations:

1. The protocol should be evaluated in light of the subject's conception of the task and the purposes of the interaction. How the subject conceives of the task and the purposes of the interaction is very frequently *deduced* from his incidental and non-scorable verbalizations. It is on the basis of these deductions that further deductions are made about the subject's dominant attitudes toward himself and others.

2. The Rorschach situation is assumed to give one a sample of the subject's handling of a stressful, problem-solving situation which takes place in the context of an interpersonal interaction.

3. The *sequence* of the subject's behavior is lawful and not fortuitous and reflects the way in which different response tendencies are related to each other.

4. The content of the responses is considered of prime importance in determining the subject's attitudes toward self and others.

5. Assumptions derived from a part of psychoanalytic theory are implicitly used as the basis for attributing meanings to and among responses, and also serve as the framework by which various conclusions are put in relation to one another.

Not all writers attach the same degree of importance to the above considerations. It will be apparent to the reader of this book, however, that thus far in our discussion of the Rorschach we have placed great emphasis on the importance of determining the relationship between any response or class of responses and the variables which operate in any interpersonal interaction, variables which we discussed at some length in earlier chapters of this book. Although these situational variables are taken into account to some degree by different workers, it is Schachtel (*146*) who explicitly places the greatest emphasis on their importance in the interpretive procedure.

In our discussion (Chapter 8) of the continua by which interpersonal behavior may be judged and categorized, we pointed out that such continua do not adequately reflect the complexity of human behavior or the major situational variables. Since, as we have tried to point out, the major scoring categories for Rorschach responses are similar to, if not identical with, these more generally stated continua, one should also not expect them to be adequate to the task of reflecting the complexities of behavior. The emphasis which has been placed on scoring in Rorschach texts has led many students to overevaluate the significance of scoring categories. The scoring categories, like the continua, reflect *aspects* of a complicated behavioral system and do not relieve the clinician of the necessity of deducing meanings and relationships which go beyond what is given by the categories. In the clinical interaction identifying variables and judging behavior on various continua are preliminary steps to the problem of understanding the personal significances of an individual's behavior. It is not enough for the clinician to say that a patient responds unrealistically, or primarily in terms of internal referents or stimuli, or with extremely strong hostile or passive tendencies. The problem of the clinician is to concretize the meanings of such responses, state their antecedents and consequences, and relate each to the others. To accomplish this the clinician utilizes, implicitly or explicitly, some kind of theory (Chapter 2). In the next chapter we shall endeavor to describe some of the major assumptions or concepts which appear necessary for understanding the data obtained or observations made in the clinical situation. We say *"some* of the major assumptions" because knowledge about what theoretical assumptions are actually utilized by or necessary for the clinician is sufficiently unclear to force one to be modest about the comprehensiveness of one's coverage. Following the next chapter we shall present step-by-step interpretations in an attempt to illustrate the ways in which these assumptions are utilized and determine one's interpretive procedure. It is also hoped that these case presentations will make more clear the role of scoring in the interpretive process.

# PART III

# Individual Interpretation

## Chapter 17

## SOME MAJOR ASSUMPTIONS

We HAVE on numerous occasions, especially in Chapters 2 and 16, stressed that the clinician utilizes explicitly or implicitly some kind of theory in his observation and interpretation of a patient's behavior. The theory may be of a haphazard or systematic nature—in either case only aspects of the overall theory may be used—but the behavior of the clinician is based on some kind of theory by means of which observations are given meanings. In the individual case the clinician's conclusions are based on more than a consideration of the subject's overt behavior or manipulation of various scores, be the score an intelligence quotient, the number of M responses, or the ratio of movement to color. The clinician's conclusions are largely concerned with the covert significances of the overt behavior and scores, significances which are deduced on the basis of theoretical assumptions concerning the dynamics of behavior. If a particular kind of overt behavior or score always had a particular covert significance, the clinician's task would indeed be an easy one. But, as we have seen in the case of the Rorschach, this is far from being the case. To base an interpretation solely or even largely on the consideration of scoring categories is a completely unjustified procedure. To the extent that the significance of certain Rorschach scoring categories has been empirically established—to the extent that their interpretative significance has a basis in controlled research—they can be used by the clinician as *starting points or guides* in his task. *We emphasize "starting points or guides" because there is no Rorschach score or combination of scores which is correlated so highly with either overt or covert behavior that the clinician need only know its frequency (or combination with other frequencies) to be able to state its significance in the individual case.*

It will be clear to the experienced clinician that most of what is contained in this chapter stems from psychoanalytic theory. However, although the major assumptions to be described are or can be embedded

293

in a systematic, comprehensive analytic theory, Freudian or neo-Freudian, it is not our intention to relate them to any wider framework. The assumptions, therefore, represent aspects or parts of a more general theory. Several considerations dictated this approach. First, there are parts of psychoanalytic theory which have too little foundation in terms of evidence to warrant applying them to the problems of this book. Second, the *logical* relationships among the different aspects of the theory are in many instances unclearly or tenuously related to the overall theory. Third, there are so many major disagreements among analytic theorists that it is impossible to talk of a psychoanalytic theory; one must talk rather of psychoanalytic theories. Blum (*21*), following a discussion and presentation of various analytic theories, has put the situation clearly (*21*, p. 190): "If one may venture a guess as to the reader's state of mind upon finishing this effort, the most appropriate word is probably 'confused.' It seems as though a large number of psychoanalysts through many years of observing patients, discussing cases, and borrowing from their own unconscious ideas have contributed to a massive, vague, yet potent personality theory. Encompassed are many controversial issues and sharp disagreements."

Although there is much in psychoanalytic theory to which one might object on various grounds, *one must distinguish clearly between the adequacy of the formulation and the problems which it attempts to clarify.* In rejecting the formulation it is all too easy to overlook the real problem which frequently confronted the formulator. One might object in psychoanalytic theory to the ways in which the concept of the unconscious is employed or formulated. Such objections should not obscure the fact that these formulations represent attempts to explain certain kinds of phenomena observed in patients. One may not like the formulation but one cannot rule out of existence the overt behavior which it attempted to understand. Freud's (*54*) formulation of the "death instinct" may be criticized on many grounds, and in the opinion of this writer may be dismissed as an untestable concept, but one should not overlook the fact that the concept was formulated in an attempt to understand (1) behavior which was destructive to self and others, (2) the tendency for painful experiences to be reëxperienced compulsively in the life of the individual, and (3) the developmental aspects of such behavior.

The foregoing is by way of saying that in this chapter the reader should try to distinguish between the adequacy of the major assumptions or concepts and the kinds of problems which they are meant to explain. To the reader who is not a clinician it should be pointed out that the clinician is expected to give some kind of answer to the problems which are presented to him, and he cannot avoid answering the problems because of uncertainties about the assumptions upon which he operates. However, because of this necessity to give solutions to the pressing problems of sick people the clinician must also take on the obligation of constantly subjecting his major assumptions to the tests of practical results and congruence with scientific procedure and experimental research. Exposing his thinking and practices to public and critical review is one way of meeting this obligation.

## PSYCHIC DETERMINISM

By psychic determinism is meant that a response (any agreed upon unit of behavior) is in part determined by the characteristics of the previous response. What one says or does depends in part on what one has just said or done. Put in another way: Consecutive or successive responses are not in a random relationship to each other but rather reflect something about past learning. The utilization of this principle in the clinical situation is most clearly apparent when the clinician is surprised or startled or puzzled by something a patient has said or done. *At such times the clinician focuses his attention on what preceded as well as on what followed the particular response.* When in the interaction a patient stutters for the first time, or begins to have difficulty responding, or suddenly changes the content or focus of his talking—when the patient's behavior discernibly changes, the clinician's attention turns to the antecedent behavior for clues which will make meaningful the sequence of behavior. The following case discussed by French (2, p. 119) indicates the way in which the principle of psychic determinism is utilized in understanding behavior in a therapeutic interaction:[1]

[This was] the case of a young unmarried woman, six months pregnant, who had been referred by the court to a social agency for financial assistance and help in making plans for her prior to her confinement. From the court the therapist, a woman, knew only that the patient had been very insistent

[1] Franz Alexander and Thomas Morton French, *Psychoanalytic Therapy*, 1946, The Ronald Press Company.

upon taking legal action against the putative father, Mr. M.; that at the time when she became aware of her pregnancy she had been living with her parents, but that her father had since died and she was now living alone with her mother. It was also learned that she had very recently stopped work on account of her pregnancy. The court worker had suggested that the agency might help the patient to find a place to live away from home during the rest of her pregnancy.

It was with this theme that the patient opened the interview, assailing the therapist with questions: What maternity home and hospital could she go to? How many homes were there? What were the names of them? Where were they located? Were they sponsored by churches? These questions were asked one after another without a break. When the therapist suggested that she could answer the questions more intelligently if she could learn more about the patient's situation, the patient stated that she was living with her mother; that her father had just died; that she didn't wish to stay home because it was too unpleasant there. Her oldest sister (fifteen years older than patient) had just come to live with the mother, bringing her child. The patient and this sister had never got along. Although her own feeling made her *want* to leave, she *could* stay with her mother as long as she liked.

After giving this information, the patient immediately returned to her barrage of questions about maternity homes and medical resources in the city. In this new series of questions the additional fact was brought out that the patient was a member of a Lutheran church which she attended regularly. "Do the Lutherans have something?" she asked. She had thought of an arrangement by which she could get her hospital care and live there too. She was rather pressing in her demand for such an arrangement but also indicated a certain resistance to the idea. She wanted to be sure to look the place over; she had never lived away from home and this in itself would be new and different; she could still stay on in her mother's home or she could make arrangements to live with any one of her three other sisters with whom she got along well.

It will be of interest at this point to consider how the therapist should handle this situation. It is evident that the patient is at the moment too disturbed to be able to give a systematic history. Moreover, it is important to form some impression as to the cause of her agitation in order not to increase her disturbance unnecessarily by inappropriate questioning. If we try to sense the dominant motive back of her importunate questions, it seems evident that she is reacting somewhat aggressively to an intense anxiety. This patient has never lived away from home, and yet she feels now under pressure to leave home on account of her sister's unpleasantness. In addition, her pregnancy has presumably exposed her not only to the critical remarks of the sister but also to unknown dangers with which she surrounds the prospect of medical care and delivery of the child. She is afraid, she doesn't know exactly of what, and is struggling to relieve her anxiety by taking the offensive, by asking a long series of questions so rapidly that they cannot be answered.

The last paragraph in the above excerpt seems primarily to be concerned with the question: *What were the antecedent factors in the immediate and near past which might make meaningful the patient's agitated (and puzzling) behavior at the beginning of the interview?* We are here not interested in how the question was answered but only in the direction of the therapist's focus of attention.

The therapist did . . . succeed in relieving the patient's anxiety considerably by assuring her that there was no imperative need for her to leave home immediately and that she and the patient would have time to consider alternative arrangements after they had thought things through a little more. In response to this reassurance, the patient was able to confide more about her situation. She had had no medical care with the exception of her first examination three months before. It was at that time that she had become aware that she was pregnant and the father of the child had taken her to the doctor with the idea of getting an abortion for her. She had refused and now he was holding this against her. She showed the therapist a picture of the child's father, whom she had met two and a half years before at a time when he was separated from his wife. She had maintained a constant relationship with him ever since, even though he had returned to his wife for a few months at one time. He had talked about a divorce for a year or more, but the patient had begun to wonder if he meant it. Even now she didn't know what to believe. He kept telling her that if she would drop the court case against him, he would get a divorce and marry her; but he had not done so before and she had no faith in his statements now.

The therapist inquired at this point how the patient happened to become pregnant at this time. The patient replied that in the last year she had felt that she did not care if she got pregnant. She thought that perhaps if she had his child he would have to take a definite stand. She thought he would have to go through with the divorce and marry her. She was very disappointed that this had not been so. She thought the wife would give him a divorce if she knew of the situation. But both Mr. M. and his wife had been to court and although the wife was quite angry about the situation she made no effort to grant him a divorce. Mr. M. employed his own private attorney and was angry that she had taken him to court. He pointed out that he would have been willing to give her the money he had to pay for a private attorney. He blamed her for her present predicament because she had refused the abortion he had tried to get for her. He had advised her to find an apartment and live by herself, so that he could keep in touch with her. She had seen him recently at church. He had rather encouraged her in coming to the agency to inquire about maternity homes. She just couldn't stay at home because of her conflict with her sister. When her father was alive things were different; he always stuck up for her.

After this burst of confidence, however, the patient returned to her rapid-fire questions about where she could get medical care.

In order to understand better just what gave rise to this second barrage of questions, let us now look back upon this series of confidences that the patient has been able to give to her therapist. We have already pointed out that the patient's anxiety was relieved considerably by the therapist's reassurance that it was not necessary to leave home immediately. Consequently, for a time, her thoughts cease to be polarized exclusively about her fears and she is able to confide in the therapist the fond hopes that had preceded her discovery that she was pregnant. Striking evidence of her increased confidence in the therapist is the fact that she is even able to confess her hope that by becoming pregnant she might put pressure upon Mr. M. to fulfill his promises to marry her. Her recital of these hopes, however, leads her back immediately to her disillusionment. Associated with her disillusionment, as we know, is an intense fear of being left alone to face unknown dangers. To this anxiety, as well as to her disillusionment, she had reacted by aggressive efforts to compel Mr. M. to fulfill his promises to her. These efforts to put pressure on Mr. M., however, only defeated her own purpose. From her account now it seems clear that Mr. M. has wished and is still quite willing to acknowledge much of his responsibilities toward her but her aggressive determination to bring him to court threatens only to estrange him from her. As she reaches this point in her recital she is again faced with anxiety at the possibility of being left alone without anyone to turn to. Her last association reveals how intensely she longs for someone to whom to cling. When her father was alive, she tells us, he always stuck up for her. But this reassuring thought is of little avail since the father is dead. Consequently, at this point a new series of questions betrays the re-emergence of her anxiety.

In this last excerpt, even more clearly than in the preceding one, we can see how shifts in the patient's behavior focuses the attention of the therapist on the antecedent overt or covert behavior.

Up to this point we have been illustrating the principle of psychic determinism in instances where a response is surprising or puzzling. One can also give examples in which successive or near-concomitant responses are considered meaningfully related only because of their time relationships. For example, French (*48*, p. 78) begins a discussion of an analytic case as follows: "During the few hours of his analysis this rather inarticulate man found talking freely about personal matters very difficult; also asthmatic wheezing made him uncomfortable. In the sixth hour *he experienced relief, when, finally voicing freely his resentments against his wife, he complained that she was fat, sloppy, and quarrelsome and neglected the two children and himself.*" In other words, the voicing resentment against his wife and relief from asthmatic wheezing are not considered a fortuitous sequence.

Requiring a patient to verbalize whatever comes into his mind, asking an individual to respond to a stimulus word with the first word that occurs to him, taking a complete record of a child's activity with people or objects during play or therapy—in each of these instances the clinician's procedure is in part based on the assumption that successive aspects of a behavioral sequence are meaningfully related to each other. Such an assumption, of course, does not in any way indicate either how these aspects are related in the present or the nature of the past learning as a result of which the relationships were formed. The significance of the assumption is that it focuses the clinician's attention *on the details of a sequence* and forces him to ask certain questions: Why does this type of behavior emerge at *this* point? What went before? What came after?

### PURPOSIVE BEHAVIOR

By purposive behavior is meant a response or sample of behavior that is related to (or has been learned in relation to) certain drives, or motives, or wishes. This relationship may be manifested in a direct or indirect way in the sense that motives either may be reflected in what an individual overtly says about them or may be deduced wholly from what the clinician observes. Even when an individual makes overt statements about his motives, the clinician makes deductions about their validity—the clinician deduces whether other motives are operative. The word "motive," then, does not refer to a *thing* (in the sense that words like "pen" and "car" refer to tangible objects) but refers to a hypothesized internal state of affairs. The following incident may be helpful as an example:

A student group at Yale invited a number of faculty members to address them at weekly meetings on the topic "Marriage and the Family." The writer, who was to address the third meeting, had been preceded by a sociologist and a biologist. Before the meeting began, the chairman of the group took the writer aside and began to explain in a faltering kind of way that the group had perhaps not made clear to the speakers what they had hoped would be discussed. With obvious embarrassment, hesitation, blushing, and discomfort the chairman related that the group had hoped that the speakers would discuss sex in a frank manner. The previous speakers had not touched on the topic and he hoped that the writer would feel free to talk about it in any way that he wanted and to use whatever terms were necessary. When the meeting began, the chairman, as ill at ease as before, falteringly told the group that the writer was going to discuss frankly some aspects of sexual adjustment and that they were to feel perfectly free to ask whatever questions occurred to them. Following this he said, "And now I would like *to resent,* Dr. Sarason." When the laughing subsided, the chairman turned to the writer and smiling weakly said, "That was a slip, wasn't it?"

The layman and the psychologist would agree that the student said something he "did not intend" to say—which is another way of saying that the student did intend to say something. In short, *he was motivated, or desired, or wished to achieve a certain goal:* to introduce the speaker in the conventional manner. The layman might not agree with the psychologist's deduction that the student was also motivated to say precisely what he did—he said both what he wanted and what he did not want to say. In addition, although the writer had not been previously aware that the student may have harbored hostile motives toward him, the comment following the slip suggests that the student had himself been aware of such motives. Although different psychologists might deduce different motives or patterns of motives from the description of the student's overt behavior, all would in effect describe a correlation between overt behavior and an internal process or event which was of an impelling, goal-directed nature.

To illustrate further how the assumption that behavior is purposive is utilized by the clinician, we will present a description based on the notes (taken during the hour) of the beginning of the first analytic hour of the patient described on page 75.

The patient was very tense. For a time he could not say anything. Then he said he felt "shaky." He asked if he could unbutton his collar. He spoke in a low, complaining tone of voice.

The above represents approximately five minutes and although the patient said very little, several questions might be asked: What was the patient thinking about during the time he could not talk? Why is his *first* verbalization about his shakiness? What was his *motive* in telling the therapist about it? What did he *hope or intend* to achieve by that verbalization? One could ask very similar questions about his request to unbutton his collar. In addition one might ask in what relation this request may stand to his previous verbalization. Is it likely that the patient *desires or is motivated* to inform the therapist about his discomfort and engage his sympathy?

After a long pause he said, "I didn't go into work today." He went on to say that he didn't like the work he was supposed to do and he was paid very little. He had looked for another job today but had no luck. "They [his present employer] don't want to give us work that pays. They treat us like dogs." (Short pause.) "I'm afraid to go in tomorrow. The boss will make a sarcastic remark. I'll choke up. I won't be able to say anything."

The patient shifts the focus from himself in the therapeutic situation to his attitudes and behavior in connection with his job and boss. He describes assertive behavior, hostile attitudes, and the consequences of both within himself. Why does he decide or become motivated to relate this to the therapist? Is it that he feels *impelled* to talk about something in order to comply with the instructions given to him? If so, why does the need or motivation to talk result in aggressive and hostile content? Are his motivations toward and relationship with his boss (and job) a reflection of his motivations toward the therapist and the therapy? Since it was known that the patient resisted coming for therapy, and it was considered very likely that he harbored a great deal of hostility toward the situation and whoever was part of it, was the shift in focus related to such motivations? It should not be overlooked that his anticipation of how he would respond (inability to talk) to his boss' sarcastic remarks is identical with what he felt in connection with the therapy.

After a very long pause the patient was asked what he was thinking about. "My wife. She said she won't eat supper till I get home. That means the little one [youngest child] will miss supper. I feed him. He can't win by me." He related that his wife gets upset with the two children. The older daughter fights with the little boy but "she don't mean anything. I told my wife not to wait but she said she would." Another long pause.

"Doctor, is it all right if I don't come dressed up each time? Will you mind?"

The therapist remarked that he did not understand what he meant.

"When I come here I like to get dressed but I won't have time. When I'm in working clothes I don't feel clean. I don't like the odor of perspiration. Other people don't like it either. Is it all right?"

Again one might ask why the long pause following his description of his relationship with his boss? Why does he again shift the focus of attention from his work and boss to his wife? Is the shift purposeful in the sense that thinking about his boss and his own inability to stand up to him engendered associations which *he did not want* to verbalize? Does the patient feel that he may not be pleasing the therapist by his talk and, *desiring to get some sign of approval* from the therapist, he goes on to a topic which he feels might achieve that goal? Would this kind of motive be the basis for his shift from his family to dress?

The questions we have asked about this fragment of an analytic hour are not all that might have been raised, and it is unimportant at this time whether they are considered the most cogent or "correct" ones that might have been asked. What we attempted to illustrate is the fact that the clinician reacts to the patient's overt behavior by making statements which are deductions about intentions, goals, motives, and the like. In the previous discussion we italicized those words which are commonly used to indicate purposive behavior.

The following example is presented because it is a rather clear instance of how inexplicable behavior might· be without the individual's overt verbalization of purpose. The case, which has been more fully described elsewhere (*139*, p. 282), is that of an institutionalized, mentally defective girl with whom a therapeutic relationship had been established:

One day Lottie came to the office wearing glasses, something which the therapist had never seen her wear before. He expressed surprise at the glasses and inquired about how she had found out that she was in need of them. To his surprise Lottie replied that she had had the glasses for a long time.

PSYCHOLOGIST.   How come you are wearing them today?

LOTTIE.   The cottage matron said I was supposed to wear them and that I couldn't go out today until I put them on.

PSYCHOLOGIST.   Why haven't you worn them before?

*(At this point* LOTTIE'S *head went down on her chest, a movement which the psychologist had learned to recognize as an indication that she did not want to answer the question)*

PSYCHOLOGIST *(After several minutes' silence).*   The reason I asked that question, Lottie, is that I was puzzled about why you haven't worn glasses before today. Now I'm puzzled about why you don't want to answer the question. You remember our agreement about talking. It may be hard for you to answer. Until you show me that you will stick to the agreement, there's nothing I can do or say.

LOTTIE *(After approximately ten minutes of silence).*   Because the girls called me four eyes.

PSYCHOLOGIST.   When the girls call you four eyes, it reminds you of what you think about yourself, that you are not pretty. *(Nods her head in agreement)* But I still don't understand why it was so hard for you to answer the question. Why couldn't you tell it to me?

LOTTIE *(After another ten minutes of silence).*   Because you wear glasses.

PSYCHOLOGIST *(Somewhat recovered from his surprise).*   You thought that I would be hurt the way you were by what the girls said.

In choosing examples for this section we endeavored to describe instances which illustrated not only the purposiveness of behavior but the utilization of the assumption of psychic determinism as well. One might almost say that focusing on the details of the behavioral sequence preceded questions about the goal-directed aspects of the behavior.

UNCONSCIOUS EXPERIENCES

By unconscious experiences we refer to those which are no longer accessible to voluntary, sustained attempts at recall—or, if there is no attempt to recall, experiences for which there is independent evidence of their previous occurrence but of which the individual is no longer aware and he does not or cannot recall them when such evidence is presented. By experiences we refer to fantasy, self-verbalizations, interpersonal interactions, perceptions of external events, dreams, and the like. We shall consider the following to be characteristics of unconscious experiences:

1. The unconscious experience was once considered by the individual to be in some way "painful," "dangerous," or "unacceptable" to himself. *To the individual* the overt act or conscious thought or fantasy in some way threatened his well-being, self-esteem, or strongly held values. Grinker and Spiegel's (63) descriptions of war casualties illustrate this characteristic.

CASE 36
*Psychogenic headaches caused by repressed fear and anger, increased by combat.*

This patient was a 28 year old bombardier who had been in the army for four years. Two years ago, he was washed out of pilot training. He was sent overseas, where he flew four combat missions of moderate severity. After his second mission, he complained to his Flight Surgeon about several frontal and temporal headaches, which had been intermittent for many years but had become constant since he had been in combat. Thorough examinations in several hospitals disclosed no organic disease. The patient became depressed, lost 30 pounds in weight and slept poorly. He was sent home by the Medical Board after failure of psychiatric treatment overseas.

The patient came from a middle class family, in which he seemed to be the favorite of the mother. His father was good to him but quite strict in many attitudes. Intermittent headaches began in high school and became more frequent; they were not relieved by medication. They reached an intense stage, although still intermittent, while he was flying in this country.

The patient had a stern facial expression and scowled frequently. He seemed not always to hear people talking to him. He recalled that he developed this trait as a child, not hearing his mother when she called so that he wouldn't have to go into the house. He also did not want to hear the boys call him "Fatty." Under pentothal it was disclosed that the patient had great fear of flying because of the danger of falling. He secretly was glad to be washed out of pilot training. He finally came to admit that he was actually terrified of flying, even as a bombardier, but could not quit and maintain his self respect. Furthermore, he had a great abhorrence of killing people, hated war and felt it was futile. Further light on his past was revealed, indicating that early in life he was rebellious to teachers and authority but later he kept his rebellion in check. He would walk away from all arguments and disputes. In reconstructing these episodes he came to realize that his intermittent headaches developed during periods of unexpressed anger. As the patient became conscious of the relationship of unexpressed fear and anger to his headaches and was assured he would not have to fly again, his symptoms disappeared and he became free of headaches.

. . . . .

Here we see the relationship between a repressed emotion and a disabling symptom, which at first caused great difficulty in differential diagnosis but finally was found to be psychogenic. Ventilation disclosed that the headaches were due to a conflict between rebellious aggression against an authoritative figure in the army and fear of retaliation. Abreaction and conscious knowledge of the problem, with environmental manipulation (grounding), effected a relief of symptoms. By this we do not mean a cure, for we have not touched the primary source of the conflict—we have only made its later causes conscious.

. . . . .

CASE 40
*Depression and anxiety of one year's duration due to loss of a buddy in combat.*

This patient was a Captain, 25 years of age, who entered the Convalescent Hospital because of objective symptoms of depression. He presented an expressionless face; his muscles were quite rigid, indicating a great deal of tension. He did not volunteer much information and never smiled, and his speech was retarded. The patient had been a flight leader in a pursuit squadron and had fought successfully until about his twenty-fifth mission, when a friend, who had been flying on his wing, went up in flames. However, he stated that he continued fighting and successfully completed his tour of duty although feeling badly depressed. He refused promotion to command a squadron. He had been reassigned to a job in the United States, which he liked very much and wanted to keep, but his depression continued and was accompanied by severe startle reactions. When anyone came into his room and made a sudden noise or turned on the light, he would jump out of bed with great anxiety. In addition to the depression and its concomitants, there was considerable insomnia, with battle dreams, which repeated some of the very severe traumatic incidents of his combat experiences. However, he maintained fairly good control of himself and continued to fly. He attempted to decrease the anxiety and depression by drinking, but the only result was an increase in anxiety. He stated that he tried hard to forget his experiences but found it impossible.

During the initial interview, it was learned that he was single, and was a university graduate, who studied hard, made excellent grades and was given a fellowship in animal genetics, which he could not complete because he entered the Air Forces. There was no history of any previous depression and no incident that showed that he could not adjust himself to his normal experiences and environment.

That afternoon he was given 0.25 Gm. of pentothal intravenously. He was then told that he was up in the air on a strafing mission and that the man on his wing was aflame, and he was then commanded: "Go ahead and talk." Immediately he went into an emotional reaction shouting to his friend, whose name was Joe, to "pull up and bail out."

"Why doesn't he pull up, why doesn't he bail out? I hope he doesn't think it's my fault. He's such a nice boy. Such a swell fellow. I hope I'm not responsible for his death. We were together all the time. He lived in the same tent with me and would share anything that he had. When we were on low rations, he would give as much as he could to everyone else." Accompanying all this were tears and sobbing and repetitions of, "I hope he doesn't think it's my fault. He wasn't a good flier. Oh, If I had only picked out another spot, a safer target, but that is where they told me to go, right over those trucks. If I had gone in some other place, he wouldn't have got it. Why did he do it? He should have stayed in formation. He didn't stay where he was supposed to. He came up and took the lead position with me. Maybe I should have given a talk before we went about staying in formation. Why didn't I do that?"

Then he talked about the letter they wrote home to Joe's family and how he couldn't bear to read it. That would start it all over again. "I can't get him out of my mind. I couldn't see his family because they had probably forgotten and I didn't want to stir them up." In this fashion he went over and over the traumatic situation, crying and sobbing.

As this reaction subsided, he was allowed to close his eyes and sleep for a few moments. Then he was handed a lighted cigarette and awakened. He looked at his watch and stated, "I must have been asleep. I had a dream about Joe." His pillow was wet with tears. He said, "Gosh, I perspired a lot."

The therapist said, "No, you were only asleep for a few minutes but you talked to me about Joe and you told me all about it. Let's talk about him some more."

Then in a conscious state he went over the situation again, just as he had done when asleep. Then the patient talked about another boy, who crashed in a low level flight, maintaining radio silence according to instructions although he was in need of help. Then he told of feeling badly about killing the Germans. The interview was ended by the therapist telling him that he had assumed responsibility for the death of Joe that did not seem to be based on fact.

The next morning the patient entered the interviewing room and stated, "I feel like a load has been lifted from my mind, like a great relief. I slept well last night, awakened once and went right to sleep again. I had no dreams. This morning I feel good." There was a silence. Then he said, "I guess I blamed myself unnecessarily." The therapist said, "Yes, you did. Now let's try to figure out why you blamed yourself. Tell me something about your background." The patient then told how he lived on a farm of 650 acres. His father was a successful farmer, who made enough to enable four children to go to college. The first child was born dead, the patient was the second and then there were two sisters, each two years apart, the elder two years younger than he. He had one brother, nine years younger. The mother was mild mannered and very religious. The children went to Sunday School and church, though not forced to do so. The father was very kind and gentle but strict in his attitudes. He rarely spanked the patient but he expected him to live up to his responsibilities. If he did not, the father would look pained and disappointed and tell him, "This was your job," and then do it himself, which the patient states was worse than a spanking. He was always on very good terms with his father and would rather work with him than anyone else.

He then began to talk about his commanding officer and told how this man was an exceptionally strong leader; a person who went on the most dangerous missions himself; a man who was fair and expected everyone to do his job.

The therapist said, "Your C.O. was very much like your father." The patient stated, "You know, I often thought he was like my father, doing things he wasn't supposed to do and doing everything to help us, but expecting the best from us. Of course, not in the same way, because he was a fighter." The psychiatrist then said, "Now let us summarize the things for which you blame yourself. Joe's death—you were ordered to hit the target, even though dangerous; you could do nothing else and could not be responsible for his death. Secondly, you blame yourself for not giving implicit formation instruction. But you were all experienced fliers and had been trained in formations for six months and every man knew his position. You blame yourself for killing the Germans, but you know that was to save the lives of our own troops. You blame yourself about the boy who crashed on the low mission, but it was agreed beforehand that radio silence was to be maintained. You blame yourself for not communicating with Joe's family, but you know that it is not good to stir up a sorrowing family again. So you have a lot of disapproving attitudes toward things which are not really your fault. You behave as if you were still reacting to a disapproving attitude that your father might have had toward you. You behave as if your father's image were looking at you with a disappointed expression."

The patient said, "Well, I have always taken responsibilities and duties seriously. I have never been able to feel that I did give my best unless I worked terribly hard."

To this the therapist answered, "And now your behavior, which is depressed and completely unhappy, is just as if you were intent on punishing yourself and never letting yourself have any fun or pleasure."

The patient stated, "That's it. I can't enjoy things. I wonder why I take his death so seriously," and terminated the interview.

The next day the patient began the interview smiling and stated that he felt as if he could carry on. He now realized that he took his responsibility too seriously but always had felt as if he didn't want to let anyone down. He then told about a younger pilot, 21 years of age, whom he had taught to fly in formation. The younger pilot looked up to him as an older man or father. He was asked, "Something like your younger brother?" and he answered, "Yes, he used to think I was a great guy; I taught him how to shoot, how to hold a gun and how to play all sorts of games. Our C.O. always spoke quite frankly about his opinion of the conduct and performance of the boys; he either disapproved or complimented. If a fellow did his work properly and if he asked for a day off, he always got every consideration."

It was explained to the patient that because of guilty feelings he was punishing himself for Joe's death (which had happened one year ago). This feeling had persisted without any cause in reality. Therefore, this sense of guilt and the punishment which he had been giving himself must be due to some inner feeling, which it was not possible to master unless it was unearthed and brought to light.

He was told, "Now you have said nothing but good things about Joe, how attached you were and what a fine fellow he was, but your guilty feelings about him are due to some negative attitudes toward Joe that you have not yet discussed. Perhaps these feelings were unconscious and a source of your sense of guilt."

The patient then said, "Of course, no one is perfect, but Joe was the easiest person to get along with. He drank frequently and had to be taken care of. Once when we were in the desert and got drunk, Joe tore up the tent in the middle of a sandstorm. There was a family quarrel with the four tentmates."

His attention was drawn to the fact that Joe was not made flight leader.

Was Joe envious of the patient? He reconstructed the flight: Joe was flying on the left wing of the patient, who was the leader. Joe flew on the left slightly behind but he veered to the right and forward, to accompany the patient in the lead position. The patient was asked whether he interpreted this as if Joe were out to take the lead as a sort of rebellion. He said he didn't think so, but that he didn't give way because he wanted to maintain the proper formation in the flight. Then he said, "Maybe that's why I feel so guilty, because I didn't give way." The result was that Joe was hit by flak and slid over the patient's plane to the right, on fire.

The next morning the patient entered the room, at ease and in good spirits, and said, "I've been thinking a good deal about Joe and some clue you gave me yesterday brought me to some sort of a conclusion. Probably it is silly, you might not think it is important, but I have been thinking about it. I always wanted to do things and get ahead. I was very ambitious. I wanted to be better than just average, and, when I decided on any ambition, I worked very hard to accomplish it. Sometimes I would win and sometimes I would lose, but I would always work for whatever I wanted. When I was in school, there were four of us on a cattle-judging team. I wanted to be top man but there was another fellow on the team who lived with me and he was awfully good. I had to fight it out with him. We fought it back and forth all year round. In my junior year I was able to beat him. The next year he beat me. There were no hard feelings about it. It was competition but we still were friends."

The patient then repeated several other incidents of competitive relationship with other men and it became clear that he took no pleasure in winning over people who gave him no struggle. He always wanted to win out over someone whom he felt to be superior to him. "When I joined my outfit, it was the same way. We had a C.O. who believed that the leadership in the squadron should come from the boys themselves. There were eight places for flight leaders and the men had to win the job. Even after a man became flight leader, he had to work hard to keep it. We were always practicing, practically all the time. Two or three would go up and try to outfly each other. When we finally went overseas, I wasn't able to take a lead position but I became an assistant flight leader. I was disappointed but worked hard just the same. Finally there were eight of us who were flight leaders, including Joe and myself. But we weren't always given the job of leading the flight. Our C.O. wanted to see how we were able to fly under somebody else's orders. We didn't always fly leader, we frequently flew wing. Once I went up with our C.O. to try to outfly him. I fought him hard and I beat him. When we came down, I didn't say a word to anybody that I had beaten the C.O."

The therapist then explained to the patient the nature of unconscious attitudes which were not tempered and modified by civilized realities; that our unconscious aggression, which arose from the instinctual depths within us, was derived from our animal backgrounds. Sportsmanlike competition was a civilized and modified type of aggression but the real hostile competitive spirit is still based, as far as the unconscious is concerned, on the concept "to kill or to be killed." As a result, victory in competition would mean, unconsciously, that the defeated person had been destroyed as the direct result of an unconscious wish to be rid of that person. Hence, when competition was followed by an actual death, the person felt as if he himself had killed that individual.

He grasped this interpretation and in the same interview was given another pentothal injection. He immediately started out by saying, "I *used* to think I was responsible for Joe's death. I *used* to feel as if it were my fault. I know now that it is just one of those things that happen and I couldn't help it. He was a fine fellow. I was scared to go on that mission. He and I went into the mess hall that night for some supper, but we just nibbled, we couldn't eat. I had no cigarettes but Joe had two packages and gave me one of them. I smoked half a package of cigarettes. Joe was generous like that. I was terribly nervous. It was a dangerous target but off we went in a tight formation. There was a terrible amount of flak over the target. The trucks blew up and I felt good when I saw it. I don't know why Joe came over and tried to take the lead from me. I flew under his lead the day before and *I* stayed in formation. I can't understand why he broke formation and came up toward me and then got into a heavy flak position. But I didn't give ground. *I know now we were jealous of each other and we were really fighting against each other for the job.*"

When he awakened he felt a little dizzy and thought he had been sleeping. We summarized the whole material of the interview again, before terminating the session.

The next day he came in and said he felt perfectly well. He had slept soundly all night, had had no dreams and felt that a great load had been lifted from him. He wanted to go back to duty and felt he could carry on. When he had gone home for overseas leave, his people recognized there was something the matter with him and didn't ask him any questions. The result was that he kept all the experiences to himself and deliberately tried to forget, but there was always that load on his stomach. He now understood that the only way one could forget was to suffer the pain of remembering first. He remembered episodes he thought were funny and amusing, incidents that happened in his squadron overseas. He began to talk about little experiences. Prior to this he had not been able to think about these because they always led his mind into situations which became painful. "It is silly for intelligent people to let things bother them the way I did." *His ego now had confidence in its strength and could dwell on the past without anxiety.* Nine months later the patient was still well and functioning as a successful pilot in this country.

2. The unconscious experience contained a wish or intention or motive. It was a purposive act in line with the discussion in the previous section. The cases taken from Grinker and Spiegel also illustrate this second characteristic of the unconscious experience. Freud's (53) *Psychopathology of Everyday Life* contains numerous examples of the wishful characteristic of the unconscious experience. His discoveries about the wishful characteristic of dreams (52), the "royal road to the unconscious," are obviously relevant here.

3. The unconscious experience is associated in an indirect and disguised way with some form of conscious expression which, because of its similarity to the unconscious experience, may itself subsequently either become unconscious or acquire the power of increasing the probability that the unconscious experience, or aspects of it, will become conscious. This similarity may be in terms of type of motivation or goal object or in terms of time, form, and space relationships. This characteristic may be put as follows:

Let us assume that the experience which is now unconscious consisted of contents which for convenience we label a, b, and c. *Before* the experience became unconscious not only were a, b, and c associated with each other but each was also related to a wide variety of external and internal referents so that a was related to $a_1$, $a_2$ . . . , b to $b_1$, $b_2$ . . . , and c to $c_1$, $c_2$. . . . Each of these subscripts, in turn, was associated with an equally wide variety of internal and external referents. Consequently, when the experience becomes unconscious it is understandable that far more than a, b, and c is affected and is no longer accessible to recall. But it is also likely that those associated contents which did not become unconscious continue to operate in the consciousness of the individual and, by their occurrence, act as stimuli which increase the likelihood that unconscious content will reach conscious awareness. Since with the passage of time and concomitant new experiences the conscious contents become associated with more and newer contents, two things take place: (1) *The number of contents which become associated with the unconscious experience (in the sense that they acquire the power of increasing the strength of the unconscious experience) tends to increase with time, and* (2) *the unconscious experience acquires an active or dynamic relationship with conscious experience.*

The following, described by Fenichel (*45*, p. 157), is a good example of how more and more experiences become associated with a focal problem. In this case the unconscious experience seemed to be concerned with masturbatory acts and fantasies and the guilt feelings aroused by them:

A young man of seventeen became neurotic as a result of his conflict about masturbation. For a time he masturbated without any guilt feeling and often also watched when his schoolmates indulged in mutual masturbation. He then heard his minister deliver a sermon, advising against association with anyone who masturbated. Since in childhood the patient's genitality had been inhibited by an excessive fear of castration, he took the minister's sermon to heart and decided to follow his advice and no longer speak to boys who masturbated. This had particular reference to a boy who, he knew, masturbated a great deal. For a while he succeeded in keeping his resolution. But then to avoid contact with the boy, he developed certain phobias and compulsive procedures to maintain the avoidance. First, whenever he met the boy, he had to spit; an obsessive decree about the number of times he had to spit was never clarified in analysis. The phobia spread; he refrained from any contact with the family and friends of "The Avoided One." (The patient gave the boy this title in order to avoid using his name.) Then, because the avoided one was the son of a barber, the patient kept away from barbershops. Later he even avoided contact with persons who let themselves be shaved by barbers, and found it imperative to stay away from the section of the city where the barbershop of the boy's father was situated.

And then the entire neurosis developed quickly into an "isolation neurosis." He made the compulsive stipulation that the members of his family, particularly the women, which meant his grandmother, mother, and sister, were not to go into the forbidden neighborhood. He suffered greatly because his relatives would not accept this restriction of their freedom. He himself followed his own prohibition implicitly; but the more stringently he limited his actions, the more intensely was he forced obsessively to *think* of the forbidden section of the city. It is easy to understand that this caused him pain. But he gave an unexpected explanation of the pain. It was painful, he said, because at home he saw his mother and grandmother, and therefore ought not to think of the forbidden localities or persons. Although he was aware of the relation between his illness and masturbation, he ignored the connection. His masturbation had been given up without much apparent difficulty. But in its stead, the neurotic effort to keep the idea of "member of the family" separated from "uncongenial persons and localities," to isolate them from each other, became more and more definite.

This isolation became the chief topic of the neurosis. The patient allowed himself to think of "uncongenial" things but tried to avoid thinking of "congenial" persons at the same time. . . .

The patient was like the man in Wedekind's play who was not supposed to think of a bear. Whenever the patient thought of the avoided one he immediately thought of his grandmother. This tormenting symptom he called connecting. He was able to use a defense to deal with it, namely, a so-called disconnecting, which is a good example for an "undoing" mechanism. After he had simultaneously thought of a forbidden locality and a congenial person, if he could form a mental picture of the uncongenial thing, completely isolated and freed from all congenial adjuncts, everything was set right again, and he was quieted. Before long, the patient was absorbed in making "disconnections" from morning till night.

Two other components which tend to increase the severity of a spreading compulsion neurosis then appeared: an immense extension of the field of symptomatology, and an invasion of the symptoms by the warded-off impulses.

The division of objects in congenial and uncongenial ones gradually embraced all persons and all localities. Thus "schoolmates" became "uncongenial," "relatives" became "congenial"; but also all other persons, through superficial associations, were placed in one category or the other and so were subject to connections and disconnections.

After having undergone a connection, he could not leave the place where he happened to be, nor could he interrupt the activity that engaged him at that moment, until he had completed disconnecting. This condition was most distressing to him. Thus it was always problematic whether he would be able to rise from the couch after his analytic hour, and he would be tortured throughout the hour by the fear that it might end just between a connection and a disconnection. Finally, the defense itself came to give expression to the rejected impulses. The compulsion to disconnect made it necessary for the patient to have a sufficient number of congenial persons, places, and things in constant readiness. The desire to put a quick end to the tormenting tension brought about a return of the repressed from the repression. The patient frequented uncongenial places and took careful notice of uncongenial persons, so that he might have them in readiness in case he needed them. However, he was not able to do this with all uncongenial objects. The avoided one, for example, remained avoided. In time he had a graduated series of differentiations. There were objects that were phobically avoided as completely uncongenial; then there were less uncon-

genial ones searched for which he had to have in readiness; then somewhat
indifferent ones, slightly congenial ones, and completely congenial ones. He
finally consciously exerted himself to think of uncongenial objects only,
hoping that he would then more easily bring about the disconnection. Since
the thought "uncongenial objects" stood for "masturbation," he now was
unconsciously masturbating continually. And in point of fact, when his
tension was greatest and he could not make a disconnection in spite of all
his effort, he would occasionally, to his great astonishment, have an ejacula-
tion.

4. Experiences which are unconscious involve a variety of motivations differing in the nature or direction of their goal directedness—
antithetical tendencies. Some experiences may reflect passive while
others involve aggressive tendencies; some reflect love while others
reflect hate. At different periods in an individual's life different motivations toward significant figures may become unconscious. Because
these different motivations involve the same or very similar figures, the
same or similar stimuli may acquire the power of engendering antithetical motives. We shall elaborate on this point later on in this
chapter when we discuss ambivalence.

THE DEFENSE MECHANISM

By defense mechanism we refer to a class of responses which have
the effect of rendering unconscious what was previously conscious but
was in one way or other "dangerous" to the individual. The defense
mechanism should be differentiated from lying, rationalization, and the
like, where the possibility of conscious awareness of one's own purposes
exists and memory disturbance is minimal or nonexistent. We shall
consider the following to be characteristic of the defense mechanism:

1. The defensive reaction is preceded by a situation which in one way
or other is "dangerous" in the sense that danger is either external or
internal to the individual. By an external danger we refer to a situation
in which the achievement of a goal would involve punishment from
external sources. Anna Freud (49, p. 60) has pointed out that defense
"motivated by dread of the outside world" is characteristic of the young
child. By internal danger we refer to the situation, characteristic of
adults, in which the achievement of a goal would involve a punishing
state of affairs due to transgression of one's strongly held values and
beliefs.

2. The situation which precedes the defensive reaction is one of conflict involving, on the one hand, pleasure-seeking tendencies and, on the other hand, considerations of the consequences of achieving the goal of such tendencies. The conflict situation may be characterized as one involving approach and avoidance tendencies: hesitation, indecision, anticipation of pleasure, and anticipation of punishment.

3. The conflict situation produces anxiety, which in turn results in the defensive reaction. Anna Freud (*49*, p. 61) has put this as follows: "In the formation of neurosis it seems to be a matter of indifference as to what that anxiety relates. The crucial point is that, whether it be dread of the outside world or dread of the superego, it is the anxiety which sets the defensive process going."

4. The effect of the defensive act, which is not one involving conscious awareness, is to render unconscious certain aspects of the conflict, which then take on the characteristics of unconscious contents previously described. A memory impairment is always a consequence of the defensive act.

5. The effect of the defensive act is to reduce the strength of some or all of the motivations which were part of the conflict. This effect may vary in terms of the duration and degree of tension reduction so that in some cases no other defensive reaction is required while in others repeated defensive acts are necessary. Anna Freud (*49*, p. 47) has described a case in which repeated and different defensive reactions were necessary in order to keep unconscious hostile motives associated with strong guilt feelings:

I will take as an illustration the case of a young woman employed in an institution for children. She was the middle child in a number of brothers and sisters. Throughout childhood she suffered from passionate penis envy, relating to her elder and her younger brother, and from jealousy, which was repeatedly excited by her mother's successive pregnancies. Finally, envy and jealousy combined in a fierce hostility to her mother. But, since the child's love-fixation was no less strong than her hatred, a violent defensive conflict with her negative impulses succeeded an initial period of uninhibited unruliness and naughtiness. She dreaded lest the manifestation of her hate should cause her to lose her mother's love, of which she could not bear to be deprived. She also dreaded that her mother would punish her and she criticized herself most severely for her prohibited longings for revenge. As she entered upon the period of latency, this anxiety-situation and conflict of conscience became more and more acute and her ego tried to master her impulses in various ways. In order to solve the problem of ambivalence she displaced . . . outwards one side of her ambivalent feeling. Her mother continued to be a love-object, but, from that time on, there was always in the girl's life a second important person of the female sex, whom she hated violently. This eased matters: her hatred of the more remote object was not visited with the sense of guilt so mercilessly as was her hatred of her mother. But even the displaced hatred was a source of much suffering. As time went on, it was plain that this first displacement was inadequate as a means of mastering the situation.

The little girl's ego now resorted to a second mechanism. It turned inwards the hatred, which hitherto had related exclusively to other people. The child tortured herself with self-accusations and feelings of inferiority and, throughout childhood and adolescence right into adult life, she did everything she could to put herself at a disadvantage and injure her interests, always surrendering her own wishes to the demands made on her by others. To all outward appearance she had become masochistic since adopting this method of defence.

But this measure, too, proved inadequate as a means of mastering the situation. The patient then entered on a process of projection. The hatred which she had felt for female love-objects or their substitutes was transformed into the conviction that she herself was hated, slighted or persecuted by them. Her ego thus found relief from the sense of guilt. The naughty child, who cherished wicked feelings against the people around her, underwent metamorphosis into the victim of cruelty, neglect and persecution. But the use of this mechanism left upon her character a permanent paranoid imprint, which was a source of very great difficulty to her both in youth and adult years.

The patient was quite grown up when she came to be analysed. She was not regarded as ill by those who knew her, but her sufferings were acute. In spite of all the energy which her ego had expended upon its defence she had not succeeded in really mastering her anxiety and sense of guilt. On any occasion when her envy, jealousy and hatred were in danger of activation, she invariably had recourse to all her defence-mechanisms. But her emotional conflicts never came to any issue which could set her ego at rest and, apart from this, the final result of all her struggles was meagre in the extreme. She succeeded in maintaining the fiction that she loved her mother, but she felt herself to be full of hatred and on this account she despised and mistrusted herself. She did not succeed in preserving the sense of being loved; it had been destroyed by the mechanism of projection. Nor did she succeed in escaping the punishments which she had feared in childhood; by turning her aggressive impulses inwards she inflicted upon herself all the suffering which she had formerly anticipated in the form of punishment by her mother.

## AMBIVALENCE

By ambivalence is meant behavior in which, as a result of past learning, particularly in relation to parents, the individual is capable of responding to significant figures with conflicting motivations. That parents love their children should not obscure the fact that at times they have less positive attitudes toward them. Similarly, while children love their parents there are times when they experience in relation to them hostile, destructive attitudes. One might put what we are trying to say as follows: The long dependence of the infant on his environment, the inevitable frustrations which he experiences, the variability in behavior of those upon whom he depends, and the requirement of all societies that the growing organism give up *some* pleasure-seeking activities—it is as a result of these experiences that the individual acquires motivations which are antithetical to each other. Love and hate, aggression and passivity, dependence and independence—these are some of the polarities which we assume to be characteristic of the individual. Which aspect of the polarity will be dominant, the mode of defense by means of which the conflicts will be resolved, and the "success" of the defensive reaction will largely be a function of cultural differences and individual peculiarities of development.

## AN ANALYTIC HOUR

In the discussion of purposive behavior we used for illustrative purposes the beginning of the first hour of analytic therapy. We will now present the entire hour, following which we shall attempt to describe how the assumptions just discussed are utilized in trying to understand an individual's behavior.

The patient was very tense. For a time he could not say anything. Then he said he felt "shaky." He asked if he could unbutton his collar. He spoke in a low, complaining tone of voice.

After a long pause he said, "I didn't go into work today." He went on to say that he didn't like the work he was supposed to do and he was paid very little. He had looked for another job today but had no luck. "They [his present employer] don't want to give us work that pays. They treat us like dogs." (Short pause.) "I'm afraid to go in tomorrow. The boss will make a sarcastic remark. I'll choke up. I won't be able to say anything."

After a very long pause the patient was asked what he was thinking about. "My wife. She said she won't eat supper till I get home. That means the little one [youngest child] will miss supper. I feed him. He can't win by me." He related that his wife gets upset with the two children. The older daughter fights with the little boy but "She don't mean anything. I told my wife not to wait but she said she would." Another long pause.

"Doctor, is it all right if I don't come dressed up each time? Will you mind?"

The therapist remarked that he did not understand what he meant.

"When I come here I like to get dressed but I won't have time. When I'm in working clothes I don't feel clean. I don't like the odor of perspiration. Other people don't like it either. Is it all right?"

(Long pause.) "I feel shaky again."

(Long pause.) The therapist asked what he was thinking about. "My foot. If I had a good foot I could get any job." He then told about a visit to a famous clinic where they suggested amputating his toes although they did not think it would do him much good. Because half of his toes are missing he cannot bend his ankle. There is a lot of pressure on his toes as a result of which he gets many callouses. He cuts them off each night because he is afraid of infection. He had three operations: at 6, 14, and 15 years of age. "They helped a little but not much." Two years ago he got an arch support which he has to fix every night.

(Long pause.) The therapist then inquired again about what he was thinking.

"My wife again. I'm wondering what the kids are doing now. I wonder if my wife is angry. I'm also thinking about the job. I'm wondering if I should go in tomorrow."

(Long pause.) "I hitch hiked to the — clinic (out of state). It took three days and three nights. It seems it was for nothing. They could have done the same at the New Haven Hospital."

The therapist then asked, "What was your feeling about coming here today, about coming to see me?"

"Nothing about you. I couldn't see enough reason for coming. Dr. M. (his wife's therapist) said I needed treatment. Why do I need treatment? Dr. M. said that I said I needed treatment but I can't remember saying that."

The therapist asked what the patient had spoken about in the preliminary interview a week ago. The patient enumerated, as he had previously, about his nervousness, shaky feelings, his inability to talk on many occasions, and the way he was treated in his job. There were two omissions: he did not mention his crying when he gets angry and frustrated and the fact "that I'm always thinking."

The therapist pointed out the discrepancy between how he says he feels and his doubts about needing treatment. "Is it that you are afraid to come? Afraid that you will choke up? I wonder if that does not make you want to believe that you don't need treatment?"

The patient weakly agreed. "But those are the only things I can think of—what I told you."

The therapist repeated his previous interpretation but this time suggesting that the patient felt about coming for treatment the way he felt about going to work tomorrow.

"I'm embarrassed. I can't talk. I don't think I'm being helpful to you or me."

"You're worried what I think of you?"

"Yes, Sir." (Long pause.) "I'm always thinking about my wife. She takes me for granted. I think she has some one else on the string. I asked Dr. M. but he wouldn't tell me. I told him I would beat her if she did. I would leave her. He wouldn't tell me." This was said in a complaining rather than an aggressive tone of voice.

"All I can think of is my foot, my wife, and the shop. I told her I didn't want to come today. She said I should. It would make me feel better. It helped her. She was sick." (He then described how his wife frequently would faint when she got up from a chair.)

Before the end of the hour the therapist indicated again that the patient had conflicts about coming for treatment and that he found it difficult to admit that he needed treatment. In response to this the patient seemed to agree and yet not to agree. When he got up from the couch he said spontaneously, "I'll see you tomorrow."

We might start by asking why the patient talks primarily about his wife, foot, and job? Put in another way: Why is *the patient aware* that he can think only of his wife, foot, and job? On the assumption that this sequence of associations was not randomly determined but reflects meaningfully related experiences (fantasies, interactions, dreams, self-verbalizations, perceptions), what are the bases upon which these different experiences have become related? From what is known about the patient in this single hour it would be foolhardy to think that one could give satisfactory answers to these questions. What needs to be noted, however, is that the patient appears to be unaware (and puzzled by the sources) of the determinants of the sequence of associations. We would tentatively assume that the determinants of the sequence are unconscious—he cannot at this point see the "connections" between his present and past experiences. He is incapable of describing how apparently disparate areas of his thinking are related to his previous personal experiences. We are assuming, then, that he is unable to recall certain previous experiences during which he was more or less aware of how "wife, foot, and job" were in some relationship to each other. Having made this assumption we then might reword our previous questions in this way: What was the threatening or painful or dangerous aspect of these previous experiences which cued off a defensive response? What were the conflicting motivations in response to which anxiety was evoked? What is there *in this therapeutic hour* which increases the strength of the unconscious contents and allows for their indirect or partial expression?

Another question arises from this hour: What is the attitude of the patient toward his wife? In the case of this patient the ambivalent motivations toward his wife are rather clear: He is concerned about whether she will be angry at him; he will beat her if she has someone else on the string; he resents her implicit rejection of him; he would reject (leave) her. Why these ambivalent attitudes? To what extent are these ambivalent attitudes in relation to his wife a reflection of similar attitudes toward significant figures in his development? How similar are these attitudes to those experienced in relation to the therapist? Although he is polite and deferent (and even obsequious) toward the therapist, and is afraid of acting in a way which would result in criticism and ridicule, his unwillingness to come for treatment suggests that he probably has previously had hostile feelings toward the therapist. The contrast between how he overtly acts during the hour and the probable hostile content of his fantasies toward the therapist—*the contrast between his unwillingness to accept treatment and his inability to refuse it*—suggests that it is extremely difficult for this man to act hostilely, assertively, or aggressively. He may feel aggressive, but he cannot act overtly in that manner. The patient has described two instances (in connection with his boss and, in the initial face-to-face interview, with his wife) in which his inability to talk, his "choking up," occurred in connection with strong hostile motivations. Was his choking up in the hour a function of similar motivations toward the

therapist? Was he aware of these motivations or were they unconscious? If he tends to repress hostile contents, then we would assume
that under certain conditions the hostile motivations are associated with
anxiety which sets off the defensive response. But why should he have
learned to be anxious about such feelings? Is the anxiety response to
anticipated retaliation from external sources or to the transgression of
his own personal values—or some combination of both?

We clearly did not present this series of questions (or the many
more that might have been asked) with the intent of answering them.
What we attempted to do was to indicate (1) that in his attempt to
understand behavior the clinician is constantly deducing covert from
overt behavior and (2) that the kinds of questions a clinician asks are
determined by certain assumptions which he makes. Differences in
the nature of one's major assumptions are reflected in differences in
what one selects for observations, the questions one asks about those
observations, and the content of whatever conclusions are drawn. The
psychologist as clinician *should not*, and the psychologist as a human
observer *does not*, concern himself solely with the recording of overt
behavior. The clinician deduces the nature of the relationship between
covert and overt behavior. This process of deduction is impossible without some major assumptions concerning the nature of human behavior.

In the pages that follow we shall attempt to make as explicit as possible the relation between the clinician's thinking and the conclusions
he draws as he interprets the Rorschach protocol of a particular individual. There are a number of studies (*58, 62, 93, 108, 110, 169*) which
indicate that there is an encouraging degree of validity to the interpretation of Rorschach protocols—although the evidence is by no means
clear cut or substantial. However, neither in valid nor invalid interpretations do we know (1) the step-by-step procedure whereby the interpretation was made or (2) the relative importance of the different
kinds of data and assumptions utilized (see p. 13). Although we shall
be using Rorschach protocols, the reader should not lose sight of the
fact that we know very little about the behavior of the psychologist as
he interprets any kind of clinical data in the individual case. The failure
to study the psychology of the psychologist has put us in the anomalous
position of knowing practically nothing about a variable which affects
not only the validity of clinical conclusions but the welfare of patients
as well. At the present time, and in the foreseeable future, we will have

to depend on the psychologist to organize and to give additional meanings to the data which he obtains in the individual case. Just as the psychologist, as another human being, affects the behavior of the individual with whom he interacts, so do his characteristic ways of thinking affect what he concludes about an individual's behavior. One can only hope that in the future there will be increasing research on the nature of the process of interpretation. Without such research the relation between theory and practice will remain obscure and the appropriateness of the nature and goals of clinical training can be questioned.

We should like to state at this point that we are not very satisfied by our attempt to make explicit the relation between the clinician's thinking and the conclusions he draws (see p. 15). We hope that despite its shortcomings it will be of some value to the reader. Needless to say, this represents the attempt of a particular clinician.

## Chapter 18

## SIX CASES

To PUT down in words the process of one's interpretation is, to this writer at least, a difficult task. This difficulty has primarily three sources: (1) We are not ordinarily trained or required to articulate in great detail the steps which are the basis for our conclusions; (2) in attempting to verbalize these steps we become acutely aware of the fuzziness of many of our concepts as well as of the number of times that we draw conclusions the evidence for which is not compelling; and (3) the desire to be correct makes for a degree of self-consciousness which has an interfering effect—we want, so to speak, to put our best foot forward, as a result of which selective factors operate to an un-known degree. However embarrassing the results may be we cannot avoid the necessity, or deny the importance, of making as explicit as possible the clinician's thinking. It is our opinion that the more we understand the deductive nature of the clinician's thinking the more will we be able to reduce the effects of an important source of error in prediction and diagnostic evaluation.

It was as a result of this conviction that the writer welcomed the opportunity to interpret blindly twenty-three protocols obtained from the inhabitants of the island of Truk in Micronesia. We interpreted the records blindly not because we thought records should ordinarily be so interpreted but in an attempt to force ourselves to make explicit our thinking in relation to another individual's verbal behavior. Our goal was not only to state conclusions but to describe explicitly the steps leading up to the conclusions. We wanted to know not only whether a conclusion was right or wrong but how we arrived at such a con-clusion. It should be emphasized that our sole justification for the blind interpretation was our belief that it would make it easier for us to make explicit the steps in our thinking—that it would make clearer, to us at least, to what aspects of verbal behavior we are set to respond, the significances we attach to these aspects, and the kinds of assump-

323

tions we utilize about the dynamics of behavior. Except as a way of aiding the student to become aware of the relation between his own thinking and the conclusions he draws, we do not recommend blind interpretations. Where the welfare of a patient is involved we cannot justify ignoring data or accepting the implicit and unproved assumption that the clinician's thinking results only in valid conclusions. In research where the focus is on the behavior of the clinician we can see some justification for the use of blind interpretations.

The results of the Truk study, primarily conceived and executed by Dr. Thomas Gladwin, have been published elsewhere (58). The published study includes an ethnographic description of Trukese culture, twenty-three Rorschach protocols together with a card-by-card analysis of each, a Rorschach summary of each case, the life histories of each of the twenty-three cases, interpretations of the TAT protocols of these same individuals, an evaluation of the congruence of the psychologist's conclusions with the ethnographic data, and a critical evaluation of the use of psychological tests in studies of culture and personality.

In the following pages we have presented four of the Truk cases. Because, as indicated in Chapter 2 (see p. 15), we felt that we had not been particularly successful in verbalizing various aspects of the interpretive process we have attempted to fill in these gaps. In no case, as the reader can readily determine for himself, has a conclusion been changed.

The Rorschach protocols of the four cases are first presented without any commentary. This has been done as an aid to the serious student who wishes to attempt to make explicit his way of approaching and thinking about these data. Of one thing the serious student may be sure: his attempt to justify explicitly whatever conclusions he draws will be frustrating but instructive—if only he sees more clearly some of the problems involved in understanding the psychology of the psychologist. Following the presentation of the protocols will be found the card-by-card analysis of each case. Because we say that the interpretations in these and the other nineteen cases seemed to be in large part correct—as seemed to be our characterization of the "Trukese personality"—we hope that the reader will not refrain from making his own independent judgment of the degree of congruence between the ethnography and life histories, on the one hand, and our test interpretations, on the other hand. Although we attempted to point out where the interpretations were wrong—and there were several clear examples where the interpretations were wrong—neither Dr. Gladwin nor the writer can be considered an unbiased judge of the degree of congruence.

The fifth and sixth cases which we shall present are those of a nine-year-old boy and a forty-one-year-old woman from our own culture.

Sam   Male, age 13.

In instruction blot, he saw a pig.

I-1   18″ Fruit bat. Another on the other side.

D     FC′     A

(Tracing.) Head, wing, leg; all this is fur but we don't see it because this is just a picture. (Why bat?) Because of the head and wings— the legs and genitals of a bat are all together so it makes a compact body.

2   Sting-ray.

dr[2]   FC′     A

(Tracing.) It is black, like the fruit bat . . . I put his line here (middle of tracing) because it is black. (Why ray?) Because of the shape of the wings.

3   Holes. (2 min.)

S     F, C′F     N

(Where?) The four white places— they are like holes in a reef. (What shall we think about them?) Like a window (or door) because the light comes through from the other side and makes it white.

II-1   1′25″     Candle—candle-holder. (3 min.)

dr, S     F, CF     Obj

(Tracing.) Candle, candle-holder, flame of candle. (Why does the flame not go over to here [in black area]?) It does go over there, because it is a little red, but not as red as it is here. (Why a candle-holder?) Because of the red flame. (What else?) Because the flame looks like this ⊤ with the wick at the bottom.

---

[1] The cases of Sam, Mike, Roger, and Andy are reprinted from T. Gladwin and S. B. Sarason, *Truk: Man in Paradise,* by permission of The Viking Fund (Wenner-Gren Foundation for Anthropological Research). The scoring system used in that study followed that of Klopfer (92).

[2] In Klopfer's scoring system there are several kinds of unusual details: di = inside detail, de = edge detail, dd = tiny detail, and dr = unusual details which are neither di, de, nor dd. In previous pages of this book we have used only one symbol, Dd.

III-1  12″ Person—two of them.

D   M   H
(See III-2 response)

(Parts of body?) Legs, arms, belly, head, (?) knee. (What sort of people?) Ghosts. (Why?) Whole body looks like it—pointed chin of skull, hairy arms and legs.

2  They are lifting these plants.

D   F   Pl

(?) Is round, with irregular outline. (?) Two plants.

3  Animals.

D   F−   A

(?) Elephant. (Why?) Trunk. (Parts of body?) Back, buttocks, tusks. (Do we know anything more about it?) No.

4  Red flower of the plant—it has fallen, and lies between the men. (3¾ min.)

D   FC   N

(Why?) It is red. (Anything else?) It is shaped like a flower.

IV-1  32″ *Nifaro* (a fishing bird—lives in burrows in the day-time).

dr   F   A

(Tracing.) Head, ears, eyes, mouth. We don't see it because the picture is black, but actually the *nifaro* is spotted—under its wings, belly and tail.

2  Oh, I am wrong: the whole thing is a fruit bat. (We'll think of both of them.) (1½ min.)

W   FM   A

(Why a fruit bat?) Because the wings are stretched out, like a bat that is flying.

V-1  46″ Animal. (1 min.)

W   FC′, FM   A

(What kind?) A black tern. (Where?) Whole thing. (Why?) Wings are long—also the legs stretched out because it is flying. We also see the belly, because it is flying over. (While the examiner was looking up the name of the bird in the dictionary, Sam remarked as a point of information that the bird was black, but he

was apparently not referring to
the blot.)

VI-1  30″ I don't know. (You           (Where?) Whole thing. (Why?)
      haven't really thought about     Wings, tail. The leaf of his wing
      it.) 55″ Skate. (1 min.)         (i.e., pectoral fins) moves when
                                       he swims. (Why do you think it
      W      F      A                  is moving?) It is not moving here,
                                       but it moves in the sea.

VII-1  1′25″ Clouds—here, here—        (Why?) The outline is irregular,
       the whole thing. (2 min.)       like a lot of trees. It has the shape
                                       of clouds.
       W      F      N

VIII-1  22″ The flower of a tree.      (What do we see?) One flower—
                                       which is red—and the trunk be-
        dr     FC     N                low it (above). (What about this
                                       [blue and grey area]?) Not a
                                       part of it. (?) It has the shape of
                                       a flower.

    2  Pig—two Pigs—they are           Why does this look so much like a
       on the tree. (1½ min.)          pig . . . ? (Parts of body?)
                                       Head, forelegs, back, flank, hind-
       D      F      A                 legs—we don't see the tail. (Why
                                       pig?) Short snout; the legs are
                                       like a cow's, but a little different.

IX-1  36″ These are people—they        (Parts of body?) Head, legs, arm,
   2  are sticking out from the        eye. (Why eye?) Here—the nose
      top of this tree—they are        is below, the forehead above, and
      not real people, but just a      the eye in the midle. (Why tree?)
      part of the tree which looks     Because the trunk goes down and
      like people. This is the tree    then the branches spread down to
      (green portion) and its          the ground (now pointing to the
      trunk. (2 min.)                  orange as well as green part).
                                       (Any other reason?) Just the
      D      F      H                  trunk going down—no other rea-
      W      F      N                  son.

X-1 11″ The whole thing is branches of a tree—this is the trunk. An American tree—there are none like this on Truk. (1 min.)

(Why?) All the parts just look like tree branches, plus the trunk.

W  F  N

*Note.* See Fig. 6, Sam's Responses, p. 330.

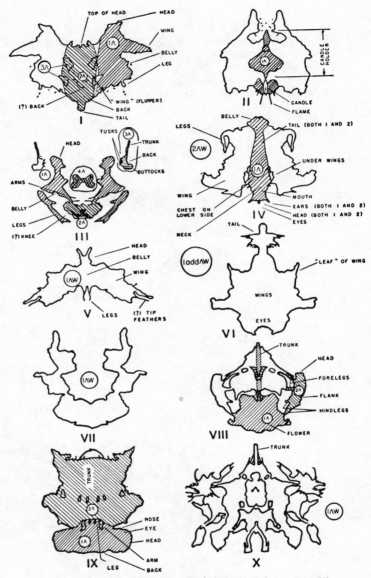

FIG. 6. Sam's Responses (Gladwin and Sarason, 58)

## MIKE

Mike  Male, age 17.

I-1  50" Island. (Looked at the card some more, but no further response. (1¾ min.)

W  F  N

(How much of it is an island?) The whole picture. (How are we looking at it?) As if from an airplane —from above. (Why is it like an island?) It just looks like one. Repeated and further questioning failed to add to this.)

II-1  (After 2¼' said) I don't know. (Look some more.) (At 6½' said) There isn't anything.

III-1  (After 4' said) I don't know this one either. (Do you understand what you are to do?) No. (Just as you saw an island in the first picture, find something in this one.) 5' Two people.

D  M  H

(Show me parts of body.) Head, legs, arms. They are standing on these rocks. Their arms are back, elbows sticking out back.

2  Rocks.

D  F  N

(Why rocks?) They are round, like rocks. (What kind of rock?) From inland (i.e., black basalt, as distinguished from coral, the only other kind of common rock). (Why?) Because people are standing on it.

3  Animals. (10 min.)

D  F  A

(What kind of animals?) Looks like a dog. (Parts of body.) Head, body, what is this long thing? . . . a tail, legs. (What shall we think about these dogs?) Nothing.

331

IV-1   5′ Like the other one, an       (Why an island?) Just looks like it.
       island. (5¾ min.)               (How are we looking at it?)
                                        From above.
       W     F     N

V-1    (After 2½′ said) I really
       don't know.

VI-1   (After 4¾′) I don't know
       this one either.

VII-1  2′28″ Rock. (2¾ min.)           (Where?) Whole thing. (Why?) I
                                        don't know.
       W     F     N

VIII-1 1′5″ I know about those         (What kind of animals?) They look
       two animals, but I don't         like pigs. (Why?) I don't know.
       know about this (center          (Parts of body.) Head, forelegs,
       portion of blot). (2½ min.)      hind legs, body. (What else do we
                                        know about them?) I looked at
       D     F     A                    them and they looked like pigs.

IX-1   (After 3¼′) I have thought
       about this, but I don't know
       (Do you think of things,
       but think they are not
       right?) Yes. (Well, what
       do you see?) Nothing.

X-1    (After 4½′) I don't know
       this either. (Not a thing
       there you know?) No.

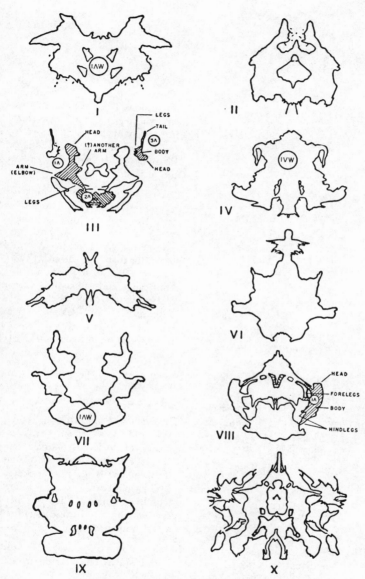

Fig. 7. Mike's Responses (Gladwin and Sarason, *58*)

Roger   Male, age 17.

I-1   28″ A tree.

W   F   N

(How much of it is the tree?) The whole thing, with the trunk in the middle. These above are twigs. (Why a tree?) The branches coming out, with leaves at the ends. (Why do they look like leaves?) Because of the serrated edges of the picture.

2   A bird.

dr   F   A

(Tracing.) These made me think of a bird—they look like a bird's feet. No, they are not feet, they are ears—one kind of bird has ears here. (What kind?) A fruit bat. (But that is not a bird. [This was an error on my part, as linguistically and apparently conceptually, the Trukese class bats with birds.]) Oh, a sea tern. (But why not a bat?) It is a bat—I really think so, but you said a bat is not a bird.

3   Rock. (2¾ min.)

dr   F   N

Five rocks. (Later, he counted up to 11 rocks.) (Why rocks?) Round. (Any other reason?) No.

II-1   2′22″ (At 1¾ min., remarked he did not see anything.) People. (3¼ min.)

W   F   H

(Tracing.) (While tracing, said) Why did I say "person" (or "people"); this looks just like a monkey. (After tracing: how about the people?) They are monkeys. (Why monkeys?) Because they look like humans. (Then why not say "human"?) Because it is not a real human being.

III-1   29″ A shark . . . here is another one.

D   F   A

Forehead, mouth, dorsal fin, tail, middle. (Any other reason?) No.

2 A plant . . . here's another.

D F N

The trunk, leaves. (Why leaves?) The edges are serrated.

3 Another plant ("butterfly"). I don't know what these (bodies of "waiters") are. (2½ min.)

D F N

The branch (or stalk) is in the middle; these are leaves.

IV-1 48″ A ghost—the whole thing. (1¼ min.)

W FC′ H

Forehead, ears, shoulders, arms, legs, penis. (Why a ghost?) It is black, like a ghost.

V-1 12″ A fruit bat—the whole thing. Ears, head, wings, legs. (1½ min.)

W F A

(What is this?) Part of the wing. (Why a fruit bat?) Has the big wings, the legs, ears, etc., of a fruit bat.

VI-1 (After ¾′) I don't know—there isn't anything.

VII-1 23″ A cloud—two of them.

W K N

The whole thing—on each side. (Why a cloud?) It is whitish and then darker in places like a cloud.

2 A house. (¾ min.)

d F Obj

(Tracing.) A pole is in the middle.

2a dr C′F N

The black on the sides (of the house) is rock. (Why?) Because it is black.

VIII-1 15″ A pig . . . another. (¾ min.)

D F A

Mouth, head, eye, back, forelegs, hind leg, tail. (Only one hind leg?) The two are together. (Why is tail big?) A few pigs have long tails. No other reason (for calling it pig).

IX-1   20″ A guitar.                          (Tracing.) It has the same shape as
       dr, S    F    Obj                      a guitar.

   2   A tree—the whole thing.                The middle is the trunk, all the rest
       (¾ min.)                               is leaves. (Why leaves?) Serrated
                                              edges.
       W     F    N

X-1    15″ (Although this was the             (Why?) It just looks like it.
       first time he had turned a
       card, he did it immediately
       and   without   hesitation.)
       The whole thing is a tree
       . . . this is the fruit . . .
       all the rest is leaves . . .
       this is the trunk. (1 min.)

       W     F     N

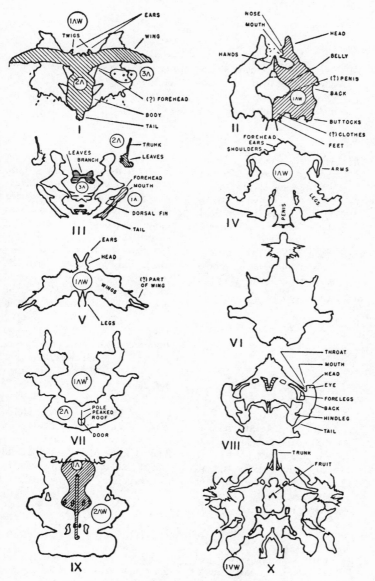

FIG. 8.  Roger's Responses (Gladwin and Sarason, 58)

Andy   Male, age 19.

I-1   34″ Animal. It flaps like a dog that is flying. I don't know what sort of an animal it is. (2 min.)

dr   FM   A

(Tracing.) (Why a dog?) Because of the shape of its head. (Why flying?) Because its forelegs are out.

II-1   41″ (Turned card down, then up.) Here is a person —two people. Their arms— they are clapping hands. Their heads, with red clothes on them? Is it blood? Are these feet? They are bloody. They are sitting. This is another foot. These are clothes. (3¾ min.)

W   M, CF, FC′   H, bl

(Tracing.) (Is it a cloth or blood on head?) I thought it was a cloth, but now I know it isn't. (What is it?) Just a head, but it looks bloody. (Why blood?) Perhaps they are fighting . . . it just looks like blood. (Why clothing [on body]?) It just looks very much like it. It is black . . . woman's clothes . . . it looked like a woman, so I decided she had clothes. (Trukese women usually wear white or prints.) (Why a woman?) It just looked like one. (How about the clothes again?) A white neck like your (i.e., the examiner's) skin, then red clothing, and then black.

2   (Having said he was finished, he looked again at the red portion of the bottom of the card.) Why does it look just like a vagina? (Pointing to middle of blood.) Holes. (This response not timed.)

dr   F, CF   Hd

(Tracing.) (Why a vagina?) Holes, blood. (Why blood?) I have seen a few women like this—I just looked at them for fun—they did not say anything. (Why blood?) Menstruating.

III-1   1′10″ Animal—two of them. Head, nose, neck,

(Tracing.) (While he was tracing, he said) Why can't we see the back, foreleg (two), tail, two hind legs (he pointed these out); leaning over with hands on something . . . holding something. I don't know about this ("butterfly" in middle).

W   M   A

2 Looks like an animal. (Pointing) Leg, waist, buttocks, two arms (demonstrated they were held out behind as if sitting and leaning back on hands), back, belly, snout like a monkey, head—the back of the head looks like a human. (7 min.)

D   M   A

IV-1 (Turned card various ways.) Nothing. (1¼ min.)

V-1 37″ Animal. Has wings like a fruit bat. I don't know about the projections above and below . . . (Long pause.) . . . Now I understand about these (upper projections). They are legs. (Turned card upright.) (Pointing) Head, ears, neck, the things which stick out on the wings (of fruit bats, i.e., the claws or hooks by which they hang themselves up). (3 min.)

W   F   A

eyes? . . . Oh, they are looking away—they are having a verbal battle. (When tracing completed: What is that?—i.e., middle lower blobs.) I don't know what sort of thing they are holding with their hands. (Why animal, not person?) Foot not like a person's foot, also nose, arms. Only the pelvic region looks human.

(Tracing.) (When he had finished the tracing, he said) Monkey. (Why a monkey?) Just looks a lot like one. (Note: although this response is more plausible in position V, he did not turn the card while talking about it either in performance or inquiry.)

(Tracing.) (Why a fruit bat?) Just looks like one—wings, legs, etc.

VI-1   (Turned card various ways.) I don't know what this may be . . . It looks as if there must be something, but I can't make it out. (1¼ min.)

VII-1   30″ (Turned card, laughed.) Clouds? It looks just like clouds. But I don't know about this (black at midline). (1½ min.)

    W    F    N

(Why clouds?) The shape—there are no objects in the picture. It looks like smoke. (Why?) It billows out (pointing to "feather in hat," "arm").

VIII-1   22″ Animal. That is all. (Look some more.) A pig.

    D    FM    A

(Why pig?) (Pointing) Legs, back, belly, ears, snout, with mouth below. One rear leg lifted to step forward. No tail. (The examiner then asked for a tracing of the head and ears only, but he did everything.)

2   I don't know what sort of a plant this is. (2½ min.)

    dr    F    Pl

(Why plant?) I just think so. (A leaf, or the whole thing?) Only a leaf. (Why leaf?) Stem in the middle. (Why stem?) Runs down the middle.

IX-1   1′25″ (Turned card various ways, pausing each time.) Person.

    D    F    Hd

(Tracing.) (Why eye?) Just looks like an eye. (What sort of person?) Woman. (Why?) Hair on head—there is lots of it.

2   Animal ("deer's head").

    D    F    Ad

(Tracing.) (What sort of an animal?) I don't know. (Why eye?) Just looks like it.

3   Rocks.

    dr    F    N

(Tracing.) (Why rocks?) Just look like them. I didn't know what they were, so I said rocks.

4  Light through branches of a tree.

   S    C'    N

(Why tree?) It doesn't matter whether it is a tree or not. I was just talking about the hole—it is white—light coming through.

5  Person. (3½ min.)

   dr    F —    H

(Tracing.) (Why person, not animal, etc.?) It just looks like a person, not an animal.

X-1  3' I don't see anything . . . (pause) . . . Animals. I don't know what they are doing with this (middle)— it looks like a cup.

   D    FM    Ad

(Tracing.) (What sort of an animal?) Elephant (he explained he saw one in a Japanese movie). It is holding a cup in its trunk. (Why is its head dark—i.e., shaded in the tracing?) I don't know whether an elephant's head is dark or not—I just showed it that way because it is so in the picture.

2  Person. Throwing arms up in play.

   D    M    H

(Tracing.) (While tracing, he laughed at the size of the arms.)

3  Plant. I don't know what kind. (7¼ min.)

   D    F    N

(Tracing.) (What is hole in branches?) Nothing. (Why a tree?) Because of the branches spreading out.

*Note.* See Fig. 9, Andy's Responses, p. 342.

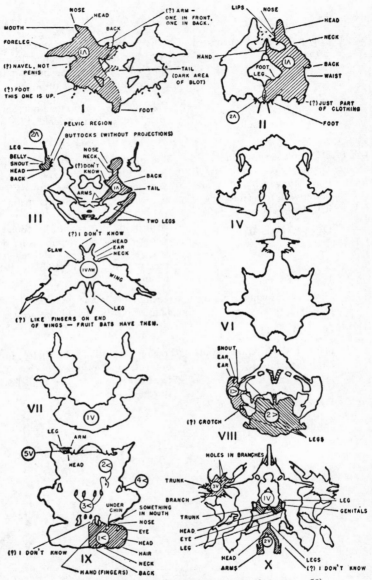

FIG. 9. Andy's Responses (Gladwin and Sarason, *58*)

CARD I

I-1  18″ Fruit bat. Another on the other side.

D    FC′    A

(Tracing.) Head, wing, leg; all this is fur but we don't see it because this is just a picture. (Why bat?) Because of the head and wings— the legs and genitals of a bat are all together so it makes a compact body.

2   Sting-ray.

dr    FC′    A

(Tracing.) It is black, like the fruit bat . . . I put this line here (middle of tracing) because it is black. (Why ray?) Because of the shape of the wings.

3   Holes. (2 min.)

S    F, C′F    N

(Where?) The four white places— they are like holes in a reef. (What shall we think about them?) Like a window (or door) because the light comes through from the other side and makes it white.

In contrast to the other records, his reaction time to this card is relatively quick and he gives more than the average number of responses. When one remembers that this is the first "real" blot he has seen—that he is being presented with a novel kind of problem-solving task—the relative quantity and speed of response suggests that this type of situation has not engendered in Sam undue anxiety or self-attitudes which interfere with overt responsiveness. Neither in the way he describes each response nor in the apparent way he feels in the situation does he manifest any feelings of inadequacy, bewilderment, or extreme caution. In fact, the spontaneous way in which he "explains" his responses would indicate a degree of self-confidence which is unusual for the Trukese. One does not have to prod him very much to get him to elaborate on his response—in contrast to some of the others where one had "to pull teeth" in order to get them to verbalize what they had seen. The fact that Sam is aware of the objective characteristic of the external stimulus, its color, and can incorporate it into his responses is another indication that this situation has not engendered in him a degree of self-consciousness which interferes with awareness of and overt responsiveness to the external stimulus. That he is not impulsive or uncritical is suggested by the fact that his responses are of acceptable form.

It should also be noted that Sam does not give up the card until he has "explained" every area: the two sides are fruit bats, the middle a sting ray, and the white spaces are holes. It is not clear at this point whether Sam conceives of the task as one in which all of the blot must be explained. Unlike some of the others, however, he is not bothered by the apparent "wholeness" of the card and can attend to the more obvious sub-configurations. If he does have a conception of a right and wrong way of responding it does not appear, at this point at least, to have had an interfering effect. One question that might be raised in this card is why he mentions the "genitals" in his first response. From the way he described the response, and traced it, it would seem that he does not see the genitals. Why, then, does he mention it? If one assumes that he did not "see" the genitals, one might ask: Of all the body parts that he could have mentioned, why did he mention the genitals?

CARD II

| II-1 | 1'25" Candle—candle-holder. (3 min.) | (Tracing.) Candle, candle-holder, flame of candle. (Why does the flame not go over to here \|in black area\|?) It does go over there, because it is a little red, but not as red as it is here. (Why a candle-holder?) Because of the red flame. (What else?) Because the flame looks like this ⊤ with the wick at the bottom. |
| | dr, S      F, CF      Obj | |

Although his response time goes up, indicating that some factor was perplexing him, he is able to produce a very well-delineated response in which color again is incorporated into the response. It is important to note that although the introduction of bright color may have perplexed him, he overcomes the difficulty and gives one of the best-organized responses in the entire series of records. He does this not by using one of the obvious details but by combining the white space and red areas in a highly creditable fashion. Again it should be noted that, in contrast to many other of his people, Sam does not have to be prodded to respond and explain—even though he was experiencing difficulty with the card. *In contrast* he appears to be spontaneous, creative, and on the extroverted side. That it was not the color *per se* that was creating difficulty for Sam is suggested by the question he asks himself: Why does not the red color go into the black area? Is it that because he sees there is some red in the black area he thinks the flame *should* have covered the black? In other words, if the flame is red and the black contains some red, why does not the flame go over into the black? Although the sources and significances of Sam's difficulty in this card are ambiguous, it should not be overlooked that the quality of his response did not suffer—a fact which supports the earlier hypothesis that Sam's feelings of adequacy and self-confidence are not as easily threatened or impaired as are those of some of his brethren. He responds to and does not withdraw from this stressful situation.

CARD III

III-1   12″ Person—two of them.

    D    M    H
    (See III-2 response)

(Parts of body?) Legs, arms, belly, head, (?) knee. (What sort of people?) Ghosts. (Why?) Whole body looks like it—pointed chin of skull, hairy arms and legs.

  2   They are lifting these plants.

    D    F    Pl

(?) Is round, with irregular outline. (?) Two plants.

  3   Animals

    D    F−    A

(?) Elephant. (Why?) Trunk. (Parts of body?) Back, buttocks, tusks. (Do we know anything more about it?) No.

  4   Red flower of the plant—it has fallen, and lies between the men. (3¾ min.)

    D    FC    N

(Why?) It is red. (Anything else?) It is shaped like a flower.

Again he responds quickly and produces more than the others. Again he responds to an external characteristic of the stimulus, the color, and for the first time he responds in a personal kind of way. Although we

know from the anthropologist that the Trukese view ghosts as ma-
levolent creatures, it is not clear in this case what *personal* significances
ghosts have for Sam. The fact that the figures are first called persons
and only under questioning become ghosts suggests that some kinds
of people may be or were as personally threatening to Sam as ghosts.
However, the fact that the response was given quickly and with no
apparent overt signs of anxiety—together with the fact that the figures
were first called persons—might be taken to mean that if persons and
ghosts were once equated in Sam's thinking, they no longer are: he
is unaware of links in a once conscious chain of associations.

Sam's "elephant" response returns us to a problem raised in the first
card. The long projection is the trunk; the little side projections are
the tusks and the rest of the area is the buttocks and the back. It is
these latter two areas which make it a whole elephant for Sam, making
it a poorly seen response. In view of the question about the genitals in
the first card, it is interesting that the part of the elephant which does
not make good sense is called the buttocks. The fact that the first indication of uncritical or unrealistic thinking involves a sexual area—taken
together with the question raised in the first card—suggests the possibility that sexuality may be an area of conflict or preoccupation. The
most cautious hypothesis would be that sexuality is of great "interest"
to Sam. Why his thinking in this area is less adequate or realistic than
when other kinds of content are engendered is not clear at this point.

CARD IV

IV-1   32″ *Nifaro* (a fishing bird—
lives in burrows in the day-
time).

dr   F   A

2   Oh, I am wrong: the whole
thing is a fruit bat. (We'll
think of both of them.) (1½
min.)

W   FM   A

(Tracing.) Head, ears, eyes, mouth.
We don't see it because the picture is black, but actually the
*nifaro* is spotted—under its wings,
belly and tail.

(Why a fruit bat?) Because the
wings are stretched out, like a bat
that is flying.

Here again we see further indication of Sam's good ability. His first
response is nicely chiseled out of the center portion. Note how easily

he explains the response: he not only tells the examiner what he sees but what he does not see and why he cannot. Unlike some of the others, Sam does not seem to be afraid of responding: he does not seem to view the examiner as a punitive, judging, authority figure.

His comment to the second response explains something that Sam has never done: *if an area has been called a certain thing then it cannot be called anything else.* Since his first response here is to an area which is also part of the second response, he wants to reject the first response. An area is $X$ and it cannot be used for $Y$—a rigidity or concreteness which is shared by the other Trukese. However, although Sam shares this concreteness and rigidity, he has it to a far less extent than the others. At least here Sam is able to use the same area for two different responses. Most of the others could not or would not show even this flexibility.

CARD V

V-1  46" Animal. (1 min.)

    W    FC', FM    A

(What kind?) A black tern. (Where?) Whole thing. (Why?) Wings are long—also the legs stretched out because it is flying. We also see the belly, because it is flying over. (While the examiner was looking up the name of the bird in the dictionary, Sam remarked as a point of information that the bird was black, but he was apparently not referring to the blot.)

The rigidity noted above shows up here. Since he uses the whole card for one response, he does not give, or try to give, another response. He gives the response and immediately relinquishes the card. But it should be noted that despite this concrete approach Sam is able to incorporate in his response a subjective or internal factor as well as an objective characteristic of the stimulus. However, it is not clear here (as it was not in the previous card) what the personal significances of the animal movement responses are. We now must qualify something that was said before. Although we have characterized Sam as being (relative to the others in the group) spontaneous and responsive, he has thus far never directly indicated what he was experiencing in this situation. Whatever we have said about his self-attitudes in this situation has been *deduced* from what he has said and done—Sam has not overtly expressed his truly personal reactions to the situation. This suggests that it is not easy for Sam to express such feelings overtly. They are expressed, at best, in a very indirect and disguised fashion.

One further question might be raised here: What is the effect of the concrete way of thinking on Sam's behavior in this situation? The most obvious answer is that it tends to reduce the quantity of his responsiveness. But when we recall that there have been times when he responded with more than the average number of responses, we might answer the question by saying that the concrete tendency makes Sam "dependent" on the external stimulus in the sense that if the stimulus lends itself to a whole response he stops responding. The concrete tendency makes it difficult for him to consider alternative ways of responding to *that* stimulus. Since he has conceived of the task in a particular way, his frequency of response will to a large degree be a function of the nature of the stimulus. That Sam shows this concrete tendency less than do many of the others suggests that he is for some undetermined reason "unusual." It is not fortuitous that this comparatively "weak" concrete tendency occurs in an individual who in this situation was relatively at ease, responsive, and self-confident.

CARD VI

| VI-1 | 30″ I don't know. (You haven't really thought about it.) 55″ Skate. (1 min.)  W    F    A | (Where?) Whole thing. (Why?) Wings, tail. The leaf of his wing (i.e., pectoral fins) moves when he swims. (Why do you think it is moving?) It is not moving here, but it moves in the sea. |

Spontaneously he rejects the card and it is the examiner's insistence that results in Sam's one response. Why was he so ready to reject the card? It is as if he wasn't trying too hard. After thirty seconds (he held cards II and V longer) he is ready to give up. One possible explanation for his rejection of the card would assume that he perceived the sexual organ. It could be argued that this card engendered an unconscious conflict against which strong inhibitory tendencies were mobilized, leaving him with a "blank" mind. This explanation does not seem to explain adequately either his readiness to reject the card or the examiner's impression that Sam was not trying hard. If he was consciously aware of the resemblance between the male sex organ and the top detail, why did he not say so, especially since he had mentioned genitals in previous responses? If sexual symbolism had nothing to do with the rejection, why was he able, relatively quickly, to give a response after some prodding? These questions cannot be answered here. What can be said is that it is likely that this boy has some kind of conflict in the sexual area. Even if one were to leave aside the possible sexual conflict, the fact still remains that at this point in the test inhibiting tendencies prevented spontaneous responding, a marked contrast to the other cards. But even this statement must be qualified: When pressed, he can respond to this card, something which other males found difficult to do.

It is apparent that much of our difficulty in understanding Sam's behavior in this card is that he gives us no idea why he does not respond. To what extent his failure to respond spontaneously was due to the possible sexual content or the presence of a foreigner we have no way of knowing. Here again one might ask why he was able to mention the genitals in card I. The mentioning of the genitals in card I, the minus response (elephants) in card III, and the rejection of card VI—the fact that each of these was in some way "unusual" leads us to conclude that a central conflict in this boy involves the sexual area, a conflict involving strong antithetical or conflicting tendencies.

CARD VII

VII-1  1'25" Clouds—here, here—  (Why?) The outline is irregular,
       the whole thing. (2 min.)     like a lot of trees. It has the shape
                                      of clouds.
       W     F     N

After what is for Sam a relatively long reaction time he produces a vague, diffuse kind of response. Since he responds to the whole, he cannot use the parts for any other response. It may be that his long reaction time, rather than being explained as a "hangover" from card VI, is due to his seeing both clouds and trees and not being sure how to decide which one it *really* is.

CARD VIII

VIII-1   22″ The flower of a tree.

        dr    FC    N

(What do we see?) One flower— which is red—and the trunk below it (above). (What about this [blue and grey area]?) Not a part of it. (?) It has the shape of a flower.

   2 Pig—two pigs—they are on the tree. (1½ min.)

        D    F    A

Why does this look so much like a pig . . . ? (Parts of body?) Head, forelegs, back, flank, hind legs—we don't see the tail. (Why pig?) Short snout; the legs are like a cow's, but a little different.

CARD IX

IX-1   36″ These are people—
   2 they are sticking out from the top of this tree—they are not real people, but just a part of the tree which looks like people. This is the tree (green portion) and its trunk. (2 min.)

        D    F    H
        W    F    N

(Parts of body?) Head, legs, arm, eye. (Why eye?) Here—the nose is below, the forehead above, and the eye in the middle. (Why tree?) Because the trunk goes down and then the branches spread down to the ground (now pointing to the orange as well as green part). (Any other reason?) Just the trunk going down—no other reason.

Sam's behavior to these cards is much as it was earlier. He must justify why his people are not real people but a part of the tree which happens to look like people. The whole thing is a tree and parts of it cannot be used for anything else. What is important is that he is able to overcome this concreteness to a certain extent, something which most Trukese could not do.

CARD X

X-1   11″ The whole thing is branches of a tree—this is the trunk. An American tree— there are none like this on Truk. (1 min.)

        W    F    N

(Why?) All the parts just look like tree branches, plus the trunk.

Although this response is on the vague, impressionistic side, he justi-
fies it in an unusual way by saying it must be an American tree. In a
sense this type of explanation typifies Sam: he has a ready, and usually
good, explanation for what he does. He is relatively resourceful in
coping with the test.

## CARD-BY-CARD INTERPRETATION: MIKE

### CARD I

I-1 50" Island. (Looked at the card some more, but no further response.) (1¾ min.)

W    F    N

(How much of it is an island?) The whole picture. (How are we looking at it?) As if from an airplane—from above. (Why is it like an island?) It just looks like one. (Repeated and further questioning failed to add to this.)

His reaction time is near the median for the male group and his one response is on the vague, diffuse side. It is possible that having given a response to the whole card he cannot give anything else—the concreteness and lack of flexibility discussed in Sam's case. If this is so then one must say that Mike suffers from this limitation to a far greater degree than Sam. The differences between Sam and Mike are striking: Whereas Sam spontaneously elaborated on his responses, Mike does not; whereas Sam responded to the examiner's questions, Mike appears to have difficulty doing so; whereas Sam's responses reflected some degree of complex or conceptual thinking, Mike's response reflects little or nothing of a sustained conceptual process. From his performance in this card one would not say that Mike is spontaneous, or self-confident, or not unduly under stress. It is difficult to say just what Mike is experiencing in this situation or how he conceives of the task and his relation to the examiner. It should be noted, however, that Mike can at least justify the response but only when pressed.

### CARD II

II-1 (After 2¼' said) I don't know. (Look some more.) (At 6½' said) There isn't anything.

Why does he reject the card? Is it that he thinks the whole card must be a "thing" and he cannot see a "thing"? Was he cowed by the examiner's questions in the inquiry of card I? Whatever the source of the difficulty—and Mike tells us nothing in a direct or indirect way about the difficulty—he is unable to be productive or creative. When Sam rejected a card (VI) he responded to the examiner's prodding by giving a response. This Mike is unable to do. Inhibitory tendencies

352

in Mike appear to be much stronger than in Sam. If Mike cannot respond unless he is sure of what he is doing—unless he is sure that what he will say will receive the examiner's approval—then one might conclude that Mike's cautiousness and inhibited behavior are means whereby he defends himself not only against "disapproved" behavior but against threats to his self-esteem as well. In other words, Mike's lack of responsiveness probably serves the purpose of protecting him from doing "wrong."

CARD III

III-1  (After 4' said) I don't know this one either. (Do you understand what you are to do?) No. (Just as you saw an island in the first picture, find something in this one.)

5' Two people.

D    M    H

(Show me parts of body.) Head, legs, arms. They are standing on these rocks. Their arms are back, elbows sticking out back.

2  Rocks.

D    F    N

(Why rocks?) They are round, like rocks. (What kind of rock?) From inland (i.e., black basalt, as distinguished from coral, the only other kind of common rock). (Why?) Because people are standing on it.

3  Animals. (10 min.)

D    F    A

(What kind of animals?) Looks like a dog. (Parts of body.) Head, body, what is this long thing? . . . a tail, legs. (What shall we think about these dogs?) Nothing.

After a very long time Mike is ready to reject this card. But in his reply to the examiner's question does he give himself away? At first he says he does not understand but when pressed he gives acceptable responses. It would appear, *especially since he did respond to card I,* that he is afraid to respond, perhaps because he does not know whether he is right or not. He is cautious, inhibited, fearful. Unless given much support when he is uncertain, he behaves in a constricted and unproductive manner. He is capable of more than he demonstrates but this situation is too stressful—too fraught with danger—to allow him to respond. The fact that Mike responded only after the examiner reassured him suggests that to Mike the examiner was an authority figure in the presence of whom one must be on guard. But why did not Sam react in such an extreme way to the examiner? Why does Mike need so much reassurance? These extreme individual differences suggest that it is not the particular examiner who is creating these differences but differences in previous life experiences.

It should be noted that Mike, unlike Sam, does not overtly respond to the objective characteristics of the stimulus, the colors. He not only does not respond to the colors but his movement response, given after he rejected the card, is on the passive side. Mike sees the people as standing whereas Sam saw them in a more active behavior. Responsiveness to the external stimulus and overt expression of internal needs do not appear to be characteristic of Mike when he is uncertain of himself —and it is likely that he frequently feels uncertain of himself.

CARD IV

IV-1  5′ Like that other one, an      (Why an island?) Just looks like it.
       island. (5¾ min.)              (How are we looking at it?)
                                       From above.
       W    F    N

After a very long reaction time he can only give the same vague response he gave to card I. It is interesting that cards I and IV both have more "whole" character than II and III and it is to the former he can respond with a whole response while to the latter he could give nothing spontaneously. In any event, Mike is unable to use his capacities in anything resembling a creative or even adequate fashion. The novel and the strange perplex and discomfort him and he can express little or nothing of himself.

CARDS V AND VI

V-1   (After 2½′ said) I really
      don't know.

VI-1  (After 4¾′) I don't know
      this one either.

The rejection of these cards adds nothing new except to emphasize the extreme constriction of the man. Whatever goes on inside him stays inside. In light of his extremely strong tendency to reject the cards it does not appear justified to attach any sexual significance to the rejection of VI. In the case of Sam we raised the "sexual problem" because (1) he rejected no other card but VI, (2) previous responses could be interpreted as indicating a specific anxiety or conflict in the sexual area, and (3) the manner in which VI was rejected was not in keeping with his behavior in other cards. However, although there is nothing in Mike's record specifically indicative of sexual conflict, it would be surprising if his extreme cautiousness, constriction, fear of authority, and low self-esteem were not in some way reflected in his sexual attitudes or behavior. By the terms "sexual anxiety" or "sexual conflict" we do not necessarily mean fear of sexual relations, or impotence, or any *specific* kind of sexual behavior. We are deliberately nonspecific (or vague) because we are dealing with a culture different from ours and we do not know what the prevailing sexual customs, sanctions, and taboos are. By sexual conflict or anxiety we mean that in thinking about, or attitudes toward, or behavior in and following sexual relations anxiety or insecurity is engendered at some point. What we are here saying is that in the sexual area strong antithetical or conflicting tendencies are engendered. On the one hand, there is a strong approach tendency and, on the other hand, a strong inhibiting tendency. How such a conflict is resolved will be in large part a function of the strength of these tendencies in the individual case, cultural factors, and modes of defense. Because we are ignorant of the culture we do not feel justified in becoming more specific about the sources and nature of Sam's and Mike's sexual conflict. We do feel justified in maintaining that in Mike's case the sexual conflict is a reflection of a more general problem than it is in Sam. Mike's inadequacies seem general while Sam's appear to be specific.

CARD VII

VII-1  2'28" (Rock. (2¾ min.)          (Where?) Whole thing. (Why?) I
     W    F    N          don't know.

Again Mike falls back on a previously given content. He plays it safe.

CARD VIII

VIII-1    1'5" I know about those          (What kind of animals?) They look
          two animals, but I don't         like pigs. (Why?) I don't know.
          know about this (center          (Parts of body.) Head, forelegs,
          portion of blot). (2½ min.)      hind legs, body. (What else do we
                                           know about them?) I looked at
          D     F     A                    them and they looked like pigs.

Here Mike tells us that he thinks he must respond to the whole card:
he tells the examiner that he "knows" about the side areas but not
about the middle. It should be noted that concreteness and rigidity are
manifested differently in this and the previous record. In Sam it appeared that he felt that he must explain the whole card either by giving
one whole response or a different response to each sub-area. Mike does
not appear to have this degree of flexibility. Although he did respond
to the details in III, it should be remembered that he initially rejected
the card and it was only after prodding and reassurance that he was
able to respond.

If, as we have hypothesized, Mike conceives of the examiner as an
authority figure who will judge his behavior, it is important to note
that, overtly at least, he responds passively and submissively. Since he
appeared to be uncomfortable and unhappy in this situation, he could
have reacted with signs of hostility, petulance, and impatience. It is
probably quite an understatement to say that such behavior in the face
of authority would be surprising both to us and to Mike.

CARDS IX AND X

IX-1    (After 3¼') I have thought
        about this, but I don't know.
        (Do you think of things, but
        think they are not right?)
        Yes. (Well, what do you
        see?) Nothing.
X-1     (After 4½') I don't know
        this either. (Not a thing there
        you know?) No.

Mike's fearfulness and unwillingness to expose his thoughts are
brought out here. He admits that he is afraid that what he thinks is
wrong but cannot bring himself to admit what these things are.

## Card-by-Card Interpretation: Roger

### Card I

**I-1  28″  A tree.**

W    F    N

(How much of it is the tree?) The whole thing, with the trunk in the middle. These above are twigs. (Why a tree?) The branches coming out, with leaves at the ends. (Why do they look like leaves?) Because of the serrated edges of the picture.

**2  A bird.**

dr    F    A

(Tracing.) These made me think of a bird—they look like a bird's feet. No, they are not feet, they are ears—one kind of bird has ears here. (What kind?) A fruit bat. (But that is not a bird. [This was an error on my part, as linguistically and apparently conceptually, the Trukese class bats with birds.]) Oh, a sea tern. (But why not a bat?) It is a bat—I really think so, but you said a bat is not a bird.

**3  Rock. (2¾′ min.)**

dr    F    N

Five rocks. (Later, he counted up to 11 rocks.) (Why rocks?) Round. (Any other reason?) No.

He responds relatively quickly and the form quality of the response is considered acceptable. (Judgments about the form quality of responses were made by the anthropologist, who was obviously better acquainted with the fauna and flora of Truk.) In contrast to Mike, but like Sam, one does not have to pull words from him. His second response is a very good one and demonstrates flexibility: even though the first response was to the whole card this does not prevent him from using part of it for his bird. It is extremely important to note that even though the examiner contradicted him, he stuck to his guns, a degree of self-confidence and assertiveness which we have not seen before. Roger does not appear to be afraid of the examiner. In terms

357

of apparent ease and security in the situation, the difference between Roger and Mike seems greater than between Sam and Mike.

Why does Roger count so many rocks? Is this a reflection of some sort of "quantity set": the more one gives the better? If so, it suggests a kind of striving and ambitiousness which is unusual for the Trukese. This possibility is not in conflict with the hypothesis that Roger is not one who is easily cowed or tends to withdraw in the face of a stressful experience. It may be important that, when Roger does become "ambitious," the quality of his responses suffers: note the difference in quality between his second and third responses.

CARD II

II-1  2'22" (At 1¾ min., remarked he did not see anything.) People. (3¼ min.)

W    F    H

(Tracing.) (While tracing, said) Why did I say "person" (or "people"); this looks just like a monkey. (After tracing: how about the people?) They are monkeys. (Why monkeys?) Because they look like humans. (Then why not say "human"?) Because it is not a real human being.

He has difficulty getting started but *without prodding* he was able to overcome it and give a good response. Roger *strives* to respond—a very great contrast to Mike. But he becomes uncertain as to whether it is a monkey or a human and decides on the monkey in a rather concrete way. That Roger wants to do well—not to be wrong—is indicated by this response as well as by the second to card I, where he is not sure whether an area is the ears or feet. It is important to note that when he is questioned by the examiner he does not change his mind and passively submit. Although he experiences uncertainty, he masters it and is not unduly affected.

In his tracing he indicates a small projection as the penis and also points out the buttocks. This is similar to what Sam did. Of all the parts that could be pointed out, why do they point out the sexual areas? Both Sam and Roger use small areas for the penis—the possible significances of this are not clear.

It should be noted that Roger gives no movement or color. Although this would suggest a tendency to be constricted—to be uninfluenced by the more obvious characteristics of the external stimulus and to inhibit a personal way of responding—this tendency does not prevent a superficial spontaneity in this situation. As in the case of Sam and Mike we must deduce how Roger conceives of and experiences this situation.

CARD III

III-1   29" A shark . . . here is an-          Forehead, mouth, dorsal fin, tail,
        other one.                             middle. (Any other reason?) No.

        D    F˘   A

    2   A plant . . . here's another.          The trunk, leaves. (Why leaves?)
                                               The edges are serrated.
        D    F    N

    3   Another plant ("butterfly").           The branch (or stalk) is in the
        I don't know what these                middle; these are leaves.
        (bodies of "waiters") are.
        (2½ min.)

        D    F    N

The inability to give the more personal kind of response is seen again in this card: he does not see the human form. But he is productive, giving three responses. The fact that he repeats a content in his third response, and tries to respond to the one area he has not used, suggests again that Roger may feel it important to respond in quantity. Although he is productive, the quality of his responses does not appear to be as good as Sam's. Since Roger does try hard to respond, but little of his needs and motivations is reflected in his responses, one may wonder how satisfying such striving is to him.

CARD IV

IV-1   48" A ghost—the whole          Forehead, ears, shoulders, arms, legs,
       thing. (1¼ min.)               penis. (Why a ghost?) It is
                                      black, like a ghost.
       W    FC'   H

He gives up on this card very quickly after he gives his one response, something which he has not done on other cards. It is not fortuitous that this happens to a response which had (for him) a relatively long reaction time and an anxious content—it is a ghost. Although in general the response is good, the penis (to the large, center-bottom detail) is disproportionately large. As in the case of Sam the first irrational element to appear is associatd with a sexual content. Why does he make it such a large penis?—in card II the penis was a small projection. Does he overevaluate the importance of the male organ? These questions, the anxious content, the lowering of productivity, and the selective manner in which he responds to this card suggest a sexual problem of some sort. If Roger does overevaluate the importance of the penis, and if he in fact is an unusually striving or "ambitious" individual, it would suggest that he may be concerned with his masculinity.

CARD V

V-1   12″  A fruit bat—the whole      (What is this?) Part of the wing.
            thing. Ears, head, wings, legs.   (Why a fruit bat?) Has the big
            (1½ min.)                          wings, the legs, ears, etc., of a
                                                fruit bat.
        W        F        A

He gives one response. Why can't he give more as on I and III. Is there a carry-over from IV? Note that he responds quickly and then holds the card for well over a minute? Whatever it was he was thinking about we have no idea. One could speculate that he may have been concerned with the projections which would have sexual significance for him—but it would be no more than speculation.

CARD VI

VI-1  (After ¾′) I don't know—
        there isn't anything.

Although he holds other cards longer before responding, he rejects this card after forty-five seconds. After what happened in IV it seems reasonable to ask in this case if the sexual area is not a conflictual one for Roger. Not only should this card be viewed with card IV but the drop in productivity beginning with IV should be kept in mind—it is not fortuitous that the rate of responding changed after card IV. Roger has petered out somewhat, in contrast to Sam, who continued to respond. What has apparently happened thus far is in line with a previous statement: Roger's overt responsiveness tends to be superficial and lacks personal expression.

In light of the fact that Roger specifically mentions the penis in previous cards, we are puzzled by his not doing so in this card—

assuming that this card did elicit sexual associations. Because he does mention the penis—he does not attempt to inhibit such responses— and because there is some indication that his reality testing in this area is somewhat impaired, we would conclude that sexuality is an area of conscious concern to Roger. If this is so then we would further conclude that his rejection of VI was a consciously purposeful act. That he rejected this card after holding it for a shorter time than other cards is also congruent with such a conclusion. What we are in effect saying is that Roger has both strong sexual drives and strong competing, inhibitory tendencies. Why this conflict should exist, what its conscious nature is, and what its unconscious determinants are we can only speculate about. It may be, as we suggested earlier, that concern about masculinity is part of the problem.

CARD VII

| VII-1 | 23″ A cloud—two of them. | The whole thing—on each side. (Why a cloud?) It is whitish and then darker in places like a cloud. |
| | W   K   N | |
| 2 | A house. (¾ min.) | (Tracing.) A pole is in the middle. |
| | d   F   Obj | |
| 2a | dr   C′F   N | The black on the sides (of the house) is rock. (Why?) Because it is black. |

He goes from a vague, undifferentiated whole to a nicely seen response to a small area. This jump from the large to the small is similar to what he did in card I (the rocks). The "jumping" may be a reflection of his desire to give responses. In connection with this one should note that he spontaneously added a response in the inquiry.

Although he uses objective characteristics of the card, the shading and color, in both instances such responsiveness is vague and diffuse. In other words, when he becomes aware of and responds to more than one aspect (i.e., form, contours) of the external stimulus, the quality of his responsiveness is lowered. In this respect Sam shows a more adequate responsiveness. One would expect Roger's handling of stressful and problem-solving situations to be more irregular and less efficient than Sam's. We should emphasize that Roger is capable of an organized solution to such situations; we would, however, expect that such capabilities would not be consistently utilized in an efficient manner.

CARD VIII

| | |
|---|---|
| VIII-1   15″   A   pig . . . another.<br>(¾ min.)<br><br>D      F      A | Mouth, head, eye, back, forelegs, hind leg, tail. (Only one hind leg?) The two are together. (Why is tail big?) A few pigs have long tails. No other reason (for calling it pig). |

He gives the popular response relatively quickly but there is no movement. Neither through the formal content of his responses nor in his incidental verbalization does Roger tell us in any clear fashion how he experiences this situation. Although in contrast to Mike he appears *relatively* at ease with the examiner, Roger says nothing about his personal reactions in this situation. The truly personal remains "private."

CARD IX

| | |
|---|---|
| IX-1   20″   A guitar.<br><br>dr, S      F      Obj | (Tracing.) It has the same shape as a guitar. |
| 2   A tree—the whole thing. (¾ min.)<br><br>W      F      N | The middle is the trunk, all the rest is leaves. (Why leaves?) Serrated edges. |

In relatively quick time he gives a very well-delineated response. In fact, his guitar in this card and his bird in card I are among the best responses in the entire series of records. Again it should be noted that he can be flexible: the fact that he gives the guitar to the middle area does not prevent him from using the whole card for the tree. Roger presents certain contrasts: he goes from the vague to the precise, from the large to the small, from responsiveness to its absence, from striving or something akin to ambitiousness to avoidance.

CARD X

| | |
|---|---|
| X-1   15″   (Although this was the first time he had turned a card, he did it immediately | (Why?) It just looks like it. |

and without hesitation.) The
whole thing is a tree . . . this
is the fruit . . . all the rest is
leaves . . . this is the trunk.
(1 min.)

W   F   N

He quickly gives a not too well delineated tree. Note that he felt
sufficiently "free" to reverse the position of the card.

## CARD-BY-CARD INTERPRETATION: ANDY

### CARD I

I-1 34" Animal. It flaps like a dog that is flying. I don't know what sort of an animal it is. (2 min.)

(Tracing.) (Why a dog?) Because of the shape of its head. (Why flying?) Because its forelegs are out.

dr    FM    A

He responds relatively quickly with a movement response. He is the first one to give a movement response so early in a record. Note that he holds the card for 1½ minutes after giving the response but we have no idea what he was thinking about. It should also be noted that he apparently does not feel that he has to respond to the whole card either by giving one whole response or a different response for each area. The form quality of the response is somewhat dubious (see tracing) but this may be due to the examiner's question about the tracing. What he gives spontaneously is better than what he adds as a result of questioning about unspecified areas.

### CARD II

II-1 41" (Turned card down, then up.) Here is a person—two people. Their arms—they are clapping hands. Their heads, with red clothes on them? Is it blood? Are these feet? They are bloody. They are sitting. This is another foot. These are clothes. (3¾ min.)

W    M, CF, FC'    H, bl

(Tracing.) (Is it a cloth or blood on head?) I thought it was a cloth, but now I know it isn't. (What is it?) Just a head, but it looks bloody. (Why blood?) Perhaps they are fighting . . . it just looks like blood. (Why clothing [on body]?) It just looks very much like it. It is black . . . woman's clothes . . . it looked like a woman, so I decided she had clothes. (Trukese women usually wear white or prints.) (Why a woman?) It just looked like one. (How about the clothes again?) A white neck like your (i.e., the examiner's) skin, then red clothing, and then black.

2  (Having said he was finished, he looked again at the red portion of the bottom of the card.) Why does it look just like a vagina? (Pointing to middle of blot.) Holes. (This response not timed.)

(Tracing.) (Why a vagina?) Holes, blood. (Why blood?) I have seen a few women like this—I just looked at them for fun—they did not say anything. (Why blood?) Menstruating.

dr      F, CF      Hd

He is the first one to turn the card so early in the record—thus far Andy has two "firsts" which when taken together suggest in this situation he does not feel under such stress that he is unable to respond in a relatively spontaneous manner: to act overtly on the basis of internal stimuli. When it occurs to him to turn the card, he does not appear to become concerned about whether it is right or wrong—he does it.

He not only gives a lively (active) movement response—in which the whole card is used—but he also uses the colors. He shows a good degree of sustained conceptual thinking. He responds in a varied manner: he is aware of and responds to the objective properties of the card and he also gives verbal expression to subjective or personal factors. Note his indecision re the content. Initially they are clapping but because of the blood it may be women fighting. The aggressive content is, so to speak, delayed and does not appear right off. There is hesitation about giving it but he does give it. This is a "Western" type of response —very un-Trukese.

Although he said he was finished after this response he did not let the card go as so many would have done. Others might have seen the vagina but would not have commented on it. There is an interesting chain of associations: clapping, fighting, women, menstruation. Note how he says he has seen a "few women" like this, as if one should not do this. What does he mean "they did not say anything"? Does this indicate that women can be aggressive re sexual matters? In any event, it indicates that Andy has a degree of assertiveness and curiosity which most Trukese males do not overtly manifest. He appears to be (relatively) spontaneous and direct, lacking the inhibitions that so many have. He can give of himself and he is aware of things, far more perceptive than others.

The ease with which Andy talks of sexuality indicates that he has strong drives in this area. The fact that Sam and Roger also give sexual responses makes us feel more strongly that for Trukese males sexuality is an activity of *inordinate* interest. But why should Andy's "sexual response" involve menstruating women in an aggressive kind of activity? Does he, and do perhaps others, view women as aggressive and as persons toward whom one in turn must be aggressive?—note that he indicates that he saw a few menstruating women and that he should not have done so.

CARD III

III-1   1'10" Animal—two of them. Head, nose, neck, back, foreleg (two), tail, two hind legs (he pointed these out); leaning over with hands on something . . . holding something. I don't know about this ("butterfly" in middle).

    W    M    A

(Tracing.) (While he was tracing, he said) Why can't we see the eyes? . . . Oh, they are looking away—they are having a verbal battle. (When tracing completed: What is that?—i.e., middle lower blobs.) I don't know what sort of thing they are holding with their hands. (Why animal, not person?) Foot not like a person's foot, also nose, arms. Only the pelvic region looks human.

2   Looks like an animal. (Pointing) Leg, waist, buttocks, two arms (demonstrated they were held out behind as if sitting and leaning back on hands), back, belly, snout like a monkey, head—the back of the head looks like a human. (7 min.)

    D    M    A

(Tracing.) (When he had finished the tracing, he said) Monkey. (Why a monkey?) Just looks a lot like one. (Note: although this response is more plausible in position $\vee$, he did not turn the card while talking about it either in performance or inquiry.)

Again he gives a well-delineated movement response with aggressive content. But note that the aggressiveness is "verbal" and that the response is given after a long reaction time. One would not expect Andy to be an overtly aggressive person in the sense of being unable to control the expression of aggressiveness. Aggressive content, as in card

II, does not come out immediately; it is more like an afterthought. He would probably be aware of aggressive tendencies but controls them fairly well.

The way in which aggressive content appears in this record (i.e., "delayed," verbal) now brings to our attention that the first three records were almost devoid of aggressive content. We previously noted that in their apparent relation to and attitudes toward the examiner Sam, Mike, and Roger showed little or no aggressiveness but rather seemed concerned about performing in a way that the examiner might think "wrong." Although Roger was more assertive than the other two, we would not conclude that assertiveness and aggressiveness were striking characteristics of his behavior in this situation. When their apparent behavior to an authority figure is viewed in the light of the relative absence of aggressive content, one might conclude that acting aggressively is not a Trukese characteristic, especially where interactions with authority figures are concerned. If this conclusion has merit, it would suggest that there are strong defenses against aggressive behavior— stronger defenses than against sexual activity of a conflictful nature. From the Rorschach protocols, at least, the Trukese appear to be able to give some expression to sexual thoughts more easily than to aggressive ones.

In his second response Andy gives a monkey in a human-like pose. The frequency with which he gives movement responses indicates that he should be able to express his needs and motivations much better than others. Although inhibitory tendencies against subjective expression are not as strong as in others, one should not overlook the amount of "mulling over" that accompanies such responses: it took him 1'10" to give his first response and he held the card for a total of seven minutes.

CARD IV

IV-1   (Turned card various ways.)
       Nothing. (1¼ min.)

One must qualify the statement re inhibitory tendencies. Why does he reject the card? On the basis of previous performance, as well as his apparent ease in the situation, one would expect him to have been able to handle the card. There are some inhibitory tendencies.

CARD V

V-1   37″ Animal. Has wings like a       (Tracing.) (Why a fruit bat?)
      fruit bat. I don't know about      Just looks like one—wings, legs,
      the projections above and be-      etc.
      low . . . (Long pause.) . . .
      Now I understand about these
      (upper projections). They are
      legs. (Turned card upright.)
      (Pointing) Head, ears, neck,
      the things which stick out
      on the wings (of fruit bats, i.e.,
      the claws or hooks by which
      they hang themselves up). (3
      min.)

      W      F      A

Although this is a "popular" response he describes it more precisely
than others.

CARD VI

VI-1  (Turned card various ways.)
      I don't know what this may
      be . . . It looks as if there
      must be something, but I
      can't make it out. (1¼ min.)

Again a rejection. From his verbalization one might deduce that he
actually sees something but he "can't make it out." Is it associations
about male sexuality that make it difficult? Note that he turns the
card several ways. He apparently tries but is blocked, whether for conscious or unconscious factors. If he can see the vagina in card II why
not the penis here or in card IV as some others do? Cards IV and VI
are striking contrasts to the rest of the record. It is difficult to determine
whether these rejections are a purposeful (and conscious) way of avoiding verbalization of "dangerous" material or a reflection of blocking
as a defense against conscious expression of certain conflictful contents
—or, as is likely, some combination of both. We would feel more secure
in our interpretation if we could evaluate the role of each possibility.
In any event, we interpret the rejections as indicating (1) extremely
strong inhibitory or defensive reactions related to (2) the arousal of

competing or antithetical tendencies involving sexuality. Since we assume that the male sexual role would involve aggressive or assertive behavior, it is likely that the inhibitory tendencies are related in some way both to sexual and to aggressive activities.

CARD VII

VII-1  30″ (Turned card, laughed.) Clouds? It looks just like clouds. But I don't know about this (black at midline). (1½ min.)

W     F     N

(Why clouds?) The shape—there are no objects in the picture. It looks like smoke. (Why?) It billows out (pointing to "feather in hat," "arm").

He gives his first vague, undifferentiated response. Is this in any way a function of Card VI? The fact that he laughs, and can turn the cards, at least indicates that whatever caused rejection of card VI has not had a marked pervasive effect. Note that although he laughs, he does not give any indication why he laughed—a reflection of the Trukese tendency for the covert response to stay covert.

CARD VIII

VIII-1  22″ Animal. That is all. (Look some more.) A pig.

D     FM     A

(Why pig?) (Pointing) Legs, back, belly, ears, snout, with mouth below. One rear leg lifted to step forward. No tail. (The examiner then asked for a tracing of the head and ears only, but he did everything.)

2     I don't know what sort of a plant this is. (2½ min.)

dr     F     Pl

(Why plant?) I just think so. (A leaf, or the whole thing?) Only a leaf. (Why leaf?) Stem in the middle. (Why stem?) Runs down the middle.

In tracing his animal he changes the outline in order to indicate the crotch. Why does he do this? Why do so many Trukese (male at least) bring in the sexual area when it is not "apparent" or make the area disproportionate in size? Again, did Andy reject cards IV and VI because of some anxiety connected with perception of the male organ?

CARD IX

IX-1  1'25" (Turned card various      (Tracing.) (Why eye?) Just looks
      ways, pausing each time.)        like an eye. (What sort of per-
                                       son?) Woman. (Why?) Hair on
          D    F    Hd                 head—there is lots of it.

   2  Animal ("deer's head").         (Tracing.) (What sort of an ani-
                                       mal?) I don't know. (Why eye?)
          D    F    Ad                 Just looks like it.

   3  Rocks.                          (Tracing.) (Why rocks?) Just looks
                                       like them. I didn't know what
          dr   F    N                  they were, so I said rocks.

   4  Light through branches of a     (Why tree?) It doesn't matter
      tree.                            whether it is a tree or not. I was
                                       just talking about the hole—it is
          S    C'   N                  white—light coming through.

   5  Person. (3½ min.)               (Tracing.) (Why person, not ani-
                                       mal, etc.?) It just looks like a
          dr   F—   H                  person, not an animal.

His first two responses are well-seen "Western" ones. In the tracing
of his first "person" there is a possibility of his having used the surface
shading, a possibility which is not found in most of the records. However, it is clear that in Andy's record responsiveness to the characteristics of the external stimulus is less frequent than the personal or
subjective way of responding, which, when taken together with indications of inhibitory tendencies, suggests that internal needs do not
easily reach overt expression. In contrast to the others, however, Andy
should be able to act more spontaneously on the basis of internal needs.

His next two responses are on the vague side and his last response,
another person, is poorly seen. He gave more responses here than he
did to any other card and it may be that when he tries for quantity, like
Roger, his control gets poorer—his judgment is not too good. It is perhaps not fortuitous that he gives so many responses after card VIII,
where we find the only instance where the examiner prodded him.
If the quantity in IX is related to the previous prodding, it would indicate the strength of Andy's desire to do well and please the examiner.
He does not appear to have "resented" the prodding—a form of aggressiveness which we would not expect even in Andy.

CARD X

X-1  3′ I don't see anything . . . (pause) . . . Animals. I don't know what they are doing with this (middle)—it looks like a cup.

D    FM    Ad

(Tracing.) (What sort of an animal?) Elephant (he explained he saw one in a Japanese movie). It is holding a cup in its trunk. (Why is its head dark—i.e., shaded in the tracing?) I don't know whether an elephant's head is dark or not—I just showed it that way because it is so in the picture.

2  Person. Throwing arms up in play.

D    M    H

(Tracing.) (While tracing, he laughed at the size of the arms.)

3  Plant. I don't know what kind. (7¼ min.)

D    F    N

(Tracing.) (What is hole in branches?) Nothing. (Why a tree?) Because of the branches spreading out.

He has a very long reaction time and then gives the elephant. What seems to have bothered him is the area which connects the two elephants. He solves the problem in an adequate fashion. He does not easily give up here—why then did he give up so much more easily in IV and VI? But even in tracing this response he points out the genitals although they are not indicated in the card. His next response is another movement response and he is aware of the size of the arms—that they are disproportionate—but it does not prevent him from giving it. (For once we know what caused the laughter.) Andy is certainly not the concrete, unimaginative, constricted person that so many of the others are.

At the conclusion of Roger's record we indicated several contrasts in his record. Andy's protocol presents somewhat different contrasts: from a very "Western" to a very Trukese way of responding, from a direct expression of sexuality (card II) to avoidance of such expression, from a very personal way of responding to one in which all expression is inhibited (rejections).

HAROLD

Harold   C. A. 9 years, 3 months

CARD I

I-1   6″ ∧ 2 elephants trying to pull   (See tracing)
a man apart.

W     FM(M?)     A,H

2  ∨ Face of monster when you      Looks like a monster. (Why a
turn it upside down.             *monster?*) Sort of looks like one.

55″ W, S     F     A

After an extremely short reaction time he is able to give an organized whole response. If he had given the popular bat or butterfly, or had responded to only one of the details, we would not consider the reaction time of extreme interest. But his response is not a simple one but rather reflects a complex conceptual process which takes place within six seconds. This is all the more surprising when one considers that this is the first card he has seen. There is no indication of hesitation, indecision, or lack of self-confidence—as was also apparent from his overt behavior in the situation. Since he responded so quickly with this response one might ask if he is not being impulsive or uncritical. The fact that the response is considered of adequate reality testing (good form quality) does not support the possibility that he is being impulsive or uncritical. Whether a quick reaction time is "good or bad" depends on the adequacy of the end product and in this instance we have judged the end product to be acceptable. If the response had been of inadequate reality testing, we would have cause to hypothesize impulsivity. If he had been impulsive, one might have expected that both elephants would be described in the·same way, but this is not the case. One elephant is seen in one direction while the other elephant is seen in another—similar areas are organized differently.

The content of the response is, to put it mildly, somewhat striking: the elephants are trying to pull a man apart. The man is the object of a hostile, destructive act. The response seems to reflect not only a destructive tendency but, we assume, fear as well: the man is the object of an act which should arouse fear and counteraggression. But Harold only describes the destructive tendency of the animals. It is

372

surprising that he says little or nothing about the man. Since the 'destructive activity is *not* attributed to the human figure, but the human figure is the *recipient* of the destructive act, we might tentatively hypothesize that this response reflects this boy's fear of the hostility of others rather than his own conscious hostile tendencies toward them. If this response had been something like "two people killing a man" —the hostile act is carried out by humans—we might have hypothesized that conscious hostility toward external figures might be a characteristic of this boy.

In the second response he turns the card and makes the whole card a monster: the upper white areas are the eyes, the side projections are ears, the inner white-gray ("buckle") is the nose, and the large bottom white is the mouth. Again we get a whole response in which the parts (of the face) are well organized. But why monster? Especially to children monsters are usually thought of as threatening, anxiety-arousing figures. Whereas in the first response we were surprised at the absence of any anxious or fearful content, we find that such content appears in the second one in connection with a nonhuman, threatening figure. But here again the anxiety is not explicit but rather "symbolically" expressed. What we are in effect saying is that this boy may conceive of others (external figures) as hostile—he does not see himself as hostile —and defends himself against experiencing undue anxiety which such hostile possibilities engender.

CARD II

II-1∧7″ 2 men in very heavy clothes —fighting so hard blood spots are there.

W       M, Fc, Cf       H, bl.

You can't see much so they must be in heavy clothes—red ink is blood spots. (Why *heavy?*) these lines look like fur—have 2 hands together—facing each other so only 1 eye.

2∨ Upside down same thing except men are trying to run away from each other.

1′10″ W       M, CF       H, bl.

Can even see eye—dripping blood.

Again in a relatively quick fashion he organizes the whole card. Although he points out in his tracing the eye, the hands together (and the top side projection is the other hand), the whole person is not clearly delineated. Harold's statement that "you can't see much so they must be in heavy clothes" suggests that he is aware that the persons are not well delineated. It is to his credit that he is able adequately to explain away why he only sees part of the person. It was as if he was aware that the response needed explaining—he spontaneously offers the explanation. Although the response suggests a certain diffuseness— which would not be unusual in a nine-year-old child—it is important that he is aware of and attempts to "correct" this tendency. He can be self-critical.

In contrast to the first card we get aggressive content involving humans, which forces us to qualify the hypothesis that Harold is not aware of strong hostile tendencies within himself. As might have been expected, the hypothesis offered in card I was too simple. Rarely is it an "either-or" proposition: either the individual conceives of others as hostile or he conceives of himself as hostile. In those cases where an individual attributes hostility to others it is likely that the very nature of such an attitude will engender counterhostility in the individual. If one feels others are hostile, one has grounds for being hostile toward them. The diagnostic problem is to try to determine which of the tendencies is the stronger. In this connection it is important to note that in the second response *the people are running away from each other*. The aggressive content in the first response is followed by an activity which rules out aggressive interaction. In the first card the aggressive content was followed by an anxious one; in the second card the second response is like a defense against the aggressive content in the first response. In both cards the second response is one which would avoid or inhibit aggressive display. Because aggressive content is given first and quickly, and because the content reflects a drive of great strength, we might conclude that Harold is probably aware of, or does have, strong hostile tendencies. That there are indications of tendencies to inhibit such activity suggests that hostility is an area of conflict for this boy. It is still reasonable to maintain that he *may* conceive of his own hostility as a reaction to the hostile acts of others toward him. In other words, this may be a case of "I am hostile because they are hostile." These questions, however, cannot be decided at this point, if they can be decided at all from this protocol.

The second response, like the first one, is not too clearly delineated and again there is the suggestion of diffuseness. This tendency is certainly not a function of any lack of ability or a lack of awareness and responsiveness to the characteristics of the stimulus. In this connection we might ask: Why has he in these first two cards responded to each first in the upright position and then turned the card for his second response? Also, why does he only give whole responses? Is it that he thinks that the whole card must be used, and having responded to the whole he can give another such response by turning the card? If he does have this whole tendency, then this may in part explain the somewhat diffuse use of the whole card—he uses the whole card because he feels he should and not because the whole card is essential for the response. What we are here in effect suggesting is that this boy has a rigid set toward the task and compulsively acts in accordance with it. If in fact this is a reflection of rigid and compulsive tendencies, then we might make the following deduction: Since rigidity and compulsiveness are learned defenses against unacceptable tendencies, it may be that in Harold's case the unacceptable tendencies are of a hostile nature —a not unusual situation in our culture.

CARD III

III-1  5″  ∧ 2 tall thin men fighting over some kind of rug.

    W    M    H    P

(Popular) I couldn't imagine other than rug—must have something on it. (What do you mean?) I don't know—2 spots of some kind.

2  ∧ 2 monkeys in circus and

    D    FM    A

Whole thing is a circus!—monkeys. (Why monkeys?) Tail hanging down from something—wouldn't be there if no monkeys.

3  ∧ 2 midgets.

    D    F−    H

They look like little people— couldn't be so small in comparison unless midgets. (?) Not really in show—not in front of audience.

4  ∨ Ugly looking heads.

    D    F    Hd

They are not pretty heads (couldn't find them at first).

5  ∨  2 Negroes with legs cut    Arms are sort of cut off—no legs—
off.                             going away from each other.
                                 (What do you mean?) Heads
W̶  M  H                          pointing opposite direction from
1'14"                            each other—trying to get away
                                 from each other—not running.

His first response again is quickly given and has aggressive content.
The prepotency of this kind of tendency is striking. But note that his
other movement response (2 Negroes) involves "getting away from
each other": the same antithetical tendencies noted in the previous card.
We feel more sure at this point that hostility is a major source of conflict in this boy—and that it is probably a conscious one which has
pervasive effects.

Although the noncontiguous nature of the areas of this card makes
the giving of a whole response difficult, it is important to note that the
tendency to organize whole responses is also present here, supporting
the earlier hypothesis that his behavior reflects rigid and compulsive
tendencies. In light of the antithetical attitudes toward hostile expression, the deduction that his rigid and compulsive tendencies are learned
defenses against extremely strong and unacceptable hostile motives
does not seem unreasonable. (The turning of the card should also be
noted—he does not relinquish the card until he has turned and responded to it.)

We are now struck by another characteristic of the content of this
boy's responses: they reflect, directly or indirectly, interest in the size of
things:

elephants are big
monsters are big
*tall, thin* men
*midgets*

Does this reflect a concern with the size of his own body? Of his own
physical adequacy? Is this connected with the fact that in his responses
something happens to or is wrong with the body? The elephants were
pulling a man apart, the men were injured (blood), *ugly* heads, and
Negroes had their legs cut off. Is the dubious form quality of his "midgets" a reflection of the interfering effect of a concern with bodily adequacy? If Harold does have concern about the adequacy of his body—

if he feels that he is physically not what he should be or would like to be—then such a concern could be a basis for fearing the hostility of others and preventing any aggressive display on his part. One could argue that he could react to such feelings by being overly aggressive. In view of his rigidity and compulsiveness (and the deductions made therefrom), in addition to the antithetical attitudes toward aggressive display reflected in his responses, we would favor the hypothesis that his concern about bodily adequacy inhibits overt aggressive display and exacerbates the conflict.

## CARD IV

IV-1 6″ ∧ Monster—giant monster.

W   F   A

Has something here. (What?) I don't know—head, arms. (Why monster?) Ugly. (What do you mean?) Not shaped correctly—ugly looking—looks like test tube but it couldn't be on monster—I don't think he has a mouth. (You said he had arms?) Well . . . I don't know for sure—but that is one reason I called him a monster.

2  ∨ Giant cat pushing away 2 people.

W   FM(M?)   A, H
35″

(Leg) Probably stumbling.

The first response reflects many things we have noted before: anxious content, emphasis on size (a *giant* monster), and attention to physical inadequacy (ugly). In addition, he quickly gives an organized whole response, being aware that some body parts (arms) are disproportionate in size. What is the significance of his "test tube" statement? Is he saying that if the whole thing is the monster then part of it cannot be a test tube? If you use the whole for one thing you cannot use it (or part of it) for something else? *He has never responded to the same area twice unless he had already turned the card—in which case it is not the "same area."* This boy's approach reflects a rigidity and compulsiveness which while not blatant (in an overt sense) appears nevertheless to be strong.

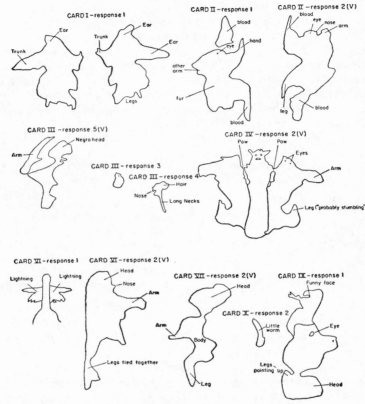

FIG. 10. Some of Harold's Traced Responses

His second response, given as usual after turning the card, is another organized whole. We are here struck by the similarity of this response to the first one in card I: a big animal performs a hostile act toward a human figure. As in the case of card I we feel that such a response—because of its "oddness" as well as the fact that people are the recipient of hostility—reflects the tendency to fear hostile display either of others or of himself. Because of other evidence indicating that Harold has strong and conscious hostile drives, in addition to what we have just said about his fear of hostile activity, we would conclude that this boy is in a state of chronic conflict: he cannot resolve it by "acting out" his feelings, and yet his own hostile thoughts continually exacerbate his anxiety and feelings of inadequacy. It is likely that one way he defends himself against recognizing the strength and sources of his own hostile feelings is by attributing such feelings to others and not to himself. "They are hostile. I am not." "They are big. I am small." "They are strong. I am weak." These statements reflect the ways in which we would expect this boy to view himself in relation to others.

Card V

V-1 ∧ 3″ Bat.                              Wings, etc. (Popular)

   W   F   A   P

2∨ Bat—has wings—bat hanging          (Why hanging?) Hanging upside
   upside down on wall.                     down from roof or eave or some-
   W    FM   A                        thing.
   40″

The strength of his rigid and compulsive tendencies is indicated here; it is as if he *must* turn the card *and* respond, even though he does not see anything that is much different from the content of the first response. It is to his credit that he can make the second response somewhat different from the first. He does not just say "another bat" and let it go at that. This boy, despite his rigidity and compulsiveness, can use his good ability in a way which masks somewhat his personal difficulties. We say good ability for several reasons: (1) He can organize a relatively complex response quickly and, in light of his age, well; (2) his verbalizations or vocabulary ("in comparison," "eave of the roof," "I couldn't imagine") seem unusual for a boy this age; (3) the fact that he knows what a test tube is (and he indicated with his finger the appropriate center area in IV) *suggests* that this is not an average boy.

CARD VI

VI-1 ∧Umh!
  1  16″ Some strange sort of building with lightning coming out of tower.
     D    Fm    N

Don't know—that's why I called it strange—has something inside that makes lightning come out— bottom does not look like building, just from here up—like skyscraper, you know how they narrow.

  2∨2 men with legs stuck together trying to pull legs apart.
    W    M    H
    1′12″

Why the long reaction time? Is it in some way related to the fact that for the first time he is unable to make a whole response? But why couldn't he fashion a whole response here when he has done it before? What selective factor is at work? If we turn to the content we find the following sequence: strange building—lightning coming out—something inside—a skyscraper (something *big*).

Before attributing any significance to this sequence we should recall the hypothesis that Harold is concerned about physical adequacy and feels that he is not physically all that he should or wants to be. If this hypothesis has merit, then one might further deduce that his concern about physical adequacy would affect his conception of "maleness" and the physical differences between boys and girls. We assume that he has thought about what a penis is for and has observed that not all penises are the same size, that girls do not have a penis, and that a penis is *important* for a man. *If Harold is concerned about the adequacy and size of his own body, then we would assume that such concern would affect or generalize to his thinking about the size and adequacy of his penis.* Since conflict about expression of hostility is related to concern about physical adequacy, it is likely that concern with the penis is also associated with the problem of hostility. We would expect, therefore, that the same antithetical tendencies which he experiences about aggressive display would be operative in his thinking in the sexual area. Because sexual and aggressive behavior is frequently punished in our culture, and because Harold's rigidity and compulsiveness reflect defenses against unacceptable (punished) tendencies, in addition to other indications of inhibitory tendencies and bodily concern, we would conclude that this boy must constantly defend himself against extremely strong but unconscious sexual-hostile drives. However, because the aggressive response (direct or indirect) is so prepotent in this boy and because of the indications of strong anxiety, in addition to lack of either "happy" or "neutral" content—in light of these factors we would conclude that his modes of defense do not result in a lowering of tension which would enable him to derive satisfaction from interpersonal and intrapersonal behavior.

The sequence noted above might be interpreted as a symbolic expression of the unconscious wish for a big, adequate penis. The big penis = strength or physical assertiveness—or the ability to act aggressively—to let out violently what is "inside." Sexuality and hostility are unconsciously equivalent or related so that what consciously affects the one also affects the other. *It should be noted that the hypothesis about concern with the penis is not necessarily dependent on our interpretation of this sequence but could be deduced from the hypothesis that Harold is concerned with the adequacy and size of his own body.*

The second response to this card—a very well-organized whole—typifies our conception of Harold: someone who feels confined, the object of aggression, and in constant struggle.

## Card VII

VII-1∧8" 2 men looking at each other—stomachs practically cut through—sitting up.

W M H

Cut through because it gets so narrow.

2∨ Monsters with huge heads and girl's body—one leg and one arm.

W M H
1'8"

(Why a girl's body?) Thin—looks like it is wearing a dress—body is facing opposite from direction of head. (What do you mean a huge head)? I don't know—another reason I called it a monster—both look exactly like each other.

Again the quickly organized whole. And again we get disfigured or injured men. The sequence in the second response is indeed odd: monsters—huge heads—girl's body. Is this Harold's conception of himself? : his body is not that of a boy and there is something wrong with his head? We will reserve further discussion of this response until later.

CARD VIII   Where do you get all this ink?

| | |
|---|---|
| VIII-1   18″  ∧  2 tigers trying to climb up funny-looking stones. | Stones not on each other—just connected—look like they would fall over. |

W      FM      A, N P

2  ∨  Same tigers going over a cliff.
W      FM      A, N P
55″

His comment (Where do you get all this ink?) was said in a somewhat petulant-quizzical tone of voice. This raises a question to which we have not paid very much attention: How did Harold overtly behave in this situation? Although he was overtly neither aggressive nor assertive, his attitude was not a friendly or warm one. He appeared to comply to directions (to the wishes of the examiner) in a manner which indicated not that he enjoyed what he was doing but that he was doing what was expected of him—it was something he had to or should do. It was this examiner's opinion that Harold felt hostile about the testing situation, but whatever covert hostility he experienced was subordinated to what the examiner, an authority figure, required of him. Overt compliance, however hostilely tinged, was the dominant overt response. Harold's initial comment to this card seemed to be said petulantly, although it was not clear why he said it in this way.

It should not be thought that Harold· appeared merely to be "going through the motions" and that he was not trying—this would be a form of hostile expression of which Harold did not seem capable. In fact, *this examiner was forcibly struck by the contrast between this boy's overt behavior and the "blood and thunder" content of his responses.* It was difficult to avoid the conclusion that (1) the expression of hostility was a conflictful area and (2) in light of the strength of the hostile response the strength of the defense against such a response would have to be unusually strong and pervasive. We shall discuss this point again later.

Nothing new is introduced by consideration of the formal responses. What becomes somewhat more striking is the strength of the rigid and compulsive tendencies.

CARD IX

IX-1  10″  ∧  6 men doing a . . .   None of these look exactly like peo-
       standing on each other's      ple—can't expect ink to drop and
       heads in circus.              look like a man.

       W    M    H
    2  ∨  Same thing—except some-   I don't know what is dripping. If
       thing is dripping from top of   my sister were here you couldn't
       them.                          ask her. (Why not?) She would
                                      be looking at doll house.
       W     M     H
       1′3″

In this card we get two more indirect expressions of hostility toward the situation. He somewhat petulantly says, "You can't expect ink to drop and look like a man"—as if he resents the examiner's questions in the inquiry. It should be emphasized that it was not what he said but how he said it which conveyed to the examiner the impression that Harold was irritable. In the inquiry of the second response it is as if Harold is saying: "I answer your questions even though I don't like them—my sister wouldn't listen to you—I do what you say—she wouldn't." One could also speculate whether Harold is at this point expressing hostility toward his sister: she is interested in doll houses; he isn't. However one interprets his statement one would not be likely to interpret it as indicative of a lack of control over expression of aggressive feeling. While it is to his credit that Harold can express *some* hostility, it is the discrepancy between the strength of the covert hostile response and the degree of its overt expression that forces one to conclude that the *"some"* that he can express is pitifully inadequate.

CARD X

X-1  5″ Tiny animals seen through   Like amoeba. (Why through a
     microscope.                     microscope?) Nothing shaped like
                                      like that which you can see with-
       D     F     A                 out a microscope.

2  Still looks like it—either ani-        I don't know—they are not on the
   mals are flying or under water.         ground—look    under    water—
                                           couldn't fly under microscope.
   D     FM     A

What should be noted is that this nine-year-old boy knows about
amoebas and microscopes. Also, it should be noted that *the major
source of stimulation to Harold in this situation was not the objective
characteristics of the cards (color, shading) but his own prepotent personal needs.* The discrepancy between the frequency of color and shading, on the one hand, and movement responses, on the other hand, is
so great that it would be surprising if awareness of the needs and feelings of others was a characteristic of Harold. One would expect him to
be much more aware of self than of others—as in his interaction with
the examiner: neither friendly, nor warm, nor responsive to the examiner, who from the start of the interaction liked and was intrigued
by Harold.

In our card-by-card analysis of this protocol we endeavored to pay
most attention to the significances of Harold's verbal responses, formal
(scored) or informal (unscored). Although we indicated briefly what
seemed to be the relation between his covert and overt behavior in this
situation, and how these relationships seemed to fit in with our conclusions based on other considerations, we feel that the examiner's use
of his observations of Harold's behavior has been incompletely described. We shall now attempt to describe in greater detail the nature
of this interaction—from the standpoint of the examiner as well as the
subject. Without such a description the process whereby alternative explanations are weighed, and diagnostic decisions made, must remain
obscure.

Harold was referred for an independent evaluation of the need for
psychotherapy. All that the examiner was told by the referring psychiatrist was that Harold was bright. He was brought for examination
by his mother. Harold appeared short for his age and wore extremely
thick glasses from which he seemed to peer as if one were at a distance
from him. When the examiner first met him and his mother, Harold
avoided looking at the examiner. Throughout the interaction Harold
did not appear to make an attempt to be friendly or to reveal *spontaneously* personal feeling. It was not that Harold was unfriendly; it
was as if he was not sure how to be friendly. From the very beginning

the examiner felt that this boy was very much aware of himself in relation to the examiner and that his self-awareness in some way inhibited
overt responsiveness. As was indicated earlier, the examiner liked Harold from the start, largely because of the cute and adult-like way he
peered at one through his thick glasses. The examiner early began to
ask himself: Why isn't he more responsive?

Harold was first given the 1937 Binet (L) and it became quickly
apparent that he was an *extremely* bright boy. His I.Q. was 182—the
brightest boy this examiner has ever seen. He talked like an adult, he
thought like an adult—it was extremely difficult for the examiner to
bear in mind that Harold was nine years old. Harold was the epitome
of the stereotype of the little "genius": undersized, pyknic build, thick
glasses, and most unchildlike in his thinking. His handwriting, however, was poorer than one would expect from a nine-year-old and in
general his motor movements seemed clumsy. When queried about
hobbies, he told of his interest in astronomy and reading. When asked
about sports, he said he liked baseball but he was too young to play and
went on to say that the other boys did not like him. He indicated that
he did not have many friends. It was on the basis of such statements,
in addition to Harold's behavior in the testing situation, that the examiner concluded that Harold did not know how (whatever the reasons) or found it very difficult to initiate and maintain an interpersonal
"give and take." That he covertly desired to do so seemed clear but it
was equally clear that he had difficulty doing so.

By the time the Rorschach was administered the examiner had come
to the following conclusions:

1. The only sources of personal satisfaction available to this boy are
of an "intellectual" nature, and these (like astronomy and reading) are
probably of a solitary rather than an interpersonal nature.

2. While his brightness brings him the praise of adults, it is very
likely that many of his peers resent and dislike him.

3. Because of his size, relatively poor vision, and clumsy motor movements, it is very likely that Harold has strong feelings of physical inadequacy which would be reinforced by the retaliatory attitudes of his
more athletic peers. In this connection it should be noted that when
asked what he wanted to be when he grew up, Harold said: "a baseball
player"—a response which the examiner felt was pathetic.

4. Harold seems to be a boy who would be unable or afraid to handle

any physical aggression directed toward him by his peers or to respond with physical aggression to verbal insults or taunts. Only in the realm of intellectual activity would one expect him to allow himself to be aggressive or competitive.

It was small wonder that when the Rorschach was administered the examiner was no little surprised at the content of the responses. From his behavior in the clinical interaction, as well as his physical appearance, one could not conclude that this content was directly mirrored in Harold's overt behavior. Although he occasionally displayed hostility—in an indirect fashion—the discrepancy between what he could display and what he apparently experienced was too marked to suggest that he could at all easily express such strong feeling. It could be argued that Harold's strong hostile drives were not overtly expressed in this interaction because the examiner was an authority figure. With other kinds of people his overt behavior might be far more hostile and uncontrolled. This possibility was rejected for several reasons:

1. The fact that he does inhibit aggressive behavior in the presence of an authority figure indicates that he does have learned antithetical tendencies against aggressive behavior which could be generalized to other kinds of figures. We are not dealing with a boy whose unacceptable tendencies are inhibited only when an external figure threatens punishment if they are expressed.

2. The content of his responses reflected tendencies against aggressive behavior which appeared to be of great strength. This was not a protocol in which only aggressive content was given.

3. The fact that his responses reflected feelings of bodily inadequacy and a fear of bodily injury, in addition to his obvious physical limitations (undersized, glasses, clumsiness), would also serve to make aggressive display very difficult.

4. His rigid and compulsive tendencies indicate not only the strength of unacceptable tendencies but the presence of strong defenses. The presence and strength of his defensive reactions further indicate that many hostile thoughts and fantasies have become unconscious and are consciously expressed in an indirect and disguised fashion.

Having concluded that Harold cannot give overt expression to his hostile feelings, we are still left with the question: How do his hostile feelings affect his attitudes toward and relationships with others? There is another question, however, which should be considered first:

What are Harold's attitudes toward or conceptions of himself? This examiner feels that the answer is succinctly given in the second response to card VII: He has a monstrous head and an inadequate body. He would rather have an adequate body than a brilliant mind—shades of his wish to become a baseball player! What he wants most is not in line with what he can do best but with what he cannot do at all well. Since he is obviously bright and because of this has undoubtedly experienced some personal satisfactions, it might be more correct to say that he has antithetical or ambivalent attitudes toward his intellectual prowess. Toward his own body his attitudes are almost exclusively of a negative content. What we are here saying is that Harold's self-attitudes have strong derogatory and hostile components—he does not like himself. From his own statement that his peers do not like him, and from our hypothesis (based on the content of his responses) that he tends to view others as hostile, we would conclude that he is probably more aware of the hostility of others toward him than of his hostility toward himself. It is less painful for him to believe that others dislike him than that he dislikes himself. We should not overlook the possibility that, among his peers at least, there is a reality basis which would facilitate the projective reaction. In any event, we would conclude that Harold is unaware of the strength of his self-derogatory attitudes and how these attitudes affect his conception of and relationship to others.

It is clear from the above that the nature of Harold's attitudes toward self and others makes it difficult for him to derive satisfaction from interpersonal contact. Such contact engenders the possibility of rejection (dislike) as well as increases the strength of self-derogatory tendencies. Consequently, he would tend to avoid initiating such contacts, preferring solitary activities (in which he is successful) rather than anxiety-arousing interpersonal contacts where his self-esteem is threatened. However, since he wishes to be successful in physical activities, the success he experiences in his intellectual pursuits is only temporarily satisfying and, by contrast, emphasizes his inadequacies in other spheres.

From all that has been said one would expect that Harold's feelings of bodily inadequacy would affect his conceptions of sexuality. It is not clear just what his conceptions of and attitudes toward sexuality are. One might speculate that it was punishment of his sexual play and curiosity which engendered strong, externally directed hostility which, together with the sexual interests, had to be inhibited. However, we do not feel it necessary to try to spell out this boy's conceptions of and attitudes toward sexuality. In terms of the reason for referral we feel that the need for psychotherapy is clearly indicated and that further analysis (which would be too speculative) would not change the nature of the interpretation or recommendation. The most important and relevant conclusion that can be made in this case is that this boy has conflicts, the handling of which does not reduce but rather reinforces the degree of his unhappiness—his preferred modes of handling his interpersonal and intrapersonal conflicts are maladaptive and self-defeating.

In subsequent discussions with the mother and referring psychiatrist it became evident that Harold had no friends, was not accepted by peers, and could not compete with them other than in the classroom. His family was concerned with his social isolation, which they felt was making him increasingly unhappy. Even in school, where he was in the fourth grade, Harold enjoyed few satisfactions. According to the mother, Harold's teachers did not particularly like him and resolved the problems caused by his brightness by leaving him alone. It was not that they treated him like other children but that they paid less attention to him. The only activities he enjoyed were solitary in nature. He did not (could not) participate in athletic activities. The mother reported that Harold was becoming increasingly irritable, moody, and unhappy and felt the need for outside guidance. She felt that something had to be done if this boy was to be able successfully and satisfactorily to be and compete with other children. Analytic therapy was begun and after several months it was the therapist's judgment that the Rorschach interpretation had been essentially correct.

Mrs. C    C. A. 41 years

Mrs. C was forty-one years of age, married, and had two children. She had first been seen in a neurological clinic to which she had been referred because of what seemed to be psychomotor epilepsy: she would become aware that she was "blacking out," would feel her arms and legs begin to stiffen, and would then black out, during which time she would become overactive, throwing things around and upsetting the furniture. According to the physician it was not clear whether Mrs. C really blacked out completely. The medical report also indicated that Mrs. C was concerned about her sexual frigidity, which presumably was of long standing. Her marriage was considered a very unhappy one, the details of which were not known. As part of a research project on epilepsy she was referred for psychological evaluation and possible psychotherapy. Following testing she was seen psychotherapeutically by the writer. Diagnostic testing was carried out by a graduate student under the writer's supervision.

CARD I

I-1    5″ That looks like a butterfly.

W    F    A    P

The wings there, this is the body. And that looks like an angel, without a head; her wings out here.

2    Someone dancing, her dress up in her hands, swirling around her feet.

W    M−    H

It looks like a dancing lady, her arms out, holding part of her skirt up. Her skirt is flaring out.

3    Something like a bat, too.

W    FM    A

It looks like a bat when it sits on a wall. (How do you mean?) With its wings outspread, and its head down. (Where is its head?) (Indicates bottom of card.) They hang upside down. (Reminded?) The outspread wings.

4    Looks like an angel without a head.

78″ W    F    A

(W; see above under 1)

389

The first question that might be asked is why Mrs. C only gives W responses. The fact that she gives more than one W suggests that whatever her conception of the task may be it does not prevent her from changing the content of her responses to the same area. However, that there are limitations to this apparent flexibility is suggested by two things: (1) In all the responses the center area is always the body and (2) the butterfly and bat have similar configurations of form (although she does see the center area of the bat differently from the way most people do), and the dancing lady and angel likewise are not very different from each other. In other words, we do not feel that her productivity reflects a genuine creative process—there is a restriction in range of content. It may be that Mrs. C feels that she must give more than one response to the card but there is no evidence to support this possibility. At this point we do not know what her conception of the task is.

What is the significance of the minus response? Part of the response (the body area) is acceptable but the rest of it is not at all clearly delineated. Why should the minus show up with this particular content? Having raised this question we are forcibly struck by certain facts about Mrs. C's appearance and behavior. The most glaring characteristic of Mrs. C is her obesity; she weighs approximately 250 pounds. Overtly, she appeared to be an unassertive, not very spontaneous woman who passively complied with the requirements of the testing situation. It is in light of these facts that one may conclude that the content of her second response describes an activity of which our subject is incapable but which she undoubtedly wishes she could perform. In addition, there are sexual overtones to the response: the dancing lady is *holding her skirt up*. Even if this particular phrase had not been verbalized we would have raised the sexual problem because dancing and sexuality are frequently associated with each other. The fact that the minus response was given with no apparent hesitation or affective concomitants, and there was no indication that Mrs. C was aware of the irrational elements in the response, suggests that certain tendencies have been inadequately defended against and continue, despite their being unconscious, to receive indirect conscious expression and interfere with reality testing. We would assume that it is sexual wishes and attitudes which are unconscious, although we do not know why such tendencies are unacceptable or dangerous. The fact that she has always been frigid would also lead one to make such an assumption. If one assumes that her obesity represents a reaction to severe frustration, then might her overt passivity and compliance indicate that it is strong hostility (and aggressive sexual wishes) against which she defends herself? Are her epileptic episodes engendered by exacerbation of her aggressive drives?

CARD II

II-1  4″ A couple of bears kissing (laughs) or dogs.

W    M    A    P

Their mouths here, these could be the ears (usual). (What gave you the impression of bears?) The shape of the mouths here, it's round (indicating under side of jaw).

2  36″ Looks like a dancing girl up there to me.

Dd    M—    FC, FC′    H

(See tracing) Tall headdress, the middle part of her body is bare, and the skirt goes down here, the same color as the headdress. (What gave you that impression?) Bare midriff. (What about that reminded you of a dancing girl?) I don't know—in India, they dance with thin dresses. (She also indicated, earlier, that most of the skirt is hidden by the "bear.")

3  Looks like a butterfly down here.

45″ D    F    A

Down here. (Reminded?) Just the outline of it.

In light of our discussion of card I we are struck by the appearance of another minus response involving another dancing woman, except here the sexual aspects of the response are more blatant. Are her unconscious sexual attitudes of an exhibitionistic, assertive content? Are these the unacceptable wishes and fantasies against which she had to defend—defenses which generalized to the expression of all strong aggressive drives? Does her statement that they dance that way "in India" reflect a denial that she (an American) is capable of such an activity? Does her laughter at the kissing dogs likewise indicate how alien such an activity is to her? It is likely that her preoccupation with her frigidity—with what she cannot do or enjoy—is a reflection of the strength of her unconscious sexual wishes, which probably have a strong assertive, hostile component. One would not doubt that Mrs. C is physically unattractive and regards herself as such. Then why has she allowed herself to become so fat? Why such self-defeating, self-punishing, and unrealistic behavior? We would conclude that whatever the conflicts and their dynamics, Mrs. C's control over them is poor. We should not overlook, however, that when nonsexual content is given her reality testing is adequate.

It is not surprising from what we have said to find that Mrs. C's responses are largely determined by internal rather than external factors. Aside from the Indian girl her responses reflect internal determinants rather than external ones.

CARD III

III-1  7″ Looks like two men in evening dress.

D    F    H

(Usual) Head, dark coat and trousers. (Why evening dress, more than some other?) They look like waiters to me, I don't know why.

2  Something like a pelvis bone there.

D    F    At

(Center red) (Impression?) The outline. (Traces around it with finger without speaking, rather thoughtfully?)

3  Looks like a couple of clowns.

D    M    H

(Lateral red) Tall hats, just to make people laugh, and he has a cigar in his mouth too, and is going through the antics of a clown. (And the rest of his body?) Something to do with his hands, here. (And is the whole body shown?) Yes.

Why does her behavior change in the second response so that the examiner considers it unusual and makes note of it? We are not surprised that the content is sexual or physical. She becomes thoughtful, although we have no idea what she is thinking about. Although we do not think the response warrants a minus scoring, it certainly is not as well delineated as her first or third responses to this card.

In the first card we suggested that the responses did not seem to reflect a genuine creative process—there seemed to be a restriction in the range of content. Although this hypothesis is not supported by the content in cards II and III, we should note that in the last two cards, where the areas are more or less noncontiguous, she relinquishes the card after each area has been explained. She does not attempt to give more responses although her approach to card I indicates that she could respond more than once to the same area. Her approach to cards II and III suggests some kind of restrictive tendency, the causes of which are not clear.

CARD IV

IV-1  9″ The head of an animal with horns. (Slightly queer tone of voice)

(Lateral projections D4 are horns; whole thing is the head)

DW      F—      Ad

2  19″ Look like the pelt of an animal that's left to dry.

W      cF      Aobj

They remove the fur pelt, tack it up to a board to dry. (What there reminds you of fur?) Well, the shade, lighter and darker like fur.

3  41″ Something like (word missed) boots down here. (Like what?) Fur boots they wear in the old country.

D      Fc      Clothing

Sometimes you see them in pictures from Europe even today. (Up to the knees.) (Why furry?) They're shaggy sort of, and shaded too.

4  62″ Looks like a face up here of a Mongolian ruler or something.

78″ Dd      Fc      Hd

These slit eyes, and sort of headgear there, and beard down here, a very stern expression.

In terms of reality testing, the first response is the poorest she has yet given. We consider this a confabulation: She starts with a recognizable detail (the horns) and uncritically uses the remainder of the card. Because she is attracted to the projections, and in light of all that we have previously said, we are inclined to conclude that the inadequacy of this response is related to the interfering effects of unconscious sexual drives. Note that her tone of voice changes—a fact which we do not consider fortuitous. In any event, we are struck by the strong evidence of in-

adequate reality testing in this woman. We consider this serious because it indicates that her control over the overt expression (be that expression direct or indirect) of strong conflictful feelings will be poor.
We would predict that in a stressful situation which engenders these
conflicts Mrs. C's behavior will be irrational. But such predictions are
not particularly meaningful unless we attempt to specify Mrs. C's conscious conflicts. We already know that Mrs. C is preoccupied with her
frigidity. Presumably she views this as *her* inadequacy and is consciously unaware of the reasons for it. Not only is she sexually less adequate than other women but she is also much more physically unattractive. We would assume that her self-attitudes are derogatory in the extreme. What we are saying is that her conscious sexual conflicts are not
between unacceptable and acceptable tendencies but rather between
acceptable tendencies and the inability to carry them out successfully.
Her unacceptable sexual tendencies, we deduce, are unconscious—their
strength being reflected in her frigidity and inadequate reality testing
in this area. If she consciously views her sexual problem in a self-derogatory manner, we would then expect that as the problem becomes
more severe the self-aggressive tendencies will become stronger and
beyond her control.

But this woman is married, and unhappily so. We assume that her
frigidity and obesity are factors in this problem area. If this woman has
been rejected by her husband, then we expect that she in turn has experienced hostility toward him. We also would expect that her obesity
has engendered critical and caustic reactions from others which in turn
have reinforced the strength of her hostility tendencies. We would predict that the handling of strong conscious hostility, toward self and
others, is this woman's core problem. If, as we hypothesized earlier, the
unacceptable unconscious tendencies involved assertive, aggressive
activity, then the conscious experience of hostility would be determined
not only by external factors but by internal (unconscious) ones as well.
Although the sexual and hostile tendencies are probably aspects of the
same problem, we would expect her major conscious problem to be
largely concerned with hostility.

The fourth response, the Mongolian ruler, brings to our attention
that Mrs. C describes men and women differently. Her women (two
dancing ladies and the angel) are more "positively" described than are
the men: a stern ruler, a clown, waiters. While such content (in con-

trast to how women are described) 'suggests hostile attitudes toward men, we are most impressed by the stern, male, authority figure. We consider this response a reflection of a tendency antithetical to the expression of hostility toward authority figures in particular. Toward her husband, for example, we would expect her to have difficulty expressing aggression, especially if he is an assertive character.

It is to Mrs. C's credit that despite beginning with an unusually poor response she is able subsequently to respond adequately and to be aware of and responsive to the characteristics of the external stimulus.

## CARD V

V-1  7″ *That* looks like a bat. (Holds card and examines it carefully.)

The head up, the feet down, the wings outspread. (Reminded?) The wings outspread.

29″  W     F     H     P

Her emphasis on the word "that" indicates that she was not particularly satisfied with her first bat response (card I). It will be recalled that in the first card we wondered if her giving of four whole responses reflected her conception of the task rather than a spontaneous flexibility in reorganizing the blot area. The fact that she now tells us that she did not see the first bat too clearly supports the contention that she may have felt compelled to give more than one response. It is to her credit that despite this presumed set she was able to describe the bat in card I in an unusual and adequate fashion. In other words, she was able to overcome her uncertainty and to respond.

## CARD VI

VI     Reject in 36″
       36″ I don't see anything.

(Suppose you look it over a little longer, and see if . . .) This looks something like a newel post, at the bottom of a staircase (the inner only).

D     F     obj

## CARD VII

VII    Reject in 48″ (after examining it carefully with back-

(Make out anything on that?) The only thing I could possibly see is

and-forth head movements)  the head of a prehistoric animal—
48″ I don't see anything.   sharp things stick up here, and
            look like the mouth open.

D  FM  Hd

To both of these cards Mrs. C appeared to be trying to respond—her overt behavior did not suggest that she was suppressing responses because of their unacceptable content. Her inability to respond to the two cards is the clearest indication thus far of how strong are the inhibitory tendencies in this woman. Put in another way: Whatever the unconscious conflicts which were engendered here, they were of such strength that extreme defensive reactions were necessary to prevent their conscious expression. Although the unconscious conflicts are kept in check, *Mrs. C cannot at all handle the problem-solving situation with which she is confronted.* We have previously hypothesized that Mrs. C's unconscious conflicts interfere with the adequacy of her reality testing— that despite defensive reactions they receive an indirect conscious expression in the process of which her critical judgment is markedly affective. In light of cards VI and VII we would now say that exacerbation of unconscious conflicts either results in irrational or uncontrolled behavior or in extreme impotence—both reactions can be expected not to resolve her conscious tensions but to increase them.

We would assume that it was an unconscious sexual conflict which was exacerbated in these cards. This assumption is made on two grounds: (1) We have previously seen that her reality testing suffered and her behavior changed (cards III and IV) when her responses were sexual in nature; (2) when she responds in the inquiry to card VI, it is to the "penis area"—describing a long, hard object; in card VII she describes a prehistoric animal which has "sharp things sticking up." Does she associate the penis (masculinity) with pain—something which did, can, or does harm her? If one makes this assumption, one would expect her to have experienced a great deal of hostility toward men—an expectation we deduced from the different ways in which she describes men and women. But since we have hypothesized that it is extremely difficult for Mrs. C to express the conscious hostility she experiences, strengthened though that is by unconscious hostile-sexual tendencies, we conclude that Mrs. C is in an almost constant state of tension. But one might then ask: Why did she not appear tense and anxious in the clinical interaction? Our answer would be that since Mrs. C was coming for help with her problems, and the examiner was a permissive, sympathetic authority figure, there was little basis for hostility and tension to be experienced. Our prediction is that when her hostility is engendered—and we would expect that in "real life" this would be frequent—her inadequacies are most glaringly apparent. We should not overlook the possibility that Mrs. C's compliant, passive behavior in this situation is a reflection of how she responds to new interpersonal interactions. She lacks the self-confidence or security to be assertive, personally revealing, or spontaneous. In fact, it is the discrepancy between the overt (what was observed) and the covert (her formal responses) that makes us feel that Mrs. C's adjustment is of an extremely precarious sort. Although we have no way of answering the question, we ask ourselves: Is there a relation between her hostility and seizures?

CARD VIII

VIII-1  7" Bears climbing up the side of a hill (hm?) . . . they're climbing.

D    FM    A    P

Here are the legs, the tail, head. They're climbing. (And the hill, was that a part of it?) No, I don't see the hill—they're just climbing.

2  22" Butterfly down here.

44" D    F, FC, Fc    Pl

Down here—outspread wings and center part of body. (What about that made you think of a butterfly?) The wings and coloring.

For the first time Mrs. C's responses to a card raise no question about sexuality, hostility, and reality testing. Although she uses color (and perhaps shading) in the second response, it should be noted that it was not given spontaneously but came after a second (and unjustified) question. We might point out here that responsiveness to the external stimulus (in the sense of using color and shading) was usually given far less quickly (and spontaneously) than the personal, subjective kind of response. Although Mrs. C is aware of and responsive to what is "out there," it is a far less prepotent response tendency than the subjective one.

CARD IX

IX-1  7″ Looks like something out
      of a medical book (laughs
      slightly). (Examines card,
      shaking head.)

      50″ W    CF    At

(Why was that?) Oh, sometimes in
medical books you see different
parts of the body in different colors, it's just the colors—I wouldn't
know what those parts were.

Why she laughs and shakes her head we do not know—she does not
easily communicate what she feels. It is not surprising that this behavior
is associated with anatomical content. This is a rather diffuse response
which reveals again how the adequacy of her response is a function of
the content. Note that in card IV (first response) she responds quickly
and poorly. In card IX she again responds quickly—not poorly but
vaguely. We consider this an indication of impulsivity—a tendency
which would facilitate the expression of strong feeling. This is a record
in which there are very strong indications of inhibitory as well as uncontrolled (minus responses, impulsivity) tendencies.

CARD X

X-1  2″ Spiders.

     D    F    A    P

(Popular) With all their legs.

2   11″ Mice—animals, that's all
    I'm seeing!

     D    F    A

(Lateral brown) Here, with a long
nose.

3   Birds.

     D    FM      A
     D    FM(M?)    A

(Top green) Birds flying, and parrots in here (the grey). (Reminded?) I don't know—they're
not flying, because their wings are
not out—the shape of the head,
the beak. (And what about these
made you think of the parrots?)
The shape of the head; they're
talking, their mouths are open.

4   45″ Canaries

     D    FC    A

The color down here reminds me
of canaries. I think it's the color
more than anything else.

It is not clear what she means by her comment in the second response. If it refers to what she has previously given to the other cards, it is clearly not a true statement. If it refers to the fact that she has given spiders and now mice, we do not know the significance of the comment. We do not feel justified in speculating further.

What is perhaps worthy of comment is that there is no sexual or anatomical content and, as in cards VIII and V, there is no question of adequacy of reality testing.

In her first therapeutic interview Mrs. C spoke almost exclusively about her hatred for her husband. According to her report, it was while she was in the hospital having her second child (eight years previously) that her husband first began going with other women. Although he has continued to go with other women, he has also continued to demand that Mrs. C have sexual relations with him. Although she resents bitterly his demandingness, she always submits. She does not enjoy the experiences in the slightest and afterwards experiences violent, hostile feelings toward herself and her husband. Aside from demanding sexual relations, her husband shows no interest in her.

Mrs. C. spontaneously stated that she should leave her husband but felt she could not do so because of her children, the feeling that she could not obtain or compete with younger girls for a job, and the fact that she could not expect any help from her family. She had married against the strong opposition of her father. Occasionally she visits her family, during which time her father's behavior is cold and formal.

Mrs. C's description of her seizures was as described earlier. From her description it did not seem as if she completely blacked out. She described in detail some of her acts during the seizures: throwing and smashing dishes, pulling the mattresses off the bed, upsetting chairs, etc. When she was asked if her seizures tended to occur at any particular time, she indicated that they usually came on after her hatred toward her husband had come to the fore.

Throughout this hour, and even during the times she was expressing the strongest hostility toward her husband, Mrs. C's overt behavior did not reflect the strength of her feeling. She spoke easily, did not appear to be suppressing any feeling—but the discrepancy between what she was saying and what she apparently was feeling was striking. At the end of the hour she indicated that she wanted to continue the interviews—she felt things could not go on as they were—and another appointment was made.

During the next three interviews Mrs. C emphasized her need to leave her husband. Having said this she would then dwell on her inability to take such a step. Before leaving the office at the end of the fourth interview she stated somewhat emphatically that she knew she had to leave her husband.

Mrs. C did not keep the next appointment and subsequently sent a message with her older child that she would not be able to come for any more interviews. Approximately a year later Mrs. C was admitted to the hospital with a cracked skull. Her husband, according to initial reports, had hit her with a hatchet after she had attacked him with a knife. Because the police were unable to determine just what had taken place, the husband, who was at first arrested, was released and "the case closed."

SOME FINAL COMMENTS

We would like to make clear that the primary reason for the card-by-card presentations was to attempt to make explicit the nature of the interpretive process. This attempt reflects the conviction that far too little is known about what a clinician does and thinks in regard to different aspects of a particular protocol. In the past a major concern of investigators has been the validity of the clinician's conclusions. While this is obviously an important problem, the amount of attention given to it has obscured the extent of our ignorance concerning how a clinician arrives at these conclusions, i.e., to what he responds in a patient's behavior, the basis for his deductions, and the status of the assumptions which determine his own selective attending to the behavior of others. It is our contention that the disappointing degree of validity of clinical descriptions and predictions—and there are few clinicians who are at all satisfied with the scientific status of their practices—is in part due to our failure to study the details of the functioning of the clinician. If we do not know what clinicians do—if there are wide differences in how clinicians arrive at their conclusions—we are in effect indicating what perhaps are some of the most important sources of the unreliability of clinicians' conclusions and predictions.

While it is important for the clinician to demonstrate that he can make valid descriptions and predictions, the scientific significance of his efforts can be legitimately questioned if he cannot demonstrate that the manner in which he arrived at his conclusions is sufficiently explicit so that other clinicians can repeat his procedures with similar results. In our card-by-card presentations we were only very secondarily concerned with the problem of validity and primarily focused on the details of the interpretive process. For reasons stated at the beginning of the chapter we are not particularly satisfied with the clarity or completeness of our efforts. One can only hope that as students become better trained to recognize and describe the relation of their thinking to the conclusions they draw, the "communication" problem will be less thorny than it now is. When such advances will have been made we will then be in the position to compare the interpretive procedures of different clinicians with the same data, with the aim of determining not only the kinds of valid conclusions which can be drawn but the manner in which they are arrived at. One might predict that as the interpretive process becomes more explicit the inadequacies of our present means of categorization (i.e., scoring systems) will become more clear and changed so as to reflect more realistically how the data are actually used by the clinician.

# Bibliography

1. Alden, P., and Benton, A. L. Relationship of sex of examiner to incidence of Rorschach responses with sexual content. *Journal of Projective Techniques,* 1951, *15*:231–234.
2. Alexander, F., and French, T. M. *Psychoanalytic therapy.* New York: Ronald Press, 1946.
3. Allen, R. M. The influence of color in the Rorschach test on reaction time in a normal population. *Journal of Projective Techniques,* 1951, *15*:481–485.
4. Allen, R. M. *Introduction to the Rorschach technique.* New York: International Universities Press, 1953.
5. Allen, R. M., Manne, S. H., and Stiff, M. The role of color in Rorschach's test: a preliminary normative report on a college student population. *Journal of Projective Techniques,* 1951, *15*:235–242.
6. Ames, L. B., Learned, J., Metraux, R. W., and Walker, R. N. *Child Rorschach responses.* New York: Hoeber, 1952.
7. Aronson, M. L., A Rorschach study of the Freudian theory of paranoia. *Journal of Projective Techniques,* 1952, *16*:397–411.
8. Atkinson, J. W., and McClelland, D. C. The projective expression of needs: II. The effect of different intensities of the hunger drive on thematic apperception. *Journal of Experimental Psychology,* 1948, *38*:643–658.
9. Auld, F. *The influence of social class on tests of personality.* Madison (N. J.): Drew University Studies, 1952, 40, No. 4.
10. Auld, F. Influence of social class on personality test responses. *Psychological Bulletin,* 1952, *49*:318–332.
11. Bach, G. R. Young children's play fantasies. *Psychological Monographs,* 1945, 59, No. 2.
12. Baker, L. M., and Harris, J. S. The validation of Rorschach test results against laboratory behavior. *Journal of Clinical Psychology,* 1949, *5*:161–164.
13. Bandura, A. A study of some of the psychological processes associated with the Rorschach white space response. Unpublished thesis, Iowa University Library, 1952.
14. Baum, M. H. A study in concept attainment and verbal learning. Unpublished Ph.D. thesis, Yale University Library, 1951.
15. Beck, S. J. Configurational tendencies in Rorschach responses. *American Journal of Psychology,* 1933, *45*:433–443.

16. Beck, S. J. *Rorschach's test.* Vol. I. New York: Grune and Stratton, 1944.

17. Beck, S. J. *Rorschach's test.* Vol. II. New York: Grune and Stratton, 1946.

18. Beck, S. J., Rabin, A. I., Thiesen, W. G., Molish, H., and Thetford, W. N. The normal personality as projected in the Rorschach test. *Journal of Psychology,* 1950, *30*:241–298.

19. Bell, J. E. *Projective techniques.* New York: Longmans, Green, 1948.

20. Binder, H. *Die helldunkeldeutungen im psychodiagnostischen experiment von Rorschach.* Zurich: Art. Institut Orell Fussli, 1932. English summary in *Rorschach Research Exchange,* 1937, *2*:37–42.

21. Blum, G. *Psychoanalytic theories of personality.* New York: McGraw-Hill, 1953.

22. Bradway, K., and Heisler, V. The relation between diagnoses and certain types of extreme deviations and content on the Rorschach. *Journal of Projective Techniques,* 1953, *17*:70–74.

23. Bray, D. W. The prediction of behavior from two attitude scales. Unpublished Ph.D. thesis, Yale University Library, 1948.

24. Cameron, N., and Magaret, A. *Behavior pathology.* Boston: Houghton Mifflin, 1951.

25. Cantril, H. *Gauging public opinion.* Princeton: Princeton University Press, 1944.

26. Carlson, V. R., and Lazarus, R. S. A repetition of Meyer Williams' study of intellectual control under stress and associated Rorschach factors. *Journal of Consulting Psychology,* 1953, *17*:247–253.

27. Coffin, T. E. Some conditions of suggestion and suggestibility: a study of certain attitudinal and situational factors influencing the process of suggestion. *Psychological Monographs,* 1941, 53, No. 4.

28. Coleman, J. V. The initial phase of psychotherapy. *Bulletin of the Menninger Clinic,* 1949, *13*:189–197.

29. Coombs, A. W. The use of personal experience in Thematic Apperception Test stories. *Journal of Clinical Psychology,* 1946, *2*:357–363.

30. Covner, B. J. Studies in the phonographic recordings of verbal material. I. The use of phonographic recordings in counseling practice and research; II. A transcribing device. *Journal of Consulting Psychology,* 1946, *6*:105–113, 149–153.

31. Cox, N., and Sarason, S. B. Test anxiety and Rorschach performance. *Journal of Abnormal and Social Psychology.* In press, 1954.

32. Cronbach, L. J. A validation design for qualitative studies of personality. *Journal of Consulting Psychology,* 1948, *12*:365–374.

33. Cronbach, L. J. Statistical methods applied to Rorschach scores: a review. *Psychological Bulletin,* 1949, *46:*393–429.
34. Dattman, P. E., and Israel, H. E. The order of dominance among conceptual capacities: an experimental test of Heidbreder's hypothesis. *Journal of Psychology,* 1951, *31:*147–160.
35. Davis, A. *Social-class influences upon learning.* Cambridge: Harvard University Press, 1951.
36. Deese, J., and Lazarus, R. S. The effects of psychological stress upon performance: a theoretical analysis and review of recent developments. Unpublished paper.
37. Dubrovner, R. J., Von Lackum, W. J., and Jost, H. A study of the effect of color on productivity and reaction time in the Rorschach test. *Journal of Clinical Psychology,* 1950, *6:*331–336.
38. Eichler, R. M. Experimental stress and alleged Rorschach indices of anxiety. *Journal of Abnormal and Social Psychology,* 1951, *46:*344–355.
39. Elizur, A. Content analysis of the Rorschach with regard to anxiety and hostility. *Rorschach Research Exchange and Journal of Projective Techniques,* 1949, *13:*247–284.
40. Erickson, M. H. Experimental demonstrations of the psychopathology of everyday life. *Psychoanalytic Quarterly,* 1939, *8:*338–353.
41. Eriksen, C. W., Lazarus, R. S., and Strange, J. R. Psychological stress and its personality correlates. *Journal of Personality,* 1952, *20:*277–286.
42. Eron, L. D. A normative study of the Thematic Apperception test. *Psychological Monographs,* 1950, 64, No. 9.
43. Eyesenck, H. J. The effects of psychotherapy. *Journal of Consulting Psychology,* 1952, *16:*319–324.
44. Fenichel, O. *Problems of psychoanalytic technique.* Albany: Psychoanalytic Quarterly, Inc., 1939.
45. Fenichel, O. *The psychoanalytic theory of neurosis.* New York: W. W. Norton, 1945.
46. Feshbach, S. The drive reducing function of fantasy behavior. Unpublished Ph.D. thesis, Yale University Library, 1951.
47. Fonda, C. P. The nature and meaning of the Rorschach white space response. *Journal of Abnormal and Social Psychology,* 1951, *46:*367–377.
48. French, T. M. *The integration of behavior.* Chicago: University of Chicago Press, 1952.
49. Freud, A. *The ego and the mechanisms of defence.* New York: International Universities Press, 1946.
50. Freud, S. Psychoanalytic notes upon an autobiographical account of a

case of paranoia. In *Collected papers,* Vol. II. London: Hogarth Press, 1924.

51. Freud, S. Analysis of a phobia in a five-year-old boy. *Collected papers,* Vol. III. London: Hogarth Press, 1933.

52. Freud, S. The interpretation of dreams. In *The basic writings of Sigmund Freud.* New York: Modern Library, 1938.

53. Freud, S. The psychopathology of everyday life. In *The basic writings of Sigmund Freud.* New York: Modern Library, 1938.

54. Freud, S. *Beyond the pleasure principle.* London: Hogarth Press, 1942.

55. Gardner, R. W. Impulsivity as indicated by Rorschach test factors. *Journal of Consulting Psychology,* 1951, *15*:464–468.

56. Gibby, R. G. The stability of certain Rorschach variables under conditions of experimentally induced sets: 1. The intellectual variables. *Journal of Projective Techniques,* 1951, *15*:3–26.

57. Gill, M., and Brenman, M. Research in psychotherapy (Round table). *American Journal of Orthopsychiatry,* 1948, *18*:100–110.

58. Gladwin, T., and Sarason, S. B. *Truk: man in paradise.* New York: Viking Fund Publications in Anthropology, Vol. 20.

59. Glueck, S., and Glueck, E. *Unraveling juvenile delinquency.* New York: Commonwealth Fund, 1950.

60. Goldfarb, W. A. A definition and validation of obsessional trends in the Rorschach examination of adolescents. *Rorschach Research Exchange* (now the *Journal of Projective Techniques*), 1943, *7*:81–108.

61. Gordon, E., and Sarason, S. B. The relation of test anxiety and other anxieties. Unpublished paper.

62. Grant, M. Q., Ives, V., and Ranzoni, J. H. Reliability and validity of judge's ratings of adjustment on the Rorschach. *Psychological Monographs,* 1952, 66, No. 2.

63. Grinker, R. R., and Spiegel, J. P. *Men under stress.* Philadelphia: Blakiston, 1945.

64. Guilford, J. P. (ed.) U.S. Army Air Forces Aviation Psychology Program Research Report. Printed classification tests. Report No. 5. Washington, D.C.: Government Printing Office, 1927, chap. 24.

65. Gurvitz, M. S. *The dynamics of psychological testing.* New York: Grune and Stratton, 1951.

66. Harrower-Erickson, M. R., and Steiner, M. E. *Large scale Rorschach techniques.* Springfield (Ill.): Charles C. Thomas, 1945.

67. Hartley, E. L., and Hartley, R. E. *Fundamentals of social psychology.* New York: A. A. Knopf, 1952.

68. Heidbreder, E. The attainment of concepts: I. Terminology and methodology. *Journal of General Psychology,* 1946, *35*:173–189.

69. Heidbreder, E. The attainment of concepts: II. The problem. *Journal of General Psychology*, 1946, *35*:191–223.

70. Heidbreder, E. The attainment of concepts: III. The process. *Journal of Psychology*, 1947, *24*:93–138.

71. Hertz, M. R. Rorschach norms for an adolescent age group. *Child Development*, 1935, *6*:69–76.

72. Hertz, M. R. *Frequency tables for scoring responses to the Rorschach inkblot test.* Cleveland, Ohio: Western Reserve University Press, 1st ed., 1936.

73. Hertz, M. R. The shading response in the Rorschach ink-blot test: a review of its scoring and interpretation. *Journal of Genetic Psychology*, 1940, *23*:123–167.

74. Hertz, M. R. Personality patterns in adolescence as portrayed by the Rorschach ink-blot method. I. The movement factors. *Journal of General Psychology*, 1942, *27*:119–188.

75. Hertz, M. R. Suicidal configurations in Rorschach records. *Journal of Projective Techniques*, 1948, *12*:3–58.

76. Hertz, M. R. Further studies of suicidal configurations. *Journal of Projective Techniques*, 1949, *13*:44–73.

77. Hoch, P. H. (ed.) *Failures in psychiatric treatment.* New York: Grune and Stratton, 1948.

78. Holtzman, W. H. Validation studies of the Rorschach test: shyness and gregariousness in the normal superior adult. *Journal of Clinical Psychology*, 1950, *6*:343–347.

79. Holtzman, W. H. Validation studies of the Rorschach test: impulsiveness in the normal superior adult. *Journal of Clinical Psychology*, 1950, *6*:348–351.

80. Howes, D. H., and Solomon, R. F. A note on McGinnies' "Emotionality and perceptual defense." *Psychological Review*, 1950, *57*:229–234.

81. Hutt, M. L. "Consecutive" and "adaptive" testing with the revised Stanford-Binet. *Journal of Consulting Psychology*, 1947, *11*:93–103.

82. Janis, M. G., and Janis, I. L. A supplementary test based on free associations to Rorschach responses. *Rorschach Research Exchange* (now the *Journal of Projective Techniques*), 1946, *10*:1–19.

83. Janoff, I. Z. The relation between Rorschach form quality measures and children's behavior. Unpublished Ph.D. thesis, Yale University Library, 1951.

84. Joel, W. The interpersonal equation in projective methods. *Rorschach Research Exchange and Journal of Projective Techniques*, 1949, *13*: 479–482.

85. Kates, S. L. Objective Rorschach response patterns differentiating

anxiety reactions from obsessive-compulsive reactions. *Journal of Consulting Psychology*, 1950, *14*:226-229.

86. Kelly, E. L., and Fiske, D. W. *The prediction of performance in clinical psychology.* Ann Arbor: University of Michigan Press, 1951.

87. Kent, G. H. *Mental tests in clinics for children.* New York: D. Van Nostrand, 1950.

88. Kimball, A. J. History of form-level appraisal in the Rorschach. *Journal of Projective Techniques*, 1950, *14*:134-152.

89. Kimball, A. J. Evaluation of form level in the Rorschach. *Journal of Projective Techniques*, 1950, *14*:219-244.

90. Klatskin, E. H. An analysis of the effect of the test situation upon the Rorschach record: formal scoring characteristics. *Journal of Projective Techniques*, 1952, *16*:193-199.

91. Klein, G. S., and Schlesinger, H. J. Perceptual attitudes toward instability. I. Prediction of apparent movement experiences from Rorschach responses. *Journal of Personality*, 1951, *19*:289-302.

92. Klopfer, B., and Kelley, D. Mc. *The Rorschach technique.* New York: World Book Company, 1942.

93. Krugman, J. I. A clinical validation of the Rorschach with problem children. *Rorschach Research Exchange* (now the *Journal of Projective Techniques*), 1942, *5*:61-70.

94. Kubie, L. S. Problems in clinical research (Round table). *American Journal of Orthopsychiatry*, 1947, *17*:196-203.

95. Lazarus, R. S. The influence of color on the protocol of the Rorschach test. *Journal of Abnormal and Social Psychology*, 1949, *44*:506-516.

96. Lazarus, R. S., Yousem, H., and Arenberg, D. Hunger and perception. *Journal of Personality*, 1953, *21*:312-328.

97. Lindner, R. M. Content analysis in Rorschach work. *Rorschach Research Exchange* (now the *Journal of Projective Techniques*), 1946, *10*:121-129.

98. Lord, E. Experimentally induced variations in Rorschach performance. *Psychological Monographs*, 1950, 64, No. 10.

99. Mandler, G., and Sarason, S. B. A study of anxiety and learning. *Journal of Abnormal and Social Psychology*, 1952, *47*:166-173.

100. Mandler, G., and Sarason, S. B. The effect of prior experience and subjective failure on the evocation of test anxiety. *Journal of Personality*, 1953, *21*:336-341.

101. Matarazzo, R. G., Watson, R. I., and Ulett, G. A. Relation of Rorschach scoring categories to modes of perception induced by intermittent photic stimulation. *Journal of Clinical Psychology*, 1952, *8*:368-374.

102. McClelland, D. C., and Atkinson, J. W. The projective expression of needs: I. The effect of different intensities of the hunger drive on perception. *Journal of Psychology*, 1948, *25*:205–222.

103. McHugh, G. Changes in I.Q. at the public school kindergarten level. *Psychological Monographs*, 1943, 55, No. 2.

104. McNemar, Q. Book review of "The prediction of performance in clinical psychology." *Journal of Abnormal and Social Psychology*, 1952, *47*:857–886.

105. Meltzoff, J., Singer, J. L., and Korchin, S. J. Motor inhibition and Rorschach movement responses: a test of the sensory-tonic theory. *Journal of Personality*, 1953, *21*:400–410.

106. Meyer, B. T. An investigation of color shock in the Rorschach test. *Journal of Consulting Psychology*, 1951, *7*:367–370.

107. Morris, W. W. Rorschach estimates of personality attributes in the Michigan assessment project. *Psychological Monographs*, 1952, 66, No. 6.

108. Munroe, R. L. Prediction of the adjustment and academic performance of college students. *Applied Psychology Monographs*, 1945, No. 7.

109. Murray, H. A. Clinical research (Round table). *American Journal of Orthopsychiatry*, 1947, *17*:203–210.

110. Palmer, J. O. A dual approach to Rorschach validation. *Psychological Monographs*, 1951, 65, No. 325.

111. Pascal, G. R., and Herzberg, F. I. The detection of deviant sexual practice from performance on the Rorschach test. *Journal of Projective Techniques*, 1952, *16*:366–373.

112. Pascal, G. R., Ruesch, H. A., Devine, C. A., and Suttell, B. J. A study of genital symbols on the Rorschach test. *Journal of Abnormal and Social Psychology*, 1950, *45*:286–295.

113. Perlman, J. A. Color and the validity of the Rorschach. *Journal of Consulting Psychology*, 1951, *15*:122–126.

114. Piotrowski, Z. The M, FM, and m responses as indicators of changes in the personality. *Rorschach Research Exchange* (now the *Journal of Projective Techniques*), 1936–37, *1*:148–157.

115. Pittluck, P. The relation between aggressive fantasy and overt behavior. Unpublished Ph.D. thesis, Yale University Library, 1950.

116. Postman, L., Bronson, W. C., and Gropper, G. L. Is there a mechanism of perceptual defense? *Journal of Abnormal and Social Psychology*, 1953, *48*:215–224.

117. Potter, E. H. An analysis of the effect of temporary situational factors upon Rorschach test results. Unpublished Ph.D. thesis, Yale University Library, 1948.

118. Raimy, V. C. The self-concept as a factor in counseling and personality. Doctoral dissertation, Ohio State University Library, 1943.

119. Raimy, V. C. Self-reference in counseling interviews. *Journal of Consulting Psychology*, 1948, *12*:153–163.

120. Rapaport, D., Gill, M., and Schafer, R. *Diagnostic psychological testing*. Vol. I. Chicago: Year Book Publishers, 1945.

121. Rapaport, D., Gill, M., and Schafer, R. *Diagnostic psychological testing*. Vol. II. Chicago: Year Book Publishers, 1946.

122. Reich, W. *Character analysis*. New York: Orgone Institute Press, 3rd ed., 1949.

123. Reik, T. *Surprise and the psycho-analyst*. New York: Dutton, 1937.

124. Rockwell, F. V., Welch, L., Kubis, J., and Fisichelli, V. Changes in palmer skin resistance during the Rorschach test. I. Color shock and psychoneurotic reactions. *Monthly Review of Psychiatry and Neurology*, 1947, *113*:129–152.

125. Roe, A. Alcohol and creative work. I. Painters. *Quarterly Journal of Studies in Alcohol*, 1946, *6*:415–467.

126. Roe, A. Artists and their work. *Journal of Personality*, 1946, *15*:1–40.

127. Roe, A. Painting and personality. *Rorschach Research Exchange* (now the *Journal of Projective Techniques*), 1946, *10*:86–100.

128. Roe, A. A psychological study of eminent biologists. *Psychological Monographs*, 1951, 65, No. 14.

129. Rogers, C. R. The use of electrically recorded interviews in improving psychotherapeutic techniques. *American Journal of Orthopsychiatry*, 1942, *12*:429–434.

130. Rogers, C. R. *Client centered therapy*. Boston: Houghton Mifflin, 1951.

131. Rust, R. M. Some correlates of the movement response. *Journal of Personality*, 1948, *16*:369–401.

132. Rust, R. M. The Levy Movement Cards. *Journal of Personality*, 1948, *17*:153–156.

133. Sanders, R., and Cleveland, S. E. The relationship between certain examiner personality variables and subjects' Rorschach scores. *Journal of Projective Techniques*, 1953, *17*:34–50.

134. Sappenfield, B. R., and Buker, S. L. Validity of the Rorschach 8–9–10 per cent as an indicator of responsiveness to color. *Journal of Consulting Psychology*, 1949, *13*:268–271.

135. Sarason, E. K. The discriminatory value of the Rorschach Test between two etiologically different, mentally defective groups. Unpublished Ph.D. thesis, Clark University Library, 1950.

136. Sarason, S. B. The TAT and subjective interpretation. *Journal of Consulting Psychology,* 1948, *12:*285–299.
137. Sarason, S. B. The test situation and the problem of prediction. *Journal of Clinical Psychology,* 1950, *6:*387–392.
138. Sarason, S. B. The psychologist's behavior as an area of research. *Journal of Consulting Psychology,* 1951, *15:*278–280.
139. Sarason, S. B. *Psychological problems in mental deficiency.* New York: Harper, 2nd ed., 1953.
140. Sarason, S. B., and Mandler, G. Some correlates of test anxiety. *Journal of Abnormal and Social Psychology,* 1952, 47, 810–817.
141. Sarason, S. B., Mandler, G., and Craighill, P. G. The effect of differential instructions on anxiety and learning. *Journal of Abnormal and Social Psychology,* 1952, 47, 561–565.
142. Sarason, S. B., and Potter, E. H. Color in the Rorschach and Kohs block designs. *Journal of Consulting Psychology,* 1947, *11:*202–206.
143. Sarason, S. B., and Sarason, E. K. The discriminatory value of a test pattern in the high grade familial defective. *Journal of Clinical Psychology,* 1946, *2:*38–49.
144. Sarason, S. B., and Sarason, E. K. The discriminatory value of a test pattern with cerebral palsied defective children. *Journal of Clinical Psychology,* 1947, *3:*141–147.
145. Schachtel, E. G. On color and affect. *Psychiatry,* 1943, *6:*393–409.
146. Schachtel, E. G. Subjective definitions of the Rorschach test situation and their effect on test performance. *Psychiatry,* 1945, *8:*419–448.
147. Schachtel, E. G. Notes on Rorschach tests of 500 juvenile delinquents and a control group of 500 non-delinquent adolescents. *Journal of Projective Techniques,* 1951, *15:*144–172.
148. Schafer, R. *The clinical application of psychological tests.* New York: International Universities Press, 1948.
149. Scheerer, M. Problems of performance analysis in the study of personality. *Annals of the New York Academy of Sciences,* 1946, *46:*653–678.
150. Schumer, F. C. Some behavioral correlates of Rorschach human movement responses. Unpublished Ph.D. thesis, Yale University Library, 1949.
151. Shaffer, G. W., and Lazarus, R. S. *Fundamental concepts in clinical psychology.* New York: McGraw-Hill, 1952.
152. Shaw, B. Sex populars in the Rorschach test. *Journal of Abnormal and Social Psychology,* 1948, *43:*466–470.
153. Sheatsley, P. B. The art of interviewing and a guide to interviewer selection and training. In Jahoda, M., Deutsch, M., and Cook, S. W.

(eds.) *Research methods in social relations.* Part 2: Selected techniques. New York: The Dryden Press, 1951.

154. Sherif, M. A study of some special factors in perception. *Archives of Psychology,* 1935, No. 187.

155. Siipola, E. M. The influence of color on reactions to ink blots. *Journal of Personality,* 1950, *18*:358–382. By permission of Duke University Press.

156. Siipola, E., Kuhns, F., and Taylor, V. Measurement of the individual's reactions to color ink blots. *Journal of Personality,* 1950, *19*:153–171. By permission of Duke University Press.

157. Siipola, E., and Taylor, V. Reactions to ink blots under free and pressure conditions. *Journal of Personality,* 1952, *21*:22–47. By permission of Duke University Press.

158. Singer, J. L., Meltzoff, J., and Goldman, G. D. Rorschach movement responses following motor inhibition and hyperactivity. *Journal of Consulting Psychology,* 1952, *16*:359–364.

159. Staff, Jewish Board of Guardians. *Primary behavior disorder in children.* New York: Family Welfare Association of America, 1945.

160. Stein, H. Scoring movement responses on the Rorschach. *Journal of Projective Techniques,* 1951, *15*:526–533.

161. Stein, M. I. Personality factors involved in the temporal development of Rorschach responses. *Rorschach Research Exchange and Journal of Projective Techniques,* 1949, *13*:355–414.

162. Sullivan, H. S. Notes on investigation, therapy, and education in psychiatry and their relations to schizophrenia. *Psychiatry,* 1947, *10*: 271–280.

163. Taylor, J. A. A personality scale of manifest anxiety. *Journal of Abnormal and Social Psychology,* 1953, *48*:285–290.

164. Terman, L. M., and Merrill, M. A. *Measuring intelligence.* Boston: Houghton Mifflin, 1937.

165. Thorne, F. C. *Principles of personality counseling.* Brandon (Vt.): Journal of Clinical Psychology, 1950.

166. Towbin, A., and Sarason, S. B. Test anxiety and examiner differences: an incidental finding. Unpublished paper.

167. Tucker, J. E. Rorschach movement responses and intelligence. *Journal of Consulting Psychology,* 1950, *14*:283–286.

168. Uehling, H. F. Rorschach "shock" for two special populations. *Journal of Consulting Psychology,* 1952, *16*:224–225.

169. Vernon, P. E. The matching method applied to investigations of personality. *Psychological Bulletin,* 1936, *33*:149–177.

170. Wallen, R. The nature of color shock. *Journal of Abnormal and Social Psychology,* 1948, *43*:346–356.

171. Watson, R. I. *The clinical method in psychology*. New York: Harper, 1951.
172. Wechsler, D. *The measurement of adult intelligence*. Baltimore: Williams and Wilkins, 3rd ed., 1941. (Also see *Journal of Abnormal and Social Psychology*, 1953, *48*:515–524.)
173. Westrope, M. R. An investigation of the relations among Rorschach indices, manifest anxiety, and performance under stress. Unpublished thesis, University of Iowa Library, 1952.
174. Wheeler, W. M. An analysis of Rorschach indices of male homosexuality. *Rorschach Research Exchange and Journal of Projective Techniques*, 1949, *13*:97–126.
175. Whittaker, E. M., Gilchrist, J. C., and Fischer, J. W. Perceptual defense or response suppression? *Journal of Abnormal and Social Psychology*, 1952, *47*:732–733.
176. Williams, M. An experimental study of intellectual control under stress and associated Rorschach factors. *Journal of Consulting Psychology*, 1947, *11*:21–29.
177. Windle, C. Psychological tests in psychopathological prognosis. *Psychological Bulletin*, 1952, *49*:451–482.
178. Wittenborn, J. R. Certain Rorschach response categories and mental abilities. *Journal of Applied Psychology*, 1949, *33*:330–338.
179. Wittenborn, J. R. A factor analysis of Rorschach scoring categories. *Journal of Consulting Psychology*, 1950, *14*:261–267.
180. Wittenborn, J. R. A new procedure for evaluating mental hospital patients. *Journal of Consulting Psychology*, 1950, *14*:500–501.
181. Wittenborn, J. R. Symptom patterns in a group of mental hospital patients. *Journal of Consulting Psychology*, 1951, *15*:290–302.
182. Wittenborn, J. R. The use of difference scores in prediction. *Journal of Clinical Psychology*, 1951, *7*:108–111.
183. Wittenborn, J. R., and Holzberg, J. D. The generality of psychiatric syndrome. *Journal of Consulting Psychology*, 1951, *15*:372–380.
184. Wittenborn, J. R., and Mettler, F. A. Some psychological changes following psychosurgery. *Journal of Abnormal and Social Psychology*, 1951, *46*:548–556.
185. Wittenborn, J. R., and Mettler, F. A. A lack of perceptual control score for the Rorschach test. *Journal of Clinical Psychology*, 1951, *7*:331–334.
186. Wittenborn, J. R., and Sarason, S. B. Exceptions to certain Rorschach criteria of pathology. *Journal of Consulting Psychology*, 1949, *13*: 21–27.
187. Wolberg, L. R. Therapeutic failures with hypnosis. In *Failures in psychiatric treatment* (ed., P. M. Hoch). New York: Grune and Stratton, 1948.
188. Zubin, J. *Manual of projective and cognate techniques*. Madison (Wis.): College Typing Co., University of Wisconsin, 1948.

INDEXES

# Author Index

419

# Subject Index

Administration of Rorschach, 109–118

Age as a variable, 64–65, 68–72

Ambivalence, 317

Animal movement responses, interpretive significance of, 222–223

scoring, 202–203

Anxiety, and shading responses, 183–201

content, 267–275

effect of age of clinician, 68–72

effect of instructions, 26–33

See also Text anxiety; Content

Assessment of clinical psychologists, 11, 20–25, 87

Assumptions, necessary for interpretation, 3, 16, 293–322

theoretical, 3, 11, 18, 293–322

Attitudes, 73–84

and prediction, 87–95

of clinician, 12, 15–16, 60–72, 276–290

of subject, 23–25, 126–128, 133, 135, 141–143, 155, 161, 165, 172–174, 195, 201, 226–227, 235, 266

Bias, see Selective responding

Binet, effect of instructions, 25–26

interpretation of, 42, 44, 47, 49–50

timing and place of, 55–59

Case studies, 323–401

Clinical interaction, variables in, 2, 3, 7

See also Attitudes; Clinician characteristics; Instructions; Place of interaction; Psychologist as a variable; Purposes of clinical interaction; Stimu-

Clinical interaction (*Continued*)

lus task and materials; Timing as a variable

Clinical psychology, growth of, 1

prediction of success in, 11, 20–25, 87

training in, 1

Clinician characteristics, 60–72, 276–290

age, 64–65

sex, 65–68

social class, 64

Clinician's behavior, concerning purposes of interaction, 38

deductive thinking, 3, 9, 13, 15–16, 142, 321–322

individual differences, 10, 11, 13, 61, 72, 232, 234

in interpretation, 293–322, 323–401

surprise reactions, 51

See also Selective responding

Color responses, achromatic, 144–180

interpretive significance, 174–176

scoring, 145

Color responses, chromatic, 144–180

and anxiety, 193–199

changes in stimulus, 161–172

interpretive significance of, 147–161, 172–174

related to human movement, 223–227

scoring, 144–146

shock, 161–172

Complexity of response, 130, 233

continuum of, 102–103

Configurations, problem of, 184–185, 251

Content, 254–275

and color, 164–171